Extreme Event Mitigation in Buildings: Analysis and Design

Brian J. Meacham
Editor

Matthew A. Johann
Associate Editor

National Fire Protection Association
NFPA® Quincy, Massachusetts

Product Manager: Brad Gray
Developmental Editor: Kathleen Richards/Khela Thorne
Editorial-Production Services: Modern Graphics, Inc.
Interior Design: Modern Graphics, Inc.
Composition: Modern Graphics, Inc.
Cover Design: Cameron, Inc.
Manufacturing Manager: Ellen Glisker
Printer: Courier/Westford

The following are registered trademarks of the National Fire Protection Association:

Building Construction and Safety Code® and *NFPA 5000®*
Life Safety Code® and *101®*
National Electrical Code® and *NEC®*
National Fire Alarm Code® and *NFPA 72®*
National Fire Codes® and *NFC®*

NFPA No.: EEMB06
ISBN-13: 978-0-87765-743-9
ISBN-10: 0-87765-743-2
Library of Congress Control No.: 2005930358

Printed in the United States of America
06   07   08   09   10   5   4   3   2   1

Contents

Chapter 6 ■ Chemical and Biological Events 173

John Haddon

Chapter 7 ■ Natural Hazards 211

Andrew C. T. Thompson
Ann M. Kammerer
Gayle M. Katzman
Andrew S. Whittaker

Chapter 8 ■ Fire Events 245

Richard Custer
Chris Marrion
Matt Johann

Chapter 12 ■ Evacuation Planning and Modeling for Extreme Events   **347**

Jeffrey S. Tubbs
David Jacoby

Chapter 13 ■ Information Technology and Telecommunications Design   **409**

Al Lyons

Chapter 14 ■ Emergency Response Planning   **433**

Stanley Dawe

Preface

On September 11, 2001, many wondered whether the future of building design had changed forever. The deliberate impact of aircraft into the World Trade Center towers in New York City, with the intent of causing the collapse of the buildings and the deaths of the civilian occupants inside, raised questions about the performance we expect from our buildings, and under what conditions, to a new level.

Throughout the history of building regulation, provision has been made for protection against the effects of extreme events, including conflagrations, floods, hurricanes, and earthquakes. As society experiences intolerable events, changes are made to building regulations and design practices to reduce the impact of future extreme events to a tolerable level. This does not mean that we stop building structures in seismic zones or in densely packed urban environments where conflagration risks exist, nor does it mean that all structures in such environments be impenetrable bunkers. Rather, it means that society looks to understand the events and the mitigation options that are available and to seek a balance between the magnitude and likelihood of potential events, the mitigation measures that are available, the costs to society, and the other attributes that society deems important, such as openness, aesthetics, and sustainability. By doing this, we will be able to continue to construct buildings that are pleasing to the eye, that provide a pleasant living or working environment, that are located where we want and need them, and that will meet our expectations for performance in terrorist-related and other extreme hazard events.

This book aims to help those in the building industry—building owners and managers, developers, financiers, insurers, building officials, fire officials, fire and emergency response personnel, architects, engineers, contractors, building material manufacturers and system developers—as well as building occupants, to recognize that a great deal of knowledge exists regarding extreme events. This book presents information on assessing the likelihood of occurrence and potential impacts; strategies for their mitigation; mechanisms for achieving a balance between tolerable levels of risk, performance, and cost; and other societal goals and expectations.

The book has been authored by subject-matter experts and is laid out in a manner that tells a complete story, while allowing readers to target specific chapters for information regarding a particular subject. Although this approach results in some differences in style and overlap in material, it is necessary so that each chapter is able to tell a complete story. Also, a large amount of information exists regarding the topics covered in this book. In order to provide a comprehensive picture without excessive detail, references are provided on a per-chapter basis.

Chapter 1, the introduction, sets the scene by describing extreme events, how they impact buildings, and what strategies generally exist to address these events. This first chapter sets the tone for the chapters that follow.

Chapters 2 through 4 examine fundamental concepts of risk and performance and how they are used in extreme event assessment and mitigation. Chapter 2 provides a discussion on the concept of risk-informed performance-based design. This discussion shows how risk assessment and characterization can be used to understand tolerable levels of performance, which then are used to establish design criteria and performance levels. Chapter 3 discusses the concept of "competing objectives" and introduces various methodologies that exist to help identify objectives and acceptability criteria and to make decisions between competing objectives. Chapter 4 provides an overview of the threat, vulnerability, and risk-assessment process. It discusses the various components in the process, provides examples of various methodologies that exist for the component parts of the process, and offers an approach for bringing threat, risk, performance, mitigation, mitigation effectiveness, and cost into the decision-making process for selecting suitable mitigation strategies.

Chapters 5 through 8 give an overview of various extreme events that can impact buildings. Chapter 5 discusses blast hazards—from devices to their effects on people and property—and existing mitigation approaches. Chapter 6 provides an overview of chemical and biological hazards, including agent characteristics, delivery mechanisms, and effects on people. Chapter 7 presents an overview of natural hazards and their assessment and mitigation. Chapter 8 discusses fire as an extreme event, both as an initiating and as a secondary event. An overview of the general fire growth, spread, and decay model is provided, along with some fundamental fire dynamics.

Chapters 9 through 13 provide an introduction to design strategies for mitigating the impact of the events discussed in Chapters 5 through 8. Chapter 9 addresses structural design. Chapter 10 examines the design of heating, ventilation, and air-conditioning systems. Chapter 11 provides a discussion of design for fire, with Chapter 12 addressing evacuation design and modeling. Chapter 13 rounds out the design section with a discussion of information technology and telecommunications design. Closing out the book is Chapter 14, which provides an overview of emergency response issues.

The nature of both extreme events and building design is that they are not static—they change with time. Hazards—especially terrorist-initiated ones—may change, societal tolerances may shift, and design practices and materials will advance with further research, development, and implementation. Although this book provides a snapshot in time of the environment of extreme event mitigation in buildings, the concepts and strategies outlined herein have a proven history and can be expected to be effective for many years to come. This book provides a comprehensive overview of the topic, as well as tools, methods and data that can be used for current analysis and design projects. We hope you find our book to be a valuable addition to your extreme event mitigation and design toolbox.

Acknowledgments

This book would not have been possible without the hard work and dedication of the chapter authors. These people are all experts in their fields and have taken time away from their busy schedules to share with others their professional perspectives on analysis and design for extreme events. I would like to extend my sincere and deep appreciation to these extremely talented and gifted individuals for helping to disseminate important building analysis and design concepts through this book. It is the sincere hope of all of the authors that this book will help lead to better performing buildings in the face of extreme events of any type.

Likewise, this book would not have been possible without the many hardworking individuals toiling behind the scenes. Associate

Editor Matt Johann is owed a debt of gratitude for leading the manuscript editing process, prior to manuscript submittal to NFPA. In addition, Amanda Moore, Andrew Woodward, and Virginia Sartanowicz worked hard to support Matt and me in formatting, reviewing, and editing the manuscript, and their assistance is greatly appreciated.

A key to making this book a reality was the support provided by Arup in allowing the many Arup authors and support staff the opportunity to help in its development. Thanks also to the various Arup staff members who helped the chapter authors with their material.

At NFPA, I would like to thank Brad Gray for giving me the opportunity to develop and publish this book and make it broadly available within the building industry. Thanks are also due to Khela Thorne for all of her hard work in developing the manuscript.

Finally, I reserve my deepest and sincerest appreciation for my wife, Sharon, who somehow always supports me when I forget the word "no" and agree to take on the effort and responsibility required to make a book such as this a reality.

Brian J. Meacham

Foreword

Those of us who personally witnessed the events of September 11, 2001, have images and emotions seared into our memories. Many others have been affected far more deeply by having escaped from the World Trade Center or the Pentagon with their lives that day or losing coworkers, friends, or family members. As understandable as feelings of grief, fear, and anger may be, building performance will not be improved by emotional responses. The tragedy of 9/11 has created an opportunity to examine these events and similar potential ones to create a logical, dispassionate, and scientific approach to improving building performance and increasing safety for building occupants and emergency responders.

For many, the term *extreme event* has become synonymous with events arising from willful and premeditated criminal acts affecting building performance in an unintended manner. This is not entirely accurate. Building codes define requirements for seismic events, high wind, heavy rains, and snow based on historical and scientific data, but we know that other events not currently defined by codes are possible. Other natural events, such as landslides and floods, are possible, as are accidental human-initiated events, such as a natural gas explosions, chemical discharges, or even vehicle impacts. These events also require consideration.

By examining the basis of building codes and the rationale for their requirements, we can understand the probabilistic approach taken in the development of codes and standards.

The decision-making sequence begins with the identification of an occupancy and its inherent hazards and then establishing a risk or threat level to the building structure and the occupants. Building codes establish limitations or requirements based on risk for issues such as maximum areas, limitation on building heights, separation from adjoining buildings, fire rating of elements, and the need for fire suppression systems. On the basis of occupancy and construction requirements, occupant-related decisions such as travel distances can be established.

Although the issues just noted describe a sequence for prescriptive codes, the similarities in methodology for performance-based fire protection and extreme event mitigation are even greater. Designing buildings for extreme events is merely a logical development in the improvement of building performance that establishes requirements for design solutions on additional risks not previously considered.

Some issues formerly considered to be extreme are finding their way into building codes, such as the New York City Building Code that now incorporates provisions dealing with the location of building air intakes and the impact resistance of stair enclosures. As research and development continues, it is likely that other requirements will pass from the category of extreme to standard and therefore be prescribed by jurisdictions.

My partners and I are now designing the signature icon, the "Freedom Tower," at the World Trade Center. We are designing other buildings with heights exceeding 1000 feet in the United States and abroad for a mix of uses. We are designing embassies for the United States and a new headquarters for NATO, as well as airport terminals around the world. As diverse as this portfolio is, the issues associated with extreme events factor prominently into discussions with clients and public officials and within our project design teams. We are certainly not the only architects and engineers engaged in such activity, and therefore the opportunity must be taken now to continue the research and the dialogue across our professions.

Continuing the dialogue in developing responses to extreme events is essential to creating a common language for communication among public officials, building owners, architects, engineers, and the public—whose safety is dependent on the issues that we explore and the solutions that we, as professionals, develop.

Informative, useful, stimulating, and reliable resources are even more important to practicing professionals. Much of my recent work has focused on research that has consumed countless hours of studying information from disparate and fragmented sources in an effort to improve the safety of our building designs. Now, at last, the professional seeking the best source of such information need look no further than this volume, which was written by some of the most distinguished experts in their fields, experts whose knowledge and commitment to building safety improves the designs of today and the entire built environment of the future.

Carl Galioto, FAIA
Partner, Skidmore, Owings & Merill LLP

1

Impact of Extreme Events on Buildings

Stuart L. Knoop

Extreme events are incidents that make demands on a building's structure and other systems beyond the usual design parameters imposed by codes, standards, and good professional practice. These events may be categorized as *natural disasters*, such as intense hurricanes, floods, and tornadoes, or *man-made disasters*, such as terrorist attacks involving bombs or automatic weapons.

Extreme events, as discussed in this book, include any natural or man-made hazards that subject a building and its systems to stresses well beyond those ordinarily anticipated by the codes and standards used by design professionals. These extremes may also exceed the margins of safety allowed for in most design processes. This chapter introduces some basic information about extreme events and explores how buildings are impacted by such events.

HAZARDS TO THE BUILT ENVIRONMENT

Physical security and safety are the basic purposes of the built environment. *Security* involves protection from human-caused events, such as data theft, burglary, and armed hostilities; *safety* involves protection from natural events, including storms, earthquakes, and fire. When people first began putting enclosures around themselves, their animals, and their possessions, the obvious purpose was to protect against natural and man-made hazards. In modern times, many building owners have also long recognized the need for some measure of physical security to manage risk and liability.

Classification of Hazards

The Federal Emergency Management Agency (FEMA), which is now part of the Department of Homeland Security, classifies hazards in its *Risk Management and Mitigation Planning* series of publications—such as its *Reference Manual to Mitigate Potential Terrorist Attacks Against Buildings* [1]—as shown in Table 1.1.

Natural Disasters

Natural disasters kill approximately a million people around the world every decade and leave millions more homeless [2]. According to FEMA, natural disasters include gale-force winds, floods, releases of deadly chemicals, damage from fire or ice, and even upheavals of the earth itself [3]. All of these events can have major impacts on buildings and the people in them. Hurricanes, forest fires, earthquakes, and blackouts command our attention in the news and beg our assistance through government and charitable relief. In

TABLE 1.1   FEMA Hazard Classifications

Type of Hazard	Examples
Natural hazards	• Precipitation, including resulting flooding and snow accumulations • Wind, including tornadoes and hurricanes • Earthquakes • Solar and temperature extremes, including drought and fires • Electrical storms with resulting fires and disruptions
Man-made hazards—accidental or technological	• Misuse or malfunction of systems or machinery • Manufacture, transport, and use of hazardous materials, including fuels • Hazardous activities, such as nuclear power generation • Pollution or contamination, such as that from the use of pesticides or fertilizers • Misuse or mishandling of toxic agents
Man-made hazards—intentional	• Criminal acts, including assault and breaking and entering • Malicious acts, including vandalism • Acts of insanity • Terrorist acts

Source: Adapted from FEMA, 2003. *Reference Manual to Mitigate Potential Terrorist Attacks Against Buildings.* Federal Emergency Management Agency, Publication 426, Washington, DC.

2004, FEMA declared 70 major disasters and 7 emergencies in the United States [4]. Figure 1.1 shows the destruction in a downtown area after an earthquake in California. (See FEMA's Web site at www.fema.gov for more detailed information.)

Man-Made Disasters

Man-made disasters are also extreme events that have major impacts on buildings and the people in them. One such example of a man-made disaster is a terrorist attack. Following the attacks on the World Trade Center in 1993 and 2001 (Figure 1.2), the attack on the Pentagon in 2001, and the destruction of the Alfred P. Murrah Federal Building in Oklahoma City in 1995, the American public has become increasingly aware of terrorism in the continental United States. Previously, terrorist actions against America had been overseas, directed at U.S. diplomatic and military missions and some businesses.

FIGURE 1.1 Damage to downtown Paso Robles, California, caused by the 6.5-magnitude San Simeon Earthquake.

(*Source:* Photo by Dane Golden/FEMA News Photo.)

FIGURE 1.2 Pedestrians flee after the World Trade Center tower collapses following terrorist attacks on September 11, 2001.

(*Source:* AP/Wide World Photos.)

Terrorism. In 2003, 208 terrorist attacks were perpetrated on U.S. interests internationally. According to the U.S. Department of State, a total of 625 people were killed in the attacks of 2003: ". . . a total of 3646 persons were wounded in the attacks that occurred in 2003, a sharp increase from 2013 persons wounded the year before. This increase reflects the numerous indiscriminate attacks during 2003 on 'soft targets,' such as places of worship, hotels, and commercial districts, intended to produce mass casualties" [5].

In 1993, with the attack on the Murrah Federal Building, and in 1995 and 2001, with the attacks on the World Trade Center and Pentagon, terrorism became a domestic threat. Figure 1.3 shows the destruction caused by the September 11, 2001, terrorist attacks at the World Trade Center in New York City.

FIGURE 1.3   Aerial view of Ground Zero shows progress made on cleanup of the site 6 months following the World Trade Center attack in New York City.

(*Source:* Photo by Larry Lerner/ FEMA News Photo.)

Department of Homeland Security Advisory System. The Department of Homeland Security (DHS) Advisory System has maintained a Code Yellow, or Elevated Threat Level ("significant risk of terrorist attacks"), for many months. Since DHS was created in 2002, it has declared a Code Orange, or High Threat Level ("high risk of terrorist attacks"), several times. See Figure 1.4 for an image of the advisory system. (Visit the DHS Web site at www.dhs.gov for more detailed information on the system.) The threat of terrorism continues to be recognized by the U.S. government.

Homeland Security Threat Advisories contain information about an incident involving or a threat targeting critical national networks

FIGURE 1.4   The DHS advisory system.
(*Source:* U.S. Department of Homeland Security, www.dhs.gov.)

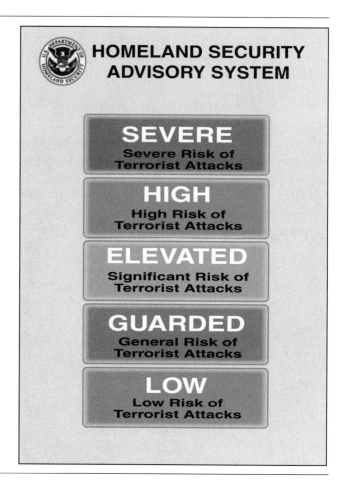

or infrastructures or key assets. They could, for example, relay newly developed procedures that, when implemented, would significantly improve security or protection. The advisories also could suggest a change in readiness posture, protective actions, or response. The DHS Threat Advisory Service includes products formerly called *alerts, advisories,* and *sector notifications.* Advisories are targeted to federal, state, and local governments; private sector organizations; and international partners.

Wars in Afghanistan and Iraq have intensified concerns about terrorist threats and the security being put in place to counter them. The creation of the DHS has focused public attention on terrorism and has helped identify ways to guard against it. Federal facilities, as well as many state and municipal facilities, are subject to the national DHS Advisory System, and many have begun physical security construction measures. Private businesses have long been cognizant of the need for physical security against criminal threats, but have been less proactive in responding to potential terrorist threats until relatively recently.

Facility Protection. U.S. government facilities overseas—both military and civilian—have long been targets of terrorist attacks. Yet even since the attacks in the United States itself—on the World Trade Center in 1993 and 2001, the Murrah Federal Office Building in 1995, and the Pentagon in 2001—most private building owners in the United States do not consider their facilities to be terrorist targets. This is mainly because the probability of a terrorist attack on any single building in the United States, and private buildings in particular, is very low. Commercial building owners and tenants often are more concerned with other types of crime, such as IT sabotage, information and identity theft, and assaults. Although few commercial facilities have invested in physical construction specifically designed to protect against potential terrorist attacks, many have installed systems and construction that protect against other crimes, such as breaking and entering, burglary, and armed robbery. Many commercial buildings attempt to prevent such crimes through the use of access control and closed circuit television (CCTV).

The views of most businesses are probably reflected by a 2003 survey of 331 businesses by The Conference Board, which found that since September 11, 2001 [6]:

- The median increase in security spending by businesses was 4 percent.
- Insurance and risk management reports were up 33 percent.
- Large-scale capital improvements that could not demonstrate an immediate return on investment were difficult to sell to management.
- Businesses were hesitant to spend more on security if they did not see it contributing directly to earnings.

Interagency Security Committee. Following the attacks on the World Trade Center in 1993 and the Murrah Federal Office Building in Oklahoma City in 1995, the federal government began to act. The U.S. Department of Justice (DOJ) surveyed federal buildings nationwide and recommended measures to reduce the vulnerability of existing federal buildings to attacks like the one that had occurred at the Murrah Building [7]. One of the DOJ's recommendations was that an Interagency Security Committee (ISC) be established to address government-wide security concerns. This was done by Executive Order 12977, and the ISC Security Criteria were developed and issued in May 2001 [8]. No special funding for actually providing physical security accompanied the criteria, so little change resulted until after September 11, 2001, when two supplemental appropriations made it possible to apply the ISC Criteria. The ISC Criteria are now in use nationwide and are being supplemented and amended by a standing committee now under the jurisdiction of the DHS.

Because the ISC Criteria are directed toward office buildings, certain agencies of the federal government, such as the National Institutes of Health and the Department of Veterans Affairs, have begun developing their own supplemental criteria for nonoffice applications, including research, laboratory animal, and healthcare facilities.

U.S. Government Publications. Over the past few years, the federal government, through the DHS and other agencies, has begun broad-based efforts to make security information available to the general public. Examples include the following publications:

- *Reference Manual to Mitigate Potential Terrorist Attacks Against Buildings* [1]
- *Integrating Man-Made Hazards into Mitigation Planning* [9]
- *Guidance for Protection of Building Environments from Airborne Chemical, Biological or Radiological Attacks* [10]
- *Guidance for Filtration and Air-Cleaning Systems to Protect Building Environments from Airborne Chemical, Biological or Radiological Attacks* [11]

These, and publications yet to come, are available to the public for application to any building, though the information is necessarily general.

Buildings Potentially at Risk. Although the issue of whether an institution needs to protect itself from terrorism should be carefully determined through professional threat and risk assessment (TARA), Table 1.2 lists representative nongovernment facilities that may be terrorist targets. (TARA is discussed briefly later in this chapter and in more detail in Chapter 4.)

TABLE 1.2 Possible Nongovernment Facility Targets for Terrorism

Type of Facility	Example or Comment
High-profile corporations and institutions where prominent or controversial public figures work or live or where symbolic value is attractive to terrorists who wish to make a point and inflict heavy casualties	The World Trade Center, though developed by and associated with an interstate agency (the Port Authority of New York and New Jersey), was a commercial complex and viewed by many as a U.S. financial icon.
Facilities housing or associated with controversial procedures or research	Clinics associated with abortions, research laboratories that use animals or study stem cells, and commercial developments and SUV dealerships are possible targets.
Facilities associated with targeted religious, racial, or ethnic groups	The potential for such incidents increase as tensions rise between the United States, Islamic countries, and activist groups.
Institutions harboring targeted individuals	These include the following: • Political figures, especially extremists against particular groups or ideologies • Criminal suspects or convicts, especially those involved with drugs or organized crime • Witnesses and survivors in hospitals or in protective custody during a trial or other legal proceeding
American corporations with overseas facilities	Petrochemical companies are possible targets.
American institutions overseas	Funded by the U.S. Agency for International Development's American Schools and Hospitals Abroad (ASHA), these include hospitals on all continents and in such turbulent areas as Lebanon, the Philippines, and Haiti.

Collateral Damage. Any building or complex located near a potential target of terrorism could be subjected to collateral damage from the primary target—as happened to large parts of lower Manhattan when the World Trade Center collapsed. The following are examples of buildings that may be subject to collateral damage in the event of a terrorist attack:

• Institutions located near refineries, ports, federal installations, or military bases

- Facilities near vital infrastructure, such as power generation stations, communications exchanges, or water treatment plants

Soft Targets. When a building not otherwise intended as a target is near a well-protected primary target, such as a federal building, it is possible that a terrorist will choose the "softer" (i.e., less protected) building to attack. For example, Timothy McVeigh originally intended to attack a building in Washington, D.C., but after assessing the level of protection in the nation's capital, he opted for the much more accessible Oklahoma City building.

Hospitals are a particularly vulnerable soft target. Because access to patient areas of hospitals and similar facilities must be maintained for visitors and medical personnel, the potential for large numbers of easily dominated captives is present. Project ER One, which is directed, managed, and coordinated by the Department of Emergency Medicine at Washington Hospital Center in Washington, D.C., addresses many aspects of security for healthcare facilities—specifically emergency departments—in disaster mitigation. Project ER One, in examining various risk scenarios, offers Scenario 9, a situation in which an emergency room (ER) is taken over by a gang and the occupants are held hostage [12]. The emotional impact of such a situation could be formidable—a condition sought in many terrorist scenarios.

Public places and schools have already been targets in Russia. The Chechen rebels who seized 700 hostages in a theater in Moscow in October 2002 certainly had the emotional impact of the event on everyday Russians in mind. In September 2004, pro-Chechnya Muslim terrorists launched an attack on a school in Russia in which more than 300 people were killed and some 700 wounded. In the Russian school attack, heavily armed Islamists took over and wired with explosives the school building in Beslan, North Ossetia. It is believed that an accidental explosion set off a battle between Russian security personnel and the terrorists, who set off several explosions and shot schoolchildren and teachers as they tried to escape.

Methods of Attack

Physical security is designed to protect against intentional man-made hazards. Although most agree as to what constitutes a criminal and malicious act, this discussion uses the term *terrorism* as it is defined in the Code of Federal Regulations; that is, ". . . the unlawful use of force and violence against persons or property to *intimidate or coerce* a government, the civilian population, or any segment thereof, *in furtherance of political or social objectives"* [13] (emphasis added to distinguish terrorism from other violence that may arise without these particular intentions).

Explosives. The attacks with vehicle-delivered explosives on the World Trade Center in 1993 and the Murrah Federal Building in 1995 brought to American soil a hazard that was, until then, known mostly in connection with attacks on U.S. embassies and military installations overseas, especially in the Middle East. Because explosives are easily and cheaply obtained and deployed, and because their use can result in spectacular and fatal consequences, attacks using explosives are a preferred tactic of terrorists. Unfortunately, it is impossible to determine whether explosives will be used against a particular facility, but because the preponderance of physical security design criteria for federal agencies is directed at preventing and mitigating blast effects on buildings, a brief overview of blast effects may be useful. (See Chapters 5 and 9 for detailed discussions of structural design for blast-related events.)

The following are key considerations in protecting people and buildings from bomb damage:

• Blast pressures and resultant damage diminish exponentially with distance from the blast. The further a potential blast source can be kept from a building, the better.

• Blasts occurring near a structural column can cause catastrophic progressive collapse, such as was seen at the Murrah Building. Parking facilities located under a building are therefore especially hazardous, because main building columns are exposed in these areas.

• Even when the main building structure is protected or designed to sustain blast effects, the cause of most casualties in an explosion is flying debris—especially glass.

• Blasts occurring inside a building are magnified by reflected and reinforced pressures. Because of this, smaller explosive charges, such as those carried in a satchel or backpack, can be lethal and cause massive damage. Areas where explosives can be covertly introduced to a building's interior, such as lobbies, mail rooms, and loading docks, must be designed to resist amplified blast loads.

• Screening of people and vehicles for explosives is feasible and is being performed at many federal installations. It is one of the best means of keeping explosive events from occurring.

- It is possible to design buildings to survive blasts and to reduce casualties in the event of an explosion. This is most effective and least costly when blast-proof design methods are incorporated into new construction. It is also possible, if more costly, to improve existing construction.

Key Point   Building components, including windows, can be designed to be less hazardous to occupants in the event of an explosion, but the more resistant the construction, the higher the costs involved.

Chemical, Biological, and Radiological Attacks. Since the anthrax episodes in 2001, much attention has been focused on developing technologies for mitigating chemical, biological, and radiological (CBR) attacks. The potential for mass casualties from a CBR attack and the role of healthcare facilities if such an event were to occur are reflected in the findings of Project ER One [12]. Although CBR agents can be delivered to a population in a number of different ways, such as by food, water, and "dirty" bombs, airborne agents have received the most attention.

In most buildings, air is intentionally introduced from the exterior and circulated internally; thus many are concerned about the spread of toxic agents in the air. Some CBR mitigation methods against airborne agents include isolation of potential sources, such as air intakes and return grilles, and zoning to keep lobbies, mail rooms, and loading areas on separate systems so that contaminated air is not distributed to other parts of the building. A number of studies are examining the use of high-efficiency filters and other methods to kill biological agents. Researchers also are searching for ways to neutralize chemical and radiological agents. Research into CBR mitigation within building systems is still in its infancy. Toxic agents also can be introduced to a building through its water supply—either from the exterior into the public supply or internally into the distribution system or point of use.

A major concern in CBR response is that with some agents by the time an attack is detected it may be very difficult to respond to it. In other words, it may be hours, or even days, before signs of an attack are evident. Detection technologies are being developed, but they are a long way from being widely available.

See Chapter 6 for a detailed discussion of chemical and biological hazards and Chapter 10 for a discussion of CBR mitigation via heating, ventilation, and air conditioning (HVAC) design.

HAZARD MITIGATION DESIGN

The design professions have included protection against hazards through the design of the building structure and envelope for centuries. This has included design against the elements and against war. Today, the design of buildings must continue to anticipate a range of hazards—some familiar and some less so.

Codes and Regulations

For the built environment, mitigation of most natural hazards is covered by fire and life safety codes, such as those of the National Fire Protection Association (NFPA); building codes, such as the *International Building Code* (IBC) [14] and *NFPA 5000®, Building Construction and Safety Code®*; and industry standards, such as those of the American Society for Testing Materials (ASTM), the American Concrete Institute (ACI), and many others. These codes and standards are commonly cited and required by most government jurisdictions. Most nongovernment building permits, licensures, and accreditations require compliance with these codes. The codes establish design requirements, including those for structural systems, means of egress, fire and smoke barriers, and electrical and mechanical systems. The codes also set minimum resistance to fire and maximum flame spread and smoke developed and other safety requirements for many building materials.

Because many of the effects of natural hazards covered by the codes also occur with those generated by intentional man-made hazards, such as bombs, the modification or amplification of some code requirements may improve the response of buildings to such events. However, fire and life safety codes do not yet mandate mitigation of intentional man-made hazards (physical security) except in terms of some of the by-products of a terrorist attack, such as fire and smoke.

Because security measures against certain criminal acts, such as forced entry or vandalism, do not usually involve construction that could afford the protection required for life safety, the codes have left most physical security measures to building owners. For example, most codes, including the IBC, do not have criteria for protection of people, such as bank tellers, from ballistic threats. However, to establish an industry-wide basis for classifying materials and assemblies by ballistic resistance, Underwriters Laboratories (UL) has developed a systematic categorization of building materials assemblies that resist certain classes of firearms. (See UL 752, *Standard for Bullet-Resisting Equipment* [15].) UL also has developed standard test methods for these products.

Most technological hazards (such as those resulting from system failures) and natural hazards are covered by building codes and standards. Factors of safety in structural design extend the coverage of these possible occurrences from the statistically probable (such as wind velocities and seismic shocks) to at least some extent.

Technological man-made hazards include such events as boiler explosions, which are generally covered by pressure-vessel design requirements. Others, such as electrical fires and blackouts, are covered by codes and standards, including UL and Factory Mutual (FM) testing and supervisory programs in manufacturing.

Physical Security Design Process

In the late 1960s and early 1970s, increases in crime in large public housing projects prompted the National Institute of Law Enforcement and Criminal Justice of the Department of Justice to commission Oscar Newman of New York University to study the influence of the physical layout of residential environments on the vulnerability of residents to crime. Based on the results of experiments on properties of the New York City Housing Authority, Newman wrote the landmark book *Defensible Space* [16]. This and subsequent studies have resulted in the concept of "Crime Prevention through Environmental Design" (CPTED), which is now cited in many physical security design guidelines. The essence of the book was that crime can be reduced by designing buildings and the spaces around them to create areas in which people take an ownership interest.

Although some forms of international terrorism are ancient, such as assassinations and horrific pogroms against populations to intimidate and rule them, modern nonmilitary violence directed at buildings as a method of influencing opinion is generally a post–World War II phenomenon.

Key Point   Buildings themselves are rarely the targets of terrorist attacks, except as symbols for what they house or represent.

Although terrorists have historically targeted an individual or a specific group, the victims of terrorism, beginning in the twentieth century, have often been innocent civilians picked at random or present by chance at the site of an attack. Terrorist attacks on buildings are relatively recent, although the Irish Republican Army (IRA) has conducted bombings of British cities on a small scale since 1939, and one of the first reported truck bombings was in 1946 by the Irgun, a Jewish group, against the British military headquarters at the King David Hotel in Jerusalem [17].

In the 1960s, with the rise of American power and presence worldwide, U.S. civilian and diplomatic properties became sites of mass protest demonstrations, sit-ins, and more destructive actions, such as the sacking and burning of the ground floor of the U.S. Embassy Chancery in Athens. As the severity of attacks against foreign service posts escalated to large-scale suicide bombings, such as those against the U.S. embassies in Kuwait and Beirut in the 1980s, the Department of State began a program of protecting its buildings and developed design criteria, including physical security measures, that are the most comprehensive in the nonmilitary sector. Military technical manuals covering security on military installations had also been published, but were directed more at combat situations and protection against sabotage and espionage. In 1988, the Federal Construction Council conducted a study of federal building security with the National Research Council and published a report [18]. The report focused on temporary and permanent upgrades, mostly to access control, for existing federal office buildings. It recommended a long-term approach to security and the establishment of security management and emergency procedures. However, the report did not result in any significant actions, mostly for lack of funding.

PHYSICAL SECURITY NEEDS ASSESSMENT

When assessing its physical security needs, an organization should review the needs of the facility, evaluate the hazards it intends to protect against, determine the amount of protection it can provide, and decide how to control access to potentially dangerous hazards.

Needs Assessment

A facility's owner or management must perform (with in-house or consultant expertise) three assessments to determine whether and how many resources to invest in physical security:

1. Threat assessment
2. Risk assessment
3. Vulnerability assessment

Threat Assessment. A threat assessment is performed to determine who might wish to harm a facility or its occupants and why, how they might do so, and what tactics they might use to succeed.

Risk Assessment. The organization would typically ask two questions to address the components of risk assessment: consequences and probability. These two questions are as follows:

1. How severe would the consequences be if an event occurred?
2. What is the probability of a particular event occurring?

Vulnerability Assessment. Having established the threats and risks, the organization must then determine how vulnerable the facility is to these risks. The organization must then decide on the response or mitigation measures needed to achieve the appropriate level of protection.

These three steps are sometimes combined under the term *risk assessment,* or *threat and risk assessment* (TARA). This three-step approach, which is discussed in greater detail in Chapter 4, may be especially appropriate when an organization combines physical security functions with other risk management such as fire safety and IT records protection. In any case, the same steps of threat, risk, and vulnerability assessment must be taken. For example, if one of the threats to be mitigated is surreptitious and forced entry to steal records, then the vulnerability analysis would examine the construction and access control surrounding those areas where records are stored and handled. This would be done in conjunction with an information technology (IT) and operations analysis of how records are handled, used, and protected. It would also take into consideration restricting access by screening operating personnel and enforcing IT security operations.

Multihazard Mitigation

Because some hazard mitigation, such as that against explosions or CBR attacks, can be costly, the concept of multihazard mitigation places physical security costs in a broader context of addressing multiple needs at the same time. The following are examples:

- Seismic design can improve a building's response to an explosion, but it is not a substitute for blast analysis and design. However, most of the construction cost for hardening the structure against blast will be covered by the seismic reinforcing.

- Windows designed to withstand the impact of wind-borne debris during hurricanes will also improve the response to an explosion. However, a blast analysis should still be done, and upgrades will probably be necessary.
- Redundancy of systems such as primary power supply and emergency power generation, water supply, and other utilities is beneficial, especially for critical facilities, under any circumstances.
- Air filtration against CBR hazards can have a general health benefit, including prevention of "sick building syndrome."
- Restricting access to the building or selected areas of it for security also supports or can be used in conjunction with separation of staff and the public.

Levels of Protection

The available financial resources to cover start-up and operating costs will determine the amount of protection that can be applied to mitigate a particular threat. For example, IT security is a major concern of many organizations. Physical protection of IT assets could include forced-entry-resistant construction not only around central archives and mainframe or server locations, but also around electrical and data panel rooms and wire closets, wiring or fiber runs, and junctions. In highly secure environments, terminals accessing secure data and all network elements should be physically secured with forced and surreptitious entry construction and be able to be readily inspected for illicit taps or damage. Obviously, the cost of this degree of security can only be justified if compromise of the information would have severe consequences, such as would be the case in the event of the disclosure of national security information.

Levels of protection are discussed further in Chapters 2 and 4, as well as in specific chapters on hazard events and mitigation strategies. The issue of benefit-cost assessment is explored further in Chapter 4.

Access Control

Many intentional man-made hazards, including firearms, explosives, and CBR agents, are mitigated initially by preventing or controlling access to a target, such as a building interior or the vicinity surrounding a target building.

Keyed Locks. The most common physical security measure is controlling access to a restricted space. The most rudimentary means of doing so is robust construction around the space and a lock on the door that enters it. Even at this basic level, the consequences of the threat being carried out will dictate whether a cheap lock or an expensive one should be installed, whether the door should be hollow or solid core, whether the door frame should be metal and reinforced against attempts to spread it to spring the lock, and whether the partition in which the doorway occurs should be reinforced against forced entry. The amount of financial resources expended will depend on how long the protection must resist the amount of effort required to break through. The required duration of resistance is related to the time necessary for someone, such as a guard, to intervene and what tools the perpetrator might use to gain entry.

Key Point   Controlling access with mechanical keyed locks is only as successful as the ability of management to control the distribution and return of keys and to prevent their duplication.

High-security locks, which cannot be duplicated by most commercial key-copying devices and which are very difficult to pick, can provide a higher level of security than typical mechanical keyed locks. However, even the best lock will not provide protection if access to the keys is not restricted. Keeping track of keys to high-security locks remains an administrative challenge.

Combination or Cipher Locks. Still greater access control can be achieved using a mechanical or electromechanical combination or cipher lock. The management issue then becomes restricting access to and changing the combination when it becomes necessary to change access privileges, such as when a combination holder leaves the employ of the facility. After all, it is even easier to pass on a combination than to duplicate a key.

With electronic card readers, authorized cardholders can open locks electronically by passing their card through the reader. Electronic card systems can track the entry and exit of card users so that if an event occurs, the system can generate a report of who entered and when. If an employee is terminated, that person's access rights can be withdrawn electronically. Such systems are already in wide use in many facilities. The extent and sophistication of the system are matters of need and cost.

Electronic systems can be augmented by various biometric identification devices, such as hand readers and retina scanners. Each layer of security that improves access control also has the potential to add inconvenience, intrusiveness, and cost.

Screening. In addition to controlling access to spaces with devices ranging from locks to biometric identification units, screening people and their belongings prior to their being allowed access to a facility (as is now routinely done at airports and many public buildings, such as courthouses) is a measure that seeks to reduce the ease with which weapons, including explosives, can be brought in. The amount and type of screening required can impact the design of lobby areas where the process is usually performed. Because screening persons, their vehicles, and their possessions is an intrusive act, any institution, especially one providing services to the public, must give great thought before implementing such measures.

PHYSICAL SECURITY DESIGN AND EMERGENCY RESPONSE

Most physical security measures are designed to buy time for a response. It is not possible to provide indefinite and undefeatable protection against any type of extreme event. However, if an incident's effects, such as those on the building's structural and fire and life safety systems, can be contained long enough for first responders to arrive and perform their tasks, the built environment will have done all it can. If progressive collapse of the structure can be prevented and evacuation and rescue thereby made possible, casualties will be greatly reduced. Similarly, control of fire and smoke and maintenance of communications and means of egress will facilitate evacuation and rescue.

The response plan must be considered when designing physical security features. See Chapter 14 for a full discussion of emergency response planning. If an intrusion detector is activated, someone must respond soon enough to interdict the intruder. If a blast occurs,

the building systems—structural and fire and life safety systems—
must remain in place and be functional long enough for evacuation
and rescue to take place.

The design of the physical features of security must increase the
demands on operations in terms of staffing of access control, surveillance and intervention, and maintenance of physical security equipment and systems. Conversely, the physical security should
minimize the number of staff needed to protect the facility. Too
many guards watching too many entrances or too many CCTV monitors cannot be sustained by most budgets. Security designs that require large staffs to operate and maintain them are vulnerable to
elimination by management or to neglect.

Key Point   Coordination of physical security design with public first responders, especially law enforcement, fire, and emergency services, is essential.

Internal guard forces and life safety personnel typically can only
manage an event until the public professionals arrive. The physical
features of security should be designed to facilitate this interaction.
Barriers designed to keep a would-be attacker out must not impair
fire and rescue personnel and equipment.

__SUMMARY__

Although providing security has always been a principal function of
the built environment, the rise in terrorism in the late twentieth and
early twenty-first centuries has given new awareness to the issue.
Everyone who travels by air has experienced airport security, and
most people have seen the vivid images from September 11, 2001.
The design community, working chiefly with the government, has
been developing new ways to protect buildings, seeking the least intrusive and least visually offensive solutions whenever possible. In
the United States, the goal is not to retreat behind fortresses, but to
protect people and activities from terrorism and other extreme
events.

Only through rational analysis of threats, vulnerabilities, and
risks can reasoned and balanced actions be taken. Physical security
may have always been the primary function of the built environ-

ment, but it is far from being the only one, and it should not become one that dominates all others in an open, democratic society.

BIBLIOGRAPHY

References Cited

1. FEMA, 2003. *Reference Manual to Mitigate Potential Terrorist Attacks Against Buildings,* Publication 426, Federal Emergency Management Agency, Washington, DC.

2. FEMA, 1997. General Disaster Statistics, www.fema.gov/pdf/library/stats.pdf.

3. FEMA, October, 2004. Disaster Fact Sheets and Backgrounders, www.fema.gov/library/factshts.shtm.

4. FEMA, 2003. Federal Disaster Declarations, www.fema.gov/news/disasters.fema?year=2003.

5. U.S. Department of State, 2004. *Patterns of Global Terrorism,* U.S. Department of State, Washington, DC.

6. The Conference Board, 2003. *Investing Against Terror: How Vulnerable is Corporate America?* The Conference Board, July 9, 2003.

7. U.S. Department of Justice, 1995. *Vulnerability Assessment of Federal Facilities,* U.S. Department of Justice, Washington, DC.

8. ISC, 2001. *ISC Security Design Criteria for New Federal Office Buildings and Major Modification Projects,* Interagency Security Committee, Washington, DC.

9. FEMA, 2003. *Integrating Man-Made Hazards into Mitigation Planning,* FEMA Publication 386-7, Federal Emergency Management Agency, Washington, DC.

10. CDC and NIOSH, 2002. *Guidance for Protection of Building Environments from Airborne Chemical, Biological or Radiological Attacks,* Centers for Disease Control and Prevention and National Institute for Occupational Safety and Health, Atlanta, GA.

11. CDC and NIOSH, 2003. *Guidance for Filtration and Air-Cleaning Systems to Protect Building Environments from Airborne Chemical, Biological or Radiological Attacks,* Centers for Disease Control and Prevention and National Institute for Occupational Safety and Health, Atlanta, GA.

12. Feied, C., 2004. *ER One Phase I Report,* Department of Emergency Medicine, Washington Hospital Center, Washington, DC, http://er1.org.

13. Title 28, Code of Federal Regulations, Part 0, "Organization of the Department of Justice," U.S. Government Printing Office, Washington, DC.

14. ICC, 2003. *International Building Code,* International Code Council, Falls Church, VA.

15. UL, 2000. *UL 752, Standard for Bullet-Resisting Equipment,* Underwriters Laboratories Inc., Northbrook, IL.

16. Newman, O., 1972. *Defensible Space: Crime Prevention through Urban Design,* Macmillan Publishing Company, New York.

17. Terrorism Research Center. July 30, 2003, www.terrorism.com.

18. Commission on Engineering and Technical Systems (CETS), 1988. *The Protection of Federal Office Buildings Against Terrorism,* National Academy Press, Washington, DC.

NFPA Codes, Standards, and Recommended Practices

NFPA Publications.   The following is a list of NFPA codes, standards, and recommended practices cited in this chapter. See the latest version of the *NFPA Catalog* for availability of current editions of these documents.

> *NFPA 5000®, Building Construction and Safety Code®*
> NFPA 730, *Guide for Premises Security*
> NFPA 731, *Standard for the Installation of Electronic Premises Security Systems*

Additional Reading

> ASHRAE Guideline 29P, *Guideline for Risk Management of Public Health and Safety in Buildings,* American Society of Heating, Refrigerating and Air-Conditioning Engineers, Atlanta, GA.

2

Risk-Informed Performance-Based Analysis and Design

Brian J. Meacham

Since the tragic events of September 11, 2001, significant discussion has focused on whether or how building design may need to change to become more resilient to extreme events, including natural hazards and terrorist attacks. Prior to September 11, 2001, efforts were already under way to help designers and engineers balance openness, aesthetics, and other design goals with safety and security [1]. In addition, there has been a shift from prescriptive-based to performance-based regulations and design (see *NFPA 101®, Life Safety Code®; NFPA 5000®, Building Construction and Safety Code®;* and the *ICC Performance Code for Buildings and Facilities* [ICCPC] [2]). In this new post–September 11 environment, a good understanding of risk and performance is critical to achieving balance between sometimes competing design objectives. This chapter will review the use of risk-informed performance-based analysis and design to address the potential impact and mitigation of extreme events on buildings.

OVERVIEW

When one considers the wide range of objectives that exist for buildings, particularly when protection in the event of extreme events is a significant concern, risk-informed performance-based design provides a framework for developing balanced designs.

Defining Risk-Informed Performance-Based Design

Risk-informed performance-based design is an extension of the performance-based design process [3]. It is a process in which the following factors are addressed:

- Stakeholder and regulatory goals and objectives are clearly stated and agreed upon.
- A threat and risk assessment is conducted to understand the events that may impact a building and its occupants.
- Analysis of building performance in response to these events provides the basis for design.

By explicitly addressing these factors, all of the parties involved in the design, approval, and operation of buildings achieve their objectives and find balance in the design without unduly compromising openness, aesthetics, safety, or other goals.

Building design considers a multiplicity of objectives, from aesthetics, to use, to resilience in the face of natural and technological hazards, such as earthquakes, high wind, flooding, and fire. In the current environment, however, owners, tenants, and design professionals are becoming more concerned with extreme events. New objectives are being considered, including those resulting from the potential for terrorist-delivered blasts and chemical or biological hazards. In considering these new factors in the design process, numerous questions for building design have been raised, from material selection (e.g., the extent of glazing and how to protect it, attributes of concrete versus steel for different load effects), to required safety features and their design (e.g., what defines "adequate" egress capacity, how chemical or biological threats can best be mitigated), to finding acceptable ways to balance the costs and risks, especially for low-probability extreme events that may have catastrophic consequences.

Balancing Risks and Costs

For many, the issue of balancing risks and costs is the most challenging. Although analytical tools and methods exist for assessing load effects and for mitigating various loads, the risk of a terrorist attack and the use of a specific weapon are much more difficult to predict than natural and technological hazards. Thus, it can be difficult to make decisions regarding the level of investment that is appropriate to the risk based on statistics alone. Furthermore, building features intended to mitigate one risk may increase another. Consider evacuation alarms, for example. If fire is the only concern, a suitable evacuation strategy might be to have a building alarm aimed at getting people out of a building in a fire situation. However, in the past terrorists have located a bomb outside of a building and then activated the fire alarm. In such a situation, the fire alarm is used to put people at risk by having them leave the safety of the building and move toward the bomb.

Several factors come into play in determining whether a building is at risk for an extreme event. Factors that can impact a building's risk of terrorist attack include its symbolic importance, its criticality, and the consequences of a successful attack. In the attacks on the World Trade Center and on the Pentagon, each of these risk factors was present. However, owners and design teams face a difficult task in designing buildings that provide protection from terrorist threats but that retain features that make them desirable spaces for working and living. For buildings located in dense urban areas, limited ability to restrict access can impact standoff distances and perimeter control [4]. In addition, architectural design aesthetics may conflict with threat-mitigation objectives. At the end of the day, however, a balance must be struck, because if financiers and tenants do not feel comfortable with the risk—or their perception of the risk—it may be difficult to obtain financing for or lease or sell the property and spaces therein [5].

In light of (a) the uncertainty about extreme events and stakeholders' perceptions of risk, (b) the architectural design and the owner's goals and objectives for the building, and (c) the limited resources available for physical protection, an approach is needed that balances these sometimes competing objectives in a way that meets stakeholder and societal objectives for occupant life safety while accepting some level of damage to the structure, operations, and other non-life-safety goals in a cost-effective manner. Because prescriptive building codes do not always address such events, a risk-informed performance-based design approach takes on greater importance.

RISK CHARACTERIZATION

Defining Risk Characterization

Risk characterization is a process that brings together analytical data (e.g., statistics, risk analysis, historical data, computational modeling, test results, cost data) and stakeholder concerns in a way that enables the parties involved to agree on levels of tolerable risk [6, 7]. It is a decision-driven activity, directed toward informing choices and solving problems. Risk characterization is an essential step in risk-informed performance-based design, because it informs the cornerstones of performance-based design—goals, objectives, and criteria.

Stakeholder Concerns

A fundamental premise of risk characterization is that adequately addressing a risk requires a broad understanding of relevant losses, harms, or consequences to interested or affected parties. In the case of extreme event mitigation, this may include various stakeholders, including the building's owner, manager, and developer; financiers; tenants; neighbors; emergency officials; and the public. Bringing the stakeholders together or, at a minimum, anticipating the diverse perspectives of these stakeholders, is critical to the success of risk characterization. A singular view of risk and its tolerability may miss important considerations, such as technical, social, economic, or perceptual impacts. If a key perspective is overlooked, the risk problem may be formulated improperly, and the ensuing analysis may omit key parameters. In addition, if all stakeholder views are not represented in the process, certain groups may disagree with various parts of the process, from the problem statement to the risk measure selected. This is not to say, however, that every stakeholder can be fully accommodated in the risk-characterization process—this is difficult to achieve in any process involving a diversity of views. Nonetheless, involvement of as many views as feasible from the outset will help minimize roadblocks to gaining agreement throughout the process.

Achieving appropriate representation of stakeholder views is just one component of risk characterization. Successful risk characterization depends on systematic analysis that is appropriate to the problem, that responds to the needs of the stakeholders, and that treats uncertainties of importance to the decision problem in a comprehensible and reasonable way. Success also depends on deliberations that formulate the decision problem, that guide analysis to improve decision participants' understanding, that seek the meaning of analytic findings and uncertainties, and that improve stakeholders' abilities to participate effectively in the risk-decision process [8]. In other words, good risk characterization requires the following:

- A well-defined risk problem that stakeholders agree with
- A sound scientific base for assessing the risk and developing acceptable mitigation strategies
- The proper use of analytical techniques, with appropriate consideration of uncertainties and unknowns
- A good understanding of the mitigation effectiveness versus cost-effectiveness

FIGURE 2.1 The Risk-Characterization Process.

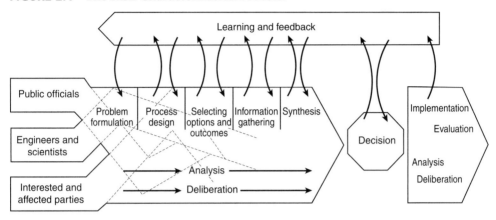

(*Source:* Adapted from Stern, P. C. and Fineburg, H. V. (Eds.), 1996. *Understanding Risk: Informing Decisions in a Democratic Society,* National Research Council, National Academy Press, Washington, DC, p. 28.)

- Sufficient discussion and deliberation so that everyone understands all of the issues involved

The risk-characterization process will likely require several iterations as new information and data become available and as participants gain a better understanding of the process and raise more issues. It needs to be an interactive process; one group should not dominate the deliberations or analysis and force a solution. The iterative nature of the risk-characterization process is illustrated in Figure 2.1.

The Risk-Diagnosis Framework

During the risk-characterization process, a number of clearly defined steps need to be taken to place boundaries around the problem. These steps include diagnosing the kind of risk and determining the state of knowledge about the risk, describing the legal mandate, articulating the purpose of the risk decision, identifying stakeholders and likely public reaction to the issues and to the solution, and developing and agreeing upon a preliminary process design [6]. These steps are illustrated in Figure 2.2.

The following text outlines the key steps (steps 5 and 6 in Figure 2.2 are primarily internal organizational resource decisions, which

FIGURE 2.2   Steps for Bounding the Risk Problem.

(*Source:* Adapted from Stern, P. C. and Fineburg, H. V. (Eds.), 1996. *Understanding Risk: Informing Decisions in a Democratic Society,* National Research Council, National Academy Press, Washington, DC, p. 143.)

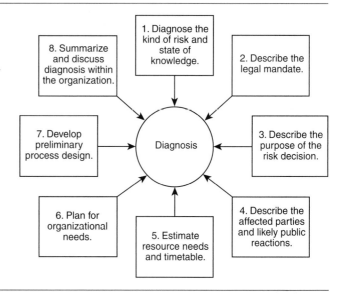

are beyond the scope of this discussion). Although not every assessment will require the level of analysis described herein for every hazard, the process and the key steps involved provide a framework for determining where to focus efforts.

Diagnosing the Risk and Determining the State of Knowledge. The first step of the process, and one that should be considered during any risk-characterization effort, is to diagnose the risk and to determine the state of knowledge about the risk. The aim of this step is to begin to identify and characterize who or what will be impacted and by what (e.g., threats, risks, and vulnerabilities). To help focus this effort, various diagnostic questions should be asked about the hazards and the risks, including the following [6]:

- Who or what is exposed? (People, property, operations, the environment, heritage?)
- If people are exposed, what specific groups are exposed? (Employees, tenants, the public? Sensitive populations, adults, everyone?)
- What is posing the risk? (Natural hazard, fire, terrorist event?)
- What is the nature of the harm? (Sudden injury or death, morbidity, delayed mortality, property loss, operational losses, threat to community welfare, loss of critical functions?)

- What qualities of the hazard may affect judgments about the risk? (Dread, individual control, vulnerability, familiarity, immediacy, degree of technical knowledge available?)
- Where is the hazard experience? (Local, national, international events? Similar facilities?)
- Where and how do hazards overlap? (Are some classes of people or facilities disproportionately exposed to one or multiple hazards? Is there a geographical component to overlapping hazards?)
- How adequate are the databases on the risks? (Solid data, some data with some judgment, few data with considerable judgment, speculation?)
- How much scientific consensus exists about how to analyze the risks? (Is there agreement on analytical methodology, theoretical basis for analysis, harms not analyzed?)
- How much scientific consensus is there about risk estimates? (Is epistemic, or knowledge, uncertainty a serious problem?)
- How much consensus is there among the affected parties about the nature of the risk?
- Has anything been omitted from the analysis? (Have possible harms, management options, or effects been left unassessed?)

Additional questions may arise based on the specific risk problem. Much of the rest of this book is focused on diagnosing the risk problems associated with individual events and threats and to provide guidance for developing appropriate mitigation strategies.

Describing the Legal Mandate. The legal mandate is important in benchmarking the regulatory environment and requirements that may impact the extreme-event analysis and design process. In some cases, building regulations will provide requirements that must be met (e.g., design requirements against natural hazards and fire). In other cases, the regulations will be silent, such as for security and resilience against terrorist actions (in the private sector). In the case of government projects, a plethora of regulations and guidance documents may be applicable to facility design. An office building with federal government tenants may need to meet aspects of local building regulations, national standards, General Services Administration (GSA) requirements, Department of Defense (DoD) guidelines, and other regulatory documents.

Key Point Sometimes application of specific analysis methods or approaches is only required when federal funding is involved; conversely, specific analysis may be imposed by potential funding entities as part of due diligence or financial risk-assessment processes.

Given the broad range of potential regulatory requirements—or lack thereof, in some cases—it is unrealistic to go into more detail on all aspects of this topic within this book. However, three examples are provided later in this chapter: *NFPA 5000*, the ICCPC [9], and the *DoD Minimum Antiterrorism Standards for Buildings* [10].

Describing the Purpose of the Risk Decision. Clearly defining the purpose of the risk decision, and therefore of the risk characterization, may seem straightforward. This step can be a challenge and may potentially lead to disagreements during stakeholder deliberations if it is not addressed collaboratively. For example, if a facility owner desires a risk-characterization effort to "demonstrate that the risk associated with consequences of a terrorist attack on his chemical facility is negligible," it may be difficult to actively engage facility neighbors and the public in a fruitful risk-characterization process. However, if the objective is to "characterize the risk associated with terrorist attack on the chemical facility for the purpose of agreeing on strategies to achieve a tolerable level of risk," the chance of success will be greater (noting again that successful implementation of an agreed-upon process does not guarantee agreement with the final outcome by all involved).

Identifying Stakeholders and Likely Public Reaction. Generally, the hazards and risks addressed by building regulations, such as natural hazards and fire, will not require much effort in the area of assessing potential public reaction, because the regulatory development process is intended to address such concerns. However, for facilities that present a high risk (real or perceived) to tenants, neighbors, or the public, the reaction of stakeholders should be an integral part of the process, because omission of stakeholder concerns can have a significant impact on the planning, design, and approval processes. For assessments and designs that are security related and designed to protect the public, it may not always be possible to have broad stakeholder participation, but consideration of stakeholder concerns should still be addressed to avoid unnecessary problems in the design and implementation processes.

Developing Preliminary Process Designs for Specific Risk Problems. Defining the process that will be used to characterize a specific risk problem for a particular facility or structure is crucial. The risk-characterization process provides a general framework of issues to consider, but for a specific risk problem, a process needs to be developed and agreed upon. This does not mean that every assessment needs to start from scratch. The challenge is finding a process that fits the problem—with or without modification—and obtaining stakeholders' agreement as to the applicability of the approach. Subsequent chapters will discuss specific processes for addressing different extreme-event hazards in more detail. These extreme events include approaches to seismic risk assessment, fire risk assessment, and terrorism-driven threat and risk assessment, including blast and chemical, biological, and radiological (CBR) threats.

PERFORMANCE CODES AND REGULATIONS

Numerous professional societies and government agencies offer approaches for characterizing and addressing risk for a number of different hazards and threats, from natural to man-made to terrorist-delivered ones. Three example approaches are discussed here: *NFPA 5000*, the ICCPC, and the *DoD Minimum Antiterrorism Standards for Buildings*. The main point of this discussion is to understand the regulatory environment within which the risk analysis will be undertaken and the facility will be constructed and operated, so as to ensure that relevant requirements have been addressed, especially when competing regulatory objectives exist (see also Chapter 3).

NFPA 5000 (Performance Option)

The performance option of *NFPA 5000* has its roots in the performance option of NFPA *101*. In brief, it allows one to undertake performance-based analysis and design as an alternative to complying with traditional, prescriptive code requirements. It does this by providing a set of objectives that must be met, along with various design scenarios that must be used to test the design alternative with respect to meeting the objectives. For example, following the prescriptive code portion of *NFPA 5000*, one would have prescribed travel distances, numbers of exits, fire-resistance ratings, and the like. Using the performance option, an engineer can propose alternative fire protection and exit strategies, and when successfully tested against the design scenarios, the alternatives can be used. As part of the analysis, the engineer is free to select design criteria against which the scenarios will be tested (some guidance on criteria is provided in the annexes of *NFPA 5000*).

The performance option of *NFPA 5000* relies on several design scenarios involving the fire protection systems, the structural systems, and the egress paths of a building. All of the design scenarios listed in Table 2.1 are applied to the proposed design independently, and for each of the design scenarios, the proposed design must achieve the selected performance criteria in order to meet the goals and objectives. See Chapter 5 of *NFPA 5000* for more detailed information.

TABLE 2.1 *NFPA 5000* **Fire Design Scenario Requirements**

Required Scenarios	Fire Scenarios Applied to Each Proposed Design
Scenario 1	Typical occupancy-specific fire. Must explicitly specify the following: • Occupant activities • Number and location of occupants • Room size • Furnishings and contents • Fuel properties and ignition source • Ventilation conditions • First item ignited and its location
Scenario 2	Ultra fast-developing fire in primary means of egress, with interior doors open at start of the fire.
Scenario 3	Fire starts in unoccupied room, may endanger large number of occupants in a large room or other area.
Scenario 4	Fire originates in concealed wall or ceiling space adjacent to a large, occupied room.
Scenario 5	Slow-developing fire, shielded from fire protection systems, in close proximity to high-occupancy area.
Scenario 6	Most severe fire resulting from the largest possible fuel load characteristic of the normal operation of the building.
Scenario 7	Outside exposure fire.
Scenario 8	Fire originating in ordinary combustibles in room or area, with each passive or active fire protection system or feature independently rendered ineffective. Not required for fire protection systems or features for which both the level of reliability and the design performance in the absence of the system or feature are acceptable to the authority having jurisdiction.

Source: NFPA, 2006. *NFPA 5000®, Building Construction and Safety Code®,* Section 5.5.2, National Fire Protection Association, Quincy, MA.

Fire Design Scenarios. Eight required fire design scenarios must be applied to each proposed design, as shown in Table 2.1. These fire design scenarios were developed through consultation with NFPA Technical Committee members, originally as part of the development of the performance-based design option in NFPA *101* and later carried over into *NFPA 5000*. The intent of the consultation was to obtain a broad perspective from a diversity of interest groups as to significant factors that may impact the severity of a fire. The expert elicitation was further supported by fire-loss statistics collected by the NFPA.

Structural Design Scenarios. In addition to the fire design scenarios, three structural design scenarios must be applied to the building. The first design scenario, the serviceability scenario, requires the application of dead loads in combination with live, impact, soil, and hydrostatic pressure; rain, flood, wind, ice, and snow; and earthquake loads in accordance with the load combinations specified in ASCE-7, *Minimum Design Loads for Buildings and Other Structures* [11]. The serviceability level of performance of the structure must be a state in which structural elements and nonstructural components do not sustain detrimental cracking or yielding or degradation in strength, stiffness, or fire resistance requiring repair, as explained in the 2006 edition of *NFPA 5000*.

The second structural design scenario requires buildings and their nonstructural components to be designed and constructed to provide the immediate occupancy performance level, which is defined as minor, repairable cracking and yielding and permanent deformation of the structure and nonstructural elements. However, the structure cannot sustain such degradation such that it is unsafe for continued occupancy. The third structural design scenario, the collapse-prevention scenario, states that "buildings shall be designed and constructed to resist collapse, and their components shall be designed to resist failure."

Building Use Design Scenarios. Two required design scenarios address safety during building use. Building Use Design Scenario 1 is an event in which the maximum occupant load is present in an assembly occupancy building and an emergency event occurs that blocks the principal exit/entrance to the building. Building Use Design Scenario 2 is a fire in an area of a building undergoing construction or demolition while the remainder of the building is occupied and in which the normal fire suppression system in the area has been taken out of service.

The International Code Council Performance Code (ICCPC)

The concept of risk characterization was used in the development of the ICCPC code to establish a performance basis that reflected a level of building safety risk tolerable to society [2, 7, 8, 12]. The result was a set of building-use groupings, importance criteria, occupant risk characteristics, and hazard events that relate broadly to levels of building performance that are tolerable for various magnitudes of hazard events. Several of the key factors addressed in the risk-characterization process, as applied to the ICCPC, are summarized in the following text.

Occupancy Groups. Which groups are exposed? This question is addressed broadly in current U.S. building codes through the use of occupancy groups or use groups. Over time, as specific losses or concerns were raised for certain groups within the population or for certain uses of buildings, occupancy- or use-specific requirements were codified [7, 8]. Some of these classifications were meant to provide additional safety for areas where large groups of people gathered, whereas others were aimed at providing additional safety for those areas occupied by people with disabilities or impairments. Still others were meant to provide protection against high or unusual hazards that could impact the occupants, whether they were aware of the hazard or not. However, as the number of specific requirements grew and exceptions were added for particular cases, it became less clear who was being protected, why they were being protected, from what, and how.

Risk Factors. In an attempt to focus on these fundamental issues, the risk-characterization process resulted in the following set of risk factors that are addressed explicitly in the ICCPC (although not addressed explicitly in *NFPA 5000*, these factors are equally important when using that code as well, for example, when applying the various design scenarios) [2, 7, 8, 9]:

- Nature of the hazard
- Number of occupants
- Length of time occupied
- Sleeping occupants

- Familiarity with building
- Vulnerable populations
- Occupants with dependent relationships

The nature of the hazard, whether it is likely to originate internal or external to the structure, and how it may impact the occupants, the structure, and the contents are important factors, because different hazards present different risks (e.g., fire versus earthquake).

The number of people normally occupying, visiting, working in, or otherwise using the building, structure, or portion of the building or structure is important, because large-loss events are perceived to be more devastating than large numbers of low-loss events. If large numbers of people will be in one location, it is expected that those people will be reasonably protected from whatever hazards might befall them. Based on past history, protection strategies are often selected that aim to prevent multiple deaths from occurring.

The length of time the building is normally occupied is intended to help address variations in the time a building is normally occupied. These time variations can range from 24 hours a day (e.g., hospitals); during business hours only (e.g., offices); rarely, if at all (e.g., storage facilities); or rarely, but with large numbers of people when in use (e.g., a sports stadium).

Whether people normally sleep in the building is also an important factor, primarily from the perspectives of potential vulnerability and response time, because hazard-induced risks are greater for people when they are asleep (e.g., reaction times may be slower and faster notification times may be needed).

Whether the building occupants and other users are expected to be familiar with the building layout and means of egress is another important factor. If a hazard is such that people need to egress a structure quickly to avoid injury or death, unfamiliar surroundings can lead to confusion, especially if lighting is lost, if people become disoriented, or if people are focused on trying to help others.

Another important factor is whether a significant percentage of the building occupants are, or are expected to be, members of vulnerable population groups such as infants, young children, elderly persons, persons with physical or mental disabilities, or persons with other conditions or impairments that could affect their ability to make decisions, egress without the physical assistance of others, or tolerate adverse conditions. This factor is aimed at establishing a level of risk appropriate to the population expected to use the building. It is critical, because the variability within a population will make some people more susceptible to a particular hazard than others, and analysis of the population can help identify whether risk-acceptability criteria should be based on the entire population or on the most vulnerable or sensitive populations.

Whether the building occupants and other users have familial or dependent relationships is another factor that should be considered. People who are dependent on others, such as infants and the infirm, are clearly at an increased level of risk. Likewise, those who are responsible for others require special attention, because they may place themselves at higher levels of risk in order to care for their dependents. In some cases, such as hospitals, protection schemes often account for this factor. In other cases, such as residences, protection schemes may not consider delays in evacuation, for example, incurred as one family member searches for another.

These risk factors play a critical role in expectations of safety provided to building occupants, and thus in the expected performance of buildings.

Direct Impacts. What is the nature of the harm? For the purpose of building regulations, the nature of the harm is often viewed as direct impacts on people or property (i.e., injury or damage). To address these impacts, code provisions specific to such factors as occupant health and safety and structural stability have been developed. Other potential issues include business continuity and community welfare. Business continuity is generally beyond the scope of building regulation, but community welfare is not. Community welfare is sometimes addressed in terms of the importance of different classes of buildings, such as hospitals.

In general, it is important to consider the importance of a building because specific structures play critical roles in providing health, safety, and welfare to communities, especially after hazard events. For these structures, society demands a higher level of protection. People expect them to remain functional after hazard events, regardless of the magnitude of the event. This concept is embodied in current codes to address expected performance after natural hazard events. In determining the importance of a building to a community, the following risk factors should be considered [7, 8, 9]:

• *The use or function of the building, structure, or portion of the building or structure in providing an essential service during normal and emergency conditions.* Such facilities may house essential safety services personnel, equipment, and communications and are expected to be functional during and after hazard events. Such facilities also include hospitals with surgery and emergency treatment facilities. These facilities are expected to: (1) contain vulnerable populations who cannot be moved during a hazard event and (2) provide emergency medical services after a hazard event. Designated emergency shelters also are considered essential facilities. In addition, power generating stations and other public utilities necessary to provide emergency power to other essential facilities are themselves considered essential.

• *The use or function of a building, structure, or portion of the building or structure in which a significant failure of the building, structure, or portion of the building or structure would present a significant hazard to human life.* A variety of facilities will be impacted by this concern, based on the risk factors listed in this chapter. In general, these facilities are characterized as containing one or more of the following: large numbers of a vulnerable population; large numbers of people in a single enclosure; very large numbers of people in the facility; restricted access or egress; or large amounts of toxic, corrosive, or infectious agents or materials.

• *The use or function of a building, structure, or portion of the building or structure in which a significant failure of the building, structure, or portion of the building or structure would present a very low hazard to human life.* This would apply to normally unoccupied buildings, such as a stand-alone garage for a single-family house. Buildings housing only electrical or mechanical systems may fall into this category as well.

Buildings of various uses that have requirements for similar levels of importance can be grouped together into *performance groups* [2, 7, 8, 9]. The ICCPC identifies four performance groups: Performance Group IV structures are deemed most important, and thus have the highest performance expectations under the highest loads (e.g., essential facilities). Buildings in Performance Group I are deemed as having the lowest performance expectations (e.g., minor storage facilities).

Tolerable Performance Levels. What is the nature of the hazard and the hazard experience? Do the hazards overlap? From a simplified perspective, the ICCPC addresses structural loads, natural hazards, and technological hazards (e.g., fire, explosion, contamination, infection, and other safety and health hazards). In theory, as long as these hazards are protected against to an agreed-upon tolerable level of performance or risk, everything should be fine.

However, for a variety of reasons, it is not easy to readily determine tolerable levels of performance or risk. From the design perspective, a primary reason is the difficulty in determining the "load" against which appropriate "resistance" is required. This is the current situation with prescriptive fire protection requirements. Almost every fire test of building materials, elements, and systems is against different, and sometimes incompatible or unrealistic, loads. Thus, when these components are assembled in a building, it is sometimes difficult to determine what level of performance (safety) is being provided. When addressing loads associated with extreme events, this becomes all the more difficult.

In an attempt to address this concern, the ICCPC uses the concepts of *magnitude of design event* and *levels of tolerable impact*. The magnitude of design events (loads) may be defined, quantified, and expressed deterministically or probabilistically; the magnitude may be expressed as a point value with confidence limits or safety factors or as a distribution. The magnitude may be strictly hazard related or it may have a frequency component (risk related). The term *design event* is used because one cannot guarantee the maximum load that a structure will be subjected to, especially in the case of hazard event–induced loads; however, one can design a structure to resist loads that are representative of probable events. In the ICCPC, design events are characterized into four classes: small (frequent), medium (less frequent), large (rare), and very large (very rare), indicating increasing magnitudes where "small" events are indicative of limited consequence events and "very large" events are indicative of significant consequence events. Specific to natural hazards, a correlation exists between event frequency and magnitude (e.g., very large magnitude earthquakes are very rare). The use of consequence, with or without frequency, allows flexibility in analysis and design.

Key Point   The definition of a *design event* also depends on the measurement of performance. As used in the ICCPC, *performance* is expressed in terms of *level of tolerable impact* (consequence) that the design event can have on structures, occupants, and contents.

Key Point   The relationship of the design event to the level of tolerable impact is important, because different events may demand different levels of performance, even if the same descriptor is used.

For example, a "mild" fire impact to an office may differ from a "mild" impact to a surgical suite in a hospital. As a result, a "small" design fire event for an office may differ from a "small" design fire event for a surgical suite.

Placing bounding conditions on the extent of impacts from design events has been obtained by defining levels of tolerable impact to which the structure must conform when subjected to design loads of various magnitudes. In order that the levels of impact can be measured or calculated, metrics were selected that reflect various limit states of damage, injury, or loss. The term *tolerable* is used to reflect the fact that absolute protection is not possible, and that some damage, injury, or loss is currently tolerated in structures, especially after a hazard event. The term *impact* is used as a broad descriptor of loss. In the ICCPC, four levels (I through IV) of tolerable impact to the structure, its contents, and its occupants are used [2, 7, 8, 9]. In this range, Level I represents a mild impact, whereas Level IV represents a severe impact. The four tolerable levels of impact are shown in Table 2.2.

Note the use of the terms *may* and *likelihood* in Table 2.2. These qualifiers reflect the fact that the levels of tolerable impact are *design* levels; some probability exists that an actual event will exceed the design impact thresholds. Although developed without specific consideration of terrorist events, these levels of tolerable impact can be used, with or without modification, for terrorist design events (e.g., blast, impact, and chemical/biological), where the design loads can be expressed in terms of forces, overpressures, concentrations, densities, or rates in a manner similar to natural and technological event loads.

Performance/Risk Matrix. The ICC developed a four-by-four matrix to tie together the concepts of *performance groups, magnitudes of design events,* and *tolerable levels of impact* [2, 7, 8, 9]. The primary reason for the matrix is to communicate the concepts of risk and related building performance. The matrix is illustrated in Figure 2.3.

The column headings represent the four *performance groups,* which embody groups of buildings with various uses for which

TABLE 2.2   Four Tolerable Levels of Impact for Buildings and Facilities

Impact Levels	Mild	Moderate	High	Severe
Structural Damage	There is no structural damage and the building or facility is safe to occupy.	There is moderate structural damage, which is repairable; some delay in re-occupancy can be expected.	There is significant damage to structural elements but no large falling debris; repair is possible. Significant delays in reoccupancy can be expected.	There is substantial structural damage, but all significant components continue to carry gravity load demands. Repair may not be technically possible. The building or facility is not safe for re-occupancy, as re-occupancy could cause collapse.
Nonstructural Systems	Nonstructural systems needed for normal building or facility use and emergency operations are fully operational.	Nonstructural systems needed for normal building or facility use are fully operational, although some clear-up and repair may be needed. Emergency systems remain fully operational.	Nonstructural systems needed for normal building or facility use are significantly damaged and inoperable; egress routes may be impaired by light debris; emergency systems may be significantly damaged, but remain operational.	Nonstructural systems for normal building or facility use may be completely nonfunctional. Egress routes may be impaired; emergency systems may be substantially damaged and nonfunctional.
Occupant Hazards	Injuries to building or facility occupants from hazard-related applied loads are minimal in numbers and minor in nature. There is a very low likelihood of single or multiple life loss. The nature of the applied load	Injuries to building or facility occupants from hazard-related applied loads may be locally significant. There is a low likelihood of single life loss and a very low likelihood of multiple life loss. The nature of the applied load (i.e., fire	Injuries to building or facility occupants from hazard-related applied loads may be locally significant with a high risk to life, but are generally moderate in numbers and nature. There is a moderate likelihood of	Injuries to building of facility occupants from hazard-related applied loads may be high in numbers and significant in nature. Significant risk to life may exist. There is a high likelihood of single life loss and a moderate likelihood

	(i.e., fire hazard) may result in higher levels of expected injuries and damage in localized areas, whereas the balance of the areas may sustain fewer injuries and less damage.	hazard) may result in higher levels of expected injuries and damage in localized areas, whereas the balance of the areas may sustain fewer injuries and less damage.	single life loss and a low probability of multiple life loss. The nature of the applied load (i.e., fire hazard) may result in higher levels of expected injuries and damage in localized areas, whereas the balance of the areas may sustain fewer injuries and less damage.	of multiple life loss. The nature of the applied load (i.e., fire hazard) may result in higher levels of expected injuries and damage in localized areas, whereas the balance of the areas may sustain fewer injuries and less damage.
Overall Extent of Damage	Damage to building or facility contents from hazard-related applied loads is minimal in extent and minor in cost.	Damage to building or facility contents may be locally significant, but is generally moderate in extent and cost. The nature of the applied load (i.e., fire hazard) may result in higher levels of expected injuries and damage in localized areas, whereas the balance of the areas may sustain fewer injuries and less damage.	Damage to building or facility contents from hazard-related applied loads may be locally total and generally significant. The nature of the applied load (i.e., fire hazard) may result in higher levels of expected injuries and damage in localized areas, whereas the balance of the areas may sustain fewer injuries and less damage.	Damage to building or facility contents from hazard-related applied loads may be total. The nature of the applied load (i.e., fire hazard) may result in higher levels of expected injuries and damage in localized areas, whereas the balance of the areas may sustain fewer injuries and less damage.
Hazardous Materials	Minimal hazardous materials are released to the environment.	Some hazardous materials may be released to the environment, but the risk to the community is minimal. No emergency relocation is necessary.	Hazardous materials may be released to the environment with localized relocation needed for buildings and facilities in the immediate vicinity.	Significant hazardous materials may be released to the environment, with relocation needed beyond the immediate vicinity.

Source: ICC, 2003. *ICC Performance Code for Buildings and Facilities,* International Code Council. Falls Church, VA.

FIGURE 2.3 Relationships Among Events, Tolerable Impacts, and Performance Groups Magnitude of Tolerable Impact.

| | | | Increasing level of performance → → → → → → → → → → → → → → → **Performance groups** | | | |
			PG I	PG II	PG III	PG IV
Magnitude of design event (Increasing magnitude of event ↑)		Very large (very rare)	Severe	Severe	High	Moderate
		Large (rare)	Severe	High	Moderate	Mild
		Medium (less frequent)	High	Moderate	Mild	Mild
		Small (frequent)	Moderate	Mild	Mild	Mild

(*Source:* ICC, 2003. *ICC Performance Code for Buildings and Facilities,* International Code Council, Falls Church, VA.)

similar performance is expected during and after a design hazard event based on the various risk and importance factors. The row headings represent the four magnitudes of design events. Within the matrix are the levels of tolerable impact. This approach enables the design team, code enforcement officials, and other stakeholders to better understand the assumed risk to occupants in buildings and the performance provided by buildings in various performance groups. The matrix provides a basis for establishing building performance objectives in terms of tolerable levels of impact. Here, the performance groups contain buildings of different uses for which similar levels of performance are desired. Performance Group I includes small, unoccupied outbuildings; Performance Group IV includes critical facilities, such as hospitals. The *magnitude of tolerable impact* reflects an expectation of building performance given a specific *magnitude of design event.*

As shown in Figure 2.3, a level of the tolerable impact is provided for each magnitude of design event in each performance group. For example, for a large magnitude design hazard event, the tolerable levels of impact are severe, high, moderate, and mild for Performance Groups I, II, III, and IV, respectively. This means a building in Performance Group IV should have only mild damage when subjected to the large design hazard event, whereas a building in Performance Group I would experience severe damage.

Key Point   For design purposes, the tolerable levels of impact can be considered the inverse of design performance levels to which the structure must conform when subjected to design loads of various magnitudes (expected performance).

The matrix embodies the following concepts:

- Society expects better performance for some buildings than for others.
- The measurement of building performance is a factor of the maximum levels of damage to be tolerated for increasing design hazard events.
- The establishment of building performance groups (levels), maximum levels of damage to be tolerated, and magnitudes of design events are based on analytical hazard and risk data, as well as public perceptions and expectations of the risk from hazards impacting buildings.

DoD Minimum Antiterrorism Standards for Buildings

The goal of the Department of Defense's *DoD Minimum Antiterrorism Standards for Buildings* [10] is to minimize the likelihood of mass casualties from terrorist attacks against DoD facilities and personnel. With its focus on minimizing mass casualties, the document is weighted heavily toward mitigation of blast effects. Although aimed at military force protection, the DoD standards can be applied in the private sector as well. The DoD standards include the following major design strategies:

- Maximize standoff distance
- Prevent building collapse
- Minimize hazardous flying debris
- Provide effective building layout
- Limit airborne contamination

- Provide mass notification
- Facilitate future upgrades

The DoD standards encompass the following areas:

- Non-worst-case baseline threats
- Variety of explosive-charge weights, based on delivery mode and target
- Improvised use of CBR weapons
- Controlled perimeters
- Levels of protection

Of particular concern are the levels of protection for new buildings. The DoD standards identify five levels of building protection:

1. Below standards
2. Very low
3. Low
4. Medium
5. High

The five levels of protection, and associated damage expectations, are described in Table 2.3.

The descriptions in Table 2.3 provide an indication of what type and level of damage and injury might occur given explosion loads of defined charge weights. As with the NFPA performance-based design options and the ICCPC matrix, the intent of Table 2.3 is to provide decision makers with information to help them establish an appropriate level of protection for a given facility based on threats, design loads, and potential damage.

As with any decision regarding performance and risk mitigation, trade-offs will be made between cost and protection level. In addition, that an actual event will be less than or equal to the design load selected is not guaranteed. This is true for the NFPA, ICC, and DoD approaches, and this issue will be addressed further in Chapter 4 and in subsequent chapters. The relationship between risk, performance, and tolerable loss is used within regulatory structures in the commercial and governmental sectors. The approaches applied can provide an excellent basis for risk-informed performance-based analysis and design for extreme events. Another resource is the *ISC Security Criteria for New Federal Office Buildings and Major Renovation Projects: A Review and Commentary* [13].

TABLE 2.3   Levels of Protection for New Buildings

Level of Protection	Potential Structural Damage	Potential Door and Glazing Hazards	Potential Injury
Below standards	Severe damage. Frame collapse, massive destruction, little left standing.	Doors and windows fail, resulting in lethal hazards.	Majority of personnel suffer fatalities.
Very low	Heavy damage. Damage results in onset of structural collapse. Major deformation of primary and secondary structural members, but progressive collapse is unlikely. Collapse of nonstructural elements.	Glazing will break and will likely be propelled into the building, resulting in serious glazing-fragment injuries, but fragments will be reduced. Doors may be propelled into rooms, presenting serious hazards.	Majority of personnel suffer serious injuries. There are likely to be a limited number of fatalities (10 to 25%).
Low	Damaged and unrepairable. Major deformation of non-structural elements and secondary structural members and minor deformation of primary structural members, but progressive collapse is unlikely.	Glazing will break but will fall within 1 meter of the wall or will otherwise not present a significant fragment hazard. Doors may fail but they will rebound out of their frames, presenting minimal hazards.	Majority of personnel suffer significant injuries. There are likely to be a few fatalities (<10%).
Medium	Damaged and repairable. Minor deformation of nonstructural elements and secondary structural members and no permanent deformation in primary structural members.	Glazing will break, but will remain in window frame. Doors will stay in frames, but will not be reusable.	Some minor injuries, but fatalities unlikely.
High	Superficial damage. No permanent deformation in primary structural members, secondary structural members, or nonstructural elements.	Glazing will not break. Doors will be reusable.	Only superficial injuries are likely.

Source: Adapted from DoD, 2003. *DoD Minimum Antiterrorism Standards for Buildings,* Unified Facilities Criteria, UFC 4-010-01, U.S. Department of Defense, Washington, DC.

—PERFORMANCE-BASED ———————————— ANALYSIS AND DESIGN

In the broadest sense, performance-based analysis and design is a process of engineering a solution to meet specific levels of performance, where performance may be stated in terms of qualitative or quantitative objectives, criteria, or limiting states of damage or injury [3].

Performance-based analysis and design has gained momentum in recent years and is being used increasingly for structural engineering for natural hazards [14]; for fire protection engineering, as explained in NFPA's *Introduction to Performance-Based Fire Safety*, the *SFPE Engineering Guide to Performance-Based Fire Protection Analysis and Design of Buildings*, and other publications [3, 15]; and for multihazard mitigation design, including extreme events [16].

Performance-Based Structural Design

The basic process for performance-based structural design is shown in Figure 2.4. In brief, the process consists of the following steps:

- Select appropriate performance objectives.
- Develop a preliminary design designed to meet the objectives.
- Verify that the design can achieve the objectives.
- Iteratively revise the design until an acceptable design is achieved.

Performance objectives are quantified statements of the severity of a design event, its probability of occurrence, and the permissible damage given that the event is experienced [14].

The design event or its probability of occurrence is often defined as the *hazard*. Probabilities of occurrence may be expressed as mean annual recurrence intervals (the average period of time, in years, between repeat occurrence of an event of a given or larger magnitude) or annual probabilities of exceedance (the likelihood in any year that a given event will be experienced, calculated as the inverse of the mean recurrence interval). Note that the two expressions of probabilities of occurrence describe the same event. For example, using the mean-annual-recurrence taxonomy, a 100-year flood would be the level of flooding expected to occur, on average, once every 100 years. Using the annual probability-of-exceedance taxonomy, a 100-year flood would have an annual probability of exceedance of 0.01. Use of a particular taxonomy is often a combination of personal preference and industry norm.

FIGURE 2.4   The Performance-Based Structural Design Process.

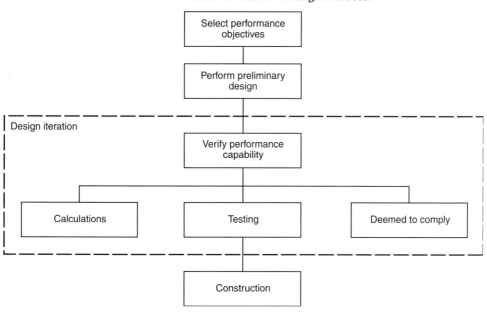

(*Source:* Hamburger, R. O., 2004. "Structural Design," in *Performance-Based Building Design Concepts,* International Code Council, Falls Church, VA, pp. 6-1–6-22.)

Associated with a design event is the amount of damage that is tolerable (performance level). As discussed previously, performance levels may be qualitative or quantitative. As used in structural design, a qualitative performance level might relate to the effect of the damage from a design event on the state of the building after the event is experienced; for example, whether the building remains safe for continued occupancy, whether it is damaged but functional or operational in its intended service, or whether the safety of occupants is threatened. Quantitative expressions of performance levels, as used in structural analysis and design, relate to specific physical states, such as the extent of strength or stiffness loss, the amount of energy dissipated, and so on. Such expressions of performance are often meaningful only to structural engineers.

Given that both qualitative and quantitative descriptions are used in practice, most authoritative documents providing guidelines for performance-based structural design provide both qualitative and quantitative descriptions of performance levels to facilitate communication between structural engineers and others, such as the lay public. More details on performance-based structural design for extreme events, including seismic events, can be found in Chapters 7 and 9.

Performance-Based Fire Safety Design

As with structural engineering, the performance-based concept has been adopted by the fire safety engineering community, where performance-based fire safety design has been defined in NFPA's *Introduction to Performance-Based Fire Safety* as follows:

> . . . an engineering approach to fire protection design based on (1) agreed upon fire safety goals, loss objectives, and design objectives; (2) deterministic and probabilistic evaluation of fire initiation, growth, and development; (3) the physical and chemical properties of fire and fire effluents; and (4) quantitative assessment of the effectiveness of design alternatives against loss objectives and performance objectives.

Although this definition is not universal, research conducted in the 1990s into the evolution of performance-based codes and performance-based fire safety analysis and design methods determined that the concepts are entrenched in more than a dozen performance-based fire safety analysis and design approaches under development or in use around the world [17].

Development of performance-based design options has in some cases also resulted in a more clearly developed set of rules for prescriptive-based designs. This is particularly true where performance-based design options require proposed solutions to be measured against the goals and objectives of the code. Codes such as NFPA *101* and *NFPA 5000* offer a detailed set of goals and objectives that apply to traditional prescriptive-based code regulations and the newer performance-based code regulations. The goals and objectives provide qualitative conditions to describe the level of performance, the intended perils considered by the code, and the expected outcome when the goals and objectives are met.

This level of detailed performance goals and objectives did not exist in U.S.–based codes until performance-based design concepts were introduced into codes beginning in 2000.

Evaluation Process

Many of these performance-based design approaches, including the one described in the *SFPE Engineering Guide to Performance-Based Protection Analysis and Design of Buildings*, contain seven interrelated steps [3, 18]:

1. Identify site or project information.
2. Identify goals and objectives.
3. Develop performance criteria.
4. Develop event scenarios, design scenarios, and design loads.
5. Develop candidate design options.
6. Evaluate candidate design options and select final design.
7. Develop final design documentation.

The basic flow of the these steps is outlined in Figure 2.5.

In Figure 2.5, the process is outlined as a sequential process. In reality, however, it often involves several iterations, especially dur-

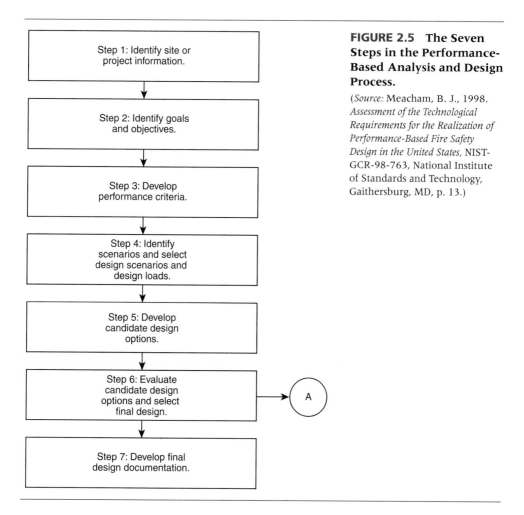

FIGURE 2.5 The Seven Steps in the Performance-Based Analysis and Design Process.

(*Source:* Meacham, B. J., 1998. *Assessment of the Technological Requirements for the Realization of Performance-Based Fire Safety Design in the United States,* NIST-GCR-98-763, National Institute of Standards and Technology, Gaithersburg, MD, p. 13.)

ing the evaluation stage (step 6). The iterative nature of the evaluation, including the possibility of revisiting the performance criteria selected, is shown in Figure 2.6. (Figures 2.5 and 2.6 both illustrate the process without reference to fire, indicating its applicability to any engineering problem.)

The advantage of the performance-based analysis and design approach lies in the flexibility that can be achieved without compromising on safety, cost, or other important factors such as aesthetics, usability, and function [18, 19]. The approach allows all parties involved to agree on the goals, objectives, criteria, and analysis and evaluation methods, resulting in a design that best fits all parameters—a performance-based design solution. The following provides a brief summary of the various steps in the process [17].

A performance-based analysis and design approach can be used in conjunction with performance-based regulations or on its own. When performance-based regulations exist, issues such as goals, objectives, criteria, and performance requirements may already be identified and will not necessarily require development as part of the analysis.

Identifying Site or Project Information. The first step in the performance-based analysis and design process is to gather information about the site, structure, facility, or process. This includes gathering information on the building's characteristics, such as size, layout, use, and construction. Particular attention should be paid to the facility's use, occupancy, construction, geographic location, symbolic importance, criticality, consequence, and threats.

Operational characteristics relate to specific functions of a facility, building, or process or to needs specific to the mission of the facility or its occupants. Facilities or areas of facilities that are very important because they contain areas of high-value equipment or areas in which down-time needs to be effectively zero should be identified. This is especially important when the facility serves a necessary community service, such as a hospital or a utility, or when a business relies on the operation of processes or equipment being protected.

Finally, it is important to characterize the occupants at this stage. Occupant characterization will vary by use of the building and should include such factors as the occupants' ages and abilities, whether people sleep in the building, and whether any or all of the occupants may be considered targets (when terrorism is a concern). Obtaining this information is extremely important, especially in cases when performance-based codes are lacking in specifics on the populations being protected and the levels of risk or safety desired.

FIGURE 2.6   **The Iterative Nature of the Performance-Based Design Evaluation Process.**

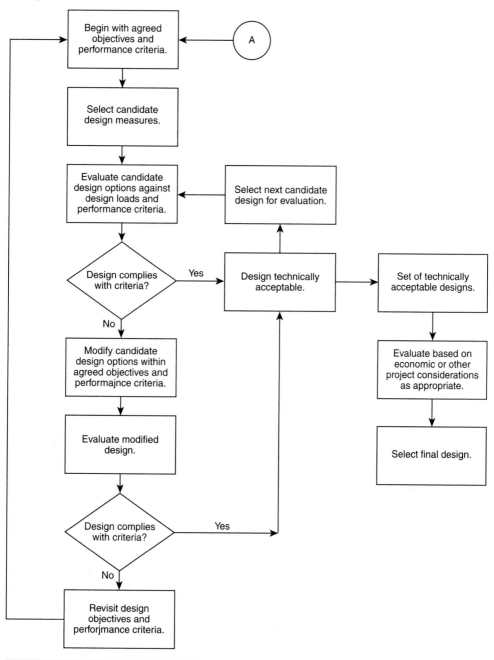

(*Source:* Meacham, B. J., 1998. *Assessment of the Technological Requirements for the Realization of Performance-Based Fire Safety Design in the United States,* NIST-GCR-98-763, National Institute of Standards and Technology, Gaithersburg, MD, p. 14.)

Identifying Goals and Objectives. After gathering site and project information, the next step is to establish goals and objectives. In general, *goals* are noncontroversial statements that reflect a common aim. They are often easy to agree with and are measured qualitatively, if at all. In a performance-based regulatory system, statements of goals are normally provided in the regulation.

Objectives are used to provide direction as to how a particular goal might be met. They are normally stated in quantifiable terms. For example, an objective may be expressed as a stakeholder objective or as a client-loss objective (some indication of the level of loss that the client can tolerate). Such an objective may be expressed as "protect the piece of equipment in Room X against the effects of a fire such that a return to full operation can occur within 2 hours." In order to meet the goal of maintaining continuity of operations, the objective is to ensure that the equipment is not out of service for more than 2 hours.

Once the stakeholder objectives or functional requirements are clearly defined and agreed upon by those involved in the design process, the level at which the building and its systems should perform in order to meet those objectives should be identified. This is done through statements called *design objectives* or *performance requirements*.

For example, a design objective for mission protection might read: "limit the temperatures in the room to less than that which would cause irreversible or unrecoverable damage to the target equipment." In this case, the fire size that will cause the damage can be estimated, and appropriate structural and other systems can be designed to meet this requirement.

In performance-based codes, one typically finds *performance requirements*, which are statements of the level of performance that must be met by building materials, assemblies, systems, components, and construction methods in order to satisfy fire safety goals and objectives. Such parameters should be quantifiable. In addition, analysts should be able to measure, calculate, and predict them as well.

Developing Performance Criteria. *Performance criteria* are the metrics against which design objectives or performance requirements are assessed. Unlike design objectives or performance requirements, which are often stated qualitatively, performance criteria must be stated in such a manner that they can be directly measured or calculated (e.g., gas temperature), because these become the criteria that form the basis for the evaluation of a design. Further, performance criteria must be described in engineering terms (i.e., quantified values for critical parameters) such that they can be used in analysis to judge performance directly against the goals, objectives, and performance requirements. This is one area where performance-based design differs significantly from many performance-based regulations.

Key Point Not all performance-based regulations include quantitative criteria, but a performance-based design cannot be undertaken or evaluated without quantitative criteria.

The need for quantitative criteria can be illustrated using a simplified example based on a life-safety goal:

- The life-safety goal is to protect those people not intimate with the initial fire from loss of life. (This is easy to agree with, yet difficult to quantify.)
- To meet this goal, one stakeholder objective (functional requirement) might be to provide people not in the room of the fire's origin with adequate protection from the effects of the fire. (This provides a little more detail; one could infer that fire protection systems must be provided.)
- To meet this requirement, one design objective (operative requirement or performance requirement) might be to limit the effects of the fire to the room of origin. (If the fire effects are contained to the room of origin, the people outside of the room will not be exposed to the threat, under most conditions.)
- To meet the design objective, an engineer (or some document within the regulatory system) needs to establish a performance criterion (or set of performance criteria), such as a maximum expected heat-release rate or fire-growth rate for the room of fire origin.

In most cases, several design criteria will be needed to demonstrate that a performance requirement has been met. Demonstrating this may be difficult, because the interrelations between requirements and criteria may be complex.

Developing Event Scenarios, Design Scenarios, and Design Loads. Another key step in the performance-based design process is to consider a range of event and design scenarios and to develop corresponding design loads. An *event scenario* is a set of conditions that defines an initiating event and its subsequent impact throughout a building or part of a building. An infinite number of event scenarios are possible for any given building. Because this range of event scenarios includes situations that may be considered highly unlikely, it is possible to pare the scenarios down into a smaller group of scenarios that can be used as part of the design process. These are called *design scenarios.*

The range of design scenarios selected for consideration should reflect both probabilistic and deterministic considerations; that is, how likely it is that the event will occur, and, if it does occur, how it is expected to impact the building. Many factors must be considered when developing event scenarios and paring them down into design scenarios, including the following:

- The pre-event situation: building, compartment, conditions
- Extension potential: beyond compartment, structure, area, or origin (including subsequent events, such as fire)
- Occupant characteristics: alert, asleep, self-mobile, disabled, infant, elderly, and so forth
- Available relevant data

Risk assessment is often the most appropriate tool for identifying event scenarios and paring them down to design scenarios.

Once a set of design scenarios has been established, a set of corresponding design loads needs to be developed. Design loads are used to evaluate the candidate design options, much the same as design loads are used in structural design to ensure that the strength of a structure is adequate. Design loads need to be developed for every design scenario considered for a compartment, building, structure, or process.

Developing Candidate Design Options. After the design scenarios and design loads have been developed, the next step is to develop design alternatives. Candidate designs should be selected from components, systems, and strategies that will ensure that the design objectives are met. In most cases, a number of candidate design options should be considered, including applicable prescriptive code requirements.

Evaluating Candidate Design Options and Selecting Final Design. After the candidate design options have been developed, the next step is to evaluate them for compliance with the design objectives and performance criteria and to select a suitable option as the final design. The evaluation process is iterative, and a variety of mitigation measures are evaluated against the design loads and the design objectives. Factors such as modifications to the ventilation systems and variations to construction materials, interior finish, and contents are evaluated in this step. In many cases, code-prescribed requirements will serve as a baseline for evaluation and review, and it is important to know if the code requirements meet the performance criteria, exceed them, or fall short of them.

Developing Final Design Documentation. The final step in the process is to document the analysis and design and to prepare equipment and installation specifications. The analysis and design report is a critical factor in the acceptance of the performance-based design. The report needs to outline all of the steps taken during the analysis and design process and present the results in a format and manner acceptable to the authorities and to the client (stakeholder). At a minimum, the report should include the following:

- Intent of the analysis or design: A narrative of why the process was undertaken.
- Statement of design approach (philosophy): A statement that describes the approach taken, why it was taken, what assumptions were made, and what engineering tools and methodologies were applied.
- Site or project information: Information on hazard and risk analysis, building characteristics, and occupant characteristics.
- Statement of client goals and objectives: A statement that describes the agreed upon goals and objectives of the performance-based analysis or design and that identifies who agreed and when.
- Performance criteria: A listing of the performance criteria and the performance requirements (design objectives) to which they relate, including any safety or reliability factors applied, and support for safety or reliability factors, where necessary.
- Event and design scenarios: A description of the event scenarios considered and the design scenarios used, the bases for selecting and rejecting event scenarios not used as design scenarios, and assumptions and design restrictions (conditions).
- Design load(s): A description of the design load(s) used, the bases for selecting and rejecting design load(s), and the assumptions, limitations, and design restrictions (conditions).

- Candidate designs: A description of the design alternative(s) se-lected, the bases for selecting and rejecting design alternative(s) (deterministic, probabilistic), and the assumptions, conditions, limitations, and uncertainties. This information should include comparison of results with the performance criteria and design objectives and a discussion of the sensitivity of the selected de-sign alternative to changes in the building use, contents, and oc-cupants.

- Uncertainty factors: A description of any uncertainty (safety, reli-ability) factors, how they were derived, and appropriate refer-ences.

- Cost-benefit analyses: When cost is a factor in the decision-making process, cost-benefit analyses should be included as well.

- Design tools and methods used: Documentation of the engi-neering tools and methods used in the analysis or design, in-cluding appropriate references (literature, date, software version), assumptions, limitations, uncertainties, engineering judgments, input data, validation data or procedures, and sensi-tivity analyses.

- Test, inspection, and maintenance requirements: All tests, inspec-tion procedures, and maintenance schedules should be detailed.

- Emergency management concerns: Discussion on changes in use, contents, or materials as well as training and education for build-ing staff and occupants.

- References: Software documentation, journal reports, handbook references, technical data sheets, and fire test results should be supplied.

With regard to both the design and the emergency-management aspects, it is important to consider the expected use of the building, throughout its lifetime, when designing mitigation measures. The design documentation should clearly indicate the limits of the design and identify any specific factors that will warrant a reevaluation or redesign. These indicators may include change of occupancy, a change of mission, or significant modifications to the building or its systems. Even though a performance-based approach may be used to identify design parameters, actual installation of resultant equip-ment, systems, and related fire protection features will not signifi-cantly change, as installation standards will be followed just as they are in a prescriptive design.

__COST AND EFFECTIVENESS ANALYSIS _____

With most risk-informed decision problems, the cost and effectiveness of mitigation are critical decision factors. As such, application of cost-benefit concepts can be helpful. In principle, if risk mitigation measures vary in both cost and benefit (effectiveness), classical economic theory can be used to help describe an "optimal" level of risk, where the optimal level is that at which the incremental or marginal cost of risk reduction equals the marginal reduction achieved in societal cost [20]. In other words, insufficient spending on risk mitigation could result in significant expected losses, whereas overspending on risk mitigation could result in expected losses that are disproportionately low when compared to the mitigation investment, with the optimal level somewhere in between. This concept is illustrated in Figure 2.7.

FIGURE 2.7 **Economic Concept of Optimal Level of Risk.**

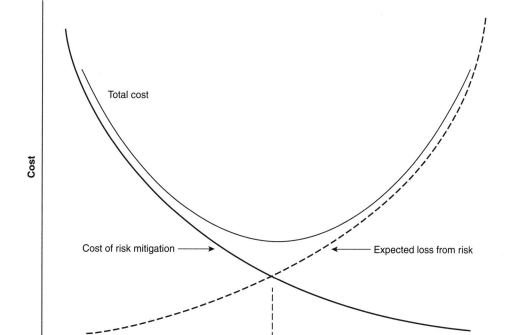

(*Source:* Adapted from Morgan, M. G., 1990. "Choosing and Managing Technology-Induced Risk," in T. S. Glickman and M. Gough (Eds.), *Readings in Risk,* Resources for the Future, Washington, DC.)

FIGURE 2.8   The Risk-Cost-Effectiveness Matrix.

	Area/ system	Threat scenario	Ease of delivery /attack potential	Operational impact	Life-safety impact	Relative risk	Relative mitigation effectiveness	Relative mitigation cost	Relative cost effectiveness	Relative risk/ cost ranking
1										
2										

(*Source:* Arup Internal Report.)

In the context of the risk-informed performance-based design process, the cost and benefit (effectiveness) of mitigation measures can be determined through the use of a simple spreadsheet to apply a ranking method to compare risks, costs, and mitigation effectiveness. This process is illustrated in Figure 2.8.

In such a matrix, the levels of risk, costs, and effectiveness can be ranked. For example, several risk- and cost-ranking approaches use a scale from 1 to 5, with 1 being *low* and 5 being *high* [10, 21], but other scales can be used as well [22]. It is important that the scale and the associated values fit the risk problem, and that the values are mathematically combined in an appropriate manner so as to provide meaningful results.

When set up appropriately, the matrix can yield useful insight for the selection of mitigation options. For example, looking at risk, cost, and effectiveness and using a ranking scale of 1 to 5, where 1 is *low* and 5 is *high,* combining the factors can quickly give one a sense for the overall risk, cost, and effectiveness. For example, if the risk is *high,* the mitigation effectiveness is *high,* and the mitigation cost is *low,* then this would be a good option to consider; likewise, if the risk is *low,* the mitigation effectiveness is *low,* and the cost is *high,* then this would probably not be a good option. Again, the most important concerns are that the ranking and the valuation match the problem, stakeholder risk, and cost tolerances. Additional discussion is provided on risk, performance-based design, and decision making in Chapter 3.

▃SUMMARY

Risk-informed performance-based analysis and design provides a comprehensive approach to addressing the potential impact and mitigation of extreme events on buildings. It involves assessing unwanted events that may impact a building, determining the likelihood of an event occurring, and predicting the potential impacts. It can provide a basis for establishing tolerable building performance, for characterizing risk for buildings, and for identifying the likelihood and consequences of various extreme event scenarios.

However, risk means different things to different people. Care must be taken to gain broad stakeholder understanding and acceptance when undertaking a risk-informed performance-based approach to minimize misunderstanding and to facilitate a design that meets all stakeholder needs. Combining risk and performance concepts into a risk-informed performance-based approach allows for risk data and engineering analysis to be coupled with stakeholder and societal risk perceptions and performance expectations in order to establish building risk and performance targets that everyone can agree with.

__BIBLIOGRAPHY_____

References Cited

1. GSA, 1999. *Balancing Security and Openness: A Thematic Summary of a Workshop on Security and the Design of Public Buildings, Sponsored by DSA and AIA,* November 30, 1999, General Services Administration, Washington, DC.

2. ICC, 2001. *ICC Performance Code for Buildings and Facilities,* International Code Council, Falls Church, VA.

3. Meacham, B. J., 1998. *Assessment of the Technological Requirements for the Realization of Performance-Based Fire Safety Design in the United States,* NIST-GCR-98-763, National Institute of Standards and Technology, Gaithersburg, MD.

4. Little, R., Meacham, B. J., and Smilowitz, R., 2001. "A Performance-Based Multi-Objective Decision Framework for Security and Natural Hazard Mitigation," *Proceedings of the National Symposium on Comprehensive Force Protection,* Society of American Military Engineers, Charleston, SC, November 1–2.

5. Meacham, B. J., 2003. "A Risk-Informed Performance-Based Approach to Tall Building Design," *Proceedings of the CIB-CTBUH International Conference on Tall Buildings: Strategies for Performance in the Aftermath of the World Trade Center,* International Council for Building Research and Innovation (CIB), Council on Tall Build-

ings in the Urban Habitat (CTBUH), and Construction Technology and Management Center, Universiti Teknologi, Malaysia, Rotterdam, Netherlands, pp. 279–286.

6. Stern, P. C., and Fineburg, H. V. (Eds.), 1996. *Understanding Risk: Informing Decisions in a Democratic Society,* National Research Council, National Academy Press, Washington, DC.

7. Meacham, B. J., 2000. "A Process for Identifying, Characterizing and Incorporating Risk Concepts into Performance-Based Building and Fire Regulation Development," Ph.D. Dissertation, Clark University, Worcester, MA.

8. Meacham, B. J., 2004. "Risk Characterization and Performance Concepts," in B. J. Meacham (Ed.), *Performance-Based Building Design Concepts,* International Code Council, Falls Church, VA, pp. 4-1–4-34.

9. ICC, 2003. *ICC Performance Code for Buildings and Facilities,* International Code Council, Falls Church, VA.

10. DoD, 2003. *DoD Minimum Antiterrorism Standards for Buildings,* Unified Facilities Criteria, UFC 4-010-01, U.S. Department of Defense, Washington, DC.

11. ASCE, 2003. *Minimum Design Loads for Buildings and Other Structures,* SEI/ASCE 7-02, American Society of Civil Engineers, Reston, VA.

12. Meacham, B. J., 2004. "Performance-Based Building Regulatory Systems: Structure, Hierarchy and Linkages," *Journal of the Structural Engineering Society of New Zealand,* Vol. 17, No. 1, pp. 37–51.

13. Board on Infrastructure and the Constructed Environment (BICE), 2003. *ISC Security Design Criteria for New Federal Office Buildings and Major Renovation Projects: A Review and Commentary,* National Academies Press, Washington, DC.

14. Hamburger, R. O., 2004. "Structural Design," in B. J. Meacham (Ed.), *Performance-Based Building Design Concepts,* International Code Council, Falls Church, VA, pp. 6-1–6-22.

15. Meacham, B. J., and Custer, R. L. P., 1995. "Performance-Based Fire Safety Engineering: An Introduction of Basic Concepts," *Journal of Fire Protection Engineering,* Vol. 7, No. 2, pp. 35–54.

16. Whittaker, A., Hamburger, R., Comartin, C., Mahoney, M., Bachman, R., and Rojahn, C., 2003. "Performance-Based Engineering of Buildings and Infrastructure for Extreme Loadings," Applied Technology Council, Redwood City, CA, www.atcouncil.org/pdfs/Whittaker2.pdf.

17. Meacham, B. J., 1998. *The Evolution of Performance-Based Codes and Fire Safety Design Methods,* GCR 98-763, National Institute of Standards and Technology, Gaithersburg, MD.

18. Meacham, B. J., 2004. "Performance-Based Building Regulatory Systems: Structure, Hierarchy and Linkages," *Journal of the Structural Engineering Society of New Zealand,* Vol. 17, No. 1, pp. 37–51.

19. Meacham, B. J., 1999. "Fire Safety Analysis and Design in a Performance-Based Regulatory System," *Proceedings of the International Convention on Global Building Model in the Next Millennium,* Victoria Building Control Commission, Melbourne, Australia, pp. 187–201.

20. Morgan, M. G., 1990. "Choosing and Managing Technology-Induced Risk," in T. S. Glickman and M. Gough (Eds.), *Readings in Risk,* Resources for the Future, Washington, DC, pp. 17–28.

21. DoD, 2000. *Standard Practice for System Safety,* MIL STD 882D, U.S. Department of Defense, Washington, DC.

22. FEMA, 2003. *Risk Management Series—Reference Manual to Mitigate Potential Terrorist Attacks against Buildings,* Publication 426, Federal Emergency Management Association, Washington, DC.

NFPA Codes, Standards, and Recommended Practices

NFPA Publications. The following is a list of NFPA codes, standards, and recommended practices cited in this chapter. See the latest version of the *NFPA Catalog* for availability of current editions of these documents.

NFPA *101®, Life Safety Code®*
NFPA *5000®, Building Construction and Safety Code®*

Additional Readings

Chapman, R. E., and Leng, C. J., 2004. *Cost-Effective Responses to Terrorist Risks in Constructed Facilities,* NISTIR 7073, National Institute of Standards and Technology, Gaithersburg, MD.

Custer, R. L. P., and Meacham, B. J., 1997. *Introduction to Performance-Based Fire Safety,* National Fire Protection Association, Quincy, MA.

SFPE, 2000. *SFPE Engineering Guide to Performance-Based Fire Protection Analysis and Design of Buildings,* National Fire Protection Association, Quincy, MA.

3

Competing Objectives

Richard G. Little

Buildings are constructed to fulfill many objectives—to make a public statement, to provide needed space, or to generate income. In addition to these basic objectives, buildings often must meet requirements to provide amenities, satisfy public or corporate missions, and be cost-efficient, among others. Buildings are also expected to protect their occupants from death and injury and to limit damage to the facility, its contents, and its mission from a broad range of natural and technological hazards, including acts of terrorism and related violence.

If only one objective, such as creating an architectural feature of great beauty or maximizing the survivability of the occupants, is deemed important, it can generally be accomplished. For most buildings, however, trade-offs must be made so that competing objectives can be addressed and satisfied, at least partially. This chapter discusses issues that arise when design or operational objectives conflict during planning for extreme events. It presents tools that can be used to help address and balance competing objectives and explores how trade-offs can be structured so that hazard mitigation is provided within a rational context of aesthetics, functionality, and cost. To a large degree, this chapter focuses on vehicle bomb attacks against buildings and the countermeasures employed to thwart them. Although trade-offs must be made when considering other hazards, such as earthquakes, hurricanes, or fire, such hazards must be addressed during the design process, because building codes have specific provisions for seismic and wind loads as well as for fire safety. At present, building owners are not required to provide physical or management measures to counter a terrorist attack. It is the element of choice implicit in such a risk-based decision that frames the ensuing discussion.

__NATURE OF THE HAZARD_____

Over their lifetimes, buildings and other structures must resist a formidable array of hazards. For example, natural hazards that routinely affect buildings include earthquakes, extreme winds, floods, snow and ice, volcanic activity, landslides, tsunamis, and wildfires. Technological hazards include fire, accidental and deliberate explosions, and failures resulting from system complexity. Although all of these hazards affect buildings in a somewhat different manner, they all have the potential to cause costly damage (sometimes total failure), loss of function, and oftentimes injury and death.

Buildings must be resistant to a wide variety of hazards and often cannot be built to address only one objective. However, some buildings have been built to meet one specific objective. For example, the Taj Mahal in India is an example of a building designed for one objective—great beauty (Figure 3.1).

Another example is the Cheyenne Mountain Operations Center (CMOC) in Colorado, which was constructed by the U.S. Depart-

FIGURE 3.1 Exterior of the Taj Mahal in India.
(*Source:* Photo by Associated Press.)

ment of Defense to survive a nuclear attack. Neither of these building programs—neither the Taj Mahal nor the CMOC—was constrained by cost and budget factors.

The main objective at CMOC was to create a complex of buildings of great strength. At the entry to the CMOC is a pair of steel blast doors each weighing 25 tons. Behind those doors, which are shown in Figure 3.2, is a complex of steel buildings built on 5.1 acres; it includes a system of excavated chambers and tunnels surrounded by 2,000 feet of granite. The inner complex is made up of 15 freestanding buildings that have no physical contact with the rock walls or roofs. Twelve of these buildings are three stories tall; the others are one and two stories [1].

Key Point Engineering design for extreme events has generally focused on first-order effects; that is, designing robust systems that can resist the static and dynamic loads imparted by a specific event, such as an earthquake, hurricane, or tornado.

FIGURE 3.2 **Blast Doors to the Cheyenne Mountain Complex.**

(*Source:* Photo by Eugene Chavez; courtesy of the U.S. Department of Defense.)

In recent years, owners, tenants, and design professionals have had to consider a new hazard in the design equation: the threat of a terrorist attack. Although the vehicle bomb is only one terrorist tactic of concern for buildings—the introduction of chemical and biological agents into the ventilation system must also be considered—it does serve as a practical surrogate for how hazard mitigation can be integrated into the broader decision process.

In both new construction and renovation, physical protection for some buildings has become a mandatory element during the planning and design process. This task is made more difficult because buildings must provide protection from terrorist threats and other hazards while retaining features that make them desirable workspaces and attractive public spaces. For example, architectural design objectives are frequently seen as being in conflict with blast mitigation objectives, because the question is reduced to a simple binary set: secure but unaesthetic on one side and attractive but vulnerable on the other. In light of the limited resources available for physical protection, and hazard mitigation in general, a better way is needed to allocate scarce resources to the highest-priority concerns.

MULTI-OBJECTIVE DECISION MAKING

Multi-objective decision making has been well explored from both a theoretical and empirical standpoint, and many excellent references are available that venture far beyond the material in this chapter [2, 3, 4]. This work all supports a general algorithm for decision making that incorporates the following five elements:

1. Define the problem.
2. Set objectives.
3. Develop a range of alternatives that meet the objectives.
4. Identify and understand the consequences of the competing alternatives.
5. Evaluate the alternatives giving consideration to the necessary trade-offs.

Stakeholder Participation

Although this algorithm appears to be relatively straightforward, in practice each step must be undertaken thoughtfully, with extra care taken to include the input and values of all stakeholders. The importance of meaningful stakeholder involvement cannot be overemphasized.

Key Point   Given the high cost of implementing effective physical security and hazard mitigation strategies, the participation and knowledge of all affected parties, including policy makers, law enforcement officials, building owners and occupants, planners, architects, engineers, first responders, and security specialists, is required.

Those discussions of security that have occurred have been largely unproductive because some believe that security must be maximized regardless of the consequences for design, cost, or accessibility, whereas others demand attractive, accessible architecture while paying minimal attention to real security issues. This debate fails to recognize the distinct differences between the technical elements of protecting buildings from hazards (e.g., terrorist threat levels, tactics, bomb sizes and delivery methods, building construction) and the community value judgments (e.g., architectural aesthetics, freedom of movement) that must be incorporated. A balance between technical elements and community values must be achieved if workable strategies are to be developed and implemented. Methods that can be used to frame this complex and often emotionally charged discussion are discussed later in this chapter. In any event, however, questions of this type are not for engineers to answer alone [5].

Physical Access Control Measures

The vulnerabilities to terrorism of our cities and public places and how best to address them have been subject to considerable discussion, debate, and reflexive defensive measures since September 11, 2001. Physical access control measures have ranged from "temporary" concrete barriers to planters and street furniture to permanent bollards, walls, and plinths. These physical access controls are usually supplemented by armed guards aided by closed-circuit TV cameras and other surveillance measures. Buildings have received retrofit window treatments and structural enhancement of columns and slabs to mitigate blast effects, and some buildings are being considered for systems of sensors and filters to guard against chemical and biological agents. Figure 3.3 shows an example of the security

FIGURE 3.3 **Perimeter Security Measures on Pennsylvania Avenue in Washington, D.C.**

(*Source:* Photo courtesy of the National Capital Planning Commission.)

measures taken after the September 11 terrorist attacks to protect the perimeter of a building in Washington, D.C.

Although these direct physical responses to the events that occurred on September 11 are certainly understandable, they are driven more by the desire to protect people and assets from what could happen rather than what is likely to happen. In other words, these measures address the vulnerability of people, buildings, and other public spaces to certain types of attack. They are not a true assessment of the risk of attack. This approach essentially removes the public from the decision process and eliminates from consideration any willingness on the part of the public to accept some portion of that risk.

SECURITY AND RISK

Risk is a concept that gives meaning to things, forces, or circumstances that pose a danger to people or what they value [6]. In the context of hazard mitigation for buildings, risk connotes the likelihood and consequences of failure of critical physical or operational systems that would lead to loss, either economic or in terms of human life. The development of effective and efficient project-specific hazard mitigation strategies requires the use of *risk assessment,* a decision technique that systematically incorporates consideration of adverse events, event probabilities, event consequences, and vulnerabilities. It assumes the participation and knowledge of all affected stakeholders, including policy makers, owners, occupants, architects, engineers, and security specialists.

Calculating Risk

Risk can be expressed conceptually as follows:

$$R = P \times C \tag{1}$$

Where:

P = Probability of an adverse event
C = Consequences of that event

Risk has classically been defined by three questions [7]:

1. What can go wrong?
2. What is the likelihood that it could go wrong?
3. What are the consequences of failure?

Although direct, in practice these questions often prove difficult to define precisely. Therefore, risk management seeks answers to a second set of questions [8]:

- What can be done and what options are available? (What is the mix of site selection and configuration, building features, and management practices that will provide the desired level of protection?)
- What are the associated trade-offs in terms of all costs, benefits, and risks? (For example, reduced risk and improved confidence in security normally would be traded off with increased cost.)
- What are the impacts of current management decisions on future options? (Policy options that seem cost-effective must be evaluated under changing conditions. For example, providing certain physical protective features may preclude building modifications to increase functionality in the future.)

These questions are particularly relevant to the discussion of competing objectives, because experience has shown that all too often "temporary" measures taken to enhance security become de facto permanent solutions [9]. Examples include measures taken at the White House, at the U.S. Capitol, and at major monuments on the Mall in Washington, D.C. In effect, these measures preclude further discussion or assessment of risk, costs, or benefits. Such physical protective features typically address the generic vulnerabilities of buildings to vehicle bombs (e.g., window breakage and facade damage) and are not generally selected based on a quantified (even if somewhat subjective) calculation of the likelihood that the building will be attacked. As mentioned previously, given the high cost of implementing an effective physical security strategy for public buildings and spaces, the participation and knowledge of all affected parties should be elicited. Much of the current debate on security in an open society is unproductive because it fails to recognize the distinct difference between the technical elements in the risk calculation.

Using Risk in Decision Making

Governments and other stewards of the public welfare have a responsibility to provide for the safety of those entrusted to their care. When considering protection levels for the safety of facilities, building owners in the public and private sectors must weigh the cost of providing a particular level of safety. Ultimately, a choice must be made whether an investment to reduce risk to those directly affected is of greater benefit to society than expending the funds for some other purpose [10]. Given the high cost of security measures and the limited availability of public funds, the decision to fund security at the expense of other valid public needs should be considered by the public at large and not be a purely administrative decision.

Fortunately, methods exist to make this task less daunting. Figure 3.4 is a simplified decision matrix that categorizes actionable outcomes of the risk-assessment process based on the probabilities of certain classes of events and their consequences. Predictably, high-probability events with serious adverse outcomes demand priority attention. Although this is useful information, it provides little insight into what countermeasures may be most appropriate in a specific application.

Event Probability. Risk-based structural design provides a means for evaluating the risks of competing hazards [11]. The probability of

FIGURE 3.4 **Probability Consequence Matrix for Evaluating Risk Levels.**

Consequence

	Catastrophic 1	Very serious 2	Serious 3	Not serious 4
Certain A	1A	2A	3A	4A
Highly probable B	1B	2B	3B	4B
Probable C	1C	2C	3C	4C
Improbable D	1D	2D	3D	4D

Likelihood

a structural failure due to the collectively exhaustive universe of n mutually exclusive hazards, H_I, can be expressed as follows:

$$P_f = \Sigma\, P(F|H_I)\, P(H_I) \tag{2}$$

Where $P(F|H_I)$ is the conditional probability of failure given that hazard H_I has occurred (failure in this case being human casualties or other descriptors of loss), and $P(H_I)$ is the probability of the hazard occurring. Putting this in terms of a terrorist attack, it can be seen that overall risk can be reduced either by avoiding or minimizing the likelihood of attack [controlling $P(H_I)$] or by designing the structure to resist the effects of attack, thereby reducing $P(F|H_I)$ to an acceptable level.

Although $P(H_I)$ cannot be predicted with the same level of confidence as, say, floods, windstorms, or even earthquakes, subjective estimates can be developed that are useful for comparative purposes. For example, during the last 20 years, including the attacks of September 11, 2001, at least 10 significant attacks have been perpetrated against U.S. interests domestically and overseas, on average one every two years. On this basis, the probability of a terrorist attack in any year could be construed to be as high as 0.5. However, this information alone provides little basis for action, because the inventory of buildings owned by the U.S. government and U.S. corporate interests approaches 1 million. Using a figure of 1,000,000 buildings yields a probability of attack against any building in a given year of about 2×10^{-6} (i.e., $1/(0.5 \times 10^{6})$). In reality, much of the building inventory cannot be considered a legitimate target due to its location, lack of significance, or other factors, so the actual probability of attack is probably higher. However, even reducing the number of potential targets by a factor of 100 yields a probability of only 2 in 10,000. This makes it still not a likely event. Although it is surely possible to bound $P(H_I)$ through more sophisticated analysis than the simplistic examples presented here, it is not really necessary to do so to develop useful countermeasure strategies.

Attack Probability Example. In the case of terrorism, overall risk can be reduced either by controlling the probability of attack or by reducing the consequences of an attack should one occur. Experience has shown that if a terrorist vehicle-bomb attack occurs in close proximity to a structure not specially prepared to withstand such a blast, a large glass and fragment load will be produced and building collapse may occur. If the building is occupied at the time of the attack, many of the occupants will be killed or injured, and $P(F|H_I)$ will be high and unacceptable. Therefore, unless the probability of attack, $P(H_I)$, can be reduced to some acceptably low value, some intervention is indicated (a probability of 10^{-7} per year has been suggested as a "de minimis" risk threshold below which society is indifferent [12]). The action taken may be to acquire additional land for greater setbacks from vehicular access ways, to provide strengthening features, to limit vehicular access and parking, or to assign security personnel to patrol the area continuously. It could even entail relocating personnel and operations to another location.

These decisions can be based on a probability of attack defined jointly by decision makers and other stakeholders and based on their individual circumstances; for example, "Highly Probable" from the risk matrix may be 10^{-1} per year for one and 10^{-3} per year for another. Consequences, in human and economic terms, could be defined as "Catastrophic," meaning total building destruction and great loss of life, or "Not Serious," representing little or no damage and only minor injuries. Other, similar definitions could also be used. Potential countermeasures can then be evaluated based on their cost, ease of implementation, and effectiveness, and security decisions can be based on realistic estimates of risk for a specific facility. The social and policy sciences provide some interesting and useful tools to frame this complex discussion, and two of these tools are discussed in the following section.

POLICY FORMULATION TOOLS

Two useful tools for goal setting and decision making within the context of protecting public spaces from extreme events are judgment analysis and the Taylor-Russell diagram [13]. Both of these tools were developed for different purposes and adapted for policy formulation over time.

Judgment Analysis

When developing a physical protection strategy for public spaces and buildings subject to extreme events, it is important to have an index or indicator of safety to measure the effectiveness of the actions taken. Judgment analysis can be used to design such an indicator that is based on a consensus judgment of a group of technical experts. The method of judgment analysis and the theory surrounding it, Social Judgment Theory (SJT), are about 50 years old [14, 15, 16, 17].

Based on historical data or experimental testing regarding the effectiveness of various countermeasure strategies in past extreme events (e.g., under a range of actual terrorist bombing attacks or test conditions), a model of building performance can be constructed with respect to the various features of the buildings and attacks (e.g., bomb size, standoff distance, building type). Once parameters are established, other buildings could be scored on how resistant they appear to be in a similar type of attack. This type of modeling requires abundant and accurate data that are often difficult or impossible to obtain for past events and that are quite expensive to gain in controlled tests. However, even without such data, it is still possible to develop an indicator by utilizing the judgment of experts.

Using judgment analysis to develop an indicator involves the following steps [14]:

1. Experts are interviewed about the attributes of the problem that constitute the cues to the judgment of safety, including active security measures, standoff distance, and building features. Although experts might differ on the importance of each of these to overall safety, they may be able to agree on a list.

2. A sample set of real buildings with various protective features is assembled.

3. Once a set of representative buildings has been gathered, each expert would rate each building for the effectiveness of the security features provided.

4. Each expert's "policy" for making judgments of safety would represent a weighted combination of important features. The importance attributed to each feature would be determined from the expert's judgment as influenced by past experience, research results, and so on. The use of statistics greatly increases the likelihood that the exercise will produce valid expert judgments.

This type of judgment analysis would provide insight into how different experts rate buildings on safety, as well as the judgment policies of different experts. For example, one expert might think that active physical security is the most important factor, whereas another might believe that passive features, such as building setback and physical hardening, are paramount. With time, research and experience with actual events would determine the relative effectiveness of different approaches. Meanwhile policy makers or advisory groups charged with developing policy recommendations for security could use the various judgment policies to create an acceptable safety indicator. The result would be an experience-based index for actions taken to enhance security.

Taylor-Russell Diagram

The second tool, the Taylor-Russell diagram, has been effectively applied to a variety of policy-formulation questions [4, 18]. Once an indicator is selected for predicting building safety, the next step is to select a safety threshold or cutoff point, such that buildings above the threshold would be considered "safe" (i.e., acceptable) and those below it would be considered "unsafe" (i.e., unacceptable).

Key Point   The Taylor-Russell diagram can be used to engage public values in a decision about the appropriate threshold for that safety indicator; that is, how much safety is "enough."

Unless the indicator is perfect, any threshold for a safe/unsafe decision will result in some buildings rated as safe when they are not (false positives) or some buildings being rated as unsafe when they are safe (false negatives). A Taylor-Russell diagram can be used to clarify the components of this situation [19, 20].

A Taylor-Russell diagram is presented in Figure 3.5. Along the horizontal axis are building safety indicator scores. Along the vertical axis are building security performance scores. Each point represents a particular building. The quality of the indicator is shown by the spread of the points around a line angled at 45 degrees.

A lower, or "lenient," threshold for an acceptable level of building security may reduce costs, but there is a risk of constructing buildings that will turn out to be unsafe if attacked (false positives). However, as the threshold for the acceptable level of security is raised or made more "strict," needless costs may be imposed on the builder as unnecessary security measures are implemented (false negatives). This trade-off between false positives and false negatives for any choice of threshold is made instantly visible in a Taylor-Russell diagram.

The number of false positives and false negatives depends not only on the threshold chosen, but also on the degree of association between the indicator and the true safety rating. The correlation between these values represents the quality of the indicator. As the quality of the indicator improves, the cluster of observations will approach a straight line, as seen in Figure 3.6.

Using a Taylor-Russell diagram, experts can select an appropriate threshold based on the quality of the indicator and the numbers of false positives and false negatives the experts are willing to accept.

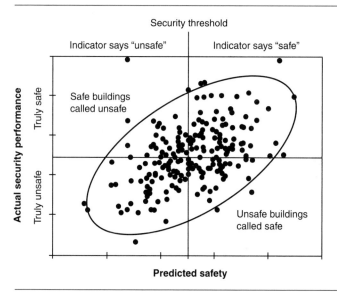

FIGURE 3.5   Taylor-Russell Diagram.

(*Source:* Little, R. and Weaver, E. A., 2004. "A Socio-Technological Approach to Determining Appropriate Levels of Protection for Public Spaces," *Proceedings of the 11th Annual Conference of the International Emergency Management Society,* May 18–21, Victoria, Australia.)

The Taylor-Russell diagram provides a means of envisioning simultaneously the connection among (1) the choice of threshold, (2) the effectiveness of an indicator, and (3) the resulting trade-offs between, for example, security and cost.

Once an indicator has been chosen and a threshold selected, there's no guarantee that the trade-off of false positives and false negatives will be satisfactory to others or that the threshold will always be appropriate. In fact, if a highly salient event occurs for which there is a false positive, such as a building turns out unexpectedly to be unsafe (i.e., it performs less well than expected, as did many steel-frame buildings in the Northridge earthquake of 1994), those concerned with safety will pressure policy makers to move the threshold higher.

This debate is ongoing with regards to the performance of World Trade Center 1 and World Trade Center 2 in New York following the terrorist attacks on those buildings, with implications for both structural design and fire protection. As additional safety measures are implemented for buildings that were already safe enough, there will be diminishing returns on investment. The community concerned with the cost of buildings might then pressure the policy makers to lower the index. In reality, the threshold will tend to oscillate as stakeholders respond to recent events and pressure policy makers to change the threshold. See Weaver and Richardson's paper entitled

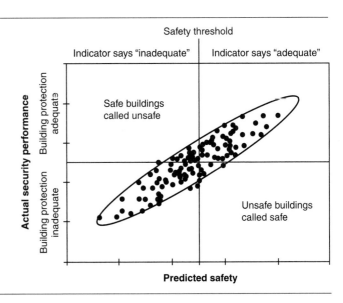

FIGURE 3.6 Taylor-Russell Diagram with a High-Quality Indicator.

(*Source:* Little, R. and Weaver, E. A., 2004 "A Socio-Technological Approach to Determining Appropriate Levels of Protection for Public Spaces," *Proceedings of the 11th Annual Conference of the International Emergency Management Society,* May 18–21, Victoria, Australia.)

"Threshold Setting and the Cycling of a Decision Threshold" for a description of how such oscillations occur [21].

Because the selection of a threshold represents a value-based decision, it may become outmoded as societal values respond to recent events and as indicators improve. In order to have a responsive policy context that is protected from too rapid and vigorous an overreaction to recent events, it may be necessary to build in administrative structures that manage or regulate the threshold in an appropriately responsive manner. This role is often played by the various building code organizations that serve to modulate regulatory cycle times so that costly changes are not introduced without prior thought and discussion.

PERFORMANCE-BASED DESIGN

The regulatory process for commercial buildings offers a possible means of addressing the oftentimes competing objectives of the planning and design process for buildings subject to extreme events. Building codes are increasingly moving toward a performance-based process that relates high-level goals to specific design solutions and allows the unique circumstances of each building to shape its design requirements—the multi-objective decision-making approach described earlier. Figure 3.7 is a model of a pyramidal performance-based building code process [22].

Performance goals for buildings are society's value statements regarding acceptable performance of buildings in terms of health, safety, welfare, amenity, and mission fulfillment. This means that desired performance (and acceptable risk) should not be driven solely by the current state of technical knowledge, but by what society or the technical experts deem to be acceptable or tolerable. In the case of buildings subject to extreme events, goals may also include mitigating the effects of various additional hazards. This may result in higher performance requirements for specific structures or for certain categories of structures.

Once goals for performance and risk have been established, and related functional and operative requirements have been developed, they can be translated into design criteria. As part of the process, it is helpful to consider whether (and how) different classes of buildings may be expected to perform under a variety of normal and emergency conditions (thus resulting in categorization into different performance groups with differing performance levels, as discussed in Chapter 2). Once the categorization is complete, and a building or a

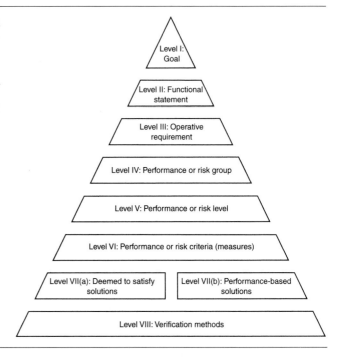

FIGURE 3.7   Elements of a Performance-Based Building Code Process.

(*Source:* Meacham, B. J., Bower, R., Traw, J., and Moore, A., 2005. "Performance-based building regulation: Current situation and future needs," *Building Research and Information,* Vol. 33, No. 2, pp. 91–106.)

building element can be described in terms of how it performs under normal conditions and under appropriate loads and methods are available to evaluate and to verify this performance, a design solution based on the desired performance requirements can be engineered.

___ SUMMARY _____

The goal of the design process for all facilities subject to extreme events should be the identification and successful and cost-effective management of all risk factors that can adversely affect the building's performance. Investigations of performance failures, whether from an engineering standpoint or with regards to user expectations for a facility, usually determine that failure is preventable. Many failures can be traced, at least in part, to poor communication between individuals or organizations involved in project delivery and missing or dysfunctional decision processes. This shortcoming is inherent in the traditional design and construction process, which is linear and compartmentalized—characteristics that tend to inhibit free and interactive communications between project elements and across disciplines. Because many different security and natural hazard issues and mitigation approaches are introduced at different steps in the facility design process, it is important that the process have sufficient flexibility to integrate this information with the facility's primary mission. An even better alternative is to keep all relevant stakeholders involved throughout the process. Although risk will always be a factor for buildings subject to extreme events, better systems can be designed to both reduce the overall level of risk and manage the residual risk more effectively.

Unfortunately, threats are unpredictable and, based on the events of September 11, 2001, and their aftermath, the full range of threats is probably unknowable. We will never be able to anticipate all possible threats and events, and even if we could, there is not enough money to deploy countermeasures to address them all. The strategy for dealing with extreme events needs to be flexible and agile—capable of addressing new threats as they emerge while still meeting the demands of the public for attractive architecture and free access to public spaces. This cannot be a one-time investment; it is an effort that will need to be revisited periodically as threats, resources, and community values continue to change and compete for attention and available resources.

BIBLIOGRAPHY

References Cited

1. DoD, 2005. U.S. Department of Defense, www.cheyennemountain .af.mil.

2. Keeney, R., 1992. *Value-Focused Thinking: A Path to Creative Decision Making*, Harvard University Press, Cambridge, MA.

3. Keeney, R., and Raiffa, H., 1993. *Decisions with Multiple Objectives: Preferences and Value Trade-offs*, Cambridge University Press, Cambridge, UK.

4. Hammond, K. R., 1996. *Human Judgment and Social Policy: Irreducible Uncertainty, Inevitable Error, Unavoidable Injustice*, Oxford University Press, New York.

5. NIST, 1994. *1994 Northridge Earthquake: Performance of Structures, Lifelines, and Fire Protection Systems*, National Institute of Standards and Technology, Gaithersburg, MD.

6. NRC, 1996. *Understanding Risk: Informing Decisions in a Democratic Society*, National Research Council, National Academy Press, Washington, DC.

7. Kaplan, S., and Garrick, B. J., 1981. "On the Quantitative Assessment of Risk," *Risk Analysis,* Vol. 1, No. 1, pp. 11–27.

8. Haimes, Y. Y., 1991. "Total Risk Management," *Risk Analysis,* Vol. 11, No. 2, pp. 169–171.

9. NRC, 2003. *Working in Olmsted's Shadow: Guidance for Developing a Scope of Services for the Update of the Master Plan for the U.S. Capitol and Grounds,* National Research Council, National Academy Press, Washington, DC.

10. NRC, 1985. *Safety of Dams, Flood and Earthquake Criteria,* National Research Council, National Academy Press, Washington, DC.

11. Ellingwood, B. R., 2001. "Acceptable Risk Bases for Design of Structures," *Progress in Structural Engineering and Materials,* Vol. 3, No. 2, pp. 170–179.

12. Pate-Cornell, E., 1994. "Quantitative Safety Goals for Risk Management of Industrial Facilities," *Structural Safety,* Vol. 13, No. 3, pp. 145–157.

13. Little, R., and Weaver, E. A., 2004. "A Socio-Technological Approach to Determining Appropriate Levels of Protection for Public Spaces," *Proceedings of the 11th Annual Conference of the International Emergency Management Society,* May 18–21, Victoria, Australia.

14. Cooksey, R., 1996. *Judgment Analysis: Theory, Methods, and Applications,* Academic Press, New York.

15. Stewart, T. R., 1988. "Judgment Analysis: Procedures," in-Brehmer, B. and Joyce, C. R. B. (Eds.), *Human Judgment: The SJT View.* North-Holland, Amsterdam.

16. Hammond, K. R., 1955. "Probabilistic Functioning and the Clinical Method," *Psychological Review,* Vol. 62, No. 4, pp. 255–262.

17. Brunswik, E., 1955. "Representative Design and Probabilistic Theory in a Functional Psychology," *Psychological Review,* Vol. 62, No. 4, pp. 193–217.

18. Swets, J. A., 1992. "The Science of Choosing the Right Decision Threshold in High-Stakes Diagnostics," *American Psychologist,* Vol. 47, No. 4, pp. 522–532.

19. Hammond, K. R. 1996. *Human Judgment and Social Policy: Irreducible Uncertainty, Inevitable Error, Unavoidable Justice.* Oxford University Press, New York.

20. Green, D. M., and Swets, J. A., 1966. *Signal Detection Theory and Psychophysics.* John Wiley & Sons, New York.

21. Weaver, E. A., and Richardson, G. P., 2002. "Threshold Setting and the Cycling of a Decision Threshold," paper presented at System Dynamics 2002, Palermo, Italy, www.wpi.edu/News/Transformations/2003Spring/pendulum.pdf.

22. Meacham, B. J., Bower, R., Traw, J., and Moore, A., 2005. "Performance-based building regulation: Current situation and future needs," *Building Research and Information*, Vol. 33, No. 2, pp. 91–106.

Additional Readings

Hopper, L. J., and Droge, M. J., 2005. *Security and Site Design*, John Wiley and Sons, Hoboken, NJ.

Owen, D. D., and R. S. Means Engineering Staff, 2003. *Building Security: Strategies and Costs*, Reed Construction Data, Kingston, MA.

4

Threat, Vulnerability, and Risk Assessment

Brian J. Meacham

This chapter discusses the activities involved in conducting a threat, vulnerability, and risk assessment—also known as a threat and risk assessment (TARA) or a threat or vulnerability assessment (TVA)—using examples from different industry sectors. The focus in this chapter is on terrorist threats; TARA for natural and technological hazards (e.g., seismic events and fire) is addressed in other chapters. However, many of the processes and approaches discussed here are applicable to natural and technological hazards as well.

Ultimately, a comprehensive assessment should consider all threats and hazards. Consideration of all potential threats and hazards is important, because, as discussed in Chapter 3, multiple threats may result in competing objectives, and the mitigation measures selected to address those threats may not be picked up in single-threat assessments. For example, blast mitigation may require that windows be strengthened to prevent glass from shattering, which would then hinder fire-fighting activities, such as ventilating a space or gaining access to an area.

OVERVIEW

Understanding risk and knowing what options exist to avoid, mitigate, or transfer it are central to risk assessment. *Risk assessment* involves identifying events of concern, determining the likelihood of those events, and predicting the potential consequences should such events occur. Risk assessment is part of risk characterization (see Chapter 2).

Threat assessment focuses on identifying and understanding the potential sources of events, particularly with respect to terrorist actions. It is equivalent to hazard assessment, for example, in considering fire or natural hazard events. In threat assessment, consideration is given to potential terrorist activity, weapons that might be used, and potential impacts from those weapons.

Vulnerability assessment focuses on identifying potential weaknesses in a facility that would allow terrorists to access it, such as a lack of building security, the ability to drive a vehicle close to a facility, and so forth. In some cases, vulnerability assessment is closely tied to consequence analysis in that it considers the response of a facility to an event of a certain magnitude, thus indicating the facility's vulnerability to that event (e.g., assessing the response of a facade to a certain size explosive load would both indicate the facade's vulnerability to a blast of that size as well as identify potential consequences that may result should the blast occur).

Together, the concepts of threat assessment and vulnerability assessment (and consequence assessment) provide input into the overall risk assessment for a facility.

THE THREAT, VULNERABILITY, AND RISK ASSESSMENT PROCESS

The intent of a threat, vulnerability, and risk assessment is to (1) identify potential threats or hazards to people, facilities, operations, and finances; (2) evaluate the likelihood of specific threat or hazard scenarios occurring; and (3) assess the consequences (severity) should a threat or hazard scenario occur. A threat, vulnerability, and risk assessment should encompass the following components:

- Asset identification and valuation
- Target potential
- Threat identification
- Threat scenarios
- Vulnerability assessment
- Consequence analysis
- Risk assessment
- Prevention and mitigation strategies
- Cost and effectiveness analyses
- Mitigation option selection

The general threat, vulnerability, and risk assessment process is depicted in Figure 4.1.

FIGURE 4.1 The Threat, Vulnerability, and Risk Assessment Process.

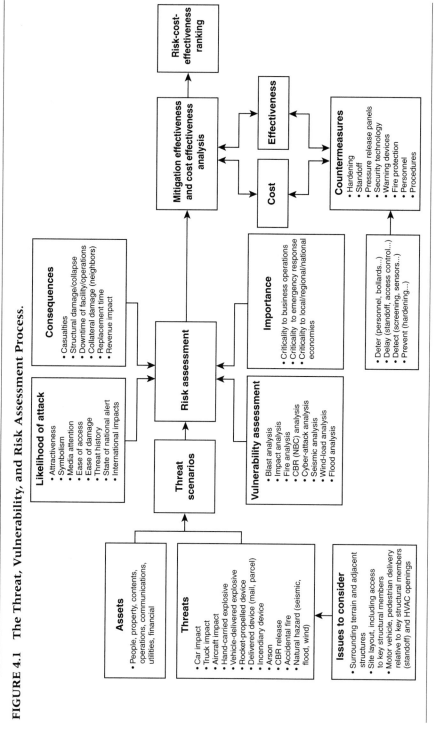

(*Source:* Arup.)

__ASSET IDENTIFICATION AND VALUATION_____

Identifying Assets

Assets include people, physical assets (property, contents, systems), financial assets, information, and operations. For a facility (one or more structures), the list of assets can be quite long, and the types of assets and their importance may vary by facility type, location, and operation. As outlined in the Federal Emergency Management Agency's *Reference Manual to Mitigate Potential Terrorist Attacks Against Buildings* [1], a two-step process can be used to identify a facility's critical assets:

1. Define and understand the facility's core functions and processes.
2. Identify critical building infrastructure, such as critical components, information systems and data, life safety systems, and security systems.

The following questions can be used to complete the identification process:

- What are the facility's core uses, services, or outputs?
- What critical activities take place within the facility?
- Who occupies and visits the building? When are they in the facility? How long do they stay? How many are present at various times?
- What internal and external reliance exists for continuous operation of the facility? These functions may include utilities, the material supply chain, and customer bases.

Valuation of Assets

Once the assets have been identified, their value needs to be determined in terms of their criticality to life safety, overall cost, criticality to operations, or other factors deemed important by the facility's management and occupants and other stakeholders. At some point, this valuation should be done in terms of real dollars or cost equivalency for budgeting and options analyses.

Key Point   During the initial assessment, assets can be ranked in terms of importance or in terms of ranges of values.

TABLE 4.1 Four-Level Asset Value Scale with Cost Levels

Descriptor	Numeric Ranking	Asset Value
Very high	4	Greater than $5,000,000
High	3	$1,000,000 to $5,000,000
Medium	2	$100,000 to $1,000,000
Low	1	Less than $100,000

Source: Arup.

Assets can be ranked in importance by assigning a numerical value to the level of importance of the asset; in most cases, a high number is assigned to an important asset and a low number to an unimportant one. This ranking can use any scale the assessor chooses, so long as the stakeholders agree on the scale and the ranking is consistent within the facility assessment. Table 4.1 illustrates a four-level asset value ranking with cost levels; Table 4.2 shows a seven-level ranking without associated costs.

In the case of Table 4.2, the Federal Emergency Management Agency (FEMA) guide provides qualitative descriptors for the asset valuation that accompanies each level; for example, *very high* reflects an expectation that loss or damage of the facility's assets would have exceptionally grave consequences, such as extensive loss of life; widespread severe injuries; or total loss of primary services, core processes, and functions. This approach couples damage states to the value of a facility's use, operations, and systems.

TABLE 4.2 Seven-Level Asset Value Scale Without Cost Levels

Descriptors	Numeric Ranking
Very high	10
High	8–9
Medium high	7
Medium	5–6
Medium low	4
Low	2–3
Very low	1

Source: Adapted from FEMA, 2003. *Risk Management Series—Reference Manual to Mitigate Potential Terrorist Attacks Against Buildings,* Federal Emergency Management Agency, Washington, DC. Table 1-1.

> **Key Point**   The coupling of a qualitative descriptor of the expected damage to some measure, such as scale, rank, or category, is not limited to asset valuation; it is also used in the assessment of event probability (frequency), consequence, and desired performance.

TARGET POTENTIAL

Evaluating Target Potential

Once the assets have been identified and valued with respect to impact on life, property, operations, and costs, the question of why the asset may be a target should be considered. Several factors should be considered during this assessment, including the following [2]:

- Value of the asset, including current and replacement value
- Value of the asset to a potential adversary
- Asset location
- How, when, and by whom an asset is accessed and used
- Impact if the asset is lost

Attractive Targets

Of particular concern in terrorist threat and risk assessment is why a particular asset may be of value to the aggressor (adversary). Several factors play a role as to why a particular asset may be an attractive target.

The symbolic meaning of a building with respect to religion, ideology (political or other), culture, and way of life is a key factor in determining the attractiveness of a target. For example, the World Trade Center in New York reflected the heights of a capitalistic culture.

Another factor is the visibility or prestige that the aggressor would gain from the destruction of or significant damage to the asset. It was known from the 1993 attack on the World Trade Center that a significant event would bring widespread visibility to the terrorists' agenda.

The potential for significant impact, not only to a single facility, but also to a community, a state, an entire nation, or multiple nations, is an important consideration. This impact could be realized in terms of asset destruction, immediate or long-term economic implications, the instilling of crippling fear throughout the population, destruction of an industry, or through some other large-scale repercussion.

The relative ease of access for ingress and egress with the equipment and personnel required for an attack is another key factor to consider when assessing the attractiveness of a potential target. As with any criminal activity, the ability to get to and from a target easily and without detection makes a target extremely attractive.

The location of the asset in terms of the city, state, or nation targeted as well as in terms of proximity to other buildings, facilities, or infrastructure is also a significant factor. The latter concern is particularly important when considering the potential for collateral damage. A facility may not necessarily be an attractive target, but it may be located adjacent to an attractive target and therefore become a target by proximate location.

The potential for mass casualties from the resulting event is important to consider when assessing the attractiveness of a facility or building.

When assessing the target potential or attractiveness of a facility, it is helpful to have a good understanding of the general level of protection afforded to similar facilities, both in the same general area and across a broader geography. This may be important from the perspective that as "attractive" targets become hardened, they may become "unattractive," and a new set of attractive targets likely will result—perhaps in locations currently viewed as being under the terrorists' radar.

THREAT IDENTIFICATION

General Knowledge

When assessing potential terrorist threats, it is helpful to have a broad understanding of various terrorist groups, where they operate, what type of terrorist events (attacks) have occurred, what weapons are available and how they have been used, and what mode of weapons delivery should be considered. These and other key factors are illustrated in Figure 4.2.

For the purposes of threat evaluation, aggressors, tools, and tactics are defined as follows: *Aggressors* include the groups and individuals who would perform hostile acts against people, facilities, and equipment in the transportation environment [2]. Their objectives often include (1) inflicting injury or death; (2) destroying or damaging facilities, property, equipment, or resources; (3) stealing

FIGURE 4.2   **Threat Evaluation for Prioritized Critical Assets.**

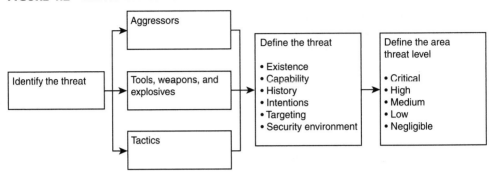

(*Source:* Fogelman, R. R. and Lupia, E. A., 2000. *Installation Force Protection Guide,* United States Air Force, www.wbdg.org/ccbAF/AFDG/afinstal.pdf, p. 6.)

equipment, material, or information; and (4) creating publicity for their cause or instilling fear in the public. Aggressors may use the first three objectives to accomplish the fourth.

To achieve their objectives, aggressors use various *tools,* such as forced-entry tools, vehicles, and surveillance mechanisms; *weapons,* such as incendiary devices, small arms, antitank weapons and mortars, and nuclear, biological, and chemical agents; and *explosives,* such as homemade bombs, hand grenades, vehicle bombs, and other explosive devices (IED).

Tactics refer to the offensive strategies employed by aggressors that reflect their capabilities and objectives. An example of a common tactic is a moving-vehicle bomb used during a suicide attack in which an explosive-laden vehicle is driven into a facility and detonated.

Threat Assessment

Aggressors who desire to undertake acts of terrorism are typically concerned with secrecy, and these types of threats do not take place as often as others. The information needed to define and analyze the threat is often more difficult to acquire than that of generic threats, such as street crimes, fires, or other hazards. To construct a composite picture of threat conditions, intelligence and law enforcement personnel gather information from numerous sources, including newspapers, academic studies and special reports, criminal records, government records, local organizations and people, and other intelligence organizations. This process is illustrated in Figure 4.3.

This threat-assessment process emphasizes five factors used in the collection and analysis of information from those sources with a bearing on terrorist threats:

- *Existence* determines whether a terrorist group is present, assessed to be present, or able to gain access to the transportation system or specific assets. The analysis of information regarding the existence of a terrorist group addresses the question: Who is hostile to existing organizations and social structure?
- *Capability* refers to the acquired, assessed, or demonstrated level of capability of the terrorist group to conduct terrorist attacks. An analysis of terrorist group capabilities addresses the questions: (1) What weapons have been used by terrorist groups in carrying

FIGURE 4.3 **Threat Assessment Process.**

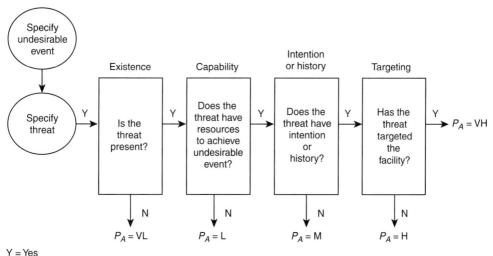

Y = Yes
N = No
P_A = Likelihood of occurrence
VH = Very high
H = High
M = Medium
L = Low
VL = Very low

(*Source:* FTA, 2003. *Security Risk Assessment Framework,*. U.S. Department of Transportation, Federal Transit Administration, Washington, DC. http://transit-safety.volpe.dot.gov.)

out past attacks? and (2) What infrastructure is necessary to train, equip, target, and execute attacks?

- *History* is the terrorist group's demonstrated terrorist activity over time. The analysis of terrorist group history addresses the questions: (1) What have the terrorists done in the past? (2) What is the terrorist group's method of operation? (3) How did they acquire the capacity they demonstrated? (4) Where did they obtain support? and (5) What additional attacks have they mounted?

- *Intentions* is the analysis of a terrorist group's recently demonstrated anti-U.S. terrorist activity or its stated or assessed intent to conduct such activity. An analysis of terrorist group intentions addresses the questions: (1) Why do groups engage in terrorist acts? and (2) What do they hope to achieve?

- *Targeting* refers to the current credible information on a group's activity, indicative of preparations for specific terrorist operations. Targeting addresses the questions: (1) Who is likely to be attacked? (2) Why are they likely to be attacked? and (3) What is the basis for accepting reports that such attacks are planned?

Whenever possible, the threat level for a specific asset is determined after information on the five threat factors has been gathered and analyzed. Various resources exist for gathering necessary data. Ignoring specific information on terrorist groups for this discussion, one can still learn a great deal about potential threats and how they might impact a facility by understanding the types of attacks that have taken place, the weapons used, and the tactics (i.e., mode of delivery) utilized. Table 4.3 provides a brief summary of various types of terrorist attacks and the weapons used.

Once the potential threats have been identified and sufficient understanding has been gained with respect to weapons, tactics, and mode of delivery, threat scenarios can be created against which to test building vulnerability.

Although detailed discussion on terrorist groups is outside of the scope of this book, various resources for obtaining general and historical data on terrorist activity are available, for example, from government sources, such as the U.S. Department of Justice (www.doj.gov), as well as from private sector sources, such as Jane's Information Group (www.janes.com). For TARA of a specific facility, working closely with law enforcement officials is recommended. This is the best way to gain up-to-date knowledge of terrorist activity and threat potential, particularly with regard to aggressor existence, capability, history, intention, and targets.

TABLE 4.3 Overview of Various Types of Attacks

Type of Attack	Historical Example(s)	Type of Weapon(s)
Explosive and incendiary devices	1995 GIA bombing of Paris Metro	Planted devices
	HAMAS suicide bombs on Israeli buses (ongoing)	Suicide bombs
	1998 bombings of U.S. embassies in Tanzania and Kenya	Vehicle bombs
	2001 World Trade Center attack; 1990s abortion clinic bombings; 1995 Oklahoma City bombing	Proximity bombs, incendiary devices, secondary devices
Exterior attacks	2001 militant assaults on Indian-held mosques in Kashmir	Rocks and clubs, improvised devices, Molotov cocktails
Stand-off attacks	Tamil Tiger's July 2001 mortar attack and bombing of Sri Lanka Airport	Antitank rockets, mortars
Ballistics attacks	Long Island Railroad shootings; Columbine High School shootings	Handguns, shotguns, submachine guns
Networked/inside access: • Forced entry • Covert entry • Insider compromise • Visual surveillance • Acoustic/electronic surveillance	Amtrak Sunset Limited derailment; 1996 Tupac Amaru Revolutionary Movement taking of Japanese Ambassador's residence and 500 guests in Peru (access through disguise as waiters)	Hand, power, and thermal tools; explosives; false credentials; stolen uniforms and identification badges; false pretenses; cell operations; binoculars; photographic devices; listening devices; electronic-emanation surveillance equipment
Cyber attack	2002 Code Red worm	Worms, viruses
Chemical, biological, radiological (CBR) release	1995 Aum Shinriyko release of Sarin gas in the Tokyo subway	Chemical, biological, radiological, or nuclear aerosolized

Source: FTA, 2003. *The Public Transportation System Security and Emergency Preparedness Planning Guide,* Final Report, U.S. Department of Transportation, Federal Transit Administration, Washington, DC.

___THREAD SCENARIOS_____

Scenario Development

Threat scenarios are developed using an interpretive methodology that encourages role-playing by facility personnel, risk and security experts, emergency responders, and others, as appropriate, to brainstorm ways that the facility in question may be attacked [2]. In brief, the approach considers the critical assets and how they may be impacted by the various threats that have been identified. By matching threats to critical assets, one can identify the capabilities required to support specific types of attacks, which in turn leads to identification of those activities that can be undertaken to prevent or mitigate the consequences of those attacks.

When developing threat scenarios or otherwise identifying unwanted events, consider the following three questions:

- What is the history of unwanted events occurring to your assets in the past?
- Have similar assets in other locations or within similar environments been compromised or attacked in the past?
- Are there Stakeholder concerns, and if so, what are they and why should they be considered?

Initially, focus should be on the most critical assets, assessing the most likely threats, the range of attack objectives, and the methods that may be used, such as pipe bombs, vehicle bombs, or release of chemical, biological and radiological (CBR) material. Ideally, when identifying the "most likely" threats, the range of perpetrators should be considered—political terrorists, radicals, right-wing extremists, disgruntled employees, disturbed copycats, and others—as well as the weapons, tactics, and mode of delivery. However, such data often are not readily available or necessarily reliable; therefore a focus on weapons, tactics, and modes of delivery can be used to create "worst-credible" scenarios that reflect a higher probability of occurrence, but not necessarily the worst possible outcome, and, where warranted, "worse-case" scenarios. Note that the likelihood of events needs to be addressed, regardless of data availability. This will be addressed later in this chapter.

Several tools can be used to develop scenarios, including event profiles, which combine the threat, method of delivery, and in some cases discussion of threat effects and mitigation options [1]. Table 4.4 lists the terrorism event profiles developed by FEMA [3].

TABLE 4.4   Event Profiles for Terrorism

Threat/Hazard	Application Mode	Duration	Extent and Effects: Static/Dynamic	Mitigating and Exacerbating Conditions
Improvised explosive device (bomb)	Detonation of explosive device on or near target via person (carried or thrown), mail, post, supply delivery, vehicle (parked or moving), or projectile.	Instantaneous; additional secondary devices may lengthen the duration of the threat/hazard.	Extent is determined by type and quantity of explosive. Effects are generally static, except for cascading consequences.	Blast energy of a given stand-off is inversely proportional to the cube of the distance from the device. Exacerbating conditions include ease of access, lack of barriers, poor construction, and ease of concealment.
Chemical agent	Liquid/aerosol contaminants can be dispersed using sprayers or other aerosol generators, liquids vaporizing from puddles/containers, or munitions.	Depends on agent and conditions, can be hours to weeks.	Contamination can be carried out of the initial target areas. Chemicals may be corrosive or otherwise damaging over time if not remediated.	Air temperature, ground temperature, humidity, precipitation, and wind can all affect extent of effects. The micrometeorological effects of buildings can alter effects, and shielding in the form of sheltering in place may protect people and property.
Arson/incendiary attack	Initiation of fire or explosion on or near target via direct contact or remotely via projectile.	Generally minutes to hours.	Extent is determined by type and quantity of device/accelerant and materials present at or near target. Effects are generally static, except for cascading consequences.	Mitigation factors include built-in fire detection and protection systems and fire-resistive construction techniques. Exacerbating conditions include inadequate security, noncompliance with fire and building codes, and failure to maintain existing fire protection systems.

(continues)

TABLE 4.4 *Continued*

Threat/Hazard	Application Mode	Duration	Extent and Effects: Static/Dynamic	Mitigating and Exacerbating Conditions
Armed attack	Tactical assault or sniper attacks from a remote location.	Generally minutes to days.	Extent varies based on the perpetrator's intent and capabilities. The effects can range from single injury to significant loss of life within the target area.	Inadequate security can give attacker(s) easy access to target.
Biological agent	Liquid or solid contaminants can be dispersed using sprayers/aerosol generators or by paint or line sources.	Depending on agent and conditions, may pose viable threats for hours to years.	Depending on the agent, contamination can be spread via wind and water. Infection can be spread via human or animal vectors.	Altitude of release above ground, sunlight, wind, and the micrometeorological effects of buildings and terrain can all influence effects.
Cyber terrorism	Electronic attack using one computer system against another.	Minutes to days.	Depending on the strain, the effects can be aggressively dynamic, spreading as affected people interact with others, serving to pass along the communication. Extent can be limited to a single entity or can be a broad attack, hitting individuals, corporations, and governments. Indirect effects in terms of down time and loss of data and communication can be significant.	Inadequate security can facilitate access to critical computer systems.

Agriterrorism	Direct, generally covert contamination of food supplies or introduction of pests and/or disease agents to crops and livestock.	Days to months.	Extent varies by type of incident. Food contamination events may be limited—relatively static events (impacting only people who eat the food); whereas, pests and diseases are more dynamic and may spread widely.	Inadequate security can facilitate adulteration of food and introduction of pests and disease agents to crops and livestock.
Radiological agent	Radioactive contaminants can be dispersed using sprayers/aerosol generators or by paint or line sources.	Depending on material used, can be seconds to years.	Initial effects will be localized to site of attack; meteorological conditions may cause dynamic behavior.	Duration of exposure, distance from source, and the amount of shielding determine exposure to radiation.
Nuclear attack	Detonation of nuclear device underground, at the surface, in the air, or at high altitude.	Light/heat flash, blast/shock wave, and electromagnetic pulse last for seconds; nuclear radiation and fallout hazards can persist for years.	Extent of effects depends on device. Initial light, heat, and blast effects of a subsurface, ground, or air burst are static; fallout of radioactive contaminants may be dynamic.	Effects can be reduced by minimizing the time of exposure, increasing distance between target and blast, and utilizing shielding.
Hazardous-material release	Solid, liquid, and/or gaseous contaminants may be released from fixed or mobile containers.	Hours to days.	Chemicals may be corrosive or otherwise damaging over time. Explosion and/or fire may be subsequent. Contamination may be carried out of the incident area by persons, vehicles, water, and wind.	Weather conditions, the micrometeorological effects of buildings and terrain, shielding, noncompliance with fire and building codes, and failure to maintain systems can all affect extent of effects.

(continues)

TABLE 4.4 *Continued*

Threat/Hazard	Application Mode	Duration	Extent and Effects: Static/Dynamic	Mitigating and Exacerbating Conditions
Unauthorized entry	Use of hand or power tools, weapons or explosives, or use of false credentials to enter a building.	Minutes to hours, depending on intent.	Effects of attack depend on goal, can be quick or long lasting. Extent is generally local to the facility being entered.	Standard physical security building design should be the minimum mitigation measure. Additional measures include CCTV or traffic flow that channels visitors past access control.
Surveillance	Standoff collection of visual, acoustic, and electronic information.	Usually months.	This is usually the prelude to the loss of an asset. A terrorist surveillance team spends much time looking for vulnerabilities and tactics that will be successful.	Building design can mitigate this hazard.

Source: Adapted from FEMA, 2002. *Integrating Human-Caused Hazards into Mitigation Planning,* Publication 386-7, Federal Emergency Management Agency, Washington, DC.

Likelihood of Attack

Scenario development will lead to potential mitigation options that are appropriate to the facility, its criticality, and the threats that have been identified. Inclusion of the likelihood of event occurrence will help in selecting the most appropriate mitigation measures from the range of options identified.

Although difficult to determine with a high degree of reliability, the likelihood of attack (event occurrence or other related measure) should be included in the threat, vulnerability, and risk assessment (a true risk assessment cannot be performed without a likelihood component, although some TARA/TVA methodologies sidestep this component). Several methods can be used to develop a measure of the likelihood of an attack, from risk ranking to more quantitative or analytical approaches. It is important that the method selected is appropriate to the threat and risk problem and to the available data.

A ranking system is often used to evaluate the likelihood of attack or event occurrence. For example, the Department of Defense's *Standard Practice for System Safety* uses a five-level ranking scale, as shown in Table 4.5 [4].

The specific values in Table 4.5 may not apply in a TARA; however, the general approach is valid and widely used. For use in a TARA, the critical factor is establishing appropriate likelihoods (probabilities) that

TABLE 4.5   Likelihood of Event Occurrence

Description	Level	Specific Item
Frequent	A	Likely to occur often in the life of an item, with a probability of occurrence greater than 10^{-1} in that life.
Probable	B	Will occur several times in the life of an item, with a probability of occurrence less than 10^{-1} but greater than 10^{-2} in that life.
Occasional	C	Likely to occur sometime in the life of an item, with a probability of occurrence less than 10^{-2} but greater than 10^{-3} in that life.
Remote	D	Unlikely, but possible, to occur in the life of an item, with a probability of occurrence less than 10^{-3} but greater than 10^{-6} in that life.
Improbable	E	So unlikely that it can be assumed that an occurrence may not be experienced, with a probability of occurrence less than 10^{-6} in that life.

Source: Adapted from DoD, 2000. *Standard Practice from System Safety,* MIL STD 882D, U.S. Department of Defense, Washington, DC.

correspond to the selected descriptor and level (ranking, category). For example, this type of approach is used in building codes, primarily for natural hazards, with the likelihood component reflected in annual return periods or recurrence intervals (see Chapters 2 and 7). This approach is also used for fire risk assessment, as reflected in Table 10-2 of the *SFPE Engineering Guide to Performance-Based Fire Protection Analysis and Design of Buildings* [5] and in various chapters in Section 5 of *The SFPE Handbook of Fire Protection Engineering* [6].

At the other end of the spectrum, various methods, including game theory [7, 8], are being explored to analytically estimate the likelihood of a threat scenario or terrorist event. The goal of such analytical approaches is to develop a probability distribution that reflects the likelihood of an attack. Probability distributions are used widely in the insurance industry, in the form of exceedance probability curves. This analytical method is becoming more widespread in engineering practice, particularly for natural hazards risk assessment, such as seismic risk assessment [9]. In the near future, it is expected that additional quantitative approaches to estimating the frequency of threat scenarios and terrorist events will be developed through the Department of Homeland Security, the Department of Defense, and other research efforts.

Design-Basis Threats

In addition to developing threat scenarios (events, event profiles, and likelihood of occurrence), design-basis threats need to be identified and incorporated into the assessment. In brief, design-basis threats represent the expected loads applied against the facility and against which the facility is expected to perform. Vulnerability assessment and consequence analysis, and ultimately risk assessment, will be benchmarked against these loads.

Table 4.4 lists a number of threats under the heading of Improvised Explosive Device, including stationary vehicle, moving vehicle, mail, supply, thrown, placed and personnel. Although these descriptors reflect modes of delivery, they do not reflect the load that will be placed on the facility or assets within the facility. Table 4.6 reflects various explosive charge weight equivalencies for delivery mechanisms of different sizes.

For the threat scenario development to be complete, consideration must be given to the range of possible loads, delivery mechanisms, and so forth, because selection of "worst credible" events (or other events), vulnerability assessment, consequence analysis, and mitigation option selection must all be benchmarked against the se-

TABLE 4.6   Explosive Load Capacities

Explosive Threat	Maximum Explosives Capacity (lb TNT Equivalent)
Semi-trailer	60,000
Box truck/water truck	30,000
Small box van	10,000
Cargo/passenger van	4,000
Full-size sedan	1,000
Compact sedan	500
Suitcase	100
Briefcase/backpack	50
Parcel	10 (+/−)
Pipe bomb	5

Source: TSWG, 1999. *Terrorist Bomb Threat Standoff,* Technical Support Working Group, Washington, DC.

lected design-basis loads. The threat scenario may include single events (e.g., single-vehicle bomb), multiple events (e.g., multiple aggressors, each with a backpack bomb), combinations of events, and combinations of targets (e.g., a public space, critical structural components, and critical utilities).

Key Point   Not all events may be considered credible, but they should be considered with rationale provided for rejecting specific scenarios or design loads.

It is worth noting that information contained in a TARA/TVA is security sensitive. Strict document- and data-control measures should be in place to prevent unauthorized access to this information. Mitigation measures can be rendered meaningless if the aggressors have access to load and protection data.

VULNERABILITY ASSESSMENT

Defining Vulnerability

Once the threats have been identified and threat scenarios developed, the vulnerability of the facility to the threat scenarios needs to be assessed. Vulnerability assessment focuses on two components:

(1) the ability of an adversary to exploit any weakness in an asset or countermeasure and (2) the ability of an asset or countermeasure to eliminate, reduce or mitigate an action, device, or system. Some TARA/TVA approaches use vulnerability to mean only one of these factors; care should be taken to understand what vulnerability means in the context of the approach used.

Vulnerability assessment requires a thorough understanding of where and how a facility, particularly critical assets within it, may be vulnerable to the various threats. For example, if progressive or disproportionate collapse is a concern (extent of damage from an explosion or other event is disproportionately greater than the load; for example, loss of a single column results in total building collapse), the assessment should determine whether and how an aggressor might gain access to critical structural components (see Chapters 5 and 9). Likewise, if a significant CBR threat is present, the ability of an aggressor to introduce an agent into the facility needs to be assessed. The next step is to determine the response of the asset to the action (e.g., blast, impact, fire, CBR release).

Aggressor Access

An assessment of the facility's vulnerability to aggressor access should consider the facility's use and criticality, its visibility, its accessibility to potential aggressors, and existing protection measures. As with the asset valuation, which was addressed earlier in this chapter, ranking scales can be used in conducting a vulnerability assessment, particularly when assessing multiple facilities or buildings within a facility. Such a ranking system enables priorities to be established for threat mitigation. Ranking scales can be established for each factor that is deemed important. Table 4.7 provides an example of ranking for aggressor access to the asset.

A vulnerability assessment must address all critical assets, including people, structures, contents, systems, operations, mission, and so forth, and can therefore be quite extensive. The use of a checklist may be helpful in conducting such an assessment. A comprehensive building vulnerability assessment checklist is provided in Appendix A.

Asset Response to Action

A broad spectrum of tools can be used to assess the vulnerability of a facility to a terrorist action. Such tools range from simple screening questions to numerical rankings to analytical methods that assess such things as structural response to an impact or blast or the move-

TABLE 4.7   Aggressor Access to Assets

Building Protection Measures	Rating Value
Fenced, guarded, protected air/consumable entry, controlled access by pass only, no parking within a designated minimum distance (such as 50 feet or 80 feet).	0
Guarded, protected air/consumable entry, controlled access of visitors and nonstaff personnel, no parking within a designated minimum distance.	1
Protected air/consumable entry, controlled access of visitors and nonstaff personnel, no unauthorized parking within a designated minimum distance.	2
Controlled access of visitors, unprotected air/consumable entry, no unauthorized parking within a designated minimum distance.	3
Open access to all personnel, unprotected air/consumable entry, no unauthorized parking within the designated minimum distance.	4
Open access to all personnel, unprotected air/consumable entry, vehicle parking within the designated minimum distance.	5

Source: FEMA, 2003. *Risk Management Series—Reference Manual to Mitigate Potential Terrorist Attacks Against Buildings,* Publication 426, Federal Emergency Management Agency, Washington, DC, Table 1-11.

ment of a CBR agent within a facility. Screening questions can be used to identify obvious critical components, such as load-bearing columns and beams; unprotected glazing; HVAC system openings and components; and fire protection, life safety, and security systems. Some of the questions in the checklist in Appendix A are useful in this regard. Once vulnerabilities have been identified, obvious mitigation measures can be implemented and analytical tools can be used, as needed, to assess the response of the critical elements to design-basis events.

Analytical assessment of facility response and mitigation response are explored in detail in later chapters. However, desired performance levels and criteria to be used to assess such performance must be agreed upon before any analytical assessment of facility response and mitigation design work.

Assessing Performance

Chapter 2 addresses how to establish performance levels and performance criteria. It is important to reiterate that identifying performance targets, in terms of facility and system performance, and determining the criteria against which performance is assessed are critical to the vulnerability assessment process. Table 4.8 (which also

TABLE 4.8 **Performance Levels for New Buildings**

Level of Protection	Potential Structural Damage	Potential Door and Glazing Hazards	Potential Injury
Below standards	Severe damage. Frame collapse, massive destruction, little left standing.	Doors and windows fail, resulting in lethal hazards.	Majority of personnel suffer fatalities.
Very low	Heavy damage. Damage results in onset of structural collapse. Major deformation of primary and secondary structural members, but progressive collapse is unlikely. Collapse of nonstructural elements.	Glazing will break and will likely be propelled into the building, resulting in serious glazing-fragment injuries, but fragments will be reduced. Doors may be propelled into rooms, presenting serious hazards.	Majority of personnel suffer serious injuries. A limited number of fatalities (10 to 25%) may occur.
Low	Damaged and unrepairable. Major deformation of nonstructural elements and secondary structural members and minor deformation of primary structural members, but progressive collapse is unlikely.	Glazing will break but will fall within 1 meter of the wall or will otherwise not present a significant fragment hazard. Doors may fail but they will rebound out of their frames, presenting minimal hazards.	Majority of personnel suffer significant injuries. Few fatalities (<10%) are expected.
Medium	Damaged and repairable. Minor deformation of nonstructural elements and secondary structural members and no permanent deformation in primary structural members.	Glazing will break, but will remain in window frame. Doors will stay in frames, but will not be reusable.	Some minor injuries, but fatalities unlikely.
High	Superficial damage. No permanent deformation in primary structural members, secondary structural members, or nonstructural elements.	Glazing will not break. Doors will be reusable.	Only superficial injuries are likely.

Source: Adapted from DoD, 2003. *DoD Minimum Antiterrorism Standards for Buildings,* Unified Facilities Criteria, UFC 4-010-01, U.S. Department of Defense, Washington, DC.

appears in Chapter 2) provides an indication of the performance levels the DoD expects from new military buildings [10].

In Table 4.8, for new buildings within the "low" level of protection, the performance target for window glazing is that it will break but fall within 1 meter of the window. Although the explosive load is not specified, the glazing performance is, thus once a design-basis explosive load has been selected, material testing and analytical modeling can be used to design windows that meet the performance objective.

Several TARA/TVA guidance documents exist, sometimes covering the same issues but with different requirements. Performance of structures and systems is one such area of difference; therefore, care must be taken to avoid mismatching performance if multiple guidance documents are used. For example, in Table 4.8 a "low" level of protection has window glazing failing but falling within 1 meter of the wall. In Table 4.9, under "Glazing Protection Levels Based on Fragment Impact Locations" from the General Services Administration's *Facilities Standards for the Public Buildings Service* [11], the level of protection afforded to occupants for the same level of glazing performance, "Glazing cracks—fragments enter space and land on floor no further than 3.3 feet from the window," is "High." Thus, the protection level of "Low" or "High" depends on the reference document.

When assessing performance, information on material performance under defined conditions contained in test standards or other reference documents can provide guidance for a specific facility TARA/TVA. For example, standards from ASTM International (formerly the American Society of Testing and Materials) and Underwriters Laboratories (UL) provide information on glazing performance against impact, ballistics, or blast pressure; door performance against impact, ballistics, blast pressure, and forced entry; and so forth. Likewise, ASTM, NFPA, UL, and others have test and installation standards for fire protection systems, security systems, and other mitigation systems and features.

CONSEQUENCE ANALYSIS

Upon completion of or concurrent with the vulnerability assessment, a consequence analysis is undertaken to characterize the impact of a terrorist or extreme event in terms of life loss, injuries, structural and nonstructural facility damage, contents damage, loss of operations or mission, and other objectives specific to the facility and assets of

TABLE 4.9 Glazing Protection Levels Based on Fragment Impact Locations

Performance Condition	Protection Level	Hazard Level	Description of Window Glazing Response
1	Safe	None	Glazing does not break. No visible damage to glazing or frame.
2	Very high	None	Glazing cracks but is retained by the frame. Dusting or very small fragments near sill or on floor acceptable.
3a	High	Very low	Glazing cracks. Fragments enter space and land on floor no further than 3.3 feet from the window.
3b	High	Low	Glazing cracks. Fragments enter space and land on floor no further than 10 feet from the window.
4	Medium	Medium	Glazing cracks. Fragments enter space and land on floor and impact a witness panel at a distance of no more than 10 feet from the window at a height no greater than 2 feet above the floor.
5	Low	High	Glazing cracks and window system fails catastrophically. Fragments enter space and impact a witness panel at a distance of no more than 10 feet from the window at a height greater than 2 feet above the floor.

Source: GSA, 2003. *Facilities Standards for Public Buildings Service,* General Services Administration, Washington, DC, Table 8-1.

concern. Whereas the vulnerability assessment indicates weaknesses and potential failure modes, the consequence analysis focuses on the extent of damage that may be expected for unmitigated design-basis threat scenarios with respect to protection targets, tolerable performance levels, tolerable loss levels, or other metrics agreed on for the TARA/TVA analysis.

The first step of consequence analysis is to ensure that protection targets, tolerable performance levels, tolerable loss levels, or other metrics have been agreed upon. This process has been discussed previously in this chapter, and Table 4.8 presented one approach to representing tolerable damage limits (in this case, in terms of performance). Another example is provided in Table 4.10.

Although the criteria in Table 4.10 may not be directly applicable to a TARA/TVA, particularly the environmental regulation component, the levels for death, disability, and financial loss reflect measures that could be used for establishing tolerable loss limits for critical assets. Depending on the facility and its mission, the financial loss levels and damage limits can vary, as can other metrics, such as facility downtime, interruption of supply chain, or other factors critical to the facility's mission.

As with the analytical tools used in vulnerability assessment, a broad spectrum of tools can be utilized for consequence analysis, from simple screening questions to a focus on tolerable damage limits to the use of analytical methods to assess such things as the extent of structural damage due to impact, injury potential due to glazing fragmentation, and loss of inventory due to fire. Many of the remaining chapters provide additional detail on the use of analytical tools for vulnerability and consequence analysis.

TABLE 4.10 Possible Severity Categories

Description	Category	Environmental, Safety, and Health Result Criteria
Catastrophic	I	Could result in death, permanent total disability, loss exceeding $1M, or irreversible severe environmental damage that violates law or regulation.
Critical	II	Could result in permanent partial disability, injuries, or occupational illnesses that may result in hospitalization of at least three personnel; loss exceeding $200K, but less than $1M; or reversible environmental damage causing a violation of law or regulation.
Marginal	III	Could result in injury or occupational illness resulting in one or more lost work days; loss exceeding $10K, but less than $200K; or mitigatible environmental damage without violation of law or regulation where restoration activities can be accomplished.
Negligible	IV	Could result in injury or illness not resulting in a lost work day; loss exceeding $2K, but less than $10K; or minimal environmental damage not violating law or regulation.

Source: DoD, 2000. *Standard Practice for System Safety,* MIL STD 882, U.S. Department of Defense, Washington, DC.

__RISK ASSESSMENT_____

After the individual threat, vulnerability, and consequence assessments have been completed, these components can be brought together in the risk assessment. Risk assessment can range from simple to complex; it may be qualitative or quantitative. For threats such as fire and natural hazards, in many cases sufficient historical data exist so that a quantitative risk assessment can be performed. For terrorist risk assessment, however, the data are sparse, and many of the quantitative methods used in this type of assessment are in their infancy (see previous discussion on methods for estimating likelihood data). However, in order to compare risk levels and to assess the effectiveness of a potential mitigation measure in reducing the risk, some level of quantification is required.

Risk Quantification

Risk can be viewed quantitatively as the combination of three components: an unwanted event, the likelihood that the event will occur, and the potential consequences should the event occur (see Chapter 3) [12]. The quantification of risk is often reflected in a simple equation, where risk is the probability of an adverse event multiplied by the consequences of that event, or $R = P \times C$. However, use of such a simple calculation may sometimes result in important factors being missed, such as perception, valuation, and criticality. For example, a high-probability, low-consequence event could have the same numerical value as a low-probability, high-consequence event, yet the risks could be perceived and valued much differently (for further discussion, see Chapter 2 and "Understanding Risk: Quantification, Perception and Characterization" [13]).

To more accurately reflect stakeholder views in the threat and risk process, the calculation of risk should go beyond the simple calculation and incorporate factors such as risk perception, asset criticality, and asset valuation to the extent appropriate to the assessment. Risk calculation, at a minimum, should include the following:

- Threat scenario (threat, likelihood of threat event, and design load)
- Vulnerability
- Consequences (including valuation)
- Importance/criticality (including perception and valuation)

Although numerous approaches to risk quantification exist, many TARA/TVA methods include most or all of these factors. In the assessment of bridge and tunnel risk, for example, the American Association of State Highway and Transportation Officials (AASHTO) [14] recommends the following equation, which specifically addresses occurrence, O (frequency); vulnerability, V (consequences); and importance, I (criticality):

$$R = O \times V \times I$$

In the general form of the risk equation, the *occurrence* is hazard oriented and will change with the nature of the hazard. In the context of the AASHTO report, occurrence approximates the likelihood that terrorists will attack the asset. It includes target attractiveness (from the perspective of the threat), level of security, access to the site, publicity if attacked, and the number of prior threats. Input into this factor typically comes from the law enforcement and intelligence communities familiar with threat and operational security measures.

Vulnerability is an indication of how much the facility or population would be damaged or destroyed based on the structural response to a particular hazard. In the context of the AASHTO report, vulnerability is the likely damage resulting from various terrorist threats (weapon type and location). It is a measure of expected damage, the outcome of the event, expected casualties, and loss of use, which are all features of the facility itself. Input into the vulnerability factor typically comes from engineering analysis and expertise.

Importance is a characteristic of the facility being protected, not the hazard, and is an indication of consequences to the facility, structure, region, or nation in the event the facility is destroyed or unavailable.

The FEMA Approach

For TARA/TVA approaches in which scales or rankings are used to reflect factors such as threat level, likelihood, vulnerability, and consequence, a similar equation can be used to provide a risk ranking. One example is the approach outlined by FEMA [1], wherein risk is defined as follows:

Risk = Asset Value × Threat Rating × Vulnerability Rating

The FEMA approach uses a seven-level risk factor scale, shown in Table 4.11 [1]. It is equally valid to select other rankings, such as a five-level scale.

TABLE 4.11   Risk Factor Rankings

Risk Factor	Numerical Ranking
Very high	10
High	8–9
Medium high	7
Medium	5–6
Medium low	4
Low	2–3
Very low	1

Source: Adapted from FEMA, 2003. *Risk Management Series—Reference Manual to Mitigate Potential Terrorist Attacks Against Buildings,* Publication 426, Federal Emergency Management Agency, Washington, DC, Table 1-18.

Given a scale and factors to be combined in the assessment, threshold levels can be established for comparison. For example, with the FEMA approach, the total risk threshold values are 1 to 60 for low risk, 61 to 175 for medium risk, and greater than 176 for high risk. An assessment of the level of risk can be obtained by calculating the risk factors of asset value, threat rating, and vulnerability rating, using FEMA's seven-level scale and equation. An example in which arbitrary ratings have been provided to a "data center" within a financial services office is shown in Table 4.12. (The "Data Center" row contains the product of the ratings for each of the three risk factor components, which combine to provide the overall risk rating for each threat.) The numbers in Bold type indicate a high risk, the numbers in italic type indicate a medium risk, and the rest indicate a low risk for the data center facility.

In this hypothetical example, the risk assessment identifies five areas of high risk for which mitigation may be warranted. The particularly high vulnerability ranking for bombs reflects that this data center is not structurally hardened. Likewise, no CBR mitigation measure is in place. In an actual TARA/TVA, more detail will be required, particularly with respect to threat scenarios (i.e., explosive charge weights, number of aggressors).

PREVENTION AND MITIGATION STRATEGIES

Once the risk has been quantified, the next step is to identify potential prevention and mitigation strategies and options. The term *poten-*

TABLE 4.12 Data Center Risk Ranking

Function	Cyber Attack	Armed Attack	Vehicle Impact	Stationary Vehicle Bomb	Package Bomb (delivered)	Briefcase Bomb (carried)	CBR	Fire
Data center	**360**	*128*	48	**280**	**432**	**432**	*144*	**200**
Asset value	8	8	8	8	8	8	8	8
Threat rating	9	4	1	5	6	6	2	5
Vulnerability rating	5	4	6	7	9	9	9	5

Source: Adapted from FEMA, 2003. *Risk Management Series—Reference Manual to Mitigate Potential Terrorist Attacks Against Buildings,* Publication 426, Federal Emergency Management Agency, Washington, DC, Table 1-20.

tial is used because of the broad range of strategies that are available—from operating procedures to physical protection systems to providing law enforcement personnel—and the various options within each strategy. For example, physical protection systems can range from access control to closed circuit television (CCTV) to structural hardening. Therefore, it is not likely that all potential strategies and options will be selected.

Primary Strategies

The four primary strategies for protecting against terrorist attack include deter, delay, detect, and prevent. *Deterrence* focuses on providing a visible presence of security. This presence can range from a security force to CCTV, bollards, lighting, or other measures that are visible to a potential aggressor. *Delay* reflects strategies that will slow an attack; such strategies include bollards or landscaping to hinder vehicle approach, access control, turnstiles, and similar measures aimed at slowing and restricting access. *Detection systems,* such as x-ray, gamma-ray and other screening tools, glass-break detectors, door contacts, smoke detectors, explosive detectors, and chemical detectors, are used to detect the presence of a threat within a facility. As a final measure, *prevention* means hardening; it is intended to mitigate consequences should a threat scenario be realized. Prevention can include a variety of physical measures, from structural hardening to fire protection systems to heating, ventilation, and air conditioning (HVAC) system filters, dampers, and controls.

Rings of Protection/Defense in Depth

In many cases, it is appropriate to implement rings of protection, with critical assets located in the core and layers of protection surrounding the asset, in concert with deter, delay, detect, and prevent strategies. The rings-of-protection concept is illustrated in Figure 4.4.

Department of Justice Security Standards

Along with the rings of protection, a variety of other security measures can be implemented, from planning and operations to physical and electronic systems. Following the Murrah Building bombing in 1995, the Department of Justice (DOJ) developed a risk-ranking and protection-level categorization system, for which they identified various security standards for the rings of protection [15]:

- *Perimeter security.* Perimeter security standards pertain to areas outside of government control. Depending on the facility type, the

FIGURE 4.4 **Rings of Protection/Defense in Depth.**

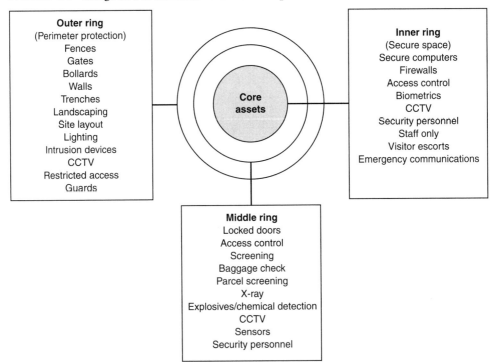

(*Source:* Arup.)

perimeter may include sidewalks, parking lots, outside walls of the building, a hallway, or simply an office door.

  • *Entry security.* Entry security standards refer to security issues related to the entry of persons and packages into a facility.

  • *Interior security.* Interior security standards refer to security issues associated with prevention of criminal or terrorist activity within the facility. This area concerns secondary levels of control after people or things have entered the facility.

  • *Security planning.* Security planning standards refer to recommendations requiring long-term planning and commitment, as well as security standards addressing broader issues with implications beyond security at a particular facility.

Table 4.13 shows the recommended minimum security standards applicable to each of the above four categories in the DOJ scheme [15].

TABLE 4.13   DOJ Recommended Security Measures by Protection Level

	Level				
Perimeter Security	I	II	III	IV	V
Parking					
Control of facility parking	▲	▲	●	●	●
Control of adjacent parking	▲	▲	▲	○	○
Avoid leases where parking cannot be controlled	▲	▲	▲	▲	▲
Leases should provide security control for adjacent parking	▲	▲	▲	▲	▲
Post signs and arrange for towing unauthorized vehicles	○	○	●	●	●
ID system and procedures for authorized parking (placard, decal, card key)	▲	▲	●	●	●
Adequate lighting for parking areas	▲	▲	●	●	●
CCTV monitoring					
CCTV surveillance cameras with time lapse video recording	▲	○	○	●	●
Post signs advising of 24 hour video surveillance	▲	○	○	●	●
Lighting					
Lighting with emergency power backup	●	●	●	●	●
Physical barriers					
Extended physical perimeter with barriers (concrete and/or steel composition)	—	—	▲	○	○
Parking barriers	—	—	▲	○	○

(continues)

TABLE 4.13 *Continued*

	Level				
Entry security	I	II	III	IV	V
Receiving/shipping					
Review receiving/shipping procedures (current)	●	●	●	●	●
Implement receiving/shipping procedures (modified)	▲	○	●	●	●
Access control					
Evaluate facility for security guard requirements	▲	○	●	●	●
Security guard patrol	▲	▲	○	○	○
Intrusion detection system with central monitoring capability	▲	○	●	●	●
Upgrade to current life safety standards (fire detection, fire suppression systems, etc.)	●	●	●	●	●
Entrances/exits					
X-ray and magnetometer at public entrances	—	▲	○	○	●
Require x-ray screening of all mail/packages	—	▲	○	●	●
Peep holes	○	○	—	—	—
Intercom	○	○	—	—	—
Entry control with CCTV and door strikes	▲	○	—	—	—
High-security locks	●	●	●	●	●

	Level				
Interior security	I	II	III	IV	V
Employee/visitor identification					
Agency photo ID for all personnel displayed at all times	—	▲	○	●	●
Visitor control/screening system	▲	●	●	●	●
Visitor identification accountability system	—	▲	○	●	●
Establish ID issuing authority	○	○	○	●	●
Utilities					
Prevent unauthorized access to utility areas	○	○	●	●	●
Provide emergency power to critical systems (alarm systems, radio communications, computer facilities, etc.)	●	●	●	●	●
Occupant emergency plans (OEPs)					
Examine OEPs and contingency procedures based on threats	●	●	●	●	●
OEPs in place, updated annually, periodic testing exercises	●	●	●	●	●
Assign and train OEP officials (assignment based on largest tenant in facility)	●	●	●	●	●
Annual tenant training	●	●	●	●	●
Day Care Centers					
Evaluate whether to locate day-care facilities in buildings with high threat activities	—	●	●	●	●
Compare feasibility of locating day care in facilities outside locations	—	●	●	●	●

TABLE 4.13 *Continued*

Security planning	Level				
	I	II	III	IV	V
Intelligence sharing					
Establish law enforcement agency/security liaisons	●	●	●	●	●
Review/establish procedure for intelligence receipt/dissemination	●	●	●	●	●
Establish uniform security/threat nomenclature	●	●	●	●	●
Training					
Conduct annual security awareness training	●	●	●	●	●
Establish standard unarmed guard qualifications/training requirements	●	●	●	●	●
Establish standard armed guard qualifications/training requirements	●	●	●	●	●
Tenant assignment					
Co-locate agencies with similar security needs	▲	▲	▲	▲	▲
Do not co-locate high- and low-risk agencies	▲	▲	▲	▲	▲
Administrative procedures					
Establish flexible work schedule in high-threat/high-risk areas to minimize employee vulnerability to criminal activity	O	O	▲	▲	▲
Arrange for employee parking in/near building after normal work hours	O	O	O	O	O
Conduct background security checks and/or establish security control procedures for service contract personnel	●	●	●	●	●
Construction/renovation					
Install Mylar film on all exterior windows (shatter protection)	▲	▲	O	●	●
Review current projects for blast standards	●	●	●	●	●
Review/establish uniform standards for construction	●	●	●	●	●
Review/establish new design standard for blast resistance	O	O	●	●	●
Establish street setback for new construction	▲	▲	O	●	●

● = Minimum standard
O = Standard based on facility evaluation
▲ = Desirable
— = Not applicable
Source: DOJ, 1995. *Vulnerability Assessment of Federal Facilities,* U.S. Department of Justice, Washington, DC.

Although Table 4.13 focuses on security systems, it does specify hardening and other measures, and one can see its utility for identifying options.

Two often-used approaches specific to security design are Crime Prevention Through Environmental Design (CPTED) and Situational Crime Prevention (SCP). Their goal is to create physical and social conditions that help to reduce both crime and the fear of crime through such strategies as well-lit areas; clear lines of sight, with few or no places to hide easily; and the visual presence of security measures and staff.

When physical or electronic security systems are insufficient or inappropriate, other measures can be taken, such as blast or impact protection, active and passive fire protection, smoke and CBR detection and management systems, protected egress systems, and so forth. The range and types of systems that are available and appropriate depend on the specific threats and hazards (e.g., ballistics, explosives, fire, and CBR).

As with the risk rankings addressed earlier in this chapter, much more detail is necessary in an actual TARA/TVA to identify mitigation alternatives for specific systems and areas of a facility. More detailed descriptions of mitigation alternatives also helps in determining which mitigation options should be selected for a particular facility.

COST AND EFFECTIVENESS ANALYSES

When selecting appropriate mitigation options, it is helpful to consider both the cost and effectiveness of the various alternatives with respect to the threat scenarios and overall risk rankings for the facility and its assets. This analysis requires a life-cycle approach to the problem due to the variations in capital versus operating costs, effectiveness of mitigation measures with time (durability and reliability issues), and other such factors.

For example, from a capital-cost perspective, installing CCTVs may appear to be more cost-effective than providing a physical protection measure, such as making a building feature inaccessible to the public. However, an effective CCTV system requires monitoring by security staff, long-term maintenance, and eventual replacement. The overall cost could be much more than that for a physical protection measure. Likewise, the cost of structural hardening may be higher at the time of construction or renovation than the installation of a feature that would provide a minimum required standoff distance. However, over time, the feature providing standoff protection may become damaged and not replaced; it may even be removed, especially if the reason for the feature is no longer remembered or deemed necessary. For example, a sacrificial covering on a column used to provide standoff for blast may be removed during a building renovation if the institutional knowledge regarding the purpose of the covering is lost or architectural and aesthetic desires change.

Numerous methods, from simple ranking approaches to cost-estimating techniques, are available for benefit-cost analysis, life-cycle cost analysis, and mitigation effectiveness analysis. With the ranking approach, one would use a scale, as discussed earlier in the chapter, that rates cost and effectiveness from low to high. If cost and effectiveness are low, the option may not be worth it. If cost is low and effectiveness high, selecting the option may be an easy decision. If the cost and effectiveness are both high, the option may require further study, with rationale needed to support the cost expenditure.

Key Point   In some cases, an option that ranks low on effectiveness may be employed because it also serves another purpose. Therefore, understanding the range of uses for the mitigation measure is important.

This approach can be used when costs are estimated in ranges or when cost estimators are used to obtain mitigation-option-specific data (in the context of the facility in which it will be installed).

＿MITIGATION OPTION SELECTION ＿＿＿＿＿＿＿＿

Finally, when all of the analyses have been completed, the available mitigation options can be reviewed and those alternatives that are most appropriate to the facility can be selected. An effective way to sort the mitigation options is to combine the risk, cost-effectiveness, and mitigation-effectiveness parameters to obtain an overall risk–cost–effectiveness ranking [16]. Such a ranking can be accomplished in a number of ways. Selection of an appropriate method will depend on the approaches used for quantification of risk, cost-effectiveness, and mitigation effectiveness. In general, however, the components simply need to be combined in a manner that is mathematically valid, that produces meaningful results, that fits the specific TARA/TVA process, and that meets stakeholders' objectives.

A simple spreadsheet that clearly lays out the risks, costs, and mitigation effectiveness can be used to compare the cost and effectiveness of mitigation measures. An example of a risk–cost–effectiveness matrix is shown in Figure 2.7 in Chapter 2.

Another approach, also addressed in Chapter 2, is to apply classical economic theory to help focus in on the "optimal" level for balancing risk and cost. In brief, this optimal level is achieved when the incremental or marginal cost of risk reduction equals the marginal reduction achieved in mitigation cost [17]. In other words, if one spends too little on risk mitigation, the result could be significant expected losses. Conversely, excessive spending on risk mitigation may not be worth it, because the expected loss would be disproportionately low when compared to the mitigation investment. The optimal level, therefore, is somewhere in between. This concept is illustrated in Figure 2.6 in Chapter 2.

SUMMARY

This chapter has provided an introduction to and overview of threat, vulnerability, and risk assessment (TARA) focused on the terrorist threat. However, the concepts presented in this chapter are equally appropriate to other extreme event threats, including earthquakes, fires, and floods.

In general, a TARA should encompass the following components: identifying and valuing the assets that are being protected; determining the viability of the facility as a target; identifying and assessing the various threats to the facility; undertaking vulnerability and consequence analyses to determine where and how the facility could be compromised and what the impacts of an event could be; assessing the overall risk to the facility; and developing cost-effective mitigation strategies.

Various approaches for completing each of these tasks have been provided. In addition, references have been provided at the end of the chapter for additional information. In the following chapters, discussion of specific terrorist threats and extreme event hazards, methods for assessing the impact of these threats and hazards, and design approaches for mitigating these threats and hazards is provided.

REFERENCES

References Cited

1. FEMA, 2003. *Risk Management Series—Reference Manual to Mitigate Potential Terrorist Attacks Against Buildings,* Publication 426, Federal Emergency Management Agency, Washington, DC.

2. FTA, 2003. *The Public Transportation System Security and Emergency Preparedness Planning Guide,* Final Report, U.S. Department of Transportation, Federal Transit Administration, Washington, DC.

3. FEMA, 2002. *Integrating Human-Caused Hazards into Mitigation Planning,* Publication 386-7, Federal Emergency Management Agency, Washington, DC.

4. DoD, 2000. *Standard Practice for System Safety,* MIL STD 882D, U.S. Department of Defense, Washington, DC.

5. NFPA, 2000. *SFPE Engineering Guide to Performance-Based Fire Protection Analysis and Design of Buildings,* National Fire Protection Association, Quincy, MA.

6. Begler, et al., 2002. *The SFPE Handbook of Fire Protection Engineering,* National Fire Protection Association, Quincy, MA.

7. Wo, G., 2002. *Game Theory and Terrorism Risk,* Risk Management Solutions, Newark, CA, paper on www.lloyds.com.

8. Major, J. A., 2002. *Advanced Techniques for Modeling Risk,* Guy Carpenter Report, Marsh McLennan Companies, New York.

9. Bachman, R. E., et al., 2003. "ATC-58 Framework for Performance-Based Design of Nonstructural Components," *Proceedings of ATC 29-2: Seminar on Seismic Design, Performance, and Retrofit of Nonstructural Components in Critical Facilities,* Los Angeles, CA, October 14–24.

10. DoD, 2003. *DoD Minimum Antiterrorism Standards for Buildings,* Unified Facilities Criteria, UFC 4-010-01, U.S. Department of Defense, Washington, DC.

11. GSA, 2003. *Facilities Standards for the Public Buildings Service,* General Services Administration, Washington, DC.

12. Kaplan, S., and Garrick, B. J., 1981. "On the Quantitative Assessment of Risk," *Risk Analysis,* Vol. 1, No. 1, pp. 11–27.

13. Meacham, B. J., 2004. "Understanding Risk: Quantification, Perception and Characterization," *Journal of Fire Protection Engineering,* Vol. 14, No. 3, pp. 199–228.

14. AASHTO, 2003. *Recommendations for Bridge and Tunnel Security,* The ASSHTO Blue Ribbon Panel on Bridge and Tunnel Security, American Association of State Highway and Transportation Officials, Washington, DC.

15. DOJ, 1995. *Vulnerability Assessment of Federal Facilities,* U.S. Department of Justice, Washington, DC.

16. Meacham, B. J., 2003. "A Risk-Informed Performance-Based Approach to Tall Building Design," *Proceedings of the CIB-CTBUH*

International Conference on Tall Buildings: Strategies for Performance in the Aftermath of the World Trade Center, International Council for Building Research and Innovation in Building and Construction (CIB), Council on Tall Buildings in the Urban Habitat (CTBUH), and Construction Technology and Management Center, Universiti Teknologi Malaysia, Rotterdam, Netherlands, pp. 279–286.

17. Morgan, M. G., 1990. "Choosing and Managing Technology-Induced Risk," in T. S. Glickman and M. Gough (Eds.), *Readings in Risk,* Resources for the Future, Washington, DC, pp. 17–28.

Additional Readings

ASHRAE, 2003. *Report of the Presidential Ad Hoc Committee for Building Health and Safety under Extraordinary Events,* American Society of Heating, Refrigerating and Air-Conditioning Engineers, Atlanta, GA.

CDC, 2002. *Guidance for Protecting Building Environments from Airborne Chemical, Biological, or Radiological Attacks,* Centers for Disease Control and Prevention, Atlanta, GA.

DoD, 1999. *Selection and Application of Vehicle Barriers,* U.S. Department of Defense, Washington, DC.

BICE, 2003. *ISC Security Design Criteria for New Federal Office Buildings and Major Renovation Projects: A Review and Commentary,* Board on Infrastructure and the Constricted Environment, National Academies Press, Washington, DC.

Rassmussen, N. C., 1990. "The Application of Probabilistic Risk Assessment Techniques to Energy Technologies," in T. S. Glickman and M. Gough (Eds.), *Readings in Risk,* Resources for the Future, Washington, DC, pp. 195–206.

USACE, 2001. *Protecting Buildings & Their Occupants from Airborne Hazards,* U.S. Army Corps of Engineers, Washington, DC.

5

Bomb Blast Hazard Mitigation

J. David Hadden
Richard G. Little
Chad McArthur

This chapter addresses physical means to mitigate the threat of vehicle bomb attacks against buildings. It presents statistics on major bombing attacks, describes the nature of the current threat, and suggests a strategic framework for addressing this threat. The responsibility of the building owner to provide safe structures is also discussed. The effects of explosions on the building frame and its components are considered, followed by a description of various measures that can be taken to reduce the vulnerability of a building to blast effects, such as strengthened windows and cladding, structural features to reduce the likelihood of a progressive or total collapse, and methods to thwart the intentions of a suicide vehicle bomber. Evacuation strategies, including the concept of shelter areas within the building, are then introduced. The final section presents various approaches to the structural analysis of blast loading on building elements.

OVERVIEW

Attacks against buildings have increased worldwide since September 11, 2001; large vehicle bombs have been detonated in Bali (2002), Jakarta (2003), Chechnya (2003), Istanbul (2003), and Baghdad (2003). Individual suicide bombers have struck repeatedly in Israel, Russia, and Chechnya. Bombs destroyed several trains in Madrid in 2004, and vehicle attacks against buildings are a continuing hallmark of the Iraq insurgency. In July 2005, bombs were detonated almost simultaneously in London on subway trains and a public bus.

Despite the frequency of vehicle bomb attacks since September 11, 2001, bombing attacks against buildings and public spaces have long been a weapon of choice used by many terrorist organizations. In 1946, in an attempt to force the British from Palestine, a Jewish terrorist group destroyed the King David Hotel in Jerusalem, killing 91 people. In 1982, Islamic terrorists used truck bombs to attack the U.S. Marine barracks in Beirut, killing 242 people. A similar attack in 1983 killed 63 people at the U.S. Embassy in Beirut.

During the early 1990s, several powerful bombs were detonated in the City of London by the Provisional wing of the Irish Republican Army. Although casualties were light because warnings were issued prior to the attack, the buildings suffered extensive damage. In 1994, the Jewish Community Center in Buenos Aires, Argentina, was destroyed by a truck bomb, and 26 persons were killed. Islamic extremists claimed responsibility. Following the first attack on the World Trade Center in New York in 1993, in which only 8 people were killed although the building was extensively damaged, 168 persons lost their lives when the Alfred P. Murrah Federal Building in Oklahoma City was destroyed in 1995 by an American terrorist using a truck bomb.

Attacks by the Al-Qaeda terrorist network against U.S. interests increased during the late 1990s with the bombing of the Khobar Towers in Saudi Arabia in 1996 (20 killed) and the bombing attacks against the U.S. Embassies in Nairobi (224 killed) and Dar es Salaam (11 killed) in 1998. Table 5.1 summarizes major vehicle bombing events since 1946.

Vehicle Bomb Threats

Despite the fact that much is known regarding the nature of the terrorist vehicle bomb threat, implementing effective countermeasures is not a straightforward technical exercise. Although people expect buildings to provide some measure of protection in the event of an attack, no consensus exists on how this can best be achieved. Building owners clearly have a responsibility to provide for the safety of those entrusted to their care, but when considering protection levels for buildings, owners must also consider the cost of providing that level of safety.

Many physical responses to the threat of terrorist attack are driven more by the desire to protect people and assets from what could happen rather than what is likely to happen. In other words, the responses address the vulnerability of people and buildings to a

TABLE 5.1 Major Terrorist Vehicle Bomb Attacks (1946–2003)

Location	Year	Size of Bomb (kg TNT Equivalent)[1]	Number of People Killed
St. David Hotel, Jerusalem	1946	350	91
U.S. Marine Barracks, Beirut	1982	5,550	242
U.S. Embassy, Beirut	1983	1,000	63
St. Mary Axe, London	1992	350	0[2]
World Trade Center, New York	1993	900	8[3]
Jewish Community Center, Buenos Aires	1994	275	26
Alfred P. Murrah Federal Building, Oklahoma City	1995	1,800	169
Khobar Towers, Dharan, Saudi Arabia	1996	2,300	20
U.S. Embassy, Nairobi	1998	275	213
Sari Club, Bali	2002	~750–1,000	202
Marriott Hotel, Jakarta	2003	220	12
Military Hospital, Mozdok, Chechnya	2003	1,000	50
HSBC Bank, Istanbul	2003	200	15

[1] Information on bomb sizes and the number of casualties was developed from a variety of published sources and may not agree in all cases with "official" figures.

[2] The bomb was detonated near midnight when few people were in the vicinity.

[3] The bomb was detonated in the parking garage in an attempt to collapse the building. Those killed were in the immediate vicinity of the blast.

certain type of attack, rather than a true assessment of the risk of that attack. This approach essentially removes the public from the decision process and eliminates from consideration any willingness on the part of the public to accept some portion of that risk. It is not surprising then, that the debate over appropriate security for buildings and public places has often degenerated into a simple binary set—secure but unaesthetic on one side and attractive but vulnerable on the other [1]. Given the high cost of providing security to buildings and public spaces, both in terms of financial cost and the impact on our built environment, this is a question that reasonably should be considered by the public at-large and not just the building owner.

As the September 11, 2001, suicide attacks on New York City and Washington, D.C., demonstrated, in some scenarios direct defense is neither practical nor realistic. Therefore, the first line of defense must be to identify and apprehend potential perpetrators before they can act. Terrorists must also be denied access to the means of attack, such as explosives and delivery vehicles. This encompasses a broad range of security-related activities, such as domestic and international intelligence and surveillance, domestic law enforcement, enhanced airport security, and improved explosives control and detection devices.

Physical Protection for Buildings

Implementing physical protection strategies requires the active collaboration of engineers, architects, landscape architects, security specialists, and others to ensure the attractive integration of site and structure in a manner that minimizes the opportunity for attackers to approach or enter a building. This protection includes such features as personnel involved in active site security and perimeter control; landscaping and earthworks that can function both as blast barriers and vehicle controls; and appropriately designed street furniture and features such as planter boxes, bollards, and plinths that prevent vehicular access. The building itself may have a range of blast-resistant features, such as additional reinforcing details, composite fiber wraps to strengthen columns and slabs, and high-performance glazing materials.

Based on experience with blast effects on buildings and people, several basic tenets of physical protection for buildings have evolved over time:

- Prevent glazing and facade materials from shattering and entering occupied spaces.
- Keep the blast energy outside the building.
- Protect occupants from injury by fragments and larger objects, blast pressure, or physical translation.
- Prevent structural collapse—global, local, and progressive.

In support of these basic principles, the following should be considered when designing buildings to protect against potential terrorist attacks [2]:

- *Deflect* a terrorist attack by showing, through layout, security, and defenses, that the chances of success for the terrorist are small.

Targets that are otherwise attractive to terrorists should be made anonymous.

- *Disguise* the valuable parts of a potential target so that the energy of attack is wasted on the wrong area, and the attack, although completed, fails to make the impact the terrorist seeks; the attack is reduced to an acceptable annoyance.
- *Disperse* a potential target so that an attack can never cover a large enough area to cause significant destruction, and thereby impact. This protection strategy is suitable for a rural, industrial installation, but probably unachievable for an inner-city building.
- *Stop* an attack from reaching a potential target by erecting a physical barrier to the method of attack; this protective design approach covers a range of measures, from vehicle bollards and barriers to pedestrian entry controls. In particular, this is the only defense that will be successful against a large vehicle bomb.
- *Blunt* the attack once it reaches its target by hardening the structure to absorb the energy of the attack and protect valuable assets.

Despite the great strides that have been made in developing new materials and innovative techniques that will reduce building damage and occupant injury in the event of a bomb attack, the enormous amount of energy generated by even modest amounts of high explosives will still cause extensive building damage and personal injury if detonated at close range. If adequate standoff distance can be established and maintained, the other tenets of building protection become realistically achievable. The importance of standoff distance in the risk management equation cannot be overemphasized. If adequate standoff cannot be established, a combination of active site security, operational procedures, and building improvements must be provided.

Responsibilities of the Building Owner

The events of September 11 made it clear that there are no safe havens from terrorism. Tragedy can strike anyone, anywhere, at any time. As we move beyond the immediate aftermath of those events, building occupants have raised expectations regarding the role of buildings in protecting people from possible future attacks. Despite the terrible loss of life, the World Trade Center towers and the Pentagon actually performed extremely well under circumstances far more severe than anything anticipated when they were designed, thus demonstrating that buildings can make a real difference in saving lives. Owners have a responsibility to design and construct buildings that will do the best possible job of protecting the people that live and work inside them.

RESPONSE OF BUILDINGS TO BLAST

In response to the major terrorist attacks of recent years, bomb blast protection has been and is increasingly included in the design of many civilian facilities. When adopting blast protection as a design requirement, it is important to consider how blast loads and their effects differ from normal and environmental loads.

Dynamic Versus Static Loads

Building structures must always be designed to resist gravity, wind, and, where it occurs, soil pressure. Wind-induced dynamic effects may be important for tall, slender structures. When designing conventional buildings, however, gravity and wind can usually be treated as static forces (i.e., sustained loads that cause deformation of the structure proportional to their magnitude). Double the load, and you double the deformation. The amount a structure deforms depends on its stiffness of the building element; the stiffer it is, the less it deforms.

All of this is familiar and feels intuitively correct, but in reality static loads are just a special case. The total resistance of a structure to an applied force is the sum of various components:

$$m.d^2x/dt^2 + c.dx/dt + k.x = F \tag{1}$$

Where:

m = mass
c = damping coefficient
k = stiffness
f = applied force

In this equation, x signifies a displacement or deflection, dx/dt indicates velocity, and d^2x/dt^2 indicates acceleration.

When there is no motion, or if any movement is very gradual, the first two terms in this general expression are zero or insignificant, leaving only the stiffness term to provide the total resistance to the applied static load. The stiffness term alone relates to stress and, if the stress exceeds the material's limit, to potential failure of the element.

Now consider the case of a dynamic load that does induce motion into a structure. This time the inertia term may contribute significantly to the total resistance to the applied load, to the extent that only a small displacement is needed to balance Equation 1. The message to draw from this is that the response of a structure or building element to a dynamic load is fundamentally different from the way it responds to a static load.

Explosion Loading

An explosion has been defined as ". . . a chemical reaction or change of state effected in an exceedingly short period of time with the generation of a high temperature and generally a large quantity of gas. An explosion produces a shockwave in the surrounding medium" [3]. To complete the picture, we can also refer to Meyer's definition of a shockwave as ". . . an intense compression wave produced by the detonation of an explosive" [3].

With these definitions in mind, we can review the nature of the loading produced by an explosion. The explosion loading to which a building may be exposed can come from several different sources. Explosive loading may be introduced by accidental events, including the following:

- Industrial processes involving inherently explosive materials
- Industrial processes involving materials (liquids, gases, or dusts) that may become explosive under certain conditions
- Storage of munitions and propellants
- Buildup of domestic gas
- Pressure-vessel explosions

Deliberate events that use the following materials and devices may also introduce explosive loading:

- Explosives for quarrying, excavation
- Explosives for demolition
- Military munitions against a target
- Improvised explosive devices (IEDs) against a target

With any type of explosion, the effect is a rapid increase in air pressure in the immediate vicinity of the event, as well as a release of heat and light. This in turn causes a wave of highly compressed air to expand outward from the seat of the explosion. The intensity of this pressure wave will decrease with increasing distance from its point of origin. At any point over which the wave passes, the air pressure will eventually return to the ambient value prior to the explosion.

Although the characteristics of the pressure wave at a given point depends on many factors, including the state, chemical composition, mass, and distance of the explosive material, explosions can be divided broadly into two groups: deflagrations and detonations.

Deflagrations. Deflagration occurs when materials undergo very rapid combustion; accidental explosions caused during industrial processes or because of a buildup of domestic gas usually are classified as deflagrations. The pressure pulse felt at a given point arising from a deflagration rises rapidly to a peak over a discernible time period before falling away again over a similar or longer duration. Figure 5.1 illustrates typical shape characteristics of a deflagration and the idealized triangular shaped pulse that may be used to approximate the load-time history of such an explosion.

Detonations. Detonation occurs when materials often referred to as high explosives undergo an extremely rapid and violent chemical reaction. In this case, the rise to peak pressure in the surrounding air happens almost instantaneously, with a subsequent rapid decay as the wave front advances away from the seat of the explosion at supersonic velocity. Figure 5.2 illustrates the typical real and idealized triangular pulse shapes for a detonation.

For both deflagrations and detonations, the initial rise in air pressure is followed by a less intense but often longer period over which air pressure falls below the ambient value before finally stabilizing. This negative, or suction, phase is generally of much less significance than the initial positive phase when designing blast protection measures, but in certain circumstances it can contribute to building damage.

The effects of accidental deflagrations on conventional buildings can be catastrophic, particularly when the deflagration is confined within elongated enclosures. The risk and possible effects of such incidents should not be dismissed. However, the focus of this chapter is on detonation caused by the willful use of high explosives to attack a building or group of buildings, particularly by terrorists using IEDs, which are often concealed within a vehicle.

Although generally composed of small amounts of military-grade explosives that act as a booster to initiate detonation in a larger mass of a more easily obtainable material, such as certain agricultural fertilizers, physical evidence from actual IEDs shows that when skill-

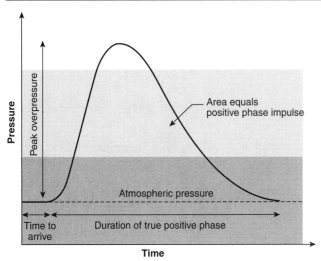

FIGURE 5.1 Typical Deflagration Pressure-Time History.

(*Source:* Arup.)

(a) True pulse shape

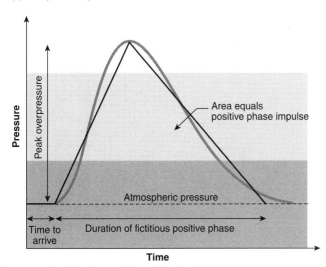

(b) Idealized equivalent triangular pulse shape

fully manufactured, they can display all of the devastating characteristics of high explosives. Therefore, in this chapter the terms *bomb blast* and *blast load* refer to a detonation that produces an air-blast pulse of the type shown in Figure 5.2, in which the peak positive pressure may be several hundred kN/m², with positive duration measured in a few thousandths of a second. As a comparison, wind loads are typically represented for design by pressures of 1 to 2 kN/m², based on a gust duration of a few seconds.

FIGURE 5.2 Typical Detonation Pressure-Time History.

(*Source:* Arup.)

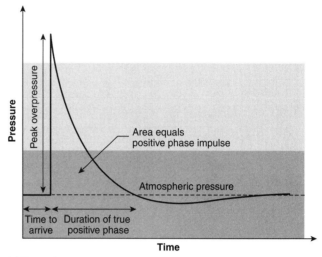

(a) True pulse shape

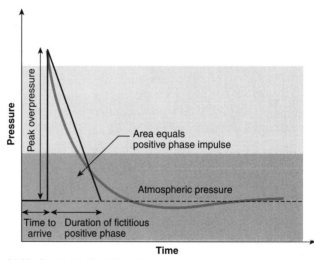

(b) Idealized equivalent triangular pulse shape

Natural Period of Vibration

So how do we decide whether to regard bomb blast, or any other transient loading, as a dynamic load? The answer to this question depends on the characteristics of the structure, and in particular its natural period of vibration. This natural period depends on two properties: stiffness and mass. If we increase stiffness while keeping mass constant, the natural period will be shortened. In other words, the structure vibrates more rapidly as stiffness increases. Conversely, if we increase mass while keeping stiffness constant, the natural period will increase.

To illustrate, think of how you used to vibrate your ruler on the desk at school. Make it shorter, and hence stiffer, and you get more rapid vibration. Add a lump of Blutack®, for example, to the end to increase the mass but keep the length the same, and it vibrates more slowly. (Blutack® is a reusable, pliable adhesive substance.)

We can show mathematically that the degree to which a structure responds to a short-duration load like a bomb blast will depend largely on the relative magnitudes of the natural vibration period of the structure and the duration of the applied blast load [4]. Figure 5.3 illustrates this effect for a triangular pulse such as that due to bomb blast.

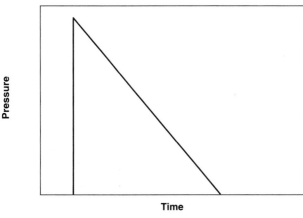

FIGURE 5.3 **Influence of Natural Period on Response to Blast Load.**

(*Source:* Arup.)

(a) Idealized triangular pressure–time plot

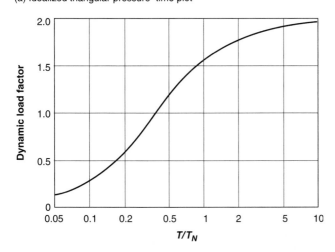

(b) Maximum response of elastic system to triangular load pulse

For a structure or element whose natural period (T_N) is significantly longer than the blast duration (T) (i.e., T/T_N is small), only a small proportion of the peak blast pressure is "felt" by the structure. In effect, due to the structure's inertia, the blast pressure pulse passes before the structure can deflect to a degree that would induce significant stress.

By contrast, if T and T_N are matched more closely, the structure will "feel" more of the applied pressure—more of the resistance is provided by the stiffness term in Equation 1. For a certain range of T/T_N values, the structure will respond up to twice as much as it would if the same peak pressure was applied statically.

As an analogy for this dynamic behavior, consider a Strongest Man in the World competition in which contestants attempt to pull a massive truck along a road from a standing start. Each competitor does not give a sudden jerk on the rope and expect it to move. If a competitor did this, the inertia of the truck would resist even the most powerful tug these formidable athletes could muster. However, by applying a large enough steady load, the truck will slowly start to roll, eventually to the point where its inertia works with the contestant as it gathers pace, maintaining motion even if the applied force should momentarily falter.

In the context of building elements, various components of a building will respond differently to a bomb blast in accordance with their dynamic characteristics. A pane of glass is usually small in scale, relatively light, and reasonably stiff; therefore, it has a short natural period of vibration, which spells trouble under blast load. The pane will respond rapidly to the blast pressure and be significantly loaded by it. Glass is also brittle and weak in bending, which is why broken windows are so common in explosions—and the single greatest source of injury.

Interestingly, it is sometimes the suction, or negative, phase of the blast pressure that breaks windows. This negative phase is less intense than the positive pulse that precedes it, but it has a longer duration. In some bomb explosions, it appears that windows have been pushed inward by the positive pressure, but not to the point of brittle failure. The pane then starts to return to its original position, still intact, when along comes the negative pressure phase to impose a relatively sustained suction in the direction it is already traveling, with the result that the pane shatters outward into the street.

Those parts of a building with a relatively long period compared to the blast duration, such as the overall lateral stability system or a long-span floor beam, will have a more limited response to the blast.

If the stability system (e.g., concrete shear walls or a braced steel frame) feels little of the applied load, then its deflection will be small, and hence the stresses generated in it will be small. Consequently, overwhelming the stability system of a large, well-engineered, robustly configured steel or concrete building to the extent that the structure topples over is unlikely to occur from terrorist explosions that have been on the scale of those seen to date around the world.

COUNTER TERRORIST MEASURES FOR BUILDINGS

What can a designer do to reduce the risk to those in and around a building in the event of an explosion? One answer is to build heavy concrete bunkers or fortresses, but buildings are occupied by people who need light, air, and an awareness of the world outside to be comfortable and able to function. A reasonable balance must be struck between blast protection and all of the other criteria for a successful building.

Threat Assessment and Blast-Protection Objectives

The starting point is for the designer and client (the developer, owner, or tenant) to agree on the level of threat to be considered and the objectives of any blast-protection measures. Assessing the terrorist bomb threat to a particular building is not an exercise in precise mathematics or statistical analysis; the range of possible combinations of device size and distance to which a building might be exposed is almost infinite. Despite the apparent difficulties in carrying out such an assessment, it is an essential first step (assessment methods are discussed in Chapter 4). Ultimately the objective of the bomb threat assessment is for the project participants to agree on one or more combinations of charge weight and location to be protected against.

The blast-protection objectives must also be realistic. To expect any building, other than perhaps a hardened military facility, to withstand a large vehicle bomb immediately outside the front door unscathed is unrealistic. However, on a large facade it may be acceptable for the windows closest to the seat of the explosion to produce a certain level of hazard on grounds of economy, with the understanding that other windows, which are offset from the seat, remain more protective. In other cases, fully protecting the exposed rooms at the closest range may be required. Building designers must decide whether to glaze the whole facade to the extent required for the most heavily loaded point at ground level or whether to adopt a graded approach to protection. Another consideration is whether the facade or other building components are expected to be reusable after the "design explosion" or whether a level of permanent damage and distortion is acceptable, necessitating replacement.

Conducting threat assessments and defining blast-protection objectives are part of a process of selecting a position on the scale of possible events from which to develop measures consistent with those objectives. This process should lead to the design of a building that offers greater protection, not only from the agreed upon threats, but also against a band of other possible scenarios than would be the case if no added protection was provided. However, those involved in the process should never lose sight of the fact that the only certainty when designing counterterrorist measures for a building is that the event used for design will not be the attack to which the building is actually exposed. Some may view this caution as a reason not to design against a specific threat, because it will inevitably be the wrong one. A more positive interpretation is to recognize that solutions based on certain design parameters need to be capable of responding well to others.

Building Design and Layout

The threat assessment should be carried out before the design progresses too far so that fundamental changes in the building can be implemented without abortive work. For example, is there any way to increase the distance of the bomb from the building—the standoff distance—identified in the threat assessment? In the battle against blast effects, every meter added to the standoff distance counts. At close proximity, and leaving aside local effects, the peak blast pressure is, broadly, inversely proportional to the square of the distance, so anything that can be done to maximize standoff, such as vehicle and pedestrian barriers, is of great value.

Other features to be treated with caution and, if possible, designed out at this stage are floors bridging over public roads, re-entrant features such as partially enclosed courtyards, and even deep window recesses. All of these features exacerbate blast effects due to confinement and reflection of the blast wave. Another issue to consider during early planning is access and egress. Ideally, doors should be well dispersed around the perimeter, as shown in Figure 5.4, to

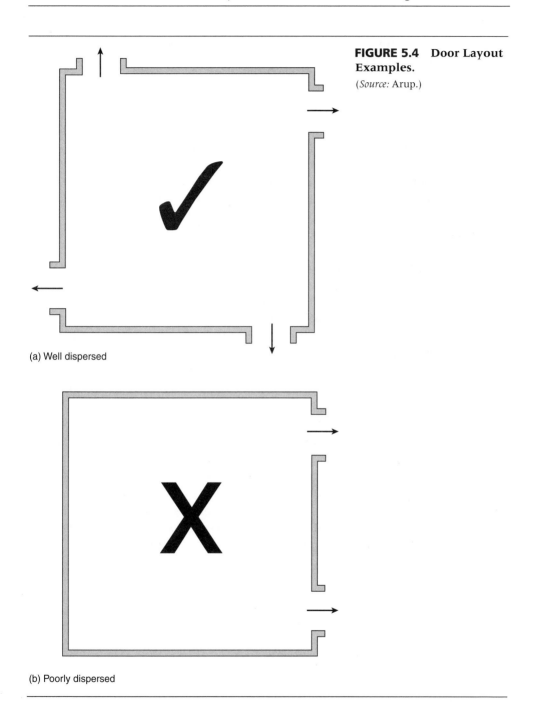

FIGURE 5.4 Door Layout Examples.
(*Source:* Arup.)

(a) Well dispersed

(b) Poorly dispersed

enable evacuation in the direction considered the safest, either before or after an explosion.

Computer Modeling and Other References

After settling on the threat, the protection objectives, and the building layout, more detailed engineering can follow. However, at this point opinions on how to proceed diverge. A topographical computer model of the building and its surroundings can be constructed. Sophisticated software can then be used to evaluate the blast pressures and impulses at points around the building for each of the agreed upon threats. However, the sheer complexity of modeling with confidence the influence of adjacent buildings, plus the uncertainties of bomb location and effective charge weight, may undermine the value of such an exercise. The response of the various building surfaces to the blast wave, which may include failure of some surfaces, can also affect the propagation of the blast wave. Merely representing these as rigid and unyielding surfaces may produce misleading results.

Alternative methods of deriving air blast pressures and impulses involve referencing published charts or tables [5]; using established, empirically based software, such as the Conventional Weapons Effects Program (ConWep) [6]; or relying on advanced computer codes, such as Air3d [7] or AutoDyne® [8] and the like, to model local conditions.

The designer should keep in mind that there are no exact answers when designing counterterrorist blast protection measures or universally established design codes to fall back on. In short, there is no substitute for a rational and realistic threat assessment backed by well-founded engineering principles and appropriate analysis.

PRACTICAL PROTECTION AGAINST BLAST

Windows

The most widespread cause of injuries and internal disruption from an external bomb blast is the fragmentation and inward projection of window glass. This has been observed in large explosions around the world, from London to Jakarta to Oklahoma to Nairobi. Plain annealed glass, which is in the majority of homes, is the most hazardous type, because it breaks into dagger-like shards. During an explosion, these shards are thrown at high speed deep into the building, causing laceration injuries. Blast pressures entering through shattered windows can also cause potentially fatal lung damage or eardrum rupture and may throw people against walls and other solid objects.

Laminated Glass. The most protective type of glazing against a blast is laminated glass. Even if cracked by blast pressures, the outer glass layers remain bonded to the inner plastic interlayer rather than forming free-flying shards. By securely bonding the glass to suitably enhanced frames, it can bulge inward (as illustrated in Figure 5.5) but stay in place, thanks to the remarkable properties of a polyvinyl butyral (pvb) interlayer.

If it remains untorn and held at its edges, the interlayer prevents blast pressures from entering the building; at most, a fine glass dust will become detached from the inner surface. The major causes of window injury are thereby removed. Eventually, if the interlayer is stretched beyond its limit, it will tear, but even after tearing has commenced the infiltrating blast wave will be restricted until the opening is substantial. The effectiveness of laminated glass due to this energy-absorbing behavior, in combination with appropriate frames and connections to the building structure, is well proven, both in tests and actual terrorist bomb explosions.

Laminated glass, even when held in normal frames with conventional neoprene gaskets, can still provide a useful reduction in blast hazard to occupants. The laminated glass may crack and even detach from its framing in the event of a blast. However, it will lose inward velocity more rapidly than individual particles or shards of nonlaminated glass and, as illustrated in Figure 5.6, it will reduce the extent of the occupied floor over which the hazard level is high.

When windows are double glazed, laminated glass should always be used in the inner layer. However, it is reasonable to use monolithic glass in the outer layer, because the inner laminate will impede the flight of the broken glass and, even if the laminate is breached, limit its throw into the building.

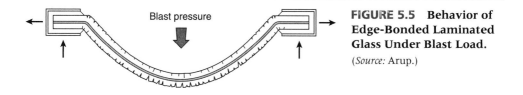

FIGURE 5.5 Behavior of Edge-Bonded Laminated Glass Under Blast Load.
(*Source:* Arup.)

FIGURE 5.6 **Laminated Glass in Conventional Frames Thrown Inward a Limited Distance by an External Explosion.**

(*Source:* U.K. Home Office Scientific Development Branch.)

Fully Tempered Glass. Toughened glass, or fully tempered glass, shatters at higher loads than annealed glass and forms dice-shaped particles rather than elongated razor-sharp shards. Although considered by some to be less hazardous than shards, these toughened "dice" may travel at even higher velocities and cause injuries deep inside a building. It is possible to design toughened glass windows (or even annealed glass if sufficiently thick) to resist a given bomb blast without cracking. However, should the blast exceed the "design bomb," the glass will shatter completely. Compared to laminated glass, solid glazing has the following disadvantages:

- Brittle failure is possible with no reserve of protection once cracking occurs.
- Once shattered, the debris is likely to detach from its frame.
- Shape and higher velocity of glazing debris makes it hazardous over a wider floor area.
- Comparatively strong, stiff frames are required to utilize the full strength of the glass.

- The glass may shatter unpredictably because of the impact of bomb fragments

Particularly in the case of a tall building, consideration is sometimes given to the height to which glazing enhancement should be extended. If the glazing selection is based on a particular explosion, it may be found that above a certain level monolithic glass of a thickness that satisfies the other design criteria would not be cracked. In such circumstances, the client may elect to install the monolithic glass if it offers cost savings. However, the client must accept that such a solution offers no reserve of protection for those floors in the event of an explosion more severe than the design event.

Antishatter Film. Fragmentation of monolithic glass can be inhibited by applying a polyester antishatter film (ASF) to its inside face. In the event of an explosion that cracks the glass, the film is intended to hold the glass together so that dangerous shards are not released. The effectiveness of ASF depends on the properties of the film itself, the manner in which it is adhered to the glass, and the care with which it is installed.

The use of polyester film to reduce the glazing blast hazard in this way was developed from the 1970s onwards, initially by the U.K. government and generally in conjunction with bomb blast-net curtains, as a retrofit measure for existing buildings. Although effective as a means of reducing widespread injury in the event of a blast, ASF is rarely an appropriate choice for blast hazard reduction in new buildings for the following reasons:

- Superior protection is provided by laminated glass, even in nonenhanced frames.
- The inevitable degradation in ASF performance over time means that peel-adhesion testing must be conducted during its service life.
- ASF must often be replaced within 5 to 10 years.
- Transparency can be reduced during service due to scratching and marking during cleaning or accidental contact.

Anchored ASF. More recently, various manufacturers have developed anchored ASF. With anchored ASF, the edges of the film are secured, either by mechanical fixings or adhesive bonding, to the perimeter frames. The objective is to generate membrane action similar to the behavior of bonded laminated glass. Although in principle this technique may enhance the level of achievable protection, the effectiveness of retrofitted ASF is highly dependent on the ability of the perimeter anchorages to resist the membrane forces generated. One important influence is the higher stiffness that polyester films generally possess compared to the pvb used as the interlayer in conventional laminated glass. This high stiffness means that polyester film can generate high edge forces, which will be onerous on the edge restraints. In addition, polyester film does not lend itself as readily as pvb to the absorption of blast energy through elongation.

Calculation methods for predicting the blast response of glass with anchored film are not yet as developed as those for laminated glass. Although some blast test data for this use of ASF exist, extrapolating these results to predict the outcome of other window sizes and/or blast-loading conditions should be undertaken with caution.

Ballistic-Rated Glazing. Ballistic-rated glazing is designed primarily to provide high impact resistance; however, it does so at the expense of the ductility and retention of debris that is desirable for blast-hazard reduction. In this category, polycarbonate is a very tough transparent material that can be used on its own or laminated together with plies of conventional glass. Although capable of resisting considerable blast loading, polycarbonate is very stiff and consequently transfers large forces to its supporting frames, which therefore must be made strong enough to avoid premature failure. The unyielding nature of polycarbonate means that its failure mode under blast load tends to be sudden detachment from its frames and vigorous inward throw of the whole pane.

Notwithstanding the amount of research on the behavior of glazing under blast load, this remains a field in which levels of expertise vary greatly and critical issues affecting clients, designers, suppliers, and constructors need to be addressed early in a project to ensure a successful outcome [9].

Building Facade

Effectiveness of Glazing Enhancement. Figure 5.7 illustrates in broad terms the relative areas (centered on a soccer stadium to give a sense of scale) over which high levels of hazard may arise from a large vehicle bomb acting on different types of glazed facade. By assuming that these areas give a measure of relative risk from an attack in an urban location, it can be seen that by progressing from thin an-

FIGURE 5.7 **Effectiveness of Different Forms of Glazing After Large Vehicle Bomb (Soccer Stadium Shown for Scale).**

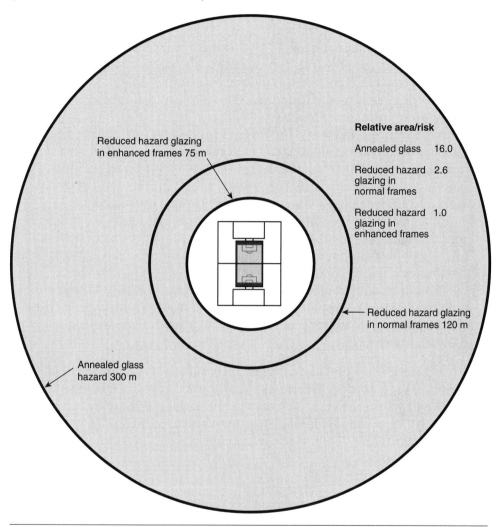

Relative area/risk

Annealed glass   16.0

Reduced hazard   2.6
glazing in
normal frames

Reduced hazard   1.0
glazing in
enhanced frames

Reduced hazard glazing
in enhanced frames 75 m

Reduced hazard glazing
in normal frames 120 m

Annealed glass
hazard 300 m

(*Source:* Hadden, D., 2002. "The Trade-Offs of Handling Risk and Resilience." *Proceedings of the Workshop on Lessons from the World Trade Center Terrorist Attack,* Technical Report, Multidisciplinary Center for Earthquake Engineering Research, MCEER-02-SP08, New York.)

nealed glass to laminated glass in normal frames and then to laminated glass in enhanced frames, the relative risk to the building occupants is significantly reduced at each step. Because costs are often building specific, it can be misleading to quote typical figures. However, it is reasonable to expect the percentage uplift in building costs at each of these steps to be in single figures. These increases compare favorably with the associated reductions in risk that can be achieved.

Nonglazed Cladding. It is logical to ensure that nonglazed areas of cladding or nonstructural walling provide comparable bomb-blast protection to adjacent glazing. Without considering the behavior of the materials in question, this may not automatically be the case. Precast reinforced concrete cladding with robust fixings to the primary structure can be effective at resisting blast load through a combination of mass and strength.

Unreinforced masonry, however, is brittle and potentially vulnerable to blast loading. Its capacity to resist out-of-plane blast load will be strongly influenced by the degree of in-plane restraint provided at the edge of each panel. Its fixings to the building structure need to be considered carefully if its full capacity is to be mobilized.

The blast resilience of lighter metal cladding depends on its bending strength and ductility, but it can be effective, especially with appropriate fixings that enable in-plane membrane action (similar to laminated glass) to be developed.

For all cladding types, fixings to the primary structure should ideally be designed to remain undamaged under blast loads so that they are reusable after an explosion, even if the cladding units themselves have to be replaced.

Interface Between Cladding and Structure. Concerns are sometimes expressed that by enhancing the building facade, more blast load will act on the main structure, thus making it more vulnerable. However, it is usually damage to a few critical members rather than an overwhelming load on the whole structure that causes buildings to collapse [10].

Key Point   By designing the cladding to span vertically between floors rather than fixing it to structural columns, any blast forces from the facade will be distributed throughout the structure by the floor slabs, which act as diaphragms with high in-plane strength and stiffness.

With the cladding arranged as shown in Figure 5.8, the blast forces will be largely resisted by the building's enormous overall inertia, thereby minimizing the risk of collapse caused by overloading the vertical load-carrying structure.

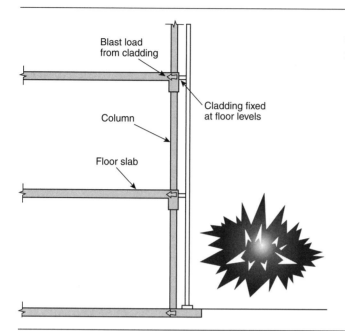

FIGURE 5.8 Cladding Spanning Between Floor Slabs.

(*Source:* Arup.)

Blast load from cladding

Cladding fixed at floor levels

Column

Floor slab

The facade of a building is the first line of defense for its occupants against the effects of an external bomb explosion. By selecting appropriate materials for both glazed and solid areas of cladding and adopting suitable methods of restraint and attachment to the building structure, significant reductions in the otherwise likely levels of blast injuries to occupants and disruption to the internal environment can be achieved at reasonable cost.

Structural Resilience

Even with the benefit of a protective facade, a building's structure can still be damaged by a bomb blast, and when extensive collapse does occur it is usually because of damage to one or more elements that are critical to resisting gravity loads.

Key Point   The structural designer's objective is to ensure that damage is limited in its extent and that any collapse is not disproportionate to its cause.

The Chamber of Shipping in St. Mary Axe, London, was built in 1967. When damaged by a nearby vehicle bomb, it suffered from a lack of robustness sometimes found in British buildings of that era, as shown in Figure 5.9.

The Alfred P. Murrah Federal Building in Oklahoma City is another example of a building that exhibited widespread collapse following bomb blast damage to critical low-level elements. This is a good illustration of the maxim coined by Arup consultant Francis Walley,[1] one of the most experienced engineers in the field of blast effects, that "structures only collapse when every possible load path has been removed."

In the United Kingdom, the lessons learned from the accidental gas explosion in 1968 at Ronan Point [11] led to building regulations and design codes that provide the framework and tools for designing robust structures with alternative load paths to reduce the risk of catastrophic or disproportionate collapse.

Bomb attacks on the Alfred P. Murrah Federal Building, Khobar Towers, and other buildings (see Table 5.1) led to the introduction of measures to reduce vulnerability to progressive collapse in new U.S. federal facilities [12]. Investigation into this aspect of building design is continuing, and design guidelines are being developed by engineers and researchers around the world.

Most steel or in-situ concrete frames have the potential to perform well under blast loads from typical terrorist vehicle bombs. Local damage can be severe, with columns or slabs close to the explosion destroyed or badly distorted, but overall catastrophic collapse is relatively rare. Some simple modifications to normal construction practice [13] will improve the blast resilience of such structures, but even with these measures, repairs and member replacement may still be required. For all but the most mission-critical facilities, when striking a balance between expenditure and protection, the designer's aim should be to avoid disproportionate damage, not to eliminate damage completely.

In any framed structure, the beam-to-column connections are critical. In a concrete frame, reinforcing bars projecting from a beam can be anchored into the upper and lower sections of a column, rather than just into the concrete at the junction of the two struc-

---

[1] Formerly Director of Civil Engineering Services of the U.K. Property Services Agency, advisor to the U.K. Explosive Storage and Transport Committee, member of U.S./U.K. Survey Unit at Hiroshima and Nagasaki, and member of wartime Ministry of Home Security Chief Scientific Advisor's Division.

FIGURE 5.9   Chamber of Shipping, London, 1992.

(*Source:* Arup.)

tural elements, where damage may be severe. In steel frames, a simple low-cost "belt-and-braces" approach can be beneficial, with a bolted end plate backed up by a welded seating cleat below, each designed to support a full beam reaction on its own.

Structural designers may also need to consider the ability of floor slabs to resist upward loads from blast. Portions of a suspended floor slab may not actually need reinforcement on its top face to resist normal downward gravity loads. However, if blast pressures enter the ground level there may be uplift on the floor slab above, which could then fail in reverse bending if it has no top reinforcement and drop back down on the level below. Figure 5.10 shows the underside of a floor slab, in this case cast on metal decking in a steel framed

FIGURE 5.10 Load Reversal in Floor Beam Due to Bomb Blast.

(*Source:* Arup; Photo by David Hadden.)

building, where blast pressure has bowed the slab upwards and caused the bottom flange of the beam, normally in tension, to buckle in compression.

The structural designer also needs to consider how precast concrete elements will behave in an explosion. If this form of construction is adopted, the precast units will need to be well tied to other robust structural elements.

Bomb Shelter Areas in Buildings

A bomb explosion, whether outside or inside a building, can cause widespread injuries and damage. The severity of the effects of an explosion will depend on the size and location of the bomb, as well as the construction of the building's structure, facades, and internal fabric. The form and materials selected for these elements, together with the layout of the building, will have a major influence on the vulnerability of occupants to explosions. In the case of a no-warning explosion, these are the primary factors that determine the degree of hazard. If a warning is received, protection, or at least hazard mitigation, can be provided against a range of potential bomb threats by complementing physical measures with suitable procedures, including inward and outward evacuation. *Inward evacuation* involves moving occupants to an area or areas within the building where they would be at lower risk than if they remained in their normal location or evacuated outward. *Outward evacuation* entails moving occupants to an area or areas of safety outside and remote from the building.

Various factors must be considered when developing appropriate strategies for a particular building. It is not unusual to find that although inward evacuation is viable for a range of potential threats, the consequences of certain major threats may be so severe that outward evacuation, even with its attendant hazards, becomes the most appropriate course of action.

Bomb Shelter Area Philosophy. In the United Kingdom, promotion by the police and other authorities of bomb shelter areas (BSAs) came about in the aftermath of large terrorist bombs in London in April 1992 and April 1993. BSAs are areas in buildings where occupants can take refuge from a bomb threat in greater safety than at their normal work location. More recent events in London Docklands in February 1996 and in Manchester in June 1996 have further emphasized the benefits of such shelter areas.

Evacuation procedures that are appropriate for fire safety may be unsuitable for city-center buildings under threat from a large explosive device because of the danger to evacuees of injury from falling glass and other debris over a wide area. As an example, it has been found that for a large vehicle-borne IED, injuries from falling glass may occur at 300 meters or more from the seat of the explosion and from metal fragments at up to 600 meters. The possibility of secondary devices being detonated at locations where occupants may evacuate to must also be considered.

Occupants may have to remain in a shelter area for a period of two hours or more from receipt of a warning until the explosion occurs or until the all clear is given. Following an explosion, police and emergency service workers may consider it necessary to delay evacuation of shelters and damaged buildings until the danger of falling debris or further explosions has receded. In this situation, it is realistic to plan for an additional period of confinement of up to one hour.

BSA Selection. It is important for building occupants to understand the qualifications and limitations of any given BSA. Currently, there is no statutory definition or specification for a BSA in either the

United Kingdom or the United States. Any recommended area should therefore be assessed in terms of the threats for which it is likely to be safe or unsafe.

Any identified BSA will provide protection only for a specific range of threats (defined by bomb size and location). More severe threats will create increasing hazards to BSA occupants. No BSA (short of a hardened "military" structure) provides complete protection against every credible threat.

Some BSAs may be directional; that is, blasts from some directions may be hazardous, whereas blasts from other directions may be protected against. The degree of protection may also vary. Injuries by one mechanism may be possible (e.g., by air blast), whereas injuries from another mechanism may be protected against (e.g., from flying glass). For threats grossly in excess of the capacity of a given BSA, it is likely that evacuation will be the less hazardous option between sheltering and outward evacuation.

BSA Design Criteria. A BSA should ideally satisfy the minimum criteria outlined in Table 5.2. Although the recommendations in Table 5.2 may be incorporated into the design of a new building, they can also guide the selection of BSAs in an existing facility. In the

TABLE 5.2   **Minimum Design Criteria for Bomb Shelter Areas**

BSA Design Criteria	Characteristics
Structural robustness	Slab-to-slab blast- and debris-resistant walls.
Ease of access and escape	Before and after the explosion.
Adequate space for occupants	Density of 0.6 to 0.8 m² of floor space or more per person.
Ventilation and cooling	Enough so that occupants can remain in BSA without serious health risk for anticipated confinement period.
Emergency lighting	Installed in shelter and its access routes.
Elevators for disabled occupants	Used to transport only disabled occupants accompanied by designated marshals to the shelter area(s); the elevator cars should then be parked at ground level.
Toilet facilities	Available near shelter areas.
Drinking water	Supplied by extending water pipes and stocking bottled water.

Source: Arup.

latter case, a survey by a suitably experienced engineer is needed to assess the availability and adequacy of potential shelter areas.

Inward Evacuation Procedures. When developing a set of responses to various bomb threats, it is desirable to strike a balance between procedures that are flexible enough to be appropriate to the threat without being so numerous and diverse that there may be confusion in implementing them during the stressful circumstances of a bomb alert. As an example of how procedures can be matched to various threats, consider the following four evacuation strategies:

A. Evacuate the entire building to a remote assembly area.
B. Evacuate inward to internal bomb shelter areas.
C. Remain in the building, away from glass.
D. Ignore the device, remain in the building.

Based on these four strategies and taking into account the resilience of the facade and the construction of the BSAs, suitable standoff distances for typical devices can be defined for each strategy, using the format shown in Table 5.3.

Outward Evacuation Procedures. To plan for circumstances in which outward evacuation of the building is the most appropriate response, it is advisable to identify muster areas remote from the

TABLE 5.3   Trigger Standoff Distances for Building Evacuation Strategies

	Evacuation Strategy			
Device	**A. Outward to Remote Assembly Area**	**B. Inward to BSAs**	**C. Remain, Stay Away from Glass**	**D. Remain, Ignore Device**
Truck bomb	≤X m	X − Y m	Y − Z m	≥Z m
Car bomb	No evacuation[1]	≤A m[2]	A − B m	≥B m
Hand-carried bomb	No evacuation[3]	≤C m[4]	C − D m	≥D m

[1] The building need not be evacuated for car bombs unless they are within the building footprint.

[2] For close-up car bombs, there may be a floor level below which on-floor BSAs should not be used. However, there may also be a higher floor level above which strategy C should be adopted instead of strategy B.

[3] Evacuation for hand-carried bombs is not necessary unless the device is internal. For internal devices, the floor on which the bomb is located should be fully evacuated and the two floors above and below the bomb location evacuated for a radius of 30 m.

[4] There may be a floor level above which strategy C could be adopted instead of strategy B.

Source: Arup.

building to which occupants can be directed. Muster areas should be sufficiently remote from the evacuated building so that the evacuees are clear of danger—not less than 500 meters, and possibly further, depending on the threat. Alternate muster areas should be identified to allow for evacuation in a direction away from the perceived threat. Finally, evacuation routes should avoid passing tall buildings.

Managing BSA Use. In-house systems and procedures should be adopted to manage the response of all building occupants to a bomb threat. Reliable communication links to emergency services outside the building should be provided, such as direct telephone lines to the shelter areas connected to alternate service providers. A dedicated internal telephone line should be installed between shelter areas. A public address system should be installed in all areas of the building so that instructions can be communicated to occupants in a bomb emergency.

An incident control room is required to accommodate the incident control officer (ICO) and the ICO's communication equipment. This room is as protected as the shelter, and preferably better protected, because the ICO is required to stay at this post throughout the incident.

The fire alarm system should be disabled during a bomb emergency to avoid the broadcast of confusing messages or signals. Incoming gas supplies to the building should also be shut off at the meter during a bomb emergency.

First aid equipment should be held in shelter areas to deal with minor injuries. A strict no smoking policy should be enforced in shelter areas during a bomb emergency.

Inward evacuation to shelter areas should be regularly practiced and amended as necessary to take into account changes in the number and distribution of occupants. Bomb emergency training for the building occupants should include discouragement of the natural inclination to look out of windows under these situations. Many victims of the 1998 U.S. embassy bombing in Nairobi were killed or injured because of their proximity to the perimeter glazing due to their inquisitiveness over the events taking place outside.

Designated marshals should be appointed for each floor to ensure that occupants respond correctly to instructions for evacuation and to assist in evacuating disabled occupants. The local police should be kept informed of current bomb emergency procedures and their advice and comments sought.

PROTECTION AGAINST SUICIDE ATTACKS USING VEHICLES

Suicide attackers using IEDs have been described as the "ultimate smart bomb." The attacker has absolutely no regard for his or her own safety or escape from the scene; these types of attacks can be carried out without any notice in any area that can be accessed. Because the attacker does not have to leave a device at the target location, he or she can respond during the course of the attack to any security measures or obstacles that are presented. It is likely that extensive reconnaissance of the intended target and of routes to be taken will be carried out in advance of such an attack.

Suicide attacks are intended to have a huge psychological impact on the population. In countries where such attacks have been carried out, many suicide attackers have targeted the public indiscriminately, attacking areas where large numbers of people congregate.

Suicide attackers may use vehicles to carry considerable quantities of explosives using a suicide vehicle-borne improvised explosive device (SVBIED), as in the 2003 attacks against a military hospital in Chechnya and HSBC offices in Istanbul (see Table 5.1). The attackers' complete disregard for their own escape or safety means that these attacks are usually carried out with no warning, and the vehicle is often used to breach a target's defenses.

If a bomb-laden vehicle is able to reach, and even breach, the facade of a building and then detonate its cargo, the likelihood of extensive collapse is significantly increased than if the device were to explode at even a modest standoff distance. Devastation within the building of both structural and nonstructural elements is also likely to be greatly magnified by confinement of an internal explosion. Consequently, barriers intended to stop SVBIEDs are becoming increasingly commonplace around buildings considered to be at risk.

Installing Vehicle and Curbside Barriers

In planning such defenses, it is important to keep in perspective the protection that they would offer. For a building with no setback from the sidewalk, the use of curbside barriers may reduce vulnerability to severe structural damage, but such barriers may not diminish the risk of widespread damage to the facade. Indeed, due to the interplay of slope distance and the angle of incidence of the blast wave, the standoff that would bring about the most extensive facade destruction by air blast may be tens of meters from the face of a building, in which case curbside barriers would do little to reduce the hazard from that particular form of damage.

Many factors need to be considered when designing vehicle barriers. The most immediate of these variables include:

- The mass and configuration of the attack vehicle
- The speed of the attack vehicle at impact
- The angle of approach of the attack vehicle
- The manner in which the barrier is intended to stop the attack vehicle, such as controlled bending, catenary action, or friction
- Available distance within which the vehicle must be stopped for the barrier system to serve its purpose

These parameters are influenced by the overall planning of the facility and its environs as well as the outcome of an appropriately focused threat and risk assessment. Further questions for the barrier designer to consider in countering the threat of SVBIEDs, especially for urban buildings, are listed in Table 5.4.

The analysis and design of various barrier types is outside the scope of this text, but it centers on the transfer of momentum and the conversion of kinetic energy into strain energy (through deformation of either the barrier system or the attack vehicle, or both) and heat (through friction). Analytical methods can range from hand

TABLE 5.4 Vehicle Barrier Design Questions for Urban Environments

Vehicle Barrier	Design Questions
Barrier design	• Credible deterrent? • Visually acceptable and not prone to rapid deterioration? • Hazard to pedestrian traffic around building? • Impeding fire evacuation routes or other life-safety provisions? • Overloading any structure below?
Barrier installation	• Excessive interruptions of existing underground services? • Interference with building elements (e.g., waterproofing systems) that may invalidate warranties? • Performance under impact likely to damage and impair structural elements, especially those outside the building?
Costs	• System design within acceptable limits? • Supply and installation within acceptable limits? • Routine maintenance within acceptable limits?

Source: Arup.

calculation to advanced numerical modeling, as appropriate. As in other fields of extreme loading, physical testing is a valuable tool to validate the methods used and to identify the more imponderable forms of system behavior. Figure 5.11 shows a vehicle-barrier test.

Protecting Building Services

Building services can be severely damaged by bomb explosions. The consequences of this damage mainly relate to the speed with which the building can be reinstated and business recommenced with adequate life safety systems in place as well as reasonable occupant comfort. Ventilation ductwork can route blast pressures into the building. When designing new buildings, locating supply and exhaust louvers at low levels should be avoided, if possible. Blast valves or dampers that react extremely rapidly to an incoming pressure pulse and close

FIGURE 5.11 **Full-Scale Vehicle-Barrier Test.**

(*Source:* Arup/Canary Wharf Group.)

off the louver can be fitted, but they are expensive and require additional space that may not be available in a commercial building.

The best protection for incoming power, gas, water, and telecommunications to a building is duplication and physical diversity so that a bomb in one place cannot take out the entire system.

For some financial organizations, disruption of information technology (IT) networks for even a brief period of time would have enormous implications in terms of loss of business. Some of these organizations have set up duplicate facilities in different buildings that are remote from each other. If one building is disabled by a bomb, the staff can transfer to another and carry on. The investment in IT hardware alone by such organizations can make it worth blast protecting main equipment rooms, even if the rest of the building's fittings are severely damaged. Figure 5.12 shows part of the blast protection Arup recently engineered for a computer room using pressed steel panels of a type used for blast walls in the offshore industry.

ANALYSIS FOR BLAST EFFECTS

Levels of Analysis

In the context of developing a new building or retrofitting an existing one, different levels of analysis are required to support each stage

FIGURE 5.12 Blast Wall to Computer Room Using Profiled Steel Panels.

(*Source:* Arup; Photo by David Hadden.)

of the design and decision-making process as it relates to the blast performance of the facility.

At an early stage, the best possible protective systems should be identified based on the funds available by prioritizing security-related countermeasures and then comparing the effectiveness of different mitigation options in terms of cost and performance. Because the modern threat environment includes numerous scenarios, these prioritizations should be conducted as part of the threat and risk assessment (TARA) studies that are ideally begun in advance of the actual design. TARA studies do require analytical input to provide estimates of the effects of an event; however, because this process occurs at a very early stage, these estimates are generally qualitative in nature and rely on the experience of the consultant providing the information. Refer to Chapter 4 for further discussion of TARAs.

Quantitative analysis is required to provide a reasonable level of confidence that the details of the developed design will offer the desired level of performance under a given design threat. Note that we assume that a performance-based approach is adopted and that appropriate design threats and desired performance criteria are agreed upon with the client in the early stages of the design process. This is the preferred approach for situations in which regulatory conditions do not govern the blast performance of the facility, as is currently typical for most counterterrorism design cases in the United States and elsewhere.

We have limited the following discussion on quantitative analysis to air-blast phenomena, which applies to situations in which there is sufficient standoff between the seat of the explosion and the target for the surrounding air to form a shock front that delivers significant pressure loads to the target. The material presented is not applicable to scenarios in which charges are placed in direct contact with the target. For contact-charge scenarios, designers may refer to guidelines on explosive demolition (FM5-250) [14]; however, this information is not wholly suitable for design purposes and must be interpreted with care.

The following discussion on the numerical analysis of structural response separates the determination of the structural loads associated with an event from the behavior of the structural element in question. In reality, these two phenomena are coupled, and the response of the structure can change the nature of the loading. In some instances this coupling can be significant, and technology is available to fully couple the fluid dynamics of the blast load with the structural response. At present, this technology sits outside the scope of common practice on a typical design project and is not discussed in detail in this chapter.

Blast-Load Phenomenology

Structures primarily experience blast events in the form of pressures applied to their exposed surfaces. In the context of design, these pressures are generally characterized in relation to the shockwave propagating away from the seat of the explosion. For those unfamiliar with air blast and associated shock loads, it may be helpful to envisage shockwave propagation by analogy to the outward propagation of the leading ripple on the surface of a pool of water after dropping a stone in it.

The initial shock loading is followed by the dynamic pressure (also known as *blast wind*). This phenomenon is associated with the velocity of the air particles after the shockwave has passed through it and results in a lower magnitude pressure, but the longer duration associated with dynamic pressure can be sufficient to affect the response of the structure. Guidance on the estimation of dynamic pressures is available (TM 5-855, TM 5-1300, PSADS) and is not discussed in further detail in the text [15, 16, 17].

The dynamic nature of blast pressures has been described earlier in this chapter, and their severity has been characterized in terms of peak amplitude and duration. The magnitude of these characteristics is dependent on variables such as the following:

- The amount of explosive material used (commonly referred to as *charge weight*)
- The placement of the device (commonly referred to as *standoff*)
- The type of explosive material used in the device
- The size, shape, and orientation of the surfaces exposed to the blast environment
- The location and orientation of adjacent reflecting surfaces
- The shape of the charge

Clearly, it is not possible to accurately predict many of these characteristics, just as the characteristics of natural hazards cannot be predicted with certainty. Furthermore, the probabilistic methods that have been used to characterize design loads related to natural hazards (i.e., wind, earthquake) are not appropriate for man-made hazards such as a terrorist attack. However, in order to proceed with a performance-based design approach, some educated assumptions as to the nature of these characteristics must be agreed upon with the client.

The most significant of these design assumptions is the determination of threat scenarios for a given facility (e.g., vehicle bomb at curbside, package bomb in lobby), which should be agreed upon with the client as part of a TARA study to identify a credible charge weight for each blast scenario in terms of its TNT equivalent. Once these scenarios and associated charge weights are established, the remaining variables can be addressed. These variables include the following:

1. The charge weight, as determined per agreement with the client, is a variable.
2. Standoff is determined on a case-by-case basis based on design features that enforce standoff (e.g., perimeter security, antiramming features, sacrificial cladding) and the level of access that a potential attacker may have to the area in question.
3. The type of explosive material used in the device is generally not considered to be a variable, because the design threat is usually defined in terms of an equivalent weight of TNT.
4. The size, shape, and orientation of the surfaces exposed to the blast environment must be evaluated on a case-by-case basis.
5. The location and orientation of adjacent reflecting surfaces must be evaluated on a case-by-case basis.

The shape of the charge is generally not considered to be a significant variable in terms of establishing pressures associated with design-level threats. For design purposes, the charge is typically assumed to be spherical. Note that thermal and fragmentation loads can also factor into the response of structure, but are usually considered to be of little significance in the design of buildings to resist terrorist event. However, they may be worth considering in regard to critical infrastructure, such as bridges and tunnels.

In addition to items 1 to 3 in the list, items 4 and 5 have a significant effect on how the loads on the structure are determined and warrant further discussion.

Size, Shape, and Orientation of Target Surfaces. The geometry of the target surface can have significant effects in terms of the loads that are experienced by the building's structural elements. We begin our discussion of the effects of these geometric features with orientation, because its effect is the easiest to envisage. Orientation effects are best illustrated at their extremes. Consider one wall that directly faces the seat of the blast (i.e., a "reflected" orientation) and another wall that is orthogonal to it (i.e., side-on, or "incident," orientation). One can easily see that the load on the wall in the reflected orientation will be more severe than the load on the wall that is in the incident orientation. The significance of this difference is illustrated in Figure 5.13, which plots the peak pressure for both reflected- and incident-oriented surfaces as a function of range (standoff) for a

FIGURE 5.13   Comparison of Peak Blast Pressures on Surfaces with Incident and Reflected Orientations as a Function of Standoff Distance for a Given Charge.

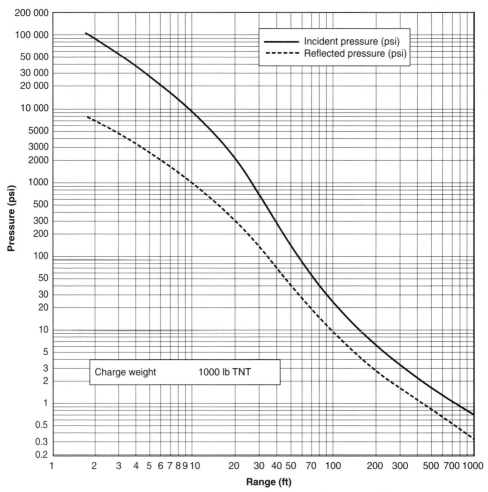

(*Source:* Hyde, D. W., 2005. *ConWep Version 2.1.0.8,* USAE Engineer Research & Development Center, Vicksburg, MS.)

given charge weight. Note that both axes are plotted on a logarithmic scale, that the difference between the two walls is more pronounced at closer standoff distances, and that the magnitude of this difference can be as much as an order of magnitude.

As the orientation angle changes from reflected to incident, the peak pressures change. However, the relationship is complex. Fully reflected pressures only begin to fall off at orientation angles greater than 45 degrees and, in some instances, there is a limited region where increasing this angle increases the effective pressures acting on the loaded element.

Figure 5.13 illustrates the peak pressure experienced at a point on a surface at a given range. Note that the magnitude is relatively independent of the size of the surface in question. However, the size of the target area can influence the duration over which the positive-pressure phase is experienced. The peak pressure and the duration form the basis of an important factor—impulse. *Impulse* is a mathematical construct that represents the area under the pressure versus time curve and is used as an indicator of the severity of the blast load.

For a flat surface, the impulse experienced at positions around the edges of the surface can decrease dramatically due to the effect of the shockwave clearing the surface. The clearing phenomenon can be envisaged as part of the load "spilling" around the edge, thereby reducing the full effect of the load in positions near the edges. The significance of this effect is demonstrated in Figure 5.14, which compares the impulse on two surfaces exposed to identical blast events. Figure 5.14 illustrates that clearing effects on an oblong surface can significantly reduce the total force that is imposed on the surface.

In the context of designing exposed elements (such as highly exposed columns, bridge piers, or other primary structural elements) to resist blast loads, in some instances the clearing effect is neglected. Although this is not rigorously correct, it is conservative to neglect this behavior (i.e., it contributes to overestimating the design loads), and if a satisfactory design solution can be found without accounting for it, it may not be necessary to further refine the design to take clearing effects into account.

Adjacent Reflecting Surfaces

Just as clearing effects can reduce the blast loads on an exposed surface, the presence of adjacent reflecting surfaces can significantly increase the loads. Amplification is attributable to two behavioral

FIGURE 5.14   **Illustration of Clearing Effects on the Impulse Distribution on Exposed Flat Surfaces.**

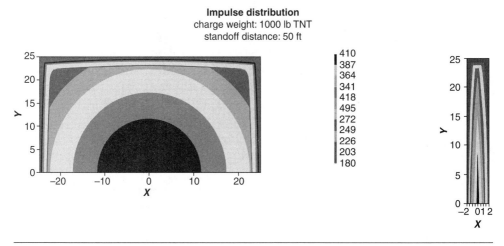

(*Source:* Hyde, D. W., 2005. *ConWep Version 2.1.0.8,* USAE Engineer Research & Development Center, Vicksburg, MS.)

characteristics of blast loading: shockwave reflection and confinement of the gas pressures. The significance of shockwave-reflection effects can be compared to dropping a pebble into a square pan of water. The size of the ripple that first hits a wall (comparable to the peak reflected pressure) is not significantly affected by the presence of adjacent walls. However, after the initial impact, waves that reflect off the other walls of the pan will hit the wall being monitored. These later waves effectively slow the decay of pressure forces, extending the duration of load and thereby increasing the effective impulse.

One only needs to perform this simple experiment to appreciate the complexity of the problem that the designer must face when addressing the effect of adjacent reflecting surfaces. Even in the pan of water, waves reflect not only off the wall of the pan, but also off other waves, creating a very complex loading environment that changes rapidly in space and time. This complexity manifests itself in the design environment when addressing scenarios that include detonations within an enclosed space (e.g., a tunnel or mail room), near a reentrant corner of any description (e.g., corner of a room, corner of a wide-flanged steel section, bottom ground/wall intersection of a building), and also within an urban environment where shockwaves can reflect off adjacent buildings.

The confinement of gas pressures can also influence the response of the structure, particularly in internal blast scenarios. The detonation of explosive material releases heat and gases as a result of the chemical reactions that take place. Release of this additional material and energy into an enclosed space causes an increase in pressure that is relieved by venting through available openings. In addition, gradual cooling occurs due to heat loss. The peak gas pressure is a function of the ratio of the volume of the explosive material to the volume of the space it is detonated in and the type of explosive material used. It can also be affected by the presence of other combustible materials in the room. The rate at which the gas pressure decays is primarily a function of the size and number of available openings that allow the pressure to vent to other spaces. Because heat loss typically occurs slowly, as compared to the pressure drop due to venting, the cooling effect is commonly neglected.

Estimating Design Blast Loads

Even though the blast loads that a given structure may experience during its service life cannot be precisely predicted and the magnitude of those loads are subject to numerous significant variables, tools are available that can help designers estimate design-level blast loads for a given scenario based on the design context and a design-level charge weight. The methods available for commercial-scale work fall into three categories: empirical, semi-empirical, and first principles.

Empirical Software. Empirical data rightfully form the basis of most estimates of blast loading that are used in the design context. The results of experimental tests have been parameterized and incorporated into computer software that enables engineers to quickly estimate structural loads for relatively simple configurations. The most widely used program for performing such analyses is ConWep, which was developed by the U.S. Army Corps of Engineers. ConWep offers a wide range of functions for evaluating blast loads. The capabilities that are most frequently used in the design and assessment of civil structures include calculation of air-blast pressure and impulse characteristics for a given charge weight and standoff and calculation of peak pressure and impulse distributions, including clearing effects on a flat surface given the size of the target's reflecting surface and the position of the seat of the explosion [6].

The advantages of applying a program such as ConWep to estimate air-blast pressures on a structure are its ease of use, the fact that it requires a minimal amount of input information from the user, and the speed at which it produces useful design-level information. In exchange for these advantages, the designer may sacrifice some accuracy with respect to the specific condition being considered based on the empirical data used to derive the loads. More specifically, the precise geometry of the target being evaluated may not be fully considered in ConWep calculations, because only flat target surfaces are considered and adjacent reflecting surfaces (except for ground) are neglected.

How the designer chooses to account for the significance of these inaccuracies must be considered on a case-by-case basis. Other tools are available that do allow for these effects to be considered more accurately, but the designer may choose to neglect the effects for exterior detonation design scenarios in relatively open surroundings. Estimating exterior blast loads in dense urban environments is a field that is not yet clearly understood. Exciting computational research is being conducted to investigate these effects, but it may be some time before there is a clear, best-practice approach for accounting for this condition in design. For lack of better information, it is currently common practice to neglect the confinement/reflection off adjacent structures at an urban scale.

At a smaller scale, these effects are somewhat better understood, and the need to account for them becomes more pronounced. This is particularly true when determining the loads on walls under an internal blast scenario such as detonation within a room or tunnel. In these instances, empirical data and simplified methods for basic geometries are available, and more complicated configurations can be accounted for with semi-empirical techniques, such as those used by the program BlastXW, which is part of the PSADS suite [17]. This type of approach offers a more realistic representation of blast loads in scenarios where the reflection and amplification of the shockwave off nearby surfaces plays a significant factor in the loads experienced on the structural surface in question. It also provides estimates for the increase in pressure associated with the buildup of gas pressures due to explosions detonated in confined spaces.

Computational Fluid Dynamic Tools. Although the approach described above offers some improvements in estimating blast loads in confined spaces, in some scenarios even this methodology may not provide a sufficiently accurate representation of the real physics of the problem at hand. One such scenario is the investigation of the behavior of the shockwave as it passes around a target and reforms at the backside of the structure. The use of computational fluid dynamic (CFD) tools, such as Autodyne [8], SHAMRC [18], Air3d [7], or CTH [19], offers improved accuracy in these scenarios. It is important to mention that although these tools can offer improved accuracy, experienced analysts must carry out these analyses, and using these tools can incur significant computational costs. In the context of conventional building design, it may be desirable to forego this level of accuracy due to time or budgetary constraints. However, as computing power continues to grow, it is clear that this level of analysis will become more common practice and should see more widespread use in the design environment.

It is important to note that all of the methods described include implicit assumptions about the behavior of the target structure that may not always be appropriate. More specifically, these methods do not account for the deformation of the structure in a detailed way, although some do make a simplified allowance for failure of boundary surfaces. For example, some tools allow for an approximate representation of glazing failure so that the effects of postfailure venting can be estimated.

More sophisticated methods are being developed that enable the coupling of detailed fluid and structural models to provide realistic simulations of blast events in which the coupled behavior is significant. Although this technology clearly represents the future of blast analysis, it has not yet been developed into a tool that can be readily used in the design environment.

To close this discussion on how blast loads are estimated, we return our focus to the context of the design environment where analysis is needed to provide a reasonable level of confidence that the design being developed will offer the desired level of performance. Given the high degree of uncertainty associated with blast loading, particularly with regard to determining design threats, the design should be developed to meet the performance criteria for these design threats as well as fail in a relatively benign way in instances where the design is overmatched. Methods for estimating the structural response to blast loading are described in more detail in the following section.

Structural Response to Blast Load

Previous sections of this chapter addressed the nature of structural response to blast loading and the behaviors that should be of most concern to a building owner. This section describes some of the methods that can be used to analytically estimate these behaviors and explains their advantages and shortcomings. Because effective protective design requires dialog across design disciplines and with the building owner, the intent here is to provide sufficient background information to facilitate this dialog and enable various members of the design team to understand and interpret the analyses that may be undertaken by a blast engineer.

The response of structures to blast loading can be described as being both dynamic and nonlinear. Although the significance of the dynamic nature of the response was addressed in earlier sections of this chapter, nonlinearity warrants further discussion. The context of this chapter precludes an in-depth discussion of nonlinear structural behavior, and for the benefit of the intended audience we have simply equated nonlinear behavior with structural damage.

Because it is absolutely essential that the blast analysis adequately represent the modes of damage that may occur, we begin with a discussion of the types of damage that are prevalent under blast-loading events for conventional (unhardened) forms of construction.

Steel. As a structural material, steel remains the stiffest, strongest material at the structural engineer's disposal. The steel alloys that are used for construction offer a significant amount of ductility. The combination of these properties demonstrates the primary characteristics that are desirable in a blast-resistant material. However, the types of damage experienced by steel structures do not stem from the vulnerability of the material itself, but from the way it is utilized in conventional construction.

Structural steel shapes and connections are optimized to support the governing design loads as efficiently as possible. Because the occurrence of blast loading may be completely different from the other design loads in terms of magnitude, direction, and location of application, typical steel construction is vulnerable to explosive attack in areas nearest to the seat of the charge. Common damage mechanisms consist of connection failure and local buckling of the structural section. If these localized vulnerabilities are properly treated, then global buckling of compression elements may still occur due to large displacements in slender elements. Note that the previous remark about load direction means that elements that are ordinarily in tension may be loaded compressively under a blast event. Stiffer elements may be prone to yield in shear near the connections rather than in plastic bending at the midspan. It is difficult for the loads associated with an air blast to rupture the material unless the charge is detonated in very close proximity to it.

Reinforced Concrete. Although reinforced concrete is softer and weaker than structural steel at the material level, the fact that it is used in volume in typical construction enables it to offer desirable characteristics under blast loading. The primary vulnerabilities of reinforced concrete columns, beams, and slabs relate to the fragility of the concrete itself. Concrete offers minimal tensile strength in the absence of reinforcing steel and crushes when loaded beyond its capacity in compression. When this crushing begins to occur, pieces of concrete can detach (spall off) from the section, which further softens and weakens the structure. This vulnerability can be reduced by providing sufficient reinforcement or jacketing the section to confine the concrete and minimize the spalling effect, resulting in a stronger, more ductile structure that can deliver suitable performance under blast loading.

It is possible for blast pressures to exceed the crush strength of concrete, particularly when a charge is detonated in close proximity to an element. In these instances, the shockwave will pulverize an area of structural material, effectively cratering it. This condition can be exacerbated by the fact that the impact of the shockwave on the front face of an element can spall material off the rear face of the element (due to internal stress wave reflection off the rear face). If the depth of the crater on the front face intersects the depth of the spall at the rear face, then a breached condition is achieved, resulting in a hole through the element. Thin walls and slabs are particularly prone to this form of damage.

Masonry. Masonry block-work, or concrete masonry unit (CMU), walls have also received significant attention from the blast engineering community because it is a common form of construction. Although these walls are often nonstructural, they can fail in a fragmentary fashion due to flexure of the wall, which may pose a significant hazard to nearby occupants. This is particularly true for non-load-bearing walls that may be only lightly reinforced, offering minimal postfailure capacity.

Glass. The vulnerability of windows to blast loading was described in earlier sections of this chapter.

Key Point If the primary structure of a building is well designed and robustly detailed, it is likely that the glazing will pose the most significant hazard to the occupants of the building.

Implementing the design details recommended earlier in the chapter (i.e., laminated panes, fully framed panes) significantly alleviates hazards from glass, but it is likely that these improved components will remain the most vulnerable elements of the building and continue to pose the most significant hazard to the occupants, albeit at a reduced level from what it would have been if these details are not adopted.

Regardless of the structural materials used, blast loading is capable of producing multiple different failure modes depending on the size and location of the charge and the configuration of the element in question. Without the benefit of significant experience examining the physical response of structures to blast loads, it is difficult to know a priori which failure modes will govern which elements given different threat scenarios. However, a number of different analytical methods are available to aid in estimating which modes of damage are most critical and most likely to occur in response to a given threat. Before proceeding with the discussion of these methods, it is important to note that the use of the term *estimate* is deliberate.

Given the significant range of uncertainties associated with the occurrence of an explosive event, it would be misleading to suggest that the nature of these analyses should be interpreted as predictive. The highest degree of certainty in the performance of a design comes when the analyses described in this section are carried out in conjunction with physical testing. In some instances, sufficient test data may be available, precluding the need to conduct project-specific blast tests. However, many conventional design details may not have been rigorously tested for resistance to blast load or, if they have been tested, the results of those tests may not be readily available if the test data are considered to be proprietary or if the test was conducted under the auspices of security-sensitive information. Just as a given project may not have a regulatory (building code) requirements to design against possible blast events, regulatory requirements may not require physical test-sensitive details. However, testing is advisable as a matter of good practice and in delivering the highest degree of confidence in the blast performance of critical elements.

Estimating Structural Response

For the purposes of this discussion, the primary evaluation tools for structural response to blast loading fall into two categories: single degree-of-freedom (SDOF) and multiple degree-of-freedom (MDOF) methods. In this context, *degree-of-freedom* refers to an analytical construct used to describe the motion of a structure. The more degrees of freedom that are included in the analysis, the higher the resolution of the solution and the more intensive the computational requirement to complete the solution.

SDOF Methods. Although real structures have a theoretically infinite number of modes of deformation, it is often possible to provide a reasonable approximation of the response of the structure based on a single dominant deformation mode. This approach is particularly appropriate for the evaluation of the response of a single element where guidance exists for common structural forms, including beams and columns, on how best to characterize the properties of the element (strength, stiffness, effective mass) and the equivalent loading. In these instances, the maximum displacement response of the element can be estimated using hand calculations or simple computer programs that require a minimal amount of input data and computation time. The simplicity of this method is the primary source of its popularity, because it enables engineers to evaluate a wide variety of scenarios and elements very quickly. It is particularly valuable at the early stages of the design, because these preliminary analyses allow the design to develop quickly. This approach will provide a reasonable representation of the response of an element as long as the formulation is consistent with the problem being solved. Some of the limitations of this approach are summarized here to provide a basic understanding of how to interpret the results from these low-resolution analyses:

- The derivations of the SDOF properties for beams and plates are typically done for a single member with defined support conditions. Thus, the effects of member coupling are lost, and global issues, such as structural stability and overall structural motions, cannot be analyzed.
- The available member geometries and support conditions in an SDOF model tend to be limited. Typical models include beams and one- and two-way plate members with various combinations of simple and fixed support conditions.

- During derivation of an SDOF model, a specific temporal and spatial variation for the loading function is assumed (i.e., the load spatial distribution, load arrival, and duration are uniform over the member's surface). Accuracy will degrade for close-in blast loads for which the load intensity, arrival, and duration vary significantly across the member's surface.

- The failure modes of SDOF models are governed by the resistance function. It is important to recognize that failure modes related to direct shear, diagonal tension, spalling, breach, reinforcing bar connections, and member joints are not included in the models and cannot be predicted.

- The output of an SDOF model consists of a time history of peak member deflection. The actual peak strains at critical points in the member are unknown and cannot be accurately determined. Thus, the adequacy of the design cannot be analytically related to strain criteria, such as reinforcing bar rupture.

- All continuous-member SDOF models will tend to give poor performance if the response is in the linear elastic range and the loads tend to excite higher modes. Performance is poor because the SDOF assumption models only a single mode. Model performance will improve if a plastic mechanism is formed, and will greatly improve if plastic mechanism behavior dominates during the response.

- Some problems cannot be adequately solved by SDOF methods simply because two or more degrees of freedom are required.

MDOF Methods. Performing a higher-resolution analysis can alleviate many of the limitations of the SDOF method. The finite element method (FEM) is the most common analytical approach for conducting a more detailed analysis. It consists of constructing a relatively detailed geometric model of the proposed design, applying appropriate approximations of the support and loading conditions, performing the computational analysis, interpreting the output results, and comparing them to the proposed design criteria. In this respect, the analysis models that are used for evaluating blast performance share similarities with the models that may be used for other structural assessments. However, there are some fundamental differences between a Finite Element (FE) model that is appropriate for blast as compared to what is modeled for conventional design loads:

- A different computational algorithm is typically used for analysis of blast scenarios. Because of the highly nonlinear behavior that can occur under blast loads, an "explicit" solution algorithm is generally more appropriate than the "implicit" formulations that are commonly used for other applications. This difference is a fundamental one, and its implication is that the analysis software that is used for the basic design and analysis of the structure is probably inappropriate for conducting an analysis of its blast capabilities.

- Because the severity of blast loading often results in a level of damage to the structural material that would not be experienced under normal design conditions, this postfailure material behavior must be input into the analysis and should include strain-rate effects. *Strain-rate effects* are the changes in the functional characteristics of the material depending on the rate at which loads are applied (e.g., significant increases in strength and stiffness are commonly observed, as is a reduction in ductility). Because blast loads occur very rapidly, the behavior of the material under these loads may be very different from behavior observed at lower speeds.

- Localized areas may require a much higher degree of resolution in terms of spatial discretization than would ordinarily be required for a conventional structural analysis. Whereas a conventional design will be developed from an analytical model constructed of one-dimensional frame elements to represent beam and column elements, the blast analysis may require localized elements to be meshed in detail using 2D shell elements or 3D solid elements. This is particularly important when considering localized failure modes, such as local buckling of steel sections.

- Depending on the level of accuracy that is required, capturing all of the spatial and temporal variations in the blast load distributed on the surface of structural elements may require substantial preprocessing efforts to adequately simulate all of the significant effects.

For all of the benefits offered by this method of analysis, a penalty may be paid in terms of computational cost. The computational size of analysis models can grow very large, and depending on the level of detail required, the time required to complete the computation can be prohibitive. Also, the success of the analysis depends on the expertise of the user, who must have substantial experience not only with nonlinear dynamic structural behavior and blast load phenomenology, but also with the subtleties of the numerical integration that is being conducted by the computer. At present, it requires an individual with fairly specialized knowledge to carry out this type of analysis and to provide the highest degree of confidence in the results. However, as the desire to design to resist explosive events becomes more popular, it should become more common for individuals to possess all of these skills.

Blast-Design Objectives

Because of the absence of clear regulatory requirements for the blast design of most construction projects, the field of blast design may be described as tumultuous. Numerous guidelines state how loading and responses should be determined, and it is not uncommon for these guidelines to offer conflicting information. Although the reader will need to rely heavily on the experience of the blast consultant to fully develop the most appropriate design solutions for the project, it is essential not to lose sight of the following primary objectives:

- Minimize blast-related hazards that contribute to casualty and loss of life.
- Minimize disruption of service associated with a blast event.
- Balance blast-design criteria with the overall design objectives of the project.

As long as the parameters that govern the blast design of a construction project remain underdefined or relatively unknown to the people that need to make critical design decisions, there is a risk that they will get lost in the analysis. Ultimately, the decision as to whether to harden a facility or its components may be somewhat subjective. Keeping in mind that structural hardening is the last line of defense against an attack, the analysis results should serve only to quantify a part of the complete solution.

SUMMARY

Urban terrorism will be with us for the foreseeable future. Engineers, architects, and their clients have a new design issue to consider when designing even the most innocuous of buildings. Clarity of definition and agreement on objectives and expectations between all stakeholders must be established at the outset of the project. The best solutions will come from an integrated approach to overall planning, physical and operational control of access, properly considered procedures for responding to an imminent threat, and the design of critical elements of the building's structure and fabric. Complex analytical procedures may help the design of blast protection in some situations, but, as in any branch of engineering, there is no substitute for sound design principles allied with the selection of the appropriate materials.

BIBLIOGRAPHY

References

1. Little, R. G., and Weaver, E. A., 2004. "A Socio-Technological Approach to Determining Appropriate Levels of Protection for Public Spaces," *Proceedings of the 11th Annual Conference of the International Emergency Management Society,* Victoria, Australia.

2. Mays, G. C., and Smith, P. D., 1995. *Blast Effects on Buildings,* Thomas Telford Publications, London.

3. Meyer, R., et al., 1987. *Explosives,* 3rd ed., Wiley-VCH, New York.

4. Biggs, J. M., 1964. *Introduction to Structural Dynamics,* McGraw-Hill, New York.

5. Kingery, C. N., and Bulmash, G., 1984. *Airblast Parameters from TNT Spherical Air Burst and Hemispherical Surface Burst,* Technical Report ARBRL-TR-02555, U.S. Army Armament Research and Development Center, Ballistic Research Laboratory, Aberdeen Proving Ground, MD.

6. Hyde, D. W., 2005. *ConWep Version 2.1.0.8,* USAE Engineer Research & Development Center, Vicksburg, MS.

7. Rose, T. A., 2001. *Air3d User's Guide,* Engineering Systems Department, Cranfield University, Royal Military College of Science, Shrivenham, UK.

8. Century Dynamics Inc., 2004. *Autodyne® Version 6.0,* Concord, CA.

9. Smith, D. C., and Hadden, D., 2004. "Problems in Specifying Glazed Facades for Blast Loading," *Proceedings of the International Conference on Building Envelope Systems & Technology (ICBEST),* Sydney, Australia.

10. Elliott, C., 2003. "Terrorism—Why Do Buildings Collapse?"

Royal United Services Institute, *Security Monitor*, Vol. 1, No. 5, pp. 5–7.

11. Ministry of Housing & Local Government, 1968. *Report of the Inquiry into the Collapse of Flats at Ronan Point, Canning Town,* Her Majesty's Stationary Office, London.

12. GSA, 2003. *Progressive Collapse Analysis and Design Guidelines for New Federal Office Buildings and Major Modernization Projects,* General Services Administration, Washington, DC.

13. ISE, 1995. *The Structural Engineer's Response to Explosion Damage,* Institution of Structural Engineers, London.

14. Department of the Army, 1998. "Explosives and Demolition," Field manual FM5-250, Department of the Army, Washington, DC.

15. Department of the Army, 1986. "Fundamentals of Protective Design for Conventional Weapons," TM5-855-1, Department of the Army, Washington, DC.

16. Departments of the Army, the Navy and the Air Force, 1990. "Structures to Resist the Effects of Accidental Explosions," TM5-1300, Departments of the Army, the Navy and the Air Force, Washington, DC.

17. DSWA, 1998. *Protective Structures Automated Design System Version 1.0,* Defense Special Weapons Agency, Alexandria, VA.

18. Applied Research Associates Inc., *Second-order Hydrodynamic Automatic Mesh Refinement Code (SHARC),* Applied Research Associates Inc., Albuquerque, NM.

19. Sandia National Laboratories, *CTH Code,* Sandia National Laboratories, Albuquerque, NM, www.cs.sandia.gov/web9232/cth/.

6

Chemical and Biological Events

John Haddon

This chapter explores the potential use of chemical and biological agents by terrorist groups. The chapter covers such topics as the types of agents available, their characteristics, and the potential for their procurement and delivery. This chapter explores the potential use of chemical and biological agents against building targets and the mechanisms of those attacks. It also presents a strategy for protecting buildings that is directly linked to the methods of attack and associated risk.

—OVERVIEW———————————————————————

Intelligence sources in the West have long been concerned over the proliferation of chemical and biological (CB) weapons in the military arena. The potential threat of attacks on a civilian population by terrorists using such weapons, however, was considered a low risk, despite the history of small-scale attacks perpetrated by various groups, including Aum Shinrikyo and the Red Army Faction. Evidence also exists to suggest that the 1993 attack on the World Trade Center included the use of cyanide packed around the bomb. It is thought that the explosion destroyed the cyanide.

Despite these incidents, most terrorist groups recognized the political dangers of using so-called weapons of mass destruction. However, the events of September 11, 2001, and reports that one of the terrorists who attacked the World Trade Center was interested in learning about crop-dusting planes, indicated a shift away from the strategies of the "classic" or "political" terrorist. The Al-Qaeda terrorists responsible for the 9/11 attacks were not seeking political compromises or concessions, and they showed that they were willing to cause mass civilian casualties. The subsequent spate of anthrax-related incidents in the United States, coupled with the discovery of a terrorist cell producing ricin in North London, also helped to change the perception of the threat.

The fear now is that terrorist groups and disaffected individuals may choose to not only unleash chemical or biological attacks, but that they will also do so without advance warning. Therefore, it is feared that the only barriers to an attack are technical, in terms of obtaining agents, producing adequate quantities of agents, and finding effective means of dispersal.

The potential for a CB attack to cause mass casualties depends on the agent selected and the means of delivery. Although sophisticated knowledge is not required to use toxic industrial chemicals, such as chlorine, a relatively high degree of expertise is required to cause mass casualties with many other agents. Terrorist groups would encounter significant difficulties if they wanted to use many of the chemical or biological agents covered by weapons conventions, because developing and storing these agents would require sophisticated facilities. Specialized knowledge is needed to acquire the correct biological agent or precursor chemicals, process the chemical or biological agent, improvise a weapon or device, and effectively disseminate the agent to cause mass casualties. In addition to overcoming these technical and operational challenges, the terrorists would run the risk of contaminating themselves and of being detected during the various stages of the process.

Given the high costs involved and the complexity of the technology, terrorist groups are unlikely to have the financial resources and industrial infrastructure for widespread attacks without the support of state sponsors. Two potential routes available to terrorists to overcome these barriers are through leakage from state-sponsored programs and through employment of individuals with the appropriate knowledge and access to the necessary equipment.

Key Point   Current U.S. intelligence estimates indicate that 10 to 12 nations may be pursuing offensive biological weapons programs; 22 to 24 countries may be exploring similar chemical weapons programs.

The continued ability of states to acquire chemical and biological materials and weapons exposes weaknesses in the Chemical Weapons Convention (CWC) and the Biological and Toxin Weapons Convention (BTWC), which are both discussed later in this chapter.

Not all countries have signed on to these agreements, and of those that have, some are clearly not acting in good faith.

In addition to the threat of a serious, large-scale chemical or biological attack from state- or non-state-sponsored groups, terrorists with less sophistication could make an improvised weapon to disseminate agents. Even relatively inefficient improvised dissemination methods could result in significant deaths and casualties, as was demonstrated by the sarin attack in the Tokyo subway in 1995. Similarly, the U.S. incidents involving the delivery of weapons grade anthrax via the postal system proved the potential for small-scale, unsophisticated attacks to cause deaths and to paralyze business and services. Furthermore, as the recent discovery of a terrorist cell producing ricin in a North London suburb demonstrated, the raw materials required to produce some agents are relatively inexpensive. The successful targeting of Al-Qaeda financing has led some experts to state that simple methods of attack relying on local resources, so-called "kitchen-tabletop" terrorism, may be the norm in the short to medium term.

Despite this change in the perception of the level of threat, and the wide range of CB agents and weapons available to terrorists, it is still likely that terrorist capabilities are more suited to the use of conventional tactics, such as vehicle bombs, when mounting large-scale attacks. Nevertheless, incidents such as the March 1995 Tokyo nerve gas attack and the anthrax attacks in the United States show the credibility of the CB threat. Although the current risk from chemical and biological attack is perceived to be low, an extrapolation of trends and emerging technologies leads to the conclusion that such an attack is both credible and a realistic possibility in the future.

The potential for chemical and biological attacks means that protective measures should be incorporated into buildings and operational procedures should plan for such eventualities. This is particularly true in the case of new buildings, in which case the likelihood of an attack in the lifetime of the building, 30 to 60 years, is much higher. However, the building designer needs to recognize that it is not possible to provide 100-percent protection against a chemical or biological attack on a building. The key in developing a design is to recognize that the most that can be achieved in a commercial environment is the management and reduction in risk from such an attack. It is therefore appropriate to categorize the types of attack that may be delivered against a building, develop strategies to combat those attacks, and then attempt to quantify the risk so that informed decisions may be taken regarding an appropriate level of mitigation. In adopting this risk-assessment-and-reduction approach, the designer must assess trends and future risks and ensure that measures that affect the building, form, planning, structure, and space are incorporated into the design on day one, because many measures will not be suitable for retrofitting to existing buildings.

___ CHEMICAL AND BIOLOGICAL AGENTS ___

The ease or difficulty with which terrorists could cause mass casualties with an improvised chemical or biological weapon or device depends on the chemical or biological agent selected. Terrorists do not need sophisticated knowledge or dissemination methods to use toxic industrial chemicals. However, terrorists face serious technical and operational challenges at different stages of the process when working with other chemical or biological agents. To cause mass casualties with many of the chemical and all of the biological agents reviewed in this chapter, terrorists would have to risk contamination and detection, overcome acquisition and production difficulties, and effectively disseminate a chemical or biological agent.

Obtaining access to the proper strains of biological agents is a difficult hurdle to overcome. Similarly, many variables may deter terrorists from using chemical agents (other than toxic industrial chemicals). For example, precursor chemicals necessary for the production of some chemical agents are controlled by the 1993 CWC, which has been in force since April 1997 [1]. Illegal acquisition of precursor chemicals would raise suspicions and attention due to the provisions of the convention. Not only are the right precursor chemicals and biological agents or strains very difficult to obtain, some chemical and many biological agents are difficult to produce, especially in sufficient quantities to cause mass casualties, except if using toxic industrial chemicals.

Threats posed by toxic industrial chemicals (TICs) should not be overlooked. The term *toxic industrial chemical* covers a wide variety of chemicals that are used in industrial processes. It is estimated that throughout the United States there are 800,000 shipments of hazardous material daily. An accidental or deliberate release of these TICs could inflict the same damage as a military chemical warfare (CW) agent, albeit larger quantities of the TIC would be required. In 1984, an accidental release of methyl isocyanate at the Union Carbide plant in Bhopal, India, killed more than 3,800 people and injured 170,000.

Chemical and biological agents pose different sets of problems for emergency planning and preparedness. For example, most chemicals quickly affect individuals directly exposed to the agent within a given geographic area. In contrast, the release of a biological agent may not be known for several days, and both perpetrators and victims may be miles away from the point of release once an incident is identified. Also, some biological agents produce symptoms that can be easily confused with influenza or other less-virulent illnesses. If communicable, the biological agent can spread throughout the population.

Chemical Agents

Chemical weapons agents have been defined by the United Nations as ". . . chemical substances, whether gaseous, liquid or solid, which might be employed because of their direct toxic effects on man, animals and plants . . ." [2]. About 70 different chemicals have been used or stockpiled as CW agents during the twentieth century. Of these CW agents, only a few are now considered likely to be used.

In recent times, chemical weapons have been grouped with biological and nuclear weapons as weapons of mass destruction. However, chemical weapons differ from their nuclear and biological counterparts. Unlike nuclear and biological weapons, the effects of chemical weapons are normally seen over a much smaller area and have a more immediate effect than biological weapons when released.

Key Point Chemical weapons use the toxic properties of chemical substances, rather than their explosive properties, to produce physical or physiological effects on an enemy.

Chemical agents fall into five broad categories:

- Choking agents
- Blood agents
- Blister agents
- Nerve agents
- Nonlethal (riot-control) agents

The principal chemical agents, with their abbreviations in parentheses, are summarized in the following sections.

Choking Agents. Choking, or pulmonary, agents are the oldest chemical warfare agents. This class of agents includes chlorine (CL) and phosgene (CG), both of which were used in World War I. In sufficient concentrations, their corrosive effect on the respiratory system results in pulmonary edema, filling the lungs with fluid and choking the victim. Phosgene is more effective than chlorine because it is hydrolyzed slowly by the water in the lining of the lungs, forming hydrochloric acid that rapidly destroys the tissue.

These agents are heavy gases that remain near ground level and tend to fill depressions. Because they are gases, they are nonpersistent and dissipate rapidly in a breeze. As a result, these chemicals are among the least effective traditional chemical agents.

Blood Agents. Blood agents, or cyanides, are absorbed into the body primarily by breathing. They prevent the normal utilization of oxygen by the cells and cause rapid damage to body tissues. Agents such as hydrogen cyanide (AC) and cyanogen chloride (CK) are highly volatile and dissipate rapidly in the gaseous state. Cyanides rapidly degrade the effectiveness of filters on protective masks. Therefore, these agents could be used to defeat a mask's protective capabilities when combined with other agents.

Blister Agents. Blister agents, or vesicants, are used primarily to cause medical casualties. Blister agents affect the eyes and lungs and blister the skin. Sulphur mustard (HD), nitrogen mustard (HN-2, HN-3), and Lewisite (L, HL) are examples of blister agents. Most blister agents are insidious in action because there is little or no pain at the time of exposure (except for Lewisite, which causes immediate pain on contact). Sulphur mustard is considered by some to be the ideal chemical agent. It presents both a respiratory and a percutaneous (skin) hazard.

Nerve Agents. Nerve agents are perhaps the most feared of all chemical weapons. Essentially, nerve agents affect the transmission of nerve impulses. Most of the agents in this category were discovered shortly before or during World War II and are related chemically to organophosphorous insecticides. Although nerve agents were not used during World War I, some reports indicate that they were used by Iraq during the Iran–Iraq War. Iraq also possessed a substantial nerve gas arsenal on the eve of the Gulf War in 1990–1991.

Similar in action to many pesticides, nerve agents are lethal in much lower quantities than the classic agents in the choking, blood, and blister categories. Nerve gases are effective when inhaled or when absorbed by the skin, or both, although there are differences in effectiveness. The rapid action of nerve agents calls for immediate treatment.

Nonlethal Agents. Nonlethal agents, such as tear gas and other riot-control agents, are generally not considered chemical weapons because they are not life threatening in all but the highest concentrations. Examples of these agents include orthochlorobenzylidene malononitrile (CS), chloroacetophenone (CN), chloropicrin (PS), and bromobenzyl cyanide (BBC). They are highly irritating, particularly to the eyes and respiratory tract, and cause extreme discomfort. Symptoms occur almost immediately upon exposure and generally disappear shortly after exposure ceases. Vomiting agents are often considered to be riot-control agents, because under field conditions they cause great discomfort, but rarely serious injury or death. Characteristic agents include adamsite (DM) and diphenyl chloroarsine (DA). In addition to causing vomiting, these arsenic-based agents may also irritate the eyes and respiratory system.

Properties of Principal Chemical Agents

The properties of the principal chemical agents are summarized in Table 6.1 [3].

TABLE 6.1 Summary of Properties of Some Principal Chemical Agents

Chemical Agent (Code Name)	Lethality	Persistence	Rate of Action	First Aid Treatment
Choking Agents				
Chlorine (CL)	Low	Not persistent	Variable	Move to fresh air. For skin contact, flush with water. No antidote. Provide supportive therapy for respiratory and cardiovascular functions.
Phosgene (CG)	Low	Not persistent	Delayed	Move to fresh air. For skin contact, flush with water.
Hydrogen cyanide (AC)	Low to moderate	Very low	Rapid	Move to fresh air. Provide supportive therapy. Provide amyl nitrite, sodium nitrite, or sodium thiosulfate.

(continues)

TABLE 6.1 *Continued*

Chemical Agent (Code Name)	Lethality	Persistence	Rate of Action	First Aid Treatment
Cyanogen chloride (CK)	Low to moderate	Low	Rapid	Move to fresh air. Provide supportive therapy. Provide amyl nitrite, sodium nitrite, or sodium thiosulfate.

Blister Agents

Chemical Agent (Code Name)	Lethality	Persistence	Rate of Action	First Aid Treatment
Sulphur mustard (HD)	Can produce incapacitation because of blistering. Can also produce death if inhaled or if a toxic dose is absorbed through the skin.	Intermediate to high	Delayed	Flush skin with water and decontaminate clothing. Provide oxygen/intubation, bronchodilators.
Nitrogen mustard (HN-2)	Can produce incapacitation because of blistering. Can also produce death if inhaled or if a toxic dose is absorbed through the skin.	Intermediate	Delayed	Flush skin with water and decontaminate clothing. Provide oxygen/intubation, bronchodilators. Provide culumine ophthalmic and topical antibiotics and dressings.
Nitrogen mustard (HN-3)	Can produce incapacitation because of blistering. Can also produce death if inhaled or if a toxic dose is absorbed through the skin.	High	Delayed	Flush skin with water and decontaminate clothing. Provide oxygen/intubation, bronchodilators.
Lewisite (L, HL)	Can produce incapacitation because of blistering. Can also produce death if inhaled or if a toxic dose is absorbed through the skin.	Intermediate to high	Rapid	Flush skin with water and decontaminate clothing. Provide British anti-Lewisite for systemic effects.

TABLE 6.1 *Continued*

Chemical Agent (Code Name)	Lethality	Persistence	Rate of Action	First aid Treatment
Nerve Agents				
Tabun (GA)	High	Intermediate	Very rapid	Move to fresh air. For skin contact, flush with water. Provide atropine or pralidoxime chloride or diazepam injections.
Sarin (GB)	High	Not persistent	Very rapid	Move to fresh air. For skin contact, flush with water. Provide atropine or pralidoxime chloride or diazepam injections.
Soman (GD)	High	Intermediate	Very rapid	Move to fresh air. For skin contact, flush with water. Provide atropine or pralidoxime chloride or diazepam injections.
GF	High	Intermediate	Very rapid	Move to fresh air. For skin contact, flush with water. Provide atropine or pralidoxime chloride or diazepam injections.
VX	Very high	High	Rapid	Move to fresh air. Provide atropine or pralidoxime chloride or diazepam injections. For skin contact, flush with water.

Source: GAO, 1999. *Combating Terrorism: Need for Comprehensive Threat and Risk Assessments of Chemical and Biological Weapons*, GAO/NSIAD-99-163, General Accounting Office, Washington, DC.

Biological Agents

Biological weapons (BWs) involve the use of living organisms or their inanimate by-products (toxins) as weapons. The subject of much research, biological agents have the potential for greater destructive impact than chemical weapons; a much smaller quantity is required to deliver a lethal dose.

Biological agents have incubation periods in the range of days or weeks. This incubation period makes a biological attack much more difficult to deal with than a chemical one, because the attack is not immediately evident. Casualties can spread an infectious agent among a much wider population before inhabitants become aware of the symptoms caused by the agent.

Similarly, biological agents are difficult to detect. At present, rapid and reliable detection methods are not available. Microorganisms can reproduce within the host after delivery and dissemination, thereby increasing and causing infection of others. The possibility of covert attacks is therefore great, and attribution of the attack may not occur until substantial implications develop. Biological weapons can also cause large numbers of casualties over a wide area in the cases where the disease is difficult to treat or highly contagious.

BWs are based on naturally occurring diseases; thus, individuals may have a natural level of resistance. In other cases, the diseases produced can be treated or vaccinated against. The agents may also be fragile outside of host cells, in which case they may be destroyed by heat or ultraviolet (UV) light. For this reason, BW agents can be difficult to weaponize. Another limitation is the undesirability of using contagious diseases as BWs due to the uncontrollable effects of such an attack and the potential rebound on the attacker. All of these factors are likely to have discouraged the use of BWs in the past.

BWs would most likely be delivered either as liquid slurry or as a powder of dried organisms or toxins. Although dissemination of biological agents by spray pressure is simple and could be used in a wide variety of terrorist applications, delivery is a complex and technically challenging process, it may perhaps be the most difficult technological obstacle to overcome in creating a robust biological weapon program. The primary challenge in weaponizing agents is keeping them alive long enough to produce their intended effects. The agent must be capable of withstanding the physical stresses involved in dissemination without losing viability or toxicity.

Covert release of a BW may only become apparent once the first cases of the disease arise. Some diseases occur so infrequently in nature that the appearance of just one case may be suggestive of deliberate release. For instance, the U.K. Public Health Laboratory Service interim guidelines note that deliberate release should be considered as a cause in the event of a single case of inhaled anthrax [4]. For diseases such as botulism, it may be more difficult to distinguish between deliberate release and (rare) natural occurrence.

Key Point The public health impact of future anthrax attacks in the United States has been minimized through good clinical awareness and early notification of the public health authorities.

The principal biological agents used as weapons can be classified into three broad groups: bacteria, viruses, and toxins. These agents are summarized in the following sections.

Bacteria. Bacteria are small free-living organisms, most of which may be grown on solid or liquid culture media. They reproduce by simple division. The diseases they produce often respond to specific therapy with antibiotics. Possible agents include anthrax, brucellosis, and plague.

Viruses. Viruses are organisms that require living cells in which to replicate. They are therefore intimately dependent upon the cells of the host that they infect. They produce diseases that generally do not respond to antibiotics. However, they may be responsive to antiviral compounds. The few antiviral compounds that are available are of limited use. Possible viral agents include smallpox and the various hemorrhagic fever viruses.

Toxins. Toxins are poisonous substances produced by and derived from living plants, animals, or microorganisms. Some toxins may also be produced or altered by chemical means. Toxins may be countered by specific antisera and selected pharmacologic agents. Possible agents include botulinum and ricin toxins.

Properties of Principal Biological Agents

The properties of the principal biological agents are summarized in Table 6.2 [3].

TABLE 6.2   Summary of Properties of Some Principal Biological Agents

Biological Agent	Lethality	Laboratory Safety Level*	Stability	Vaccine	Treatment
Bacterial Agents					
Anthrax (pulmonary)	Very high	Level 3	Spores are very stable. Resistant to sun, heat, and some disinfectants.	Yes, primate tested. Some sources view efficacy for inhalation anthrax as questionable.	Virtually always fatal once symptomatic. Treatable very early with antibiotics and supportive therapy.
Plague (pneumonic)	Very high	Level 3	Can be long-lasting, but heat, disinfectants, and sun render it harmless.	No	Very early treatment with antibiotics can be effective, supportive therapy.
Tularemia	Moderate untreated, low treated	Level 3	Generally unstable. Resists cold but is killed by mild heat and disinfectants.	Investigational new drug.	Antibiotics very effective in early treatment.
Glanders	Moderate to high	Level 3	Very stable.	No	Antibiotics, but no large therapeutic human trials.
Brucellosis	Very low	Level 3	Very stable. Long persistence in wet soil or food.	No	Antibiotics moderately effective if given soon after infection.
Q Fever (rickettsial organism)	Very low, if treated	Level 3	Stable. Months on wood and in sand.	Investigational new drug. Tested in guinea pigs. Produces adverse reactions.	Self-limited illness without treatment. Antibiotics shorten illness.
Viral Agents					
Smallpox	Moderate to high	Level 4	Very stable	Yes	One potential antiviral, but generally no effective therapy.

TABLE 6.2 *Continued*

Biological Agent	Lethality	Laboratory Safety Level*	Stability	Vaccine	Treatment
Hemorrhagic fevers (e.g., Ebola)	Depending on strain, can be very high	Level 4	Relatively unstable.	No	Antiviral drug and aggressive supportive care. Effectiveness of any treatment is questionable.
Venezuelan equine encephalitis	Low	Level 3	Relatively unstable. Destroyed by heat and disinfectants.	Investigational new drug.	Supportive therapy, anti-convulsants. Antimicrobial therapy ineffective.
Toxins					
Botulinum (Types A–G)	High without respiratory support	Level 3	Stable. Survives weeks in nonmoving water and food. Deteriorates in bright sun.	Investigational new drug. Tested in primates. Toxoid vaccine against some types (A–E).	Antitoxin (IND) and respiratory support.
Ricin	Very high	Not available	Stable	No, but candidate under development.	None (unless ingested).

* Laboratory Safety Level refers to the working procedures in research laboratories. Biosafety level 3 applies to agents that may cause serious or potentially lethal disease as a result of exposure by inhalation. Among the many precautions is a ducted exhaust air-ventilation system that creates directional airflow that draws air from clean areas into the laboratory toward contaminated areas. The exhaust air is not recirculated to any other area of the building and is discharged to the outside with filtration and other optional treatment. Passage into the laboratory is through two sets of self-closing doors and a changing room. Showers may be included in the passageway. Biosafety level 4 is required for work with dangerous and exotic agents that pose a high risk of aerosol-transmitted laboratory infections and life-threatening disease. A dedicated nonrecirculating air-ventilation system is provided. The supply and exhaust components are balanced to ensure directional airflow from the area of least hazard to the areas of greatest potential hazard. The differential pressure/directional airflow between adjacent areas is monitored and alarmed. The airflow in the supply and exhaust components is monitored, and the components are interlocked to ensure inward, or zero, airflow. A specially designed suit area requires a one-piece positive pressure suit that is ventilated by a life-support system. Entry to the area is through an airlock fitted with airtight doors. A chemical shower is provided to decontaminate the surface of the suit before the worker leaves the area.

Source: GAO, 1999. Combating Terrorism: Need for Comprehensive Threat and Risk Assessments of Chemical and Biological Weapons, GAO/NSIAD-99-163, General Accounting Office, Washington, DC.

USE OF CHEMICAL AND BIOLOGICAL WEAPONS

State Use

Although it is an oversimplification to suggest, as much of the media does, that chemical and biological weapons are the "poor man's atom bomb," the raw materials used to produce viable weapons are relatively inexpensive, and the technology for weaponization, although challenging, is widely available.

Although the "nuclear club" remains relatively small, exclusive, and expensive to join, the continued ability of pariah states and organizations and individuals not associated with a nation state to acquire chemical and biological materials and weapons exposes weaknesses in the CWC and the BTWC. Not all countries have signed up to the agreement, and of those that have, some are clearly not acting in good faith.

Chemical Weapons. The compounds involved in the manufacture of chemical weapons are controlled by the CWC, which was opened for signature in Paris on January 13, 1993. Presently, 174 states have signed or acceded to the convention, which went into effect on April 29, 1997 [1]. However, a number of states suspected of having clandestine chemical weapons stocks have refused to join the CWC.

Although forms of chemical weapons attacks date back to antiquity, much of the lore of chemical weapons, as viewed today, has its origins in World War I. During that conflict, "gas" (actually an aerosol or vapor) was used effectively on numerous occasions by both sides to alter the outcome of battles. The Geneva Protocol, which prohibits the use of chemical weapons in warfare, was signed in 1925. Several nations, the United States included, signed with a reservation forswearing only the first use of such weapons and reserved the right to retaliate in kind if chemical weapons were used against them. The United States did not ratify the Geneva Protocol until 1975.

Key Point Chemical weapons were used in 11 campaigns after World War I, often delivered from aircraft rather than artillery, thus reducing the fear that the weapons would rebound against those who used them.

Since World War I, chemical weapons have been used in the following events:

- Britain's intervention in the Russian Civil War in 1919
- Spain in Morocco from 1923–1926
- Soviet Union in China during 1934 and from 1936–1937
- Italy in Ethiopia from 1935–1940
- Japan in China from 1937–1945
- Iraq, under Saddam Hussein, against Iran during the 1980–1988 war and against Iraqi Kurds in 1987–1988

Biological Weapons. At the height of the Cold War, biological weapons were developed by both superpowers with the aim of producing weapons that would have a capacity for mass destruction comparable to nuclear weapons. It is not clear, however, that development of BWs ever reached this level. The United States unilaterally discontinued its biological weapons program in 1969, for reasons that are not entirely clear. Possibly, the United States did not see this line of development worth pursuing further.

The production and stockpiling of BW agents has been prohibited under the BWC since 1972. The BWC is also known as the BTCW, and its full name is the "Convention on the Prohibition of the Development, Production and Stockpiling of Bacteriological (Biological) and Toxin Weapons and on Their Destruction." It was signed in Washington, London, and Moscow on April 10, 1972, and entered into force on March 26, 1975 [5]. Although there are 140 state signatories to this treaty, about a dozen, including possible state sponsors of terrorism, are suspected of possessing or actively seeking biological weapons. In addition, although the Soviet Union was a signatory to the BWC, it was admitted following its breakup that the Soviets had a very active biological weapons program up until about 1992. It is not clear to what extent this program has been fully dismantled, the extent to which stockpiles of biological agents have been destroyed, and if former Soviet BW scientists are now working for other state BW programs.

Because many of the BW agents involved are infectious human diseases, they are also monitored by other bodies, such as the Center for Disease Control in the United States and the World Health Organization.

Biological weapons can be very difficult to produce and disseminate. Because of this, they have seen little use in open conflict.

Limited information exists about historical BW attacks and their effectiveness.

Key Point   The only known case of biological weapon use in open conflict was by Japan against China during World War II.

Prior to the Gulf War, U.K. sources identified the most likely BW threat as coming from bacterial sources, notably anthrax, plague, and botulinum toxin (BTx). U.K. forces were vaccinated against both anthrax and plague; serum for treating exposure to BTx was also taken to the Gulf. U.S. planners did not concur with the U.K. analysis over the risk of exposure to plague, but U.S. forces did receive both anthrax and BTx vaccines. Neither U.K. nor U.S. planners saw a credible threat of smallpox attack at that time. The threat posed by BW agents, however, remains considerable, particularly because advances in bioengineering present the possibility of genetically modified BWs emerging in the future.

Terrorist Attacks

With many states pledging to put chemical and biological weapons beyond use, or not develop these devices in the first place, concern now focuses on militant groups and other so-called "nonstate actors," including groups supported by rogue states. Recent incidents using chemical or biological weapons include the following:

- Japanese sect Aum Shinrikyo released nerve gas on the Tokyo subway in March 1995, killing 12 and injuring thousands.
- In June 1994, Aum Shinrikyo released sarin nerve gas in a residential building in Matsumoto, a small town, killing 7 and injuring over 300.
- The militant leftist German group the Red Army Faction is believed to have tried to develop botulism toxin, with some success, in the 1980s.
- A raid on a Red Army Faction safe house in Paris in 1984 uncovered a makeshift laboratory containing toxins.
- Members of a religious cult in Oregon succeeded in poisoning local restaurant salad bars with salmonella in 1994, injuring more than 700 people. No one is believed to have died as a result of the attack.

- Recent attacks in the United States involving the delivery of anthrax spores via the postal system.

The amount of chemical weapons needed for use in military versus terrorist incidents differs greatly. Although hundreds of tons may be needed for use in battle, the Aum Shinrikyo nerve gas attack demonstrated that only small quantities are needed for terrorist or unconventional applications.

THREAT ASSESSMENT

Current Threat Levels

Media concern over chemical and biological weapons reached new heights following the anthrax attacks in the United States. Although intelligence sources in the United States and the United Kingdom have long been concerned over the proliferation of these weapons, a mass-casualty attack by terrorists using chemical or biological weapons has been considered a low risk. In the past, intelligence sources stated that it was difficult to see what political ends killing large numbers of civilians would serve and that there were inherent technical difficulties in using biological weapons of mass destruction. However, after the attacks in the United States, it appears that only technical barriers, in terms of obtaining virulent strains of an agent, producing adequate quantities of the agent, and finding effective means of dispersal, remain a deterrent. Estimates suggest that 10 grams of anthrax spores are more deadly than a ton of sarin agent, the nerve gas that killed 12 people in a terrorist attack on the Tokyo underground in 1995.

Key Point Reports from U.K. and U.S. intelligence sources indicate that the risk of terrorist chemical and biological attack is credible, although low.

Terrorist groups seeking to use chemical or biological weapons would encounter significant difficulties, because developing and storing these weapons requires sophisticated facilities. However, some are concerned that chemical and biological weapons could be stolen from the countries that possess them. Even if a militant group obtained a nonconventional agent it would be difficult to deliver it effectively. However, even relatively inefficient dissemination methods could result in significant deaths and casualties, as was demonstrated by the sarin attack in the Tokyo subway in 1995. If a biological or chemical attack were to occur, it could encompass a wide variety of forms, including attacks on crops; sabotage of fuels and machinery; poisoning of food, water, and medicine; assassination attacks on individuals; and attacks on groups of people in public transportation, individual rooms, buildings, government or industrial complexes, or even whole cities.

Chemical Threats

The U.S. General Accounting Office (GAO), which is now the Government Accountability Office, is the body responsible for carrying out threat assessments for Congress. The GAO evaluated the potential threat from chemical and biological agents in its 1999 report *Combating Terrorism: Need for Comprehensive Threat and Risk Assessments of Chemical and Biological Attacks* [3]. Part of the aim of this assessment was to guide public spending programs on mitigation of CBW attacks, because there was some concern that expenditures were not in proportion to the level of threat. As part of the same initiative, the Centers for Disease Control and Prevention (CDC), an operating division within the U.S. Department of Health and Human Services, has developed a national pharmaceutical stockpile to prepare for terrorist incidents involving chemical or biological agents.

For chemical weapons, the GAO report assigns two levels of risk: "likely" and "not likely," as shown in Table 6.3 [3]. Toxic industrial chemicals can cause mass casualties and require little, if any, expertise or sophisticated methods to obtain or disperse them. Generally,

TABLE 6.3   GAO Threat Assessment for Chemical Weapons

Chemical Agent	Ease of Manufacture and Precursor Availability	Level of Risk
Choking Agents		
Chlorine (CL)	Industrial product. No precursors required.	Likely agent due to availability as a commercial product.
Phosgene (CG)	Industrial product. No precursors required.	Likely agent due to its availability as a commercial product.
Blister Agents		
Sulphur mustard (HD)	Easy to synthesize. Large quantity buys of precursor chemicals without detection difficult. Precursors are covered by CWC.	Not likely agent due to difficulty in obtaining precursor materials and moderate production requirements.

TABLE 6.3 *Continued*

Chemical Agent	Ease of Manufacture and Precursor Availability	Level of Risk
Nitrogen mustard (HN-2)	Easy to synthesize. Large quantity buys of precursor chemicals without detection difficult. Precursors are covered by CWC.	Not likely agent due to difficulty in obtaining precursor materials and moderate production requirements.
Nitrogen mustard (HN-3)	Easy to synthesize. Large quantity buys of precursor chemicals without detection difficult, but available.	Not likely agent due to difficulty in obtaining precursor materials and moderate production requirements.
Lewisite (L, HL)	Moderately difficult to manufacture and moderately difficult to acquire precursor chemicals.	Not likely agent due to difficulty in obtaining precursor materials and moderate production requirements.
Blood Agents		
Hydrogen cyanide (AC)	Industrial product. Precursor chemicals covered by CWC.	Likely agent due to its availability as a commercial product. Precursor availability may be a problem.
Cyanogen chloride (CK)	Not easily produced. Available as commercial product.	Likely agent, although precursor availability may be a problem.
Nerve Agents		
Tabun (GA)	Not readily available manufacturing instructions, but precursors available. Relatively easy to manufacture.	Likely agent due to availability of precursor chemicals and relative ease of manufacture.
Sarin (GB)	Moderately difficult to manufacture. Precursor chemical covered by CWC.	Likely agent due to demonstrated use by Aum Shinrikyo, although restrictions on precursors could create difficulties for production.
Soman (GD)	Difficult to manufacture. Precursor chemical covered by CWC.	Not likely agent due to difficulty of manufacture and control of precursor chemical.
GF	Moderately difficult to manufacture. Precursor chemical covered by CWC.	Not likely agent due to difficulty of manufacture and control of precursor chemical.
VX	Difficult to manufacture. Precursor chemicals covered by CWC.	Not likely agent due to difficulty of manufacture and control of precursor chemical.

Source: Adapted from GAO, 1999. *Combating Terrorism: Need for Comprehensive Threat and Risk Assessments of Chemical and Biological Weapons*, GAO/NSIAD-99-163, General Accounting Office, Washington, DC.

toxic industrial chemicals can be bought on the commercial market or stolen, thus avoiding the need to manufacture them. Chlorine, phosgene, and hydrogen cyanide are examples of toxic industrial chemicals.

Unlike toxic industrial chemicals, most G and V chemical nerve agents would be challenging for terrorists to acquire or manufacture. Developing nerve agents requires synthesis of multiple precursor chemicals, and some steps in the production process are difficult and hazardous. Although tabun production is relatively easy, containment of a highly toxic gas (hydrogen cyanide) is a technical challenge. Production of sarin, soman, and VX requires high temperatures and generates corrosive and dangerous by-products. Moreover, careful temperature control, cooling of the vessel, heating to complete chemical reactions, and distillation could be technically unfeasible for terrorists lacking access to a sophisticated laboratory infrastructure.

Blister chemical agents, such as sulphur mustard, nitrogen mustard, and Lewisite, can be manufactured with ease or with only moderate difficulty. However, buying large quantities of the precursor chemicals for these agents is difficult due to the CWC.

Chemical agents falling into the GAO's "likely" category are the toxic industrial chemicals (chlorine, phosgene, and cyanogens), principally due to their relatively wide availability. Other "likely" chemicals include the more easily produced nerve agents tabun and sarin. Chemical agents falling into the "not likely" category are the vesicants and the nerve agents soman and VX, due to the difficulty in producing and acquiring precursor chemicals.

It should be noted that the assumptions on which the GAO assessments were made are somewhat conservative. For example, the GAO assumes that the would-be attackers would not have state sponsorship, would have no more than first-year undergraduate knowledge of the relevant chemistry, and that in excess of 1,000 casualties would be produced by the attack. The experience of September 11, 2001, indicates that this might not be the case, and the threat from highly educated, resourceful state and possibly state-sponsored groups, as well as independent networks and individuals, is significant. In practice, all of the chemical agents—perhaps with the exception of VX, which is very difficult to produce—may present a significant threat.

Biological Threats

For biological agents, the GAO assessment is less specific, with the use of terms such as *possible; potential; possible, but not likely; may not be highly likely;* and so on. In general, the GAO report appears to consider use of any biological agent more or less unlikely, including anthrax, for which it concludes: "Possible terrorist biological agent, but requires sophistication to effectively manufacture and disseminate to create mass casualties. Use could indicate state sponsorship" [3]. This report was issued in 1999, without the benefit of hindsight in the light of recent events. It is therefore likely that the GAO assessment is somewhat conservative with respect to biological agents as well.

The CDC has also made some assessments of the risk associated with different biological agents and has classified agents into categories A, B, and C, in descending order of priority of risks to U.S. national security [6]. The CDC defines these categories as shown in Table 6.4.

The results of the GAO and CDC assessments are summarized in Table 6.5 [3, 6].

TABLE 6.4   CDC Classification of Biological Diseases and Agents

Type of Diseases/Agents	Comments
Category A	The U.S. public health system and primary healthcare providers must be prepared to address various biological agents, including pathogens that are rarely seen in the United States. High-priority agents include organisms that pose a risk to national security because they • Can be easily disseminated or transmitted from person to person • Result in high mortality rates and have the potential for major public health impact • May cause public panic and social disruption • Require special action for public health preparedness
Category B	Second-highest priority agents include those that • Are moderately easy to disseminate • Result in moderate morbidity rates and low mortality rates • Require specific enhancements of CDC's diagnostic capacity and enhanced disease surveillance
Category C	Third-highest priority agents include emerging pathogens that could be engineered for mass dissemination in the future because of • Availability • Potential for high morbidity and mortality rates and major health impact

Source: Adapted from CDC, 2004. Centers for Disease Control and Prevention, U.S. Department of Health and Human Services, www.cdc.gov.

TABLE 6.5   **GAO Threat Assessment for Biological Weapons with CDC Classification**

Biological Agent	Ease to Acquire and Process	GAO Observation and CDC Classification
Bacterial Agents		
Anthrax (pulmonary)	Difficult to obtain virulent seed stock and to successfully process and disseminate.	Possible terrorist biological agent, but requires sophistication to effectively manufacture and disseminate to create mass casualties. Use could indicate state sponsorship. Category A
Plague	Very difficult to acquire seed stock and to successfully process and disseminate.	Possible agent, but not likely. Fairly difficult to acquire suitable strain and difficult to weaponize. Transmissible disease. Category A
Tularemia	Difficult to acquire correct strain. Moderately difficult to process.	Possible agent, but difficult to stabilize. Low lethality when treated. Category A
Glanders	Difficult to acquire seed stock. Moderately difficult to process.	Potential agent, but not easy for a nonstate actor to acquire, produce, and successfully disseminate. Category B
Brucellosis	Difficult to acquire seed stock. Moderately difficult to produce.	May not be a highly likely agent because of difficulty in obtaining virulent strain, long incubation period, and low lethality. Category B
Q Fever (rickettsial organism)	Difficult to acquire seed stock. Moderately difficult to process and weaponize.	Not a likely agent. Low lethality. Category B
Viral Agents		
Smallpox	Difficult to acquire seed stock. Only confirmed sources in the United States and Russia. Difficult to process.	Very high-consequence agent, but likelihood of usage questionable due to limited access to the pathogen beyond state actors. Category A
Hemorrhagic fevers (e.g., Ebola)	Very difficult to obtain and process. Unsafe to handle.	Unlikely agent due to difficulty in acquiring pathogen, safety considerations, and relative instability. Category A
Venezuelan equine encephalitis	Difficult to obtain seed stock. Easy to process and weaponize.	Possible agent if seed stock can be acquired, but unstable with low lethality. Category B

TABLE 6.5 *Continued*

Biological Agent	Ease to Acquire and Process	GAO Observation and CDC Classification
Toxins		
Botulinum (Types A–G)	Widely available, but high-toxin producers not readily available or easy to process or weaponize.	Difficult to weaponize; not considered a mass-casualty agent. Category A
Ricin	Readily available. Moderately easy to process, but requires ton quantities for mass casualties.	Not a mass casualty agent. Category B

Sources: Adapted from GAO, 1999. *Combating Terrorism: Need for Comprehensive Threat and Risk Assessments of Chemical and Biological Weapons,* GAO/NSIAD-99-163, General Accounting Office, Washington, DC; CDC, 2004. Centers for Disease Control and Prevention, U.S. Department of Health and Human Services, www.cdc.gov.

Terrorists lacking access to a state-run laboratory infrastructure would have to overcome a number of technical and operational challenges to deliver a biological weapon and cause mass casualties. They would require specialized knowledge from a wide range of scientific disciplines to successfully conduct biological terrorism.

Seed stocks for some biological agents are readily available in the natural environment and from culture collections in the industrialized and in some developing nations. This availability is evident by the recent outbreaks of Ebola in Africa and Hanta virus infections in Asia and North and South America. In addition, many organisms are held in national collections [e.g., American Type Culture Collection (ATCC) and European collections]. Many biological agents, such as smallpox, are difficult to obtain, and in the case of other agents, such as anthrax and tularemia, it is difficult to acquire a virulent strain. However, recent cases in the United States of pulmonary anthrax show that it is possible to obtain virulent, weaponized strains. Other agents, such as plague, are difficult to produce.

To survive and be effective, a virulent biological agent must be grown, handled, and stored properly. This stage requires time and effort for research and development. Terrorists would need the means to sterilize the growth medium and dispose of hazardous biological wastes. Processing the biological agent into a weaponized form requires even more specialized knowledge. Furthermore, toxins such as ricin require large quantities to cause mass casualties, thereby increasing the risk of arousing suspicion or detection prior to dissemination.

Most industrialized nations manufacture equipment and materials necessary for the production, containment, purification, and quality control of these materials. However, the precautions associated with a particular biochemical processing plant may give important signals of covert biological agent production. Containment of the biological material during processing is of special interest.

> **Key Point**   A clear distinction exists between processing materials for biological or toxic agent weaponization and processing protective agents to be used for countermeasures or personnel-performance enhancement.

For the production of biological agents for offensive military activities, processing containment is required to prevent the infectious agent from entering the environment. For the production of biomaterials such as vaccines, biological response modifiers, antibiotics, and antiviral agents for defensive military activities, containment is required to protect the processed biomaterial from contaminating the environment. The effectiveness of countermeasures is enhanced by achieving high levels of purity and cleanliness in the product before it is administered to friendly personnel. In contrast, an unpurified biological agent that will be used as a biological weapon is generally more stable than the purified agent that is needed to produce vaccines and biological response modifiers (BRMs). Consequently, a proliferant does not require a high level of purity if production is for biological weapons use only.

In summary, it would appear that the simpler chemical agents and the biological toxins may present the greatest threat due to the ability to acquire and implement such weapons with a relatively low level of sophistication of technology. However, use of biological agents, particularly the principal bacterial agents, cannot be ruled out due to their high impact potential.

Proliferation of Chemical and Biological Weapons

In the last decade, a series of events, including developments in India, Pakistan, and North Korea, have drawn attention to the proliferation of nuclear, biological, and chemical weapons. Along with continuing uncertainty regarding the surety and safety of former Soviet programs, these events have raised global awareness at virtually every government level. Many experts stress that the nature of terrorism in the twenty-first century may undergo a fundamental shift away from the objectives, methods, and strategies of the "classic" or "political" terrorist that existed during the height of the Cold War. Rather than fighting for political freedom or related social-justice agendas, terrorists may now choose to unleash chemical or biological attacks for nebulous reasons. Accordingly, such groups or individuals may not give advance warning of their attack, trumpet their cause, or seek compromise or concessions from authorities.

The 1995 attack by Aum Shinrikyo in the Tokyo subway using the chemical nerve agent sarin killed 12 and injured many more. Some experts have noted that despite substantial financial assets, well-equipped laboratories, and educated scientists, Aum Shinrikyo did not cause more deaths because of the poor quality of the chemical agent and the dissemination technique used. Therefore, the general belief was that the bigger risk emanated from nation states, particularly those involved in long-standing political disputes. However, Al-Qaeda's aspirations to develop such weapons mean that this is probably no longer the case and that an attack is more likely from a terrorist source.

Although the cost and technical complexity associated with efficient delivery may well preclude widespread attacks without the support of state sponsors, routes through leakage from state-sponsored programs and disaffected individuals are still possible. This still may not result in city-scale devices, but it could give rise to small, local devices that would contaminate the immediate surrounding area or building.

The catalog of chemical agents will be relatively slow to evolve. By contrast, new technologies related to the production and development of biological agents is increasing in capability at a rate exceeding most other technologies. The pharmaceutical industry is relying on biotechnology for new therapeutic products to improve prophylaxis and therapy for many different diseases. One aspect that has attracted international attention is the need to define the boundaries of how biological agents are used in drug control. Recently, biological agents have been used for narcotic crop eradication in South America and in Asia.

New technologies, such as genetic engineering, are more likely to affect fabrication, weaponization, or difficulty of detection than to produce a "supergerm" of significantly increased pathogenicity. General robustness or survivability of a pathogen under the environmental stresses of temperature, UV radiation, and desiccation (drying) can also be genetically improved to promote stability during dissemination. Nutrient additives are used to enhance survival of selected biological agents in aerosols. Controlled persistence of a pathogen to permit survivability under specified environmental conditions may eventually be possible. The potential also exists for the development of so-called "conditional suicide genes," which could program an organism to die following a predetermined number of replications in the environment. Thus, an affected area may be safely reoccupied after a predetermined period of time.

The BTWC was originally established in 1972 to ban the development of biological weapons. Its goal was to control the use of genetically modified biological weapons and the development of all biological agents and toxins used for hostile purposes. Since 1972, more than 140 countries have signed the BTWC. The majority of these states have subsequently begun to introduce national legislation to enhance the aims of the convention. As with many UN conventions, however, there was no way to enforce the BTWC. This changed in 1995 when a protocol was introduced to ensure the convention could be enforced. This protocol, known as the Cartagena Biosafety Protocol, was eventually adopted in January 2000 and was opened for signing in May 2000. Despite the fact that many states expressed their intention to sign the protocol, the U.S. withdrawal from the first round of negotiations of the BTWC in July 2001 has crippled any efforts to establish global measures against biological weapons.

Despite all of the options available for attack with chemical or biological weapons, many intelligence sources believe that terrorists mounting a large-scale attack are more likely to use conventional tactics. Eliza Manningham Buller, the Director General of the U.K.'s Security Service has stated that the conventional vehicle bomb and the suicide bomber remain the most effective tools in the terrorist arsenal [7]. However, she also stated that Al-Qaeda has the ambition to carry out unconventional attacks against the West, and that the threat of a chemical, biological, radiological, or nuclear (CBRN) attack is a realistic possibility. In her opinion, it is only a matter of time before a crude version of a CBRN attack is launched in a major Western city. In this respect, although it is likely that the recent anthrax attacks in the United States were the work of an individual, this incident and the March 1995 Tokyo nerve gas attack demonstrate the credibility of the threat.

Methods of Delivery

The primary route of dissemination for most CBW agents is by airborne transfer as a vapor or aerosol of solid particles or liquid droplets. Most agents act principally by inhalation, although some also work by absorption through the skin.

The most effective way for a terrorist to mount an anthrax attack that would likely cause pulmonary anthrax, for example, would be to spray an anthrax-containing aerosol from an aircraft or automobile. The spray would be easier to disperse if the anthrax could be made into a dry agent. In 1993, a U.S. government report stated that up to three million people could die if 100 kilograms of anthrax were released over a city the size of Washington, DC [8].

Other methods of delivery could include dissemination from devices such as pressurized agricultural sprayers, commercial dispensers, air compressors, or even suitcases or bags holding powdered or liquid samples of agents. Inserting agents in a ventilation system in an enclosed building or arena would be a simple, yet effective, method of causing mass casualties with a chemical or biological weapon. Alternatively, the spores could be put into a container, such as an envelope (as seen recently in the United States), and released on unknowing victims. The amount of anthrax needed to infect a city's water supply makes this tactic impractical.

The properties developed to make CBW agents most effective in battlefield situations, particularly those relating to persistence, which enable agents to be disseminated effectively in an open environment, may be less critical within buildings or other enclosed or semi-enclosed public spaces, where the confined nature of the space and the natural pathways and building services may aid dispersal.

Chemical Attack. Chemical agents need to be in vapor or aerosol form, to cause optimal inhalation exposure, to cause an effect. Vapors and aerosols remain suspended in the air and are readily inhaled deep into the lungs. Another dispersal method is to spray large droplets or liquids for skin penetration. A chemical agent could be disseminated by explosive. However, the agent would need to be able to withstand the heat developed during such an explosion. An alternative method is a mechanical form of delivery such as commercial sprayers or improvised devices. Improvised dissemination methods could use simple containers such as glass bottles with sprayers attached to them or fire extinguishers.

The successful use of chemical agents to cause mass casualties requires high toxicity, volatility (tendency of a chemical to vaporize or give off fumes), and stability during storage and dissemination. Rapid exposure to a highly concentrated agent in an ideal environment would increase the number of casualties. Disseminating a chemical agent in a closed environment is the best way to produce mass casualties. Weather conditions, particularly sunlight, moisture, and wind, affect exterior dissemination. Some chemical agents can be easily evaporated by sunlight or diluted by water. Table 6.6 shows the persistency of selected chemical agents in various climatic conditions [9].

It is also difficult to target an agent with any precision or certainty to kill a specific percentage of individuals outdoors. For example, wind could transport a chemical agent away from the designated target area.

Key Point   In the only two chemical attacks attributed to a terrorist group, relatively low-tech methods of delivery were used.

In the June 1994 attack carried out by Aum Shinrikyo on a residential building in Matsumoto, 7 were killed and over 300 were injured. The sarin vapor was disseminated by an improvised system involving a heater, a fan, and a drip system venting from the window of a disguised delivery truck. In March 1995, a second, highly publicized attack on the Tokyo subway system killed 12. A further 500 people required hospital admission and over 5,000 sought medical

TABLE 6.6   Persistency of Selected Liquid Chemical Agents

Liquid Chemical Agent	Persistence in Sunny, Light Breeze, Temperature Around 15°C	Persistence in Windy and Rainy Climate, Temperature Around 10°C	Persistence in Calm and Sunny Climate, Snow on Ground, Temperature Around −10°C
Sarin	15 minutes to 4 hours	Fifteen minutes to 1 hour	1 to 2 days
Tabun	1 to 4 days	Half a day to 6 days	1 day to 2 weeks
Soman	2 and half to 5 days	3 to 36 hours	1 to 6 weeks
Mustard gas	2 to 7 days	Half a day to 2 days	2 to 8 weeks
V Agent	3 to 21 days	1 to 12 hours	1 to 16 weeks

Source: Adapted from Swedish National Defense Research Unit (FOI), 1992. *Briefing Book on Chemical Weapons,* Swedish National Defense Research Establishment, Stockholm.

advice, most with psychosomatic symptoms; 242 medical staff also reported symptoms, which were caused by exposure to contaminated casualties. Sect members had placed sarin, in double-layered plastic bags, onto the floors of five subway trains, had pierced the bags with sharpened umbrella tips, and disembarked. The low purity (30 percent) and ineffective dissemination of the sarin meant that casualties were low, although the overall impact was high.

Biological Attack. The most effective way to disseminate a biological agent is by aerosol. This method allows the simultaneous respiratory infection of a large number of people. Microscopic particles that are dispersed must remain airborne for long periods and may be transported by the wind over long distances. The particles are small enough to reach the tiny air sacs of the lungs (alveoli) and bypass the body's natural filtering and defense mechanisms. If larger particles are dispersed, they may fall to the ground, causing no injury, or become trapped in the upper respiratory tract, possibly causing infections, but not necessarily death. From an engineering standpoint, it is easier to produce and disseminate the larger particles than the microscopic particles. Other critical technical hurdles include obtaining the proper equipment to generate proper size aerosols, calculating the correct output rate, and having the correct liquid composition.

Biological agents can be processed into liquid or dry forms for dissemination. Both forms pose difficult technical challenges for terrorists, who seek to effectively cause mass casualties. Liquid agents are easy to produce; however, it is difficult to effectively disseminate aerosolized liquid agents with the right particle size without reducing the strength of the mixture. Furthermore, liquid agents require larger quantities and dissemination vehicles, which can increase the possibility of raising suspicion and detection. In contrast, dry biological agents are more difficult to produce than liquid agents, but easier to disseminate. Dry biological agents could be easily destroyed when processed, rendering the agent ineffective for causing mass casualties. The whole process entails risks for the perpetrators. For example, powders easily adhere to rubber gloves and pose a handling problem. Effectively disseminating both forms of agents can pose technical challenges in that proper equipment and energy sources are required. A less sophisticated product and dissemination method could still produce some illnesses or deaths. Exterior dissemination of biological agents can be disrupted by environmental (e.g., pollution) and meteorological (e.g., sun, rain, mist, and wind) conditions. Table 6.7 shows the persistency of selected biological agents in vari-

TABLE 6.7   **Survival of Potential Biological Agents in Aerosol**

Biological Agent	Biological Decay of Aerosol, Percent per Minute			
	Darkness at 75°F		Sunlight at 75°F	
	30% RH	85% RH	30% RH	85% RH
Liquid anthrax	0.0%	0.0%	≤0.1%	≤0.1%
Dried anthrax	—	0.0	≤0.1	≤0.1
Liquid Q fever	0.0	0.0	≤0.1	≤0.1
Dried Q fever		0.0	≤0.1	≤0.1
Liquid tularemia	6.8	2.3	22	14
Nonstabilized liquid tularemia		2.3	18	13
Dried tularemia	2.5	5–7	—	—
Nonstabilized dried tularemia	2–2.5	2.5	—	—
Liquid plague	—	—	21	53

Source: U.S. Congress Office of Technology Assessment, 1993. "Technical Aspects of Chemical Weapon Proliferation," *Technologies Underlying Weapons of Mass Destruction,* U.S. Congress Office of Technology Assessment, Washington, DC.

ous climatic conditions [8]. Relative humidity (RH) is an environmental term that quantifies the amount of moisture in the air.

Once released, an aerosol cloud gradually decays and dies as a result of exposure to oxygen, pollutants, and UV rays. If wind is too erratic or strong, the agent may dissipate too rapidly or fail to reach the desired area. Table 6.8 shows the effect of various environmental factors on the lethality of a biological agent aerosol attack [8].

Mechanism of Attack on Buildings

The vulnerability of buildings to CB attack lies in their accessibility. The effectiveness of an attack depends on knowledge of the security procedures and systems, particularly the ventilation systems, of a given building. A CB attack could come in many guises, ranging from a passerby releasing an agent into a low-level external air intake to person-to-person transmission from a deliberately infected suicide terrorist. In addition, such an attack could be launched via release of an agent from vehicles or a projectile attack.

Buildings are most vulnerable to CB attack because of the relative ease of disseminating agents via the ventilation systems, and hence throughout the building. Although water supplies and other

TABLE 6.8 Environmental Factors Affecting Lethality of Aerosol Biological Attack

Environmental Factor	Affect on Aerosol Attack Lethality
Terrain	
Open, flat	Maximizes lethal dispersion of agent.
Hilly	Atmospheric turbulence impedes even distribution and increases vertical dilution of agent, reducing casualties.
City	Atmospheric turbulence impedes even distribution and increases vertical dilution of agent, reducing casualties. Buildings partially shelter from agent.
Weather	Wind may blow agent away from or toward targets. Air temperature and temperature gradient effect dispersal. High winds disperse agent farther, but may dilute lethal concentrations sooner. Rains may clear air, wash away deposited agent. Sunlight or drying rapidly destroys some agents.

Source: U.S. Congress Office of Technology Assessment, 1993. "Technical Aspects of Chemical Weapon Proliferation," *Technologies Underlying Weapons of Mass Destruction,* U.S. Congress Office of Technology Assessment, Washington, DC.

water-based systems could provide access and transportation within buildings for CB agents, the more likely method of attack would involve the use of mechanical or natural ventilation pathways such as HVAC systems, opened windows, or fortuitous air pathways such as lift and riser shafts. Air-exchange rates within a building could affect the dissemination of a CB agent, but this method of attack has the potential to produce wide exposure of the building occupants to the agent, which could result in high morbidity and mortality rates, as well as contamination of large areas of the building. Many experts believe that in order to guarantee success, testing would be necessary to determine if the agent was virulent and disseminates properly. Any attempts to reconnoiter the building or test the delivery method would increase the chances of a terrorist being detected. However, this approach would not preclude an untested attack on a building and the potential to cause significant casualties. Once again, the sarin attacks in Japan showed the potential for casualties even with relatively poorly processed agents and poor methods of attack.

A building can be attacked in many different ways, and it is important to note that a CB attack does not have to be directly against a particular building for it to have a great effect on the building and the occupants. An attack on a city area or a particular building could have serious consequences for adjacent buildings.

The advantage of a CB attack against a building from a terrorist's viewpoint is that that attack does not have to be an overt, large-scale incident, such as the use of a crop-spraying plane or "dirty" vehicle bomb, to cause casualties. The ideal terrorist device would be small, resemble a familiar object, and contain a highly toxic CB agent. Such devices would not necessarily resemble "suspicious" items such as unattended bags or briefcases. A CB device could be constructed to resemble a piece of equipment that belongs in the building. The risk of an attack emanating from a source within the building is therefore of equal concern to one that originates from outside the building. A device including an ultrasonic nebulizer, timer, or radio-controlled mechanism would enable the terrorist to make his or her escape before activation. Similarly, the risk of attack by means of a delivered item (e.g., letter or parcel) also needs to be considered. Table 6.9 summarizes some of the possible methods of attacking a building.

PROTECTIVE MEASURES IN COMMERCIAL BUILDINGS

In a military situation, the source of threat and the likely method of attack are well known and predictable. In addition, battlefield detection technology is available and well tested. Battlefield protection can be provided by prophylactics, often administered as a preventative measure, and by protective clothing. Troops are also rigorously trained to not only respond to a CB attack, but to continue operating in as normal a manner as possible subsequent to an attack.

> **Key Point** When assessing the risks associated with a CB attack on a commercial building, it is useful to consider the differences between a military scenario and a terrorist incident involving a civilian population.

An attack on a civilian population by a terrorist group is likely to have a number of major differences. The source and likely types of agent are less well known. Unlike a military attack, a terrorist attack is likely to use improvised means of delivery. Taken as a whole, the threat is much less predictable. Unlike in a military environment, the options for protection in the form of pre-administered medication and personal protective clothing are either undesirable, in the case of mass inoculation of a large civilian population, or impractical. Detection in a commercial situation is also impractical given the state of current technology. Although work has been carried out in the

TABLE 6.9   Possible Mechanisms for CB attack on a Building

Target	Source of Attack
Mechanical Ventilation Systems	
Air intakes—low level	External: Hand-delivered devices, vehicle-borne devices, projectiles, airborne (e.g., crop-spraying planes).
Air intakes—high level	External: Projectiles, airborne (e.g., crop-spraying planes) Internal: Hand-delivered device by intruder*
HVAC plant rooms	Internal: Hand-delivered device by intruder*
Ductwork	Internal: Hand-delivered device by intruder*
Lift shafts	Internal: Hand-delivered device by intruder*
Service risers	Internal: Hand-delivered device by intruder*
Building Areas	
Building entrances—reception	External: Hand-delivered devices, vehicle-borne devices, projectiles, airborne (e.g., crop spraying planes) Internal: Hand-delivered device by intruder*
Building entrances—loading bays	External: Hand-delivered devices, vehicle-born devices, projectiles, airborne (e.g., crop-spraying planes); delivered goods, contamination of refuse bins Internal: Hand-delivered device by intruder (e.g., briefcase left in reception area)*
Stairwells	Internal: Hand-delivered device by intruder*
Mailrooms	Internal: Couriered packages
Inner building areas	External: Person-to-person contamination because of infected passerby Internal: Contamination of surfaces by intruder (e.g., keyboards, telephones),* device left in familiar item or package (e.g., briefcase), person-to-person contamination because of infected intruder
Building Fabric	
Facade	External: Projectile, explosive device, vehicle crashing into building, leaky facade, opened windows
Services	
Water utilities	External: Contamination of incoming water supplies Internal: Contamination of water storage tanks
Supplies	External: Contamination of food and bottled water supplies, contaminated hand towels, etc.

* This includes a person who has gained entrance illegally or who has legitimate access rights to the building (e.g., a contractor).

development of commercial detectors, reliable, cost-effective detectors with low false alarm rates, which are vital in a commercial environment, are somewhere off in the future. Similarly, although emergency services have trained for a response to a terrorist CB incident, the civilian population and, to a large extent, security and facilities staff of most commercial organizations are untrained in response measures against a real or suspected CB attack. Therefore, in order to protect a building and its occupants against a CB attack, a "whole-building" approach (i.e., one that looks at all aspects of the building design and operation) is required.

Measures to protect a commercial building against CB attack must be led by risk considerations and be practicable in the business environment. The threat from a terrorist source is unpredictable, and a risk assessment should be applied to evaluate the threat posed by simple, "passive," hand-delivered devices outside a building or inside a building in vulnerable spaces, such as reception areas, goods delivery yards, and mailrooms. Also, more sophisticated, active devices involving aerosol or vapor generation delivered by means of bombs, projectiles, or airborne systems need to be considered. An assessment of the credibility of the various methods of attack can be made and appropriate mitigation measures introduced. These mitigation methods should include conventional security measures, such as manned guarding, CCTV, access control, and physical security, as well as measures affecting building planning, ventilation systems, and operational procedures. These measures can be categorized in terms of the method of attack (i.e., simplistic or determined/mechanistic). Table 6.10 lists some of the building-enhancement measures that can be taken against simplistic attacks.

TABLE 6.10   **Whole-Building Enhancement Measures Against Simplistic Attacks**

	Level 1	Level 2	Level 3
Strategy	• Good-practice measures, choice of locations for plant	• Simple control of spread of agents • EL1 Measures plus:	• Proactive mitigation • Detection of agents • Control of spread of agents • EL2 Measures plus:
Building planning	• Secure location for HVAC plant rooms • Secure location for water storage plant rooms	• All mail and packages, including couriers, to one location	• Specialist mail handling and screening rooms

TABLE 6.10 *Continued*

	Level 1	Level 2	Level 3
Physical and electronic security	• Camera observation of air inlets • Controlled access to building, including car parks	• Physical separation between semipublic and private areas	• Monitoring of all HVAC plant rooms and other vulnerable areas • Chemical agent detectors in vulnerable areas and at air intakes • Biological agent detectors in vulnerable areas and at air intakes
Procedures	• Procedures for dealing with suspected devices • Train staff in CB attack contingency plans • Conduct regular tests of the plans • Train onsite facilities staff in the operation of the building the event of a CB incident or threat • Permit to work system in HVAC and water storage plant rooms	• Staff display identification at all time • Escort visitors when on site • Procedures for checking of bags • Security checks on contractors, cleaners • Survey of contamination levels	• Smart evacuation procedures • Provision for screening of all bags • Response plans to agent detection
Ventilation	• Protection of air intakes and outlets • Secure location, away from public access • Away from flat surfaces • Resistant to thrown projectiles/intruders • Zero recirculation to main system • Good spatial separation of air intakes and outlets	• Separate zoning of vulnerable areas • Separate HVAC systems and sealed walls for vulnerable areas: reception, mailrooms, and goods entrances • Manually triggered shut off system for HVAC systems with automatic dampers	• Active HVAC control • Automatic initiation by the building attack system. System to close dampers and stop recirculation of air • If inlet is uncontaminated, run HVAC to positively pressurize

TABLE 6.11   Whole-Building Enhancement Measures Against Determined Attacks

	Level 4	Level 5
Strategy	• Safe refuges with positive pressurization and filtration • EL3 Measures plus:	• Positive pressurization and filtration for whole building • EL4 Measures plus:
Building planning	• Internal refuges • Hardened security control rooms • Enhanced facades	• Tightly sealed building fabric • Blast-resistant facade • Air locks on external doors
Physical and electronic security	• Comprehensive camera observation of building perimeter • Comprehensive communications system • Air inlets to be resistant to fired projectiles	• Remote monitoring of building
Procedures	• Contingency plans for inward evacuation	• Automatic messaging to staff • Offsite mail screening
Ventilation	• Positive pressurization of refuges • Filtered air provided to refuge areas • Positive pressurization of control rooms • Filtered air provided to control rooms	• Positive pressurization of the entire building • Filtered air supplied to the entire building

Table 6.11 lists some building-enhancement measures that can be taken against determined attacks. In contrast to simplistic hand-delivered weapons, these attacks may involve active devices using aerosol or vapor generation.

Finally, in considering a "whole-building" approach to commercial CB protective measures, the response of staff and building management to an attack should be considered. CB agents pose different sets of problems for emergency planning and preparedness. The response and contingency plans for a potential CB attack will therefore be complex and wide-ranging and should be given at least as much priority and effort as plans dealing with other extreme events that can impact the business.

__SUMMARY__

This chapter explores the credibility of threats posed by the use of chemical and biological agents by terrorist groups. The types of agents, their characteristics, and the potential for their procurement and delivery were discussed. Their potential use against building targets and the mechanisms of attack were examined, together with a strategy for protecting buildings that is directly linked to the methods of attack and associated risk.

Many of the building protective guidelines proposed in this chapter can be classified as "good practice" measures that, if adopted at an early stage in the design of a new building, will have no, or minimal, impact on construction costs.

__BIBLIOGRAPHY_____

References

1. OPCW, 2005. *Convention on the Prohibition of the Development, Production, Stockpiling and Use of Chemical Weapons and on Their Destruction*, Organisation for the Prohibition of Chemical Weapons, www.opcw.org/html/db/cwc/eng/cwc_frameset.html.

2. United Nations Report of the Secretary General, 1969. *Chemical and Bacteriological Weapons, and the Effect of Their Possible Use, A7575/REV1*. United Nations, New York.

3. GAO, 1999. *Combating Terrorism: Need for Comprehensive Threat and Risk Assessments of Chemical and Biological Weapons*, GAO/NSIAD-99-163, General Accounting Office, Washington, DC.

4. "Convention on the Prohibition of the Development, Production and Stockpiling of Bacteriological (Biological) and Toxin Weapons and on Their Destruction," signed at Washington, London, and Moscow on April 10, 1972, entered into force March 26, 1975.

5. Harling, R., Twisselmann, B., Asgari-Jirhandeh, N., Morgan, D., Lightfoot, N., Reacher, M., and Nicoll, A., for the Deliberate Release Teams, Public Health Laboratory Service, London, England, 2001. "Deliberate Releases of Biological Agents: Initial Lessons for Europe from Events in the United States," *Eurosurveillance Monthly*, Vol. 6, No. 11–12, pp. 166–171.

6. CDC, 2004. Centers for Disease Control and Prevention, www.bt.cdc.gov.

7. Manningham, E. B., 2003. *Countering Terrorism—An International Blueprint*, Royal United Services Institute, London.

8. U.S. Congress Office of Technology Assessment, 1993. "Technical Aspects of Chemical Weapon Proliferation," *Technologies Underly-*

ing Weapons of Mass Destruction, U.S. Congress Office of Technology Assessment, Washington, DC.

9. Swedish National Defense Research Unit (FOI), 1992. *Briefing Book on Chemical Weapons,* Swedish National Defense Research Establishment, Stockholm.

Additional Readings

CDC, 2002. *Guidance for Protecting Building Environments from Airborne Chemical, Biological, or Radiological Attacks,* Department of Health and Human Services, Centers for Disease Control and Prevention, Atlanta, GA: National Institute for Occupational Safety and Health, Washington, DC.

Federation of American Scientists, http://fas.org/nuke/intro/cw/agent.htm.

Hinton, H. L., 1999. *Combating Terrorism: Observations on the Threat of Chemical and Biological Terrorism.* Statement of Assistant Comptroller General, National Security and Internal Affairs Division, GAO/T–NSIAD-00-50, General Accounting Office, Washington, DC.

Jane's Information Group, 1999. *Chemical–Biological Defense Guidebook,* Jane's Information Group, Alexandria, VA.

Miller, J. D., 2003. "Defensive Filtration," *ASHRAE,* Vol. 44, No. 12, pp. 18–23.

Parliamentary Office of Science and Technology, 2001. *Bio-Terrorism,* Postnote 166.

Parliamentary Office of Science and Technology, 2001. *Chemical Weapons,* Postnote 167.

WHO, 2001. *Health Aspect of Biological and Chemical Weapons,* World Health Organization, Geneva, Switzerland (Draft).

7

Natural Hazards

Andrew C. T. Thompson

Ann M. Kammerer

Gayle M. Katzman

Andrew S. Whittaker

Great catastrophes in the form of earthquakes, fires, floods, and other natural events are a reality of existence on our planet. As society continues to develop densely populated cities with complex and interdependent infrastructures, the exposure to loss from such catastrophic events is ever increasing. However, in parallel with this increase in risk, scientists and engineers are improving tools and gaining the knowledge needed to reduce the risk posed by natural hazards. Over the past quarter century in particular, methodologies and technologies have been developed that represent significant improvements in our ability to design natural-hazard-resistant structures and infrastructures. In some disciplines, such as earthquake engineering, the field has matured as past events have taught valuable lessons that are now being incorporated into design practice. In other cases, current knowledge could be improved significantly if the funding to support scientific research increases.

This chapter discusses issues related to natural hazards that affect buildings, with an emphasis on understanding a risk-informed performance-based design for such extreme events. The chapter will first present an overview of a number of natural hazards, followed by a description of risk-assessment techniques. The chapter will conclude with a discussion of the methods for designing for such events from the prescriptive code and performance-based points of view.

___OVERVIEW_____

It is important to begin this discussion with an overview of natural hazards. Natural hazards are caused by geology, weather, and seismicity and can be exacerbated by human behavior. Earthquakes, floods, and hurricanes are all examples of these types of events. Because many hazards are interrelated, they can occur as both isolated and combined events. Some of these types of extreme events are localized in nature, whereas others are regional. Natural hazards can impact structures and infrastructure, producing casualties and large financial losses.

In addition to an increased understanding of natural hazards and engineering-design techniques, new methodologies, such as performance-based design and risk management, have been developed to provide frameworks that move from prescriptive code-based designs to project-specific designs. These methodologies, which are covered later in this chapter, allow for the design of structures that better address the needs of owners and other stakeholders and that can reduce levels of overall regional damage during events.

Earthquakes

The Earth's crust is composed of tectonic plates that move relative to one another, typically at tens of millimeters per year, accumulating strain energy. An earthquake occurs when the strength of the rock forming the crust is exceeded by the accumulated strain energy, which causes the rock to break. When the rock ruptures, seismic waves are propagated in all directions. In addition to the direct fault rupture and strong shaking that are typically associated with seismic events, other devastating secondary events are frequently triggered. Earthquakes can cause landslides, liquefactions, tsunamis, fires, and dam failures. Earthquakes are more prevalent at plate boundaries, although very large intraplate earthquakes also have occurred.

Although earthquakes typically cause less annual economic loss than other hazards (e.g., floods), they have the potential to cause unanticipated regional devastation in just minutes, because there is currently no proven method for their short-term prediction. Earthquakes can impact all types of structures and infrastructures, including housing and commercial buildings; transportation elements (railroads, highways, tunnels, and bridges); utilities (water, gas, and sewer lines); industrial facilities; power plants; and dams. Globally, the risk of death and injuries from an earthquake varies greatly depending on local construction practices and the availability of emergency services. In addition to the short-term impacts, social, physical, and economic impacts result in long-term economic and social consequences.

Magnitude and Intensity. Seismic activity is commonly described in terms of *magnitude* and *intensity.*

> **Key Point**   *Magnitude* characterizes the total energy released during the earthquake. *Intensity* describes effects on people and property at a particular location.

An earthquake has only one magnitude, but its intensity varies throughout the affected region. Although the Richter magnitude scale is the most widely known magnitude scale, several other magnitude scales are more commonly used in the scientific community. The most widely used scale in the United States is the Moment magnitude scale, which is based directly on the energy released by a quake. It provides a more robust quantification of the earthquake's energy. Earthquakes with magnitudes of 5, 6, 7, and greater than 8 are often referred to as *moderate, strong, major,* and *great* earthquakes, respectively. Clearly, some moderate and strong events have had devastating consequences where construction quality is poor. Because magnitude uses a logarithmic scale, each whole number increase in magnitude represents a tenfold increase in measured ground motion.

A number of intensity scales are used worldwide. For example, in the United States, the Modified Mercalli Intensity scale (MMI) is used [1]. The MMI scale is composed of 12 increasing levels of intensity, ranging from no or very little impact to complete destruction (see Figure 7.1). Each level qualitatively describes the impact and severity of ground motion at a given location based on the effects it has on the earth, people, and property. It provides a consistent methodology to summarize and compare what happened at different locations and allows for an understanding of how site-specific elements, such as soil, affect damage.

Effects. On a regional scale, the most devastating effect of an earthquake is typically related to the shaking of the ground. In general, the severity of ground motion increases with the amount of energy released and decreases with distance from the ruptured fault. The

FIGURE 7.1   Abbreviated Modified Mercalli Intensity Index.

MMI		Description
I		Not felt, except rarely under especially favourable conditions.
II		Felt only by a few persons at rest, especially on upper floors of buildings.
III		Felt noticeably by persons indoors, especially on upper floors of buildings. May not be recognized as an earthquake. Standing motor cars may rock slightly.
IV	Pictures move	Felt indoors by many, outdoors by a few. At night, some awakened. Dishes, windows, and doors are distrubed. Walls make creaking sound. Pictures swing. Vibration like that due to passing of heavy trucks. Standing motor cars rock noticeably.
V	Objects fall	Felt indoors by almost all, outdoors by many. Awakens many or most. Frightens some. Buildings shake throughout. Some dishes and windows broken. Unstable objects overturned. Hanging objects or doors swing. Small objects and furnishings moved.
VI	Non-structural damage	Felt by all. Many frightened. Awakens all. Broken dishes, glassware, in considerable quantity. Some windows broken. Fall of knick-knacks, books, pictures. Some heavy furniture moved and lighter furniture overturned. Damage slight to poorly constructed buildings.
VII	Light structural damage	Most frightened and find it difficult to stand. Noticed by persons driving motor cars. Overturned heavy furniture, with some damaged. Damage negligible in buildings of good design and construction, slight to moderate in well built ordinary buildings, considerable in poorly built or badly designed buildings. Cracked chimneys to considerable extent, walls to some extent. Numerous windows broken. Weak chimneys broken. Fall of cornices from towers and high buildings. Dislodged bricks and stones.
VIII	Moderate damage	Fright general (alarm approaches panic). Persons driving motor cars disturbed. Damage slight in specially designed structures, considerable in ordinary substantial buildings. Twisting or fall of chimneys, columns, monuments, factory stacks, and towers. Very heavy furniture moved significantly or overturned.
IX	Heavy damage	Panic general. Damage considerable in specially designed structures; well designed frame structures thrown out of plumb. Damage great in substantial buildings, with partial collapse. Buildings shifted off foundations. Underground pipes broken.
X	Extreme damage	Damage severe to well built wooden structures and bridges. Some destroyed. Destroyed most masonry and frame structures, also their foundations. Bent railroad rails, significant damage to pipe lines buried in earth. Open cracks and broad wavy folds in cement pavements and asphalt road surfaces.
XI		Damage severe to wooden-frame structures, especially near shock centers. Damage great to dams, dikes, embankments, often for long distances. Few, if any, masonry structures remained standing. Destroyed large well built bridges by the wrecking of supporting piers or pillars. Pipelines buried in earth completely out of service.
XII	Total damage	Almost all constructed works significantly damaged or destroyed. Falls of rock of significant character, slumping of river banks, and the like, numerous and extensive. Objects thrown into the air.

(*Source:* Adapted from Wood, H.O., and Newman, F., 1931. "Modified Mercalli Intensity Scale of 1931," *Seismological Society of America Bulletin,* Vol. 21, No. 4, pp 277–283.)

soil present at a site can also have a large impact on the amplitude of ground shaking.

Key Point   Ground motion is the principal concern when designing earthquake-resistant structures, and it is ground motion that is typically characterized in seismic-hazard studies.

Strong shaking hazard is analyzed through either a probabilistic seismic-hazard assessment [2] or a deterministic seismic-hazard assessment. Probabilistic values are determined for a specific return period (time frame) of interest and have been used to develop seismic-hazard maps, such as those published by the U.S. National Earthquake Hazards Reduction Program (NEHRP) [3].

Surface faulting (sometimes called *ground rupture* or *surface rupture*) is a visible expression of the fault rupture on the ground surface. Deep earthquakes do not always produce surface faulting, particularly if soft, deformable soils are present near the earth's surface. Surface faulting is a very direct hazard to structures and utilities built across active faults. The displacements, lengths, and widths of surface faulting vary widely. The relative displacement between materials on each side of the fault can be on the order of many meters, and the length of the fault rupture can be on the order of hundreds of kilometers for large earthquakes. Most fault displacements are confined to a narrow zone or shear band ranging in width from a few meters to a few hundred meters (see Figure 7.2).

Liquefaction is a phenomenon that occurs during some earthquakes that can lead to foundation failure, as shown in Figure 7.3. It can also lead to lateral ground movement, settlement, and sand boils, which are vents of sediment-laden water, when specific materials behave like a viscous fluid. Liquefaction occurs when water-saturated cohesionless soil deposits (sand and silts) experience shaking strong enough to increase the density of the soil fabric. If drainage of water in the pores of the soil is limited due to the short time frame associated with seismic loading, densification of the soil fabric causes pore-water pressure to increase. If the pore-water pressure rises such that it approaches the confining pressure of the surrounding soil, the material behaves like a fluid rather than a solid until the pore water pressures dissipates. Generally, the younger and looser the sediment and the higher the water table, the more susceptible a soil is to liquefaction.

FIGURE 7.2 Fault Rupture of the 1999 Izmit Turkey Earthquake.

(*Source:* Photo by A. Whittaker, courtesy of the Pacific Earthquake Engineering Research Center.)

Liquefaction can impact both the deformation and strength of a material. Lateral spreads and flow failures involve the lateral movement of volumes of soil as a result of liquefaction of an underlying layer. Lateral spreads generally develop on gentle slopes or near a free face (such as a sea wall) and can exhibit large movements of up to tens of meters, depending on soil and site conditions. Flow failures can move even farther on steeper slopes. Damage caused by lateral spreads seldom results in loss of life, but it can have a very great long-term financial impact. Loss of bearing strength can occur, allowing the settlement and tipping of structures with foundations on the liquefied material. In addition to lateral spread and bearing-capacity failure, liquefaction is strongly associated with breakage in buried pipes, which leads to loss of water and gas-line fires.

Floods

As evidenced in New Orleans during Hurricane Katrina (2005), flooding can produce extensive and costly damage to property.

FIGURE 7.3 Foundation Failure Due to Liquefaction in the 1999 Izmit Turkey Earthquake.
(*Source:* Photo by J. Stuart and J. Bray; courtesy of the Pacific Earthquake Engineering Research Center.)

Floods are capable of damaging and undermining buildings and infrastructure, generating large-scale erosion, and causing loss of life and injury. Loss of life results principally from the sudden destruction of structures, washout of access routes, and motorists attempting to cross swollen streams. Flooding is typically caused by a variety of events, particularly large weather systems that produce sustained and sometimes intense rainfall or storm surges. On a smaller scale, floods can be caused by local effects, such as intense thunderstorms and rapid snowmelt. Seismically based hazards, such as tsunamis and dam failures, can also create flood conditions on rare occasions.

Flooding can be separated into a large number of categories: riverine flooding, which includes overflow from a river channel, flash floods, alluvial-fan floods, and ice-jam floods; dam and levee-break floods; local drainage or high groundwater levels; fluctuating lake levels; coastal flooding, including storm surges and tsunamis; debris flows; and subsidence [4].

Riverine Flooding. River-based flooding is the most common form of flooding; it can occur in a wide variety of landscape types. Narrow channels may experience fast-moving, deep flooding, whereas flat areas may accumulate water and remain inundated with shallow water over long periods of time. In some cases, local heavy precipitation can produce flooding in areas other than known floodplains or drainage channels.

Flash floods occur rapidly and without warning and are capable of significant damage due to high water velocities and large amounts of floating debris. Flash flooding is principally affected by the intensity and duration of rainfall and the topography of the affected area. Intense localized precipitation, dam brakes, ice-jam floods, and alluvial-fan floods can cause flash-flood conditions.

Coastal Flooding. In contrast to riverine flooding, storm surge typically occurs at a coastline due to large storms, such as tropical cyclones and severe winter storms. Storm-surge levels are strongly influenced by four factors: high wind speeds that drive large amounts of water onto the coastline, low barometric pressure that causes the water surface to rise, timing of landfall in relation to peak tides, and coastal shoreline configurations [5]. In addition to the storm-surge level, resulting damage is also influenced by the velocity of the storm center (with slow-moving storms doing the most damage); the nature of the coastal geology, vegetation, and slope; previous storm damage; and human activity. Storm surge can result in loss of life and in significant damage to structures, infrastructure, and the coastline.

Tsunamis are large sea waves that usually are generated by underwater earthquakes that result in a rapid drop or uplift of the ocean floor. Tsunamis can also result from volcanic activity, submarine landslides, and, on very rare occasions, from a meteor or other space debris hitting the ocean. Tsunami waves can be more destructive than wind-developed surface waves, because they often have a pressure front that reaches deep into the water column. Most tsunami waves resulting from large seismic events have high speeds, long wavelengths, and low amplitudes as they travel across the ocean, making them difficult to detect. As a tsunami reaches coastal waters, the waves slow and pile up where the ocean bottom becomes shallower. The wave height can increase greatly during the run-up. The damaging effect of the wave is increased significantly as waterborne debris is collected and forced to move with the water mass, battering any objects in its path.

Although damage from tsunami waves is often limited to the immediate vicinity of the affected coastline, large tsunami waves have damaged and flooded areas up to a mile inland. Tsunami waves can travel very long distances with little energy dissipation. As a result, tsunamis can have significant impact on regions far from the source of the tsunami.

The 2004 Indian Ocean tsunami was a reminder of the potential for destruction and loss of life that a tsunami represents. An example of the damage from this event is shown in Figure 7.4. Although tsunamis of large magnitude are rare on a human scale, many such

FIGURE 7.4   Damage from the 2004 Indian Ocean Tsunami.

(*Source:* Photo by J. Borrero; courtesy of the University of Southern California Tsunami Research Center.)

events have occurred in recorded history, often with great loss of life. As populations and the built environment increase in coastal areas, the risk posed by tsunamis increases as well. However, robust warning systems combined with a vigilant, educated public can reduce the potential for large numbers of fatalities. In addition, specific elements that increase structural resistance to tsunamis can be incorporated into design.

Key Point   Loss of property due to flooding can only be reduced on a regional level by large-scale measures, such as limiting development in areas prone to flooding and implementing flood-control measures.

Flood-hazard-assessment procedures are outlined in the United States principally by the Interagency Advisory Committee on Water

Data (IACWD) Bulletin 17B [6] and Federal Emergency Management Agency (FEMA) Report 37 [7]. Computed water-surface elevations are combined with topographic mapping data to develop flood-hazard maps. These maps are used as flood insurance rate maps (FIRMs), which detail zones of interest based on risk levels. The FIRMs show the elevation associated with the level of a 100-year flood, in addition to other information. The FIRMs are updated continually and are available (along with tutorials on understanding the maps) online from FEMA [8].

High Winds

Tropical Cyclones. Hurricanes, tropical storms and typhoons are all classifications of tropical cyclone. Hurricanes and typhoons describe the same phenomena, with the appropriate terminology depending on the location of the event. Tropical cyclones affect coastal areas worldwide, often with devastating effect. Tropical cyclones are regions of atmospheric low pressure that originate over warm tropical waters and are characterized by winds circulating around an eye. Generally, the number of tropical cyclones is seasonal and peak as sea and surface temperatures peak. Tropical cyclones are commonly associated with severe winds, storm-surge flooding, high waves, coastal erosion, extreme rainfall, thunderstorms, lightening, and tornadoes. Storm surge and extreme rainfall cause coastal, riverine, and flash flooding; contamination of land, groundwater, and water supplies; agricultural, structural, and utility damage; coastal erosion and landslides; and loss of life due to drowning. High winds also impact utilities and transportation, cause fatalities due to downbursts and tornadoes, create large volumes of debris, and result in agricultural losses and building damage.

Key Point A tropical cyclone begins as a tropical depression (winds below 30 mph/48 kph) and can intensify into a tropical storm. Further intensification can produce a hurricane or typhoon. Once a hurricane travels over land or colder water, it begins to weaken.

The Saffir/Simpson hurricane scale, shown in Figure 7.5, is used in the United States to classify tropical cyclones based on central pressure, wind speed, storm-surge height, and damage potential [9].

Classification	Maximum wind speed mph (km/h)	Storm surge ft (m)	Damage level
Tropical depression	<39 <61	Not applicable	None or minimal
Tropical storm	39–73 61–117	Not applicable	Minimal
Category 1 hurricane/typhoon	74–95 118–153	1.0–1.7 4–5	Minimal
Category 2 major hurricane/typhoon	96–110 154–177	1.8–2.6 6–8	Moderate
Category 3 major hurricane/typhoon	111–130 178–209	2.7–3.8 9–12	Extensive
Category 4 major hurricane/typhoon	131–155 210–248	3.9–5.6 13–18	Extreme
Category 5 major hurricane/super typhoon	>155 >248	>5.6 >18	Catastrophic

FIGURE 7.5 Abbreviated Saffir/Simpson Hurricane Scale.
(*Source:* Adapted from 1969 research by H. Saffir and B. Simpson.)

Advanced computer models and radar technologies, coupled with an ever-increasing data set, have improved significantly the prediction of storm impact and cyclone landfall location in recent years. This improved prediction capacity has greatly reduced the number of fatalities in recent storms. However, an increase in the lead time in which accurate landfall locations can be predicted would significantly reduce the scale of necessary evacuations and is still an area of active research.

Wind speed and high-magnitude coastal flooding are the most common measures of hazard from tropical cyclones. In some areas, coastal flood elevations from historic hurricanes have been combined with tsunami flood-inundation information to determine the total 100-year coastal flood elevation. The frequency of occurrence of tropical cyclones at a specific location is determined by tabulating the number of direct and indirect hits recorded over a given period. Storms in which the eye passes directly overhead are considered a direct hit. If the site is close enough to the eye to experience either hurricane-force winds or storm-surge tides of 4 to 5 feet (1.2 to 1.5 meters) it is considered an indirect hit.

Tornadoes. A tornado is a rapidly rotating funnel of air that is typically spawned by a severe thunderstorm. Tornadoes often form in convective cells, such as thunderstorms or hurricanes, which are themselves rotating. Tornadoes are almost always accompanied by heavy precipitation and may be associated with large hail and lightening in some cases. Large fires may also produce local (usually small) tornadoes. In general, the vast majority of tornado-borne damage occurs in the central United States in an area often referred to as Tornado Alley. Figure 7.6 shows a map of the United States and those areas most at risk for tornados.

Although most tornadoes remain aloft, they are capable of great destruction when they touch the ground. Tornadoes can lift and move very large objects, including homes and cars, and can generate a tremendous amount of debris, which becomes airborne, causing additional damage. Tornadoes have also been known to siphon large volumes of water from bodies of water. The path of a single tornado is generally very localized, though it can range up to dozens of kilometers. The severity of tornado damage is measured by the Fujita tornado scale, which ranges from light to complete damage [10]. The National Weather Service provides an early warning system to help reduce fatalities from tornados.

In addition to storms associated with hurricanes and tornadoes, severe thunderstorms can produce wind downbursts and mi-

FIGURE 7.6   General Tornado Hazard Map of the United States.

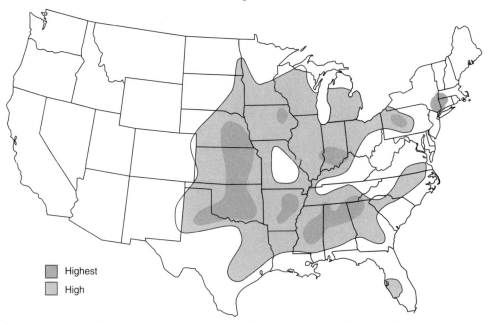

Highest
High

(*Source:* United States Geologic Survey.)

crobursts capable of causing property damage. Additional wind hazards, known as foehn-type winds, also occur for a short duration on a localized level due to down-sloping windstorms in mountainous terrain.

Other Extreme Events

A number of other naturally induced extreme events occur worldwide. Many are meteorological events, such as hailstorms, snowstorms, ice storms, and lightning. Others are associated with multiple causes. For example, fires and landslides may be caused by weather patterns or earthquakes. Avalanches may be triggered by humans, vibration, or simple buildup of a snow pack. Volcanic eruptions lead to a wide variety of potential hazards related to ash, lava flow, landslides and mudflows, fast-moving gaseous clouds, projectiles, and other effects. Heat waves cause the highest number of fatalities in the United States each year, but have limited impact on the built environment.

RISK ANALYSIS

The natural hazards introduced in the previous section can damage the built environment in a variety of ways. Partial collapse following a seismic event, foundation erosion following floods or hurricanes, or roof damage from strong winds can occur to property. Risk-analysis techniques can be used to understand the level of damage possible for various natural-hazard events and to allocate scarce resources for protection. The risk-assessment tools described in this section evaluate the level of risk posed by natural hazards for a particular building or group of buildings. Several risk-management methodologies can aid decision making for protection against natural hazards.

The Risk-Analysis Process

Risk can be defined as the product of a probability of an extreme event occurring and the severity or criticality of the consequences of the event integrated over all possible extremes. Criticality includes both the valuations of the stakeholders and the resistance of the building to the hazard. Risk analyses may be quantitative or qualitative, relative or absolute.

Key Point For natural hazards, quantitative risk-analysis methods are available because historical data exists on the probability of events in terms of return period for various locations around the country.

The risk-analysis process consists of two phases: risk assessment and risk management. Figure 7.7 shows an outline framework for a risk analysis.

Risk Assessment

The first step in a risk assessment requires gaining an understanding of the probability of the external hazards as well as the internal vulnerabilities (criticality) of and owner objectives for the facility to arrive at a relative value of risk. Valuations by owners and other parties interested in the building's performance and the characteristics of the building determine criticality. Probability is estimated using historical data. Extreme events, such as the 250- or 500-year windstorm, are usually considered for scenario-based risk analysis.

The risk assessment seeks to answer the following set of questions:

- What can happen?
- What is the likelihood that what can happen will happen?
- What are the consequences of it happening?

Assuming that the natural hazards posing risk in a particular location are known, the performance objectives for the facility should be determined. Building codes aim to ensure life safety, mainly by preventing substantial loss of life. For extreme events, building codes offer little protection against building damage or economic loss. Performance objectives can focus on a number of considerations, including the following:

- Building occupants
- Building structure and systems
- Neighboring buildings
- Environment against release of hazardous materials
- Business operations
- Access to the building (physical and electronic)
- Historic fabric
- Key assets

FIGURE 7.7   Risk Analysis Framework.

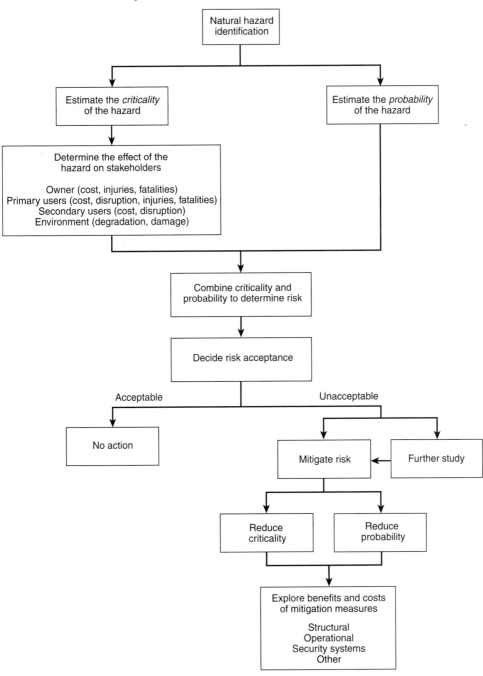

(*Source:* Arup.)

For natural hazards, performance means the behavior of the building during or following an extreme event, historically defined in terms of the level of damage experienced by the building when subjected to an extreme load. The effort by the owner and important stakeholders to define performance is a new dialogue that is taking place between architects/engineers and owners.

Key Point   In some cases, different performance objectives for nonstructural and structural elements are set in an attempt to cost-effectively meet targets.

Risk is the product of event likelihood and the severity of event consequences, integrated over all possible events. Estimating the likelihood of natural hazards is more straightforward than for other types of risk, such as technological hazards or terrorism, because frequency and severity data are often available.

Key Point   Hazard maps of the United States show that most areas of the country are vulnerable to at least one of the three major natural hazards—earthquakes, floods, or wind.

Regional probabilities are generally higher than local ones, because extreme events at any single location are relatively unlikely. The severity of the consequences of an event can be measured quantitatively, using an agreed-upon metric, or qualitatively. Metrics such as extent of structural damage, repair costs, likelihood of injuries or fatalities, and business-disruption time, can be used to measure criticality quantitatively. Figure 7.8 provides an example of a semi-quantitative risk analysis using relative values for probability and criticality that range from 1 to 5. The assessment took the form of a failure modes, effects, and criticality analysis (FMECA), in which particular failure modes were identified for each type of hazardous event. A range of natural hazards was considered, and five different building components were identified based on unique characteristics, requirements, and structural systems. For each unacceptable performance (i.e., failure) scenario listed, the probability was based on historical data, and criticality was estimated based on the characteristics of the building and the performance goals of the owner and

FIGURE 7.8 Sample FMECA Risk Assessment for a Building.

Natural hazards failure modes, effects, and criticality analysis									Building structure		Building users	
Event	#	Building component					Failure scenario	Probability ranking	Criticality ranking	Risk ranking	Criticality ranking	Risk ranking
		A	B	C	D	E						
500-year earthquake	1	X				X	500-year earthquake: Damage to foundations	3	2	6	3	9
500-year earthquake	2	X					500-year earthquake: Damage to roof	3	3	9	2	6
500-year earthquake	3		X		X		500-year earthquake: Damage to columns	3	4	12	4	12
2500-year earthquake	4	X				X	2500-year earthquake: Damage to foundations	4	2	8	3	12
2500-year earthquake	5	X					2500-year earthquake: Damage to roof	4	1	4	1	4
2500-year earthquake	6		X		X		2500-year earthquake: Damage to columns	4	3	12	3	12
100-year wind	7			X			100-year wind: Damage to main roof	2	3	6	5	10
125-year wind	8			X			125-year wind: Damage to roof	3	2	6	3	9
100-year ice storm	9	X	X	X	X	X	100-year ice storm: Damage to pipes	2	0	NA	3	6
10-year ice storm	10	X					10-year ice storm: Damage to pipes	1	0	NA	3	3

Note: High risks (with low risk rankings) are highlighted to focus attention for mitigation.

(*Source:* Arup.)

other important stakeholders. High risks (with low risk rankings) are highlighted to focus attention for mitigation.

The matrix in Figure 7.9 provides another framework for a risk assessment, this time using the suggested qualitative categories. These categories describe structural damage that can be estimated by an engineer based on evaluating the performance. The categories include (1) catastrophic, (2) very serious, (3) serious, and (4) not serious. Events in dark shading are unacceptable and require mitigation during the risk-management phase. Events in lighter shades are of less concern, but all scenarios will benefit from exploration of risk-reduction options.

Figure 7.9 can also be set up with performance groups along the top axis, if goals are defined according to desired performance rather than acceptable damage. Whatever metric is chosen, levels of damage range from 1 through 4.

A comparison of building-code performance to the performance levels defined reveals that a typical code-performing building likely behaves at a level 3 (i.e., threat to human life is minimal, but the building is both structurally and nonstructurally damaged). Special-purpose buildings, such as hospitals and schools, are required by code to perform better. Designing to code is the "minimum" baseline for conventional building structures.

FIGURE 7.9   Qualitative Risk Assessment Performance Matrix.

Consequence

Likelihood		Catastrophic 1	Very serious 2	Serious 3	Not serious 4
	Certain A	1A	2A	3A	4A
	Highly probable B	1B	2B	3B	4B
	Probable C	1C	2C	3C	4C
	Improbable D	1D	2D	3D	4D

(*Source:* Arup.)

Risk Management

Once the risk is understood, it can be managed in the second step, risk management. The decision of whether to accept the risk is made by the stakeholders. If the outcome is unacceptable (i.e., the risk is intolerable), a diverse range of risk-mitigation or risk-transfer measures can be explored. It is generally not possible to reduce the likelihood of natural events. Efforts are usually aimed at reducing the severity of the consequences of the event, usually through engineered solutions or perhaps by simply selecting a new site for the building.

Risk assessment leads to the prioritization of components for risk mitigation. Risk management seeks to answer a second set of questions:

- What can be done to address the risk?
- What options are available, and what are the associated trade-offs?
- What are the impacts of current decisions on future options?

Risk management involves the prioritization of risks so that decision makers can make recommendations. Owners can compare the cost of doing nothing with the cost of countermeasures over the facility's lifetime. Mitigation can include one or many of the following methods:

- Engineered solutions
- Operational procedures or solutions
- Financial methods, either incentives or insurance

This book focuses on engineered solutions, but other options should also be explored (e.g., insurance), depending on the function of the building. Engineered solutions can cover almost all design disciplines involved in the facility, including site planning, architectural details, structural schemes, mechanical and electrical systems, and landscaping.

Figure 7.10 repeats the sample FMECA assessment of Figure 7.8 for a building structure, with added columns for revised risk ranking. The updated risk values represent the predicted reduction in risk when various structural and other types of mitigation measures are incorporated. This presentation allows owners to clearly see where risk has been reduced. For natural hazards, the probability cannot be reduced; however, criticality can be reduced through a range of mitigation measures.

FIGURE 7.10   Sample FMECA Assessment for an Upgraded Building.

Event	#	Building component A	B	C	D	E	Failure scenario	Building structure Probability ranking	Criticality ranking	Risk ranking	Building structure Revised criticality ranking	Revised risk ranking
500-year earthquake	1	X				X	500-year earthquake: Damage to foundations	3	2	6	3	9
	2	X	X				500-year earthquake: Damage to roof	3	3	9	4	12
	3		X		X		500-year earthquake: Damage to columns	3	4	12	5	15
2500-year earthquake	4	X				X	2500-year earthquake: Damage to foundations	4	2	8	2	8
	5	X	X				2500-year earthquake: Damage to roof	4	1	4	3	12
	6		X		X		2500-year earthquake: Damage to columns	4	3	12	4	16
100-year wind	7			X			100-year wind: Damage to main roof	2	3	6	4	8
125-year wind	8			X			125-year wind: Damage to roof	3	2	6	4	12
100-year ice storm	9	X	X	X	X	X	100-year ice storm: Damage to pipes	2	0	NA	0	NA
10-year ice storm	10	X					10-year ice storm: Damage to pipes	1	0	NA	0	NA

Natural hazards failure modes, effects, and criticality analysis

Note: High risks (with low risk rankings) are highlighted to focus attention for mitigation.
(*Source:* Arup.)

Cost-Benefit Analysis. Design decisions must ultimately be made with cost in mind. A design that incorporates additional risk-reduction measures almost always results in increased design and/or construction costs. If mitigation measures are incorporated early in the design process, they will likely be less intrusive and have a lower cost impact.

> **Key Point**   One useful tool for deciding between mitigation options is a relative or absolute cost-benefit analysis.

The cost of protection, when it is added, must be evaluated over the life of the building. As with performance objectives, the decision of whether to include a mitigation measure relies on the owners' goals for the facility. Budget, aesthetic implications, and the value perceived in reducing risk will also factor into owners' decisions. Once a set of potential mitigation options has been developed, the optimal options are selected, and design proceeds. Various tools can be used to select the best option, including benefit-cost analysis, or risk-cost analysis, which provide a mechanism to understand the relative cost-effectiveness of mitigation options.

Figure 7.11 provides a simplified format for a risk-management effort that includes cost. Relative values for cost and effectiveness of the mitigation measure are assigned. Based on the risk level, the matrix format can transparently prioritize measures that can be incorporated into the facility to reduce risk. The highest values of relative risk/cost ranking can be explored further, because these represent mitigations that reduce the significant risks in a cost-effective manner.

Figure 7.12 provides a sample risk analysis for a building subject to a 500-year windstorm. In the first four columns on the left, risk is

---

FIGURE 7.11   **Cost-Benefit Risk-Analysis Framework.**

	Space/ function	Natural hazards scenarios	Operational impact	Life safety impact	Relative risk	Mitigation measures	Relative mitigation effectiveness	Relative mitigation cost	Relative cost effectiveness	Relative risk/ cost ranking
1										
2										

(*Source:* Arup.)

calculated as a function of the probability of the natural hazard event and the criticality of the event. As described in this chapter, criticality is based on the stakeholders' valuation of the building and the capacity of the building to perform adequately during the extreme event.

For the wind hazard analyzed in Figure 7.12, seven sample mitigation options are considered. These options all aim to improve the performance of the building should the event occur and are in line with the owner's objectives. For each mitigation option, the relative effectiveness and cost are estimated based on the engineers' evaluation, resulting in a value for relative cost-effectiveness. The resulting final right-hand column in Figure 7.12 provides a relative risk/cost ranking for the seven measures proposed to mitigate the risk. Measures with dark highlighting are most cost-effective and should be adopted. Measures in medium highlighting are also cost-effective and are strongly recommended. Although measures with no highlighting have lower cost-effectiveness, they should also be considered for adoption. All measures included in the analysis are relevant.

Loss Estimation. During the risk-management process, it is often necessary to predict the financial losses associated with various natural-hazard events. Various forms of loss estimation exist that can account for direct physical damage (structural and equipment), business interruption, economic loss, and social impact. The term *probable maximum loss* (PML), popularized in the insurance industry in the 1980s, has long been used in the industry to quantify maximum loss associated with a catastrophic event. PML estimations are often quoted as a percentage of value of the building or contents. Over the past two decades, many definitions for PML have been developed, with no industry or professional consensus on what PML means or how it is computed. For this reason, ASTM standard E 2026-99 recommends that new terms be used for earthquake loss estimation— *probable loss* and *scenario loss* [11].

HAZUS-MH is a comprehensive loss-estimation tool that was developed by FEMA, in conjunction with the National Institute of Building Sciences (NIBS). It is used to analyze potential losses from floods, hurricane winds, and earthquakes. HAZUS-MH provides for three levels of analysis, ranging from probabilistic to deterministic [12].

- *Level 1:* High-level probabilistic loss assessment is based on nationwide databases.
- *Level 2:* Assessment incorporates the input of local emergency management personnel, city planners, and other local officials.

FIGURE 7.12 Risk Assessment and Management Example for a 500-Year Wind.

Probability	Importance (stakeholder values)	Resistance of building (engineering assessment)	Risk	#	Mitigation options	Relative mitigation effect	Relative mitigation cost	Relative cost effect	Relative risk/cost ranking
2	5	2.4	4.2	1	Improve connections by adding welded plates.	2	2	1	4.2
				2	Option A to increase capacity of lateral-load resisting system.	2	3	0.67	2.8
				3	Option B to increase capacity of lateral-load resisting system.	3	4	0.75	3.15
				4	Option C to increase capacity of lateral-load resisting system.	4	5	0.8	3.4
				5	Connect exterior elements to base, such as trash containers.	2	1	2	8.4
				6	Improve connections for large windows.	3	3	1	4.2
				7	Provide protection against fragmentation for windows.	2	3	0.67	2.8

Note: Mitigation measures are highlighted in order of cost-effectiveness. The darker the shade, the more cost-effective the measure.

(*Source:* Arup.)

- *Level 3:* Analysis requires engineering and other expertise to provide the most accurate estimate of loss.

Various other catastrophic loss models are available, some incorporating advanced computer modeling. For individual buildings and facilities, site-specific loss assessments should be performed. For a large portfolio of buildings or facilities, catastrophe loss models can be used. Once mitigation measures have been explored and prioritized based on risk level and cost-effectiveness, they can then be designed. Design can range from prescriptive to performance based.

DESIGNING FOR NATURAL HAZARDS

Techniques for the design of buildings to mitigate risk associated with natural hazards have improved substantially in recent years. From developments in life safety design to the incorporation of more financially driven performance-based techniques, designers have a wealth of knowledge and tools at their disposal.

Design Philosophies

Prescriptive Design. Building codes rely on simple analysis methods and prescriptive details to achieve a reasonable level of life safety during hazardous events. The methods and details are broadly applicable to general building construction. The rules of building codes are those deemed necessary to provide a minimum performance level to ensure pubic safety. Although several prescriptive code provisions exist for improved performance of critical facilities (e.g., importance factors for hospitals), the design provisions are for standard types of structures and often do not take specific aspects of the structure into account.

Performance-Based Design. Performance-based design provides a means of making design decisions applicable to life safety, damage reduction, and business continuity as they relate to exposure to natural and man-made hazards. Performance-based design can provide a means for considering the unique qualities of each building and meeting stakeholders' needs.

Key Point Stakeholders should be involved from the beginning of a project and should be educated in the trade-offs and meaning of design decisions so that they can establish the acceptable level of risk.

A performance-based design approach provides the basis for the selection of design options based on the specific needs of the project and provides a mechanism for determining what levels of safety and associated costs are acceptable to the stakeholders.

The performance-based design procedure, which is described in detail in Chapter 2, begins with establishing the acceptable risk and appropriate performance levels for the building. Acceptable risk is the maximum level of damage that can be tolerated for a realistic risk-event scenario or probability. For each natural hazard, methods are available to measure the magnitude of such events and their probability. Terminology is also available to describe levels of damage or performance levels.

For example, the *SFPE Engineering Guide to Performance-Based Fire Protection* [13] provides a variety of both life safety and non-life safety criteria that can be considered during the design process. Life safety criteria include thermal effects, toxicity, and visibility. Non-life safety criteria include thermal effects, fire spread, smoke damage, fire barrier damage and structural integrity, damage to exposed properties, and damage to the environment. For each criterion, quantifiable performance levels can be set based on the needs of the individual project.

The *ICC Performance Code for Buildings and Facilities* [14] identifies four performance levels, each of which can address structural damage, nonstructural systems, occupant hazards, overall extent of damage, and hazardous materials. The levels of damage are as follows:

- Mild impact
- Moderate impact
- High impact
- Severe impact

When brought fully into the decision process, many owners are prepared to pay for higher levels of performance. For example, a hospital owner or a chip manufacturer (to maintain market share following an event) may want to design for better performance. In contrast, the owner of a warehouse with easily replaceable inventory may wish to design for the code-based minimum.

Key Point   Performance-based design is currently most advanced in seismic design, and substantially less developed for floods and high winds.

Over the past 10 to 15 years, performance-based seismic design has been formalized, with performance levels specifically defined. Advances in materials science, physical research, observations of building damage, and analytical studies have led to a better understanding of building behavior. Studies continue throughout the world.

Seismic Design

The design of buildings for seismic events has evolved significantly over the past 75 years in the United States (and throughout the world). This has been most evident in the development of seismic building codes. Most agree that based on California's earthquake experiences, regulation through a properly enforced seismic code has largely fulfilled the intent of ensuring an acceptable level of safety against death and injuries.

Code History. Initial regulations for the protection of buildings against earthquakes first appeared in the Uniform Building Code (UBC) in California in 1927. In the 1960s, the earthquake-resistant design provisions of the three model codes [National Building Code (NBC), Standard Building Code (SBC), and the UBC] began to be based on recommendations developed by the Structural Engineers Association of California (SEAOC). SEAOC's "Blue Book" [15] was first published in 1959 [16].

Following the 1971 San Fernando earthquake, FEMA provided support for the development and update of a document developed by the Applied Technology Council, now titled the *NEHRP Recommended Provisions for Seismic Regulations for New Buildings and Other Structures* [17]. The seismic provisions of the recently developed International Building Code (IBC) [18] are based primarily on the NEHRP provisions. The American Society of Civil Engineers (ASCE) publishes ASCE 7, *Minimum Design Loads for Buildings and Other Structures* [19], which provides dead, live, seismic, and other loading criteria. The National Fire Protection Association has also developed a model building code, *NFPA 5000®, Building Construction and Safety Code®*.

Most existing building codes were developed to reduce risk to health and safety, not to reduce property loss. However, the high-level goals and objectives contained in *NFPA 5000* do address the concept of property protection. In particular, property protection is a consideration as it relates to achieving a primary goal—safety, health, building usability, and public welfare. Flood-resistant design and construction criteria are examples of public-welfare goals. These features help to determine site conditions for buildings, among other criteria, to minimize property loss; insurance payouts; and, in the most drastic case, relocation of entire cities or towns. Providing this level of protection is in the best interest of the public welfare. As the codes have evolved, they have indirectly and directly assisted in reducing building damage.

Prescriptive Code-Based Seismic Design. In the traditional prescriptive code-based approach, the lateral load for analysis and design of a structure is determined for a certain level of earthquake. The earthquake level is selected based on the probability of exceedance (i.e., an event has an X percent chance of being exceeded in Y years) or on the return period (i.e., an event that happens approximately every Z years), both are measures of the frequency of occurrence of a certain magnitude of earthquake. In many code-based applications on the West Coast of the United States, the intended life of the structure is 50 years, and an earthquake with a probability of exceedance equal to 10 percent in 50 years is selected for design. The corresponding return period (calculated by a mathematical relationship) is 475 years. This earthquake level is sometimes termed as the *design-basis earthquake,* or DBE. The structure is designed such that the strength capacity is more than the demand due to the lateral load from the design-basis earthquake, reduced for the expected ductility and reserve strength in the framing system.

As discussed earlier, prescriptive methods may not fully consider the stakeholders' interests, and a performance-based approach may be more appropriate. The 1994 Northridge, California earthquake provides a good example of the need for performance-based design. Many buildings in the epicentral region had been designed to standards current at the time of the earthquake. It could be considered that these structures performed well, because there were relatively few deaths (58). However, approximately 100,000 people were displaced from their homes following the earthquake, and the earthquake caused hundreds of millions of dollars in building damage [16]. Figure 7.13 shows an example of damage to a building in Northridge following the earthquake.

FIGURE 7.13 Reinforced Concrete Structure at S. Barrington Avenue Following the Northridge Earthquake.

(*Source:* Courtesy National Information Service for Earthquake Engineering, University of California, Berkeley.)

Performance-Based Seismic Design. Discrete performance levels of the structure are defined based on the condition and engineering judgment.

Key Point In a performance-based design approach, the condition of the structure after an earthquake is used to assess the performance level of the structure.

The defined performance levels of a reinforced concrete frame may be as follows:

- Operational: No visible damage
- Immediate occupancy: Minor cracking in the members without any crushing
- Life safety: Spalling of concrete from columns and extensive cracking in beams
- Collapse prevention: Extensive cracking in columns and formation of hinges, permanent deformation of the structure

For analysis of a building, performance is quantified through deformation demands on the structure, which are often calculated by a lateral-load analysis. The target performances of the structure for different earthquake levels are selected from a representative matrix, such as that shown in Figure 7.14 [16].

To achieve the desired deformation, provisions for ductility are introduced in the structural components. The performance-based approach also provides a guideline for seismic rehabilitation and risk assessment.

Design for Other Natural Hazards

The same degree of research is not available for other natural hazards, as well as associated flooding and high winds, as there is for earthquakes. Most design for non-earthquake events is based on prescriptive code-based methods, some of which are effective for life safety but may not reflect stakeholder interests.

Designing for Floods. Existing minimum requirements in model building codes and regulations are based on the National Flood

---

FIGURE 7.14   **Performance Matrix for Seismic Loads.**

Earthquake level in probability of exceedance	Return period (years)	Target structure performance levels			
		Operational	Immediate occupancy	Life safety	Collapse prevention
50% in 50 years	72				
20% in 50 years	225				
10% in 50 years	474				
2% in 50 years	2475				

(*Source:* FEMA, 2000. *Guidelines for the Seismic Rehabilitation of Buildings,* Publication 356, Federal Emergency Management Agency, Washington, DC.)

Insurance Program (NFIP), dating back to 1968 [20]. Evidence of the effectiveness of the NFIP minimum requirements is found in flood insurance claim payment statistics. Buildings that predate the NFIP requirements are not necessarily constructed to resist floods.

> **Key Point**   Buildings that postdate NFIP legislation, which was originally passed in 1968, are designed to resist floods.

NFIP reports state that buildings meeting minimum NFIP requirements experience 70 percent less damage than do buildings that predate the NFIP. The NFIP's performance requirements for site work are as follows [16]:

- Building sites shall be reasonably safe from flooding.
- Adequate site drainage shall be provided to reduce flood exposure to flooding.
- New and replacement sanitary sewage systems shall be designed to minimize or eliminate infiltration of floodwater into the system and discharge from the systems into floodwaters.
- Development in floodways shall be prohibited unless engineering analyses show that there will be no increases in flood levels.

The NFIP's performance requirements for new buildings proposed for flood-hazard areas are as follows [16]:

- Buildings shall be designed and adequately anchored to prevent flotation, collapse, or lateral movement resulting from hydrodynamic and hydrostatic loads, including the effects of buoyancy.
- Buildings shall be constructed by methods and practices that minimize flood damage (primarily by elevating to or above the base flood level or by specially designed and certified floodproofing measures).
- Buildings shall be constructed with electrical, plumbing, heating, ventilation, and air-conditioning equipment and other service facilities that are designed and/or located so as to prevent water entering or accumulating within the components.

The first codes to include comprehensive provisions to address flood hazards were the 2000 IBC [18] and *NFPA 5000,* and they are consistent with the minimum provisions of the NFIP. These codes refer to standards such as those in ASCE 7 [19], which require that applicable loads be accounted for in the design. The designer must identify the pertinent, site-specific characteristics and then use ASCE 7 to determine the specific and combined loads. The 1998 edition of ASCE 7 was the first version of the standard to explicitly include flood loads, including hydrostatic loads, hydrodynamic loads (velocity and waves), and debris impact. The 2000 IBC and *NFPA 5000* also refer to a standard first published by the ASCE in 1998, ASCE 24, *Flood Resistant Design and Construction* [16, 21].

As with the design for seismic loads, designing for floods is usually based on a specific return period. Typically, the return period considered in design is 100 years. To determine the magnitude of the hazard, a probabilistic assessment is usually conducted, considering meteorological sources such as precipitation and storm surge. In some areas, run-up from tsunami is also included in the probabilistic analysis. Failure of dams and levees is not considered in regional probabilistic studies of flooding. Other magnitudes that are often considered are shown in Table 7.1 [21].

Designing for High Winds. In the United States, building code design criteria for high wind has been expanded greatly since the mid-1980s. Some of the major changes relate to roof coverings and roof equipment. The majority of these additional provisions were added after Hurricanes Hugo (1989) and Andrew (1992). The 2003 editions of *NFPA 5000* and the IBC were the first model codes to address wind loads on parapets and rooftop equipment [16, 22].

In general, ASCE 7 has been more reflective of the current state of knowledge for wind design loads than the model codes. Adoption of ASCE 7 for wind design loads has typically resulted in higher design loads [16].

The 2000 edition of the IBC was the first model code to address glazed protection, or wind-borne debris requirements for buildings

TABLE 7.1 NFIP/ASCE 24/ICC Criteria for Flood Hazard

Magnitude of Event	Frequency of Occurrence
Very large	Determined on a site-specific basis
Large	Determined on a site-specific basis
Medium	500 years
Small	100 years

Source: NFIP/ASCE 24/CC Criteria for Flood Hazard.

located in hurricane-prone regions (based on the 1998 edition of ASCE 7). The 1995 edition of ASCE 7 was the first edition to address wind-borne debris requirements [16].

The 2003 editions of the IBC and the *NFPA 5000* are considered reasonable for design against hurricanes except that the *IBC* does not account for water infiltration due to puncture of the roof membrane, nor does it adequately address the vulnerabilities of brittle roof coverings (such as tile) to missile-induced damage and subsequent progressive cascading failure. The 2003 IBC and the *NFPA 5000* do not address tornadoes, and they are ineffective for this type of storm [16].

NFPA 5000, the IBC, and the ASCE 7 do not require buildings to be designed for tornadoes, nor are occupant shelters mandated in buildings located in tornado-prone regions. This is mainly due to the fact that because of the extremely high pressures and missile loads, constructing tornado-resistant buildings is very expensive. When tornado design is considered, the emphasis typically is on occupant protection, which is achieved by "hardening" portions of a building for use as a safe haven. FEMA Publication 431 should be used for guidance [16, 23].

For design, probabilistic studies of high winds typically consider return periods of 50 or 100 years. These studies often consider hurricane and topographically based windstorm conditions. Tornadoes are often considered in separate probabilistic studies due to the localized and extreme nature of tornado damage.

Assessment of the wind resistance of the building envelope and rooftop equipment and the corresponding damage susceptibility is a challenge, and analytical tools are currently not available for many envelope systems and components. Many elements require physical testing to determine their load-carrying capacity. Finite element simulations may begin to replace physical testing in the future.

SUMMARY

Natural hazards are recurring events; various magnitudes of events are associated with specific frequencies. Because of their relative predictability, natural hazards are ideally suited for risk-informed performance-based design. Risk can be assessed, quantified, managed, and designed for in a relatively direct manner. More research is needed, especially for flood and high wind loads, to more accurately quantify the nature of the hazards and associated building response. When possible, a multihazard approach should be taken in risk assessment and design, both with other natural hazards and other extreme events presented in this book.

As we become more able to mitigate the risks of natural hazards, associated disasters should perhaps be called "human-induced" as opposed to "natural" disasters.

BIBLIOGRAPHY

References Cited

1. Wood, H. O., and Neumann, F., 1931. "Modified Mercalli Intensity Scale of 1931," *Seismological Society of America Bulletin,* Vol. 21, No. 4, pp. 277–283.

2. Cornell, C. A., 1968. "Engineering Seismic Risk Analysis," *Bulletin of the Seismological Society of America,* Vol. 58, pp. 1583–1606.

3. U.S. National Earthquake Hazards Reduction Program (NEHRP) National Seismic Hazard Maps, http://earthquake.usgs.gov/hazmaps/.

4. L. R. Johnson Associates, 1992. "Floodplain Management in the United States: An Assessment Report, Vol. 2; Full Report," FIA-18, Federal Interagency Floodplain Management Task Force, Washington, DC.

5. Coch, N. K., 1995. *GEOHAZARDS: Natural and Human,* Prentice Hall, Upper Saddle River, NJ.

6. Interagency Advisory Committee on Water Data, 1982. "Guidelines for Determining Flood Flow Frequency," Bulletin 17B of the Hydrology Subcommittee, Department of Interior, U.S. Geological Survey, Office of Water Data Coordination, Reston, VA.

7. FEMA, 1995. "Flood Insurance Study Guidelines and Specifications for Study Contractors," Publication 37, Federal Emergency Management Agency, Washington, DC.

8. FEMA, 2005. Flood Mapping Resources, www.fema.gov/fhm/ot_main.shtm and www.fema.gov/fhm/tsdindex.shtm.

9. Neumann, C. J., Jarvinen, B. R., McAdie, C. J., and Elms, J. D., 1993. Supplements (1994) to *Tropical Cyclones of the North Atlantic Ocean—1871 to 1992,* National Oceanographic and Atmospheric Administration, National Climactic Data Center, Ashville, NC, and National Hurricane Center, Coral Gables, FL.

10. Golden, J., and Snow, J., 1991. "Mitigation Against Extreme Windstorms," *Review of Geophysics,* Vol. 29, No. 4, pp. 477–504.

11. ASTM, 2005. *Standard Guide for the Estimation of Building Damageability in Earthquakes,* ASTM E 2026-99, ASTM International, West Conshohocken, PA.

12. FEMA, HAZUS, www.fema.gov/hazus.

13. SFPE, 2003. *SFPE Engineering Guide to Performance-Based Fire Protection Analysis and Design of Buildings.* Society of Fire Protection Engineers, SFPE Task Group on Performance-Based Analysis and Design, National Fire Protection Association, Quincy, MA.

14. ICC, 2003. *International Performance Code for Buildings and Facilities,* International Code Council, Falls Church, VA.

15. SEONC, 1999. "Recommended Lateral Force Requirements and Commentary," Seismology Committee, prepared by SEONC, published by the International Conference of Building Officials, Whittier, CA.

16. FEMA, 2004. *Design Guide for Improving School Safety in Earthquakes, Floods, and High Winds,* Publication 424, Federal Emergency Management Agency, Washington, DC.

17. BSSC, 2003. "The 2003 NEHRP Recommended Provisions for New Buildings and Other Structures, Part 1: Provisions (FEMA 450)," Building Seismic Safety Council, Washington, DC.

18. ICC, 2000. *International Building Code,* International Code Council, Falls Church, VA.

19. ASCE, 2005. *Minimum Design Loads for Buildings and Other Structures,* ASCE/SEI 7-05, American Society of Civil Engineers, Reston, VA.

20. National Flood Insurance Program (NFIP), www.floods.org/stcoor.htm.

21. ASCE, 2000. *Flood Resistant Design and Construction,* ASCE/SEI 24-98, American Society of Civil Engineers, Reston, VA.

22. ICC, 2003. *International Building Code,* International Code Council, Falls Church, VA.

23. FEMA, 2003. *Tornado Protection: Selecting Refuge Areas in Buildings,* Publication 431, Federal Emergency Management Agency, Washington, DC.

NFPA Codes, Standards, and Recommended Practices

NFPA Publications. The following is a list of NFPA codes, standards, and recommended practices cited in this chapter. See the latest version of the *NFPA Catalog* for availability of current editions of these documents.

NFPA 5000®, Building Construction and Safety Code®

8

Fire Events

Richard Custer
Chris Marrion
Matt Johann

The objectives of this chapter are to discuss potential ways that fires may start from or lead to extreme events and to identify some of the key components of the quantification of these fires and their effects on people, property, and business continuity. Although the majority of fire events are not classified as extreme events, some fires can be extreme events or they can lead to or stem from other types of extreme events. This chapter provides some perspective regarding how fire fits into extreme events and how fire can be predicted in order to determine its impact and to design for protection against it. Rational design concepts and risk-assessment techniques, as detailed in Chapters 2 and 4, are discussed as methods for considering fire in performance-based design for extreme events.

This chapter helps set the stage for further discussion regarding building design to address extreme events, as presented in Chapter 11. Because fire is an important component of many extreme events, it is a critical consideration when developing mitigation strategies. This chapter discusses how this consideration can be accomplished, and Chapter 11 combines this into the design process.

EXTREME EVENTS AND FIRE

Fire Origin and Cause

The *origin* of a fire is the point or area where the ignition source and the first fuel ignited come together resulting in a fire. The origin of a fire may be virtually anywhere that fuels and ignition sources exist. The *cause* of a fire is represented by the circumstances and factors that brought the ignition source and the fuel together. Origin and cause analysis of fires is discussed in detail in NFPA 921, *Guide for Fire and Explosion Investigations.*

Fires are caused by a number of circumstances and factors, some accidental or unintentional, some natural, and others by deliberate acts. Accidental fires include smoking-related ignitions and equipment failures (either due to design or misuse). They are characterized by the lack of intent for the fire to be initiated or spread. Fires from natural causes are those in which human intent or intervention is not involved in the initiation of the event. Natural fires arise from occurrences such as lightning, wind, landslides, and earthquakes. Deliberately caused fires, often called *incendiary fires,* come about as the result of direct, purposeful human action.

Fire-Related Extreme Events

Typically, fire-related extreme events can be placed into two categories. The first category includes fires that arise from intentional events related to arson or to terrorist activity involving the use of explosives, bombs, aircraft or missile assault, or other attacks that typically generate heat or an ignition source resulting in combustion. Intentional acts such as chemical or biological terrorism also may result in the initiation of a fire through the use of heat-generating delivery mechanisms or devices, such as explosives or thermal charges. The second category includes fires that result from accidental or natural causes. Fire following an earthquake, which is addressed in NFPA's "Fire Investigation Report: Kobe Earthquake" [1] and other sources [2, 3], is a widely known example. Fires initiated by lightning or by fallen power lines during a storm are also common.

Table 8.1 lists the major causes of fires in the United States between 1994 and 1998. It is evident that incendiary or suspicious causes resulted in the largest proportion of fires and led to the largest proportions of both deaths and injuries, as well as the most property damage (in terms of monetary value).

Unintentional Events. In some instances, the initial fire is not a large, single event, and in the absence of other circumstances, it would not constitute a large or critical loss that could be characterized as an extreme event. However, a small unintentional (accidental) fire in the right place at the right time can have extreme consequences, even if did not arise from a natural event or intentional act. Extreme event fires may also be unintentional fires of low

TABLE 8.1 Major Causes of U.S. Structure Fires Reported to Fire Departments, 1994–1998 annual average

Cause	Civilian Deaths	Civilian Injuries	Direct Property Damage (in million dollars)	Fires
Defined by Heat Source				
Smoking material (i.e., lighted tobacco product)	990	2,540	430	35,400
Electric-powered equipment	970	7,670	2,484	208,900
Open flame (e.g., match, lighter, torch, candle)	820	5,550	1,563	106,000
Fueled equipment	640	3,580	1,149	119,300
Defined by Equipment Involved				
Heating equipment	490	1,910	839	75,700
Electrical distribution system	350	1,670	1,028	58,100
Cooking equipment	330	5,120	560	116,300
Defined by First Ignited Item				
Upholstered furniture	640	1,670	272	15,000
Mattress or bedding	540	2,890	373	29,700
Structural member or framing	320	880	1,111	48,700
Defined by Material in First Ignited Item				
Fabric, textile, or fur	1,570	6,490	1,077	89,700
Wood or paper	920	3,580	2,947	174,100
Flammable or combustible liquid	300	2,160	505	30,000
Defined by Behavior or Event				
Mechanical or electrical failure	670	3,700	2,078	158,300
Incendiary or suspicious causes	640	2,530	1,680	94,500
Abandoning something (e.g., cigarette)	610	1,960	374	35,300
Child playing	300	2,170	284	23,500

Source: Cote, A. (Ed.), 2003. *Fire Protection Handbook,* National Fire Protection Association, Quincy, MA, Table 2.1.9.

frequency but high severity, such as a major fire resulting from a train derailment and ignition of hazardous cargo in a heavily populated urban area.

Key Point Extreme consequences caused by fire are often not directly related to the size of the fire. For instance, a small accidental fire in the right place at the right time can have extreme consequences, even if it did not arise from a natural event or intentional act.

Intentional Events. As is evident from Table 8.1, *incendiary,* or suspicious, causes are the largest source of fire injuries, deaths, and property damage in the United States. A carefully thought out intentional small fire, or one resulting from a terrorist act, could result in extreme consequences. For example, small fires can generate corrosive or conductive products of combustion that could, if strategically initiated, cripple telecommunications systems. Another example of an intentional fire leading to an extreme event is the setting of forest fires or fires that lead directly to forest fires. Arson is the leading cause of wildland fires, and such fires can destroy multiple homes and burn hundreds of acres of land. Such fires could be set to impact critical facilities, such as the watersheds of power distribution systems.

Arson or *incendiary fires* often involve some type of accelerant, usually a combustible or flammable liquid. The accelerant is typically used as the initial fuel source and is selected by the arsonist to create a fast-developing fire that spreads rapidly. Accelerants may be widely distributed and involve secondary combustible items to speed fire spread to other locations while at the same time increasing heat release rates and fire duration.

Extreme Event Fire Scenarios

Serious earthquakes frequently lead to ignitions from various sources, including gas line breaks and electrical short circuiting [2–4]. Other events, such as bomb blasts and lightning, can also lead to fires. Historical examples of fires caused by other extreme events are listed in Table 8.2 [2, 3, 4]. Please refer to Chapter 7 for further information regarding natural events that can lead to fires and other extreme events.

Fires can also cause other extreme events. A common example is an explosion initiated by a fire. Table 8.3 provides various historical examples of extreme events that were initiated by fires [5, 6]. Characteristics of some specific extreme event scenarios are presented in the following sections.

Key Point In fire safety planning and design, it is important to consider both fires resulting from extreme events and extreme events that can arise from fires.

Earthquakes. When an earthquake occurs, fire may result from the introduction of new ignition and fuel sources. To make matters worse, many building fire safety features can be compromised by earthquake forces. For instance, although modern sprinkler systems are designed to resist earthquakes of certain magnitudes, some older systems may not be adequately designed. In addition, city water mains often break and interrupt the water supply, and water supplies to fire hydrants may not be available for fire service operations [7, 8].

TABLE 8.2 Selected Historical Fires Caused by Extreme Events

Location	Date	Event	Result
California	April 18, 1906	Earthquake (M 8.3)	59 ignitions
Japan	September 1, 1923	Earthquake (M 7.9)	277 ignitions
Alaska	March 28, 1964	Earthquake (M 8.3)	7 ignitions
California	February 9, 1971	Earthquake (M 6.7)	149 ignitions
Illinois	September 24, 1977	Lightning	Explosion and fire: Two fuel tanks
California	October 1, 1987	Earthquake (M 6.0)	38 ignitions
California	October 17, 1989	Earthquake (M 7.1)	58 ignitions
New York	February 26, 1993	Terrorist attack	1 ignition
California	January 17, 1994	Earthquake (M 6.8)	92 ignitions
Japan	January 17, 1995	Earthquake (M 6.9)	237 ignitions
New York	September 11, 2001	Terrorist attack	6 ignitions

Sources: Data compiled from Borden, F. W., 1995. "Kobe Earthquake: Lessons for the United States," *Fire Engineering*, Vol. 148, No. 5, pages 43–45, 48, NISTR, 1997. *Fires Following the Northridge and Kobe Earthquakes*, NISTIR 6030, National Institute of Standards and Technology, Gaithersburg, MD; Scawthorn, C., Eidinger, J., and Schiff, A., (Eds.), 2005. *Fire Following Earthquake*, Technical Council on Lifeline Earthquake Engineering, Monograph 26, American Society of Civil Engineers, Reston VA.

TABLE 8.3   Selected Historical Extreme Events Caused by Fires

Location	Date	Cause	Result
Japan	June 16, 1964	Crude-oil fire	Explosion: 97 tanks damaged
France	January 4, 1966	Car fire near butane tank	BLEVE: 5 tanks damaged
Pennsylvania	August 17, 1975	Crude-oil fire	Explosion: 4 tanks damages
New Jersey	January 7, 1983	Gasoline fire	Explosion: 4 tanks damaged
Italy	December 21, 1985	Gasoline fire	Explosion: 24 tanks damaged
Nevada	May 4, 1988	Ammonium perchlorate fire	Explosion: Numerous buildings damaged

Sources: Data compiled from Garrison, W. G. (Ed.), 1988. *100 Large Losses: A Thirty-Year Review of Property Damage Losses in the Hydrocarbon Chemical Industries,* M&M Protection Consultants, Chicago, IL; Zalosh, R. G., 2003. *Industrial Fire Protection Engineering,* John Wiley & Sons, West Sussex, England.

Failures in power and gas distribution systems have been identified as factors contributing to the initiation of fires following past earthquakes [9]. For instance, electrical lines may be severed and introduce an ignition source through overheating, arcing, or sparking. Other electrical ignition sources include uninterruptible power sources and large battery-based power supplies, such as those found in telecommunications facilities.

Gas mains and lines may rupture both outside and inside buildings; if ignition sources are present, the gas may ignite. Both city gas and bottled gas, such as propane, are subject to release. In addition to the release of flammable gases, stored ignitable liquids, such as heating oil, may be released from "day" tanks that may contain 250 gallons of liquid or more. Once ignited, these fires may propagate to adjacent combustible materials.

Key Point   In earthquake-prone facilities, locations where flammable gas or ignitible liquid releases are possible should be identified, and measures should be taken to provide means to confine or control earthquake-related fires.

The technical feasibility of seismically operated shutoffs and control mechanisms should be assessed along with a cost-benefit analysis for the use of such systems. Further, guidelines for the installation and use of these devices should be developed. As a part of this analysis, the susceptibility of gas leaks to ignition should be examined.

Secondary Incidents After Impact. Fires may also begin as a secondary incident after an impact. These fires have many of the same consequences as fires after earthquakes, but they are generally confined to the impacted structure. In addition to being an ignition source for fuels contained within the impacted structure, the vehicle or device creating the impact may itself contain liquid fuels or combustible materials (seating, insulation, hydraulic fluids, etc.) that could ignite and initiate a building fire. Depending on the quantity, containment, force of impact, and so on, liquid fuels may spread to a relatively large area and ignite at impact or when reaching other ignition sources. Combustible materials remote from the area of impact may be ignited along with materials in the vicinity. The impact forces may also affect sprinkler and standpipe systems, as well as firewalls and other interior fire barriers, such as occurred in World Trade Center Towers 1 and 2 in the events of September 11, 2001 [10].

The structure being impacted may also contain fuel sources that ignite. This may include a fire starting due to gas lines being broken and igniting or severed electrical power lines sparking, arcing, or overheating and coming into contact with combustible materials.

Bomb Blasts. The heat generated by bomb blasts can also start fires. As with earthquakes and impacts, bomb blasts can affect building sprinkler systems, built-in fire barriers, and compartmentation, including stair shafts. In all of these situations, compromised fire-safety features can result in greater fire growth and increased spread of fire and smoke. Initial bomb blast damage is generally much more localized than, say, earthquakes and conflagrations involving many buildings; however, it is largely dependent on the size of the bomb, where it was detonated, the construction type of the building, and other factors.

Chemical, Biological, and Radiological Incidents. As with bombs, some devices employed to deliver chemical, biological, and radiological (CBR) agents can act as ignition sources.

Key Point In situations where fire exists with the release of chemical, biological, or radiological agents, convection from the flow of heated gases can distribute agents throughout a building or area.

If a building is equipped with a smoke management system, as is the case in many recently constructed high-rise buildings, the system may confine a CBR agent and the accompanying smoke to the area of fire origination. If, however, a CBR agent and the accompanying spreads significantly before the smoke management system begins to operate, the system may actually enhance contamination. When developing plans for managing CBR incidents, consideration should be given to the effects of the building heating, ventilation, and air-conditioning systems.

The operation of automatic sprinkler systems during a fire following a CBR event may act to dilute soluble hazardous materials, but it may also spread contamination, possibly into drains or runoff areas. Consideration should be given to providing containment. Refer to Chapter 6 for more information regarding CBR incidents.

QUANTIFYING FIRES

When designing building systems for fire safety or for emergency fire response and evacuation planning, it is important to understand how fires are initiated, how they grow and spread, their maximum heat release rates, and how long they may last.

Fire Development

Fire is essentially an energy transfer process—first from the ignition source to the initial fuel, and then from the first burning item to adjacent items as the fire spreads. If the fire occurs in a compartment, temperatures will rise and the fire may spread by radiation and convection to adjacent compartments where items will be ignited, and in the absence of intervention through fire safety design or manual suppression, the process will continue until the structure is fully involved or the available fuels are consumed. As the fire grows and spreads, energy transferred to the building structure may cause weakening that could lead to local or full building collapse (refer to Chapter 9 for further discussion of fire's effects on structures).

The energy or severity of a fire is characterized in terms of its heat output or heat release rate (HRR). The HRR of a fire in the open may be constant (steady state), as with a candle flame or a steadily burning pan of ignitable liquid, or it may increase as the fire grows and involves additional fuel and decrease as the fire decays due to lack of fuel. Various HRR curves are provided in Figure 8.1. Note that the curves in this figure are not to scale and that the figure is not intended to provide specific HRR data, but instead convey the general burning behavior of different types of fires. A number of resources

FIGURE 8.1   **Heat Release Rate Curves.**

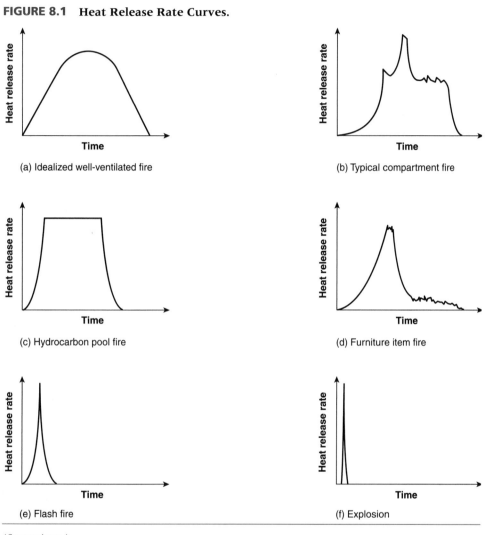

(a) Idealized well-ventilated fire

(b) Typical compartment fire

(c) Hydrocarbon pool fire

(d) Furniture item fire

(e) Flash fire

(f) Explosion

(*Source:* Arup.)

are available that provide HRR data for a variety of products and materials, including *Heat Release in Fires* [11] and Chapter 3-1, "Heat Release Rates," in the *SFPE Handbook of Fire Protection Engineering* [12].

When quantifying potential fires, ignition is often defined as the beginning of the HRR curve. Ignition is achieved when self-sustaining combustion occurs in the absence of the ignition source. This is usually when the flame reaches a height of about 10 inches (25 centimeters) [13].

Fire in the Open

When a fire is in the open or in the very early stages of development in a building, it is not confined by walls or ceilings. Hot combustion products (e.g., carbon monoxide, carbon dioxide, and hydrogen cyanide), superheated air, and particulates (smoke) produced by combustion rise from the fire, and air from the surrounding area is drawn into its base at a low level. The rising column of hot air and fire products is called the *plume*. This is depicted graphically in Figure 8.2.

As the hot gases in the plume rise, cool air from the surroundings is drawn into the plume through a process called *entrainment*. The entrained air has two effects. First, the entrained air reduces the temperature of the plume gases such that the temperature along the centerline of the plume decreases as the height above the fire increases. The second effect is to increase the volume of heated air in the plume, resulting in an increase in the plume diameter with height above the fire and an increase in the volume of smoke.

Fire Under a Ceiling

If there is a ceiling above the fire, the rising plume is trapped and the smoke and hot gases will begin to turn and spread away laterally from the centerline of the plume, forming a hot upper layer. As the smoke and gases move away from the plume along the ceiling, heat is transferred to the ceiling, raising its temperature to some degree and lowering that of the smoke and gases. This process is shown in Figure 8.3.

Fire in a Compartment

For a fire in a compartment, the fire development process can be broken down into a number of phases. Typically, these phases are ig-

FIGURE 8.2   Fire in the Open.

(*Source:* Cote, A. (Ed.), 2003. *Fire Protection Handbook,* National Fire Protection Association, Quincy, MA, Figure 2.4.2.)

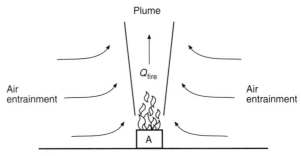

Note: A = source of fire, Q_{fire} = heat produced by the fire.

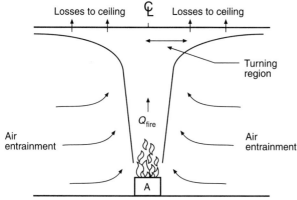

FIGURE 8.3 Fire Under a Ceiling Far from Walls.

(*Source:* Cote, A. (Ed.), 2003. *Fire Protection Handbook,* National Fire Protection Association, Quincy, MA, Figure 2.4.3.)

Note: A = source of fire, Q_{fire} = heat produced by the fire.

nition; growth, or preflashover; flashover; fully developed; and decay and extinction. Figure 8.4 combines these phases to construct a simplified complete fire curve. The phases of fire development are detailed in the following subsections. Note that not all fires involve flashover. Fuel, ventilation, or other factors may limit the size of a fire and prevent flashover.

Ignition. For ignition to occur, three components need to be present: fuel, an ignition source, and an oxidizer, usually oxygen in the air. The ignition source must be at a temperature at or above the ignition temperature of the fuel, and it must have enough energy to raise the fuel to that temperature. Because energy transfer drives the

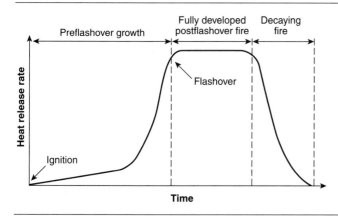

FIGURE 8.4 Phases of Fire Development.

(*Source:* Arup.)

fire process, the length of time that the fuel is exposed to a given energy source is crucial to ignition. A given fuel may require long exposure to reach ignition from a low energy source, even though the source is at its ignition temperature. Therefore, when assessing the credibility of potential ignition scenarios, the temperature, energy, area of contact, and duration of contact with potential fuel sources should be considered.

Numerous ignition sources are present throughout most buildings. These sources typically include electrical wiring and equipment, lighting, and cooking appliances. Ignition sources also include those items or processes that may only be present intermittently during the life cycle of a building (e.g., cutting and welding activities).

Growth (Pre-flashover) Stage. Once the ignition source has been identified, further analysis can lead to an understanding of how the fire will initially develop. For flaming fires, the initial rate of growth is determined by characteristics of the initial and secondary fuels and is considered to be fuel controlled. It is assumed that ventilation is sufficient such that the maximum amount of oxygen that the fire can use for combustion (the stoichiometric fuel-air ratio) is present, and the burning rate of the fire will depend only on the characteristics and arrangement of the fuels.

With regard to initial fuel sources, the rate of growth depends on a number of factors, which are addressed in Chapter 3.7, "Fire Hazard Analysis," of NFPA's *Fire Protection Handbook* [14]:

- Fuel type: Cellulosic, plastic, ignitible liquid, etc.
- Fuel state: Solid, liquid, gas
- Fuel configuration: For example, solid wood block versus sawdust (see Figure 8.5)
- Fuel location: In the open, against a wall, in a corner, against the ceiling
- Rate of heat release
- Rate of production of combustion products (smoke, CO, CO_2, HCl, HCN, etc.)

The combination of these parameters determines how a fire will develop during its initial phase. Any variation in one or more of these parameters will lead to a variation in fire development, and thus a wide range of fire development scenarios is possible. Different potential fuel sources involve different combinations of these para-

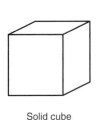  

Solid cube   Sticks (crib)   Sawdust

FIGURE 8.5 Variation of Fuel Configuration.

(*Source:* Cote, A. (Ed.), 2003. *Fire Protection Handbook,* National Fire Protection Association, Quincy, MA, Figure 3.7.3.)

meters, and thus exhibit unique fire growth characteristics, as shown in Figure 8.6.

The initial (growth) phase of a fire in a compartment results in the development of an upper layer of smoke and hot gases near the ceiling of the space. Early in the fire, this layer may be thin and may not form a continuous layer that reaches all boundaries of the room. Figure 8.7 shows this early condition. Note that the two boxes in the figure, A and B, represent generic fuel packages: fuel package A is burning, whereas fuel package B is not initially involved in the fire.

As the fire continues to grow, additional smoke and hot gases will be driven to the ceiling layer. The ceiling layer will begin to thicken,

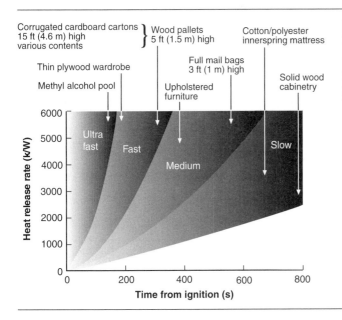

FIGURE 8.6 Variation of Fire Growth Rates.

(*Source:* Cote, A. (Ed.), 2003. *Fire Protection Handbook,* National Fire Protection Association, Quincy, MA, Figure 3.7.2.)

FIGURE 8.7   **Early Fire Development.**

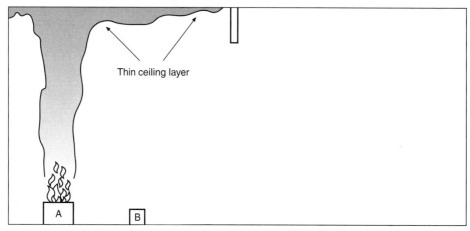

Note: A = source of fire.
        B = target fuel.

(*Source:* Cote, A. (Ed.), 2003. *Fire Protection Handbook,* National Fire Protection Association, Quincy, MA, Figure 2.4.4.)

FIGURE 8.8   **Initial Smoke Flow from Fire Compartment.**

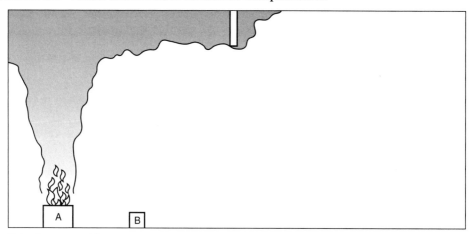

Note: A = source of fire.
        B = target fuel.

(*Source:* Cote, A. (Ed.), 2003. *Fire Protection Handbook,* National Fire Protection Association, Quincy, MA, Figure 2.4.5.)

with its lower boundary descending toward the floor. This may cause gases and smoke to flow out of open doors or other openings into adjacent spaces, as shown in Figure 8.8.

Assuming that the fire continues to grow, the upper layer will continue to increase in depth, and additional gases and smoke will flow from the compartment's openings. At the same time, temperatures within the compartment will continue to rise, and radiation from the hot upper layer will also increase, thus exposing other potential fuel packages to increasing heat fluxes.

Compartment fires result in a specific set of airflows. The fire's consumption of oxygen during the combustion process results in fresh (cool) air being drawn into the compartment near the floor. At the same time, buoyant flows of hot gases and smoke from the fire continue to enter the upper layer, which in turn expands. When openings are present, this leads to an outflow of hot gases and smoke. In an idealized model of this behavior, a neutral plane exists between the inflow of cool air and the outflow of hot gases and smoke; this neutral plane represents an area of zero net flow, as shown in Figure 8.9.

Eventually, the fire will produce sufficient conductive, convective, and/or radiant energy to ignite adjacent combustible material.

FIGURE 8.9 **Flows Within a Fire Compartment.**

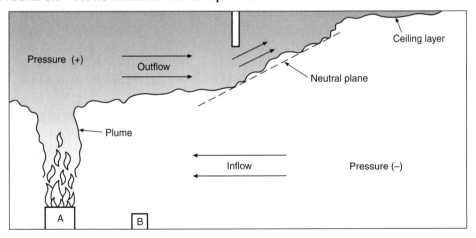

(*Source:* Cote, A. (Ed.), 2003. *Fire Protection Handbook,* National Fire Protection Association, Quincy, MA, Figure 2.4.8.)

Key Point Factors that affect the likelihood of spread to secondary fuel packages include the location of secondary fuels relative to initial fuels; the amount, distribution, and ignitability of the secondary fuels; and the heat transfer available, either through radiation, convection, or conduction, to result in ignition.

If secondary fuels are ignited or if there is a sufficient fuel supply in the initial fuel package, the fire may continue to grow to the point where significant heat fluxes radiate from the upper layer throughout the compartment. This condition results in the heating and eventual ignition of other fuel packages within the compartment.

Flashover. One of the critical aspects in assessing the potential severity of a fire is whether it reaches flashover. *Flashover* is the point at which the radiant energy in the hot gases in the upper portions of the compartment raises the temperature of unignited fuels, all items burning, or resulting in rapid transition from only one or two items burning to full room involvement. In general, flashover is characterized by an upper layer temperature of approximately 930 to 1110°F (500 to 600°C) and a radiant flux of approximately 105 Btu/ft²/sec (15 to 20 kW/m²) from the upper layer to unignited materials within the compartment [15]. Figure 8.10 shows the flashover condition.

Prior to flashover, excess air is typically available beyond that needed for combustion of the fuel. Thus, the fire growth rate and HRR are controlled by the chemical properties and physical arrangement of fuel (i.e., a fuel-controlled fire). After flashover, more fuel becomes involved, and the heat release rate, temperature, and smoke production rate increase rapidly to the point where there is insufficient air available for continued growth in the room. At this point, the burning rate becomes steady and is limited by the ventilation conditions. This fire condition is known as *ventilation-controlled burning*, or *steady-state burning*. This condition will continue until the fuel is consumed or until ventilation conditions change. Heat and smoke conditions in the compartment of origin quickly become untenable, and the fire spreads to adjacent compartments and remote areas of the building.

Evacuation of the area before flashover occurs is important for life safety. Several factors indicate whether flashover may occur in an enclosure, as described in Chapter 3-6, "Estimating Temperatures in Compartment Fires," of the *SFPE Handbook of Fire Protection Engineering* [12]. These factors include the following:

FIGURE 8.10 **Flashover Conditions Within a Fire Compartment.**

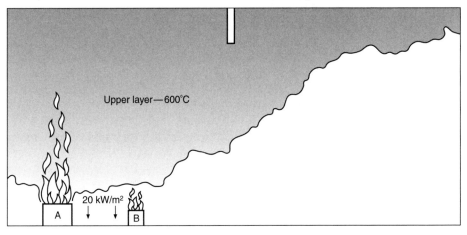

Upper layer—600°C

20 kW/m²

A   B

(*Source:* Cote, A. (Ed.), 2003. *Fire Protection Handbook,* National Fire Protection Association, Quincy, MA, Figure 2.4.9.)

- Surface area of the enclosure
- Area of enclosure openings
- Heat release rate
- Ventilation

Note that flashover is not always necessary for large-scale fire development. In fact, high-volume spaces, such as entire floors of buildings or warehouses, can reach full involvement without flashover simply by direct item-to-item spread (a process known as *spreadover*).

In extreme events such as earthquakes, impacts, and bombings that may leave large openings in the exterior shell of a building, a fire may be largely fuel controlled, even subsequent to flashover, due to the abundance of ventilation, particularly near the openings.

Fully Developed Fires. The next stage in a fire occurs when the fire is fully developed and reaches a steady state. At this point, the heat release or burning/mass loss rate depends on ventilation rather than the characteristics of the fuel. This fire stage is addressed further in Chapter 4-8, "Fire Temperature-Time Relations," of the *SFPE Handbook of Fire Protection Engineering* [12]. In this post-flashover phase, all combustible materials within the space are surface burning, as shown in Figure 8.11. This phase also results in the production of excess fuel vapors that cannot be consumed within the compartment due to lack of oxygen. For more information about this phase, see Chapter 2.4, "Dynamics of Compartment Fire Growth," in NFPA's *Fire Protection Handbook* [14].

Because the burning rate of a post-flashover fire is nearly constant and controlled by the amount of air that is available through the ventilation openings, the fire duration will be a function of the amount of fuel available. It should be noted that if the ventilation increases, perhaps as a result of windows breaking or walls collapsing, the heat release or burning rate will also increase.

Building designers can use the fully developed part of the fire curve to help them accomplish the following tasks:

- Determine the potential for structural failures that might endanger life safety or cause unacceptable building or contents damage.
- Design smoke management systems to control or exhaust the smoke produced.
- Determine radiation through exterior openings and the potential ignition of exposed buildings or their contents.
- Determine the likelihood of fire spread to parts of a building through convected and radiated heat.

FIGURE 8.11   Fully Developed Fire.

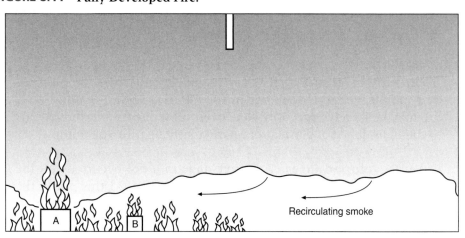

(*Source:* Cote, A. (Ed.), 2003. *Fire Protection Handbook,* National Fire Protection Association, Quincy, MA, Figure 2.4.10.)

- Evaluate the potential for failure of fire-resisting compartment elements designed to prevent fire spread to other parts of the building.

The fully developed stage may last for a short or extended period of time, depending on the quantity of fuel available and the potential for the fire to spread to adjacent combustible items. For some design-related issues, such as structural fire resistance, the duration of the fire may need to be known. To determine this value, it is necessary to determine or estimate a fuel load for design purposes. Fuel load is generally expressed in terms of mass of fuel per unit area.

The methods and data for prediction of the fully developed HRR for this stage of the design fire curve can be found in various references, such as Chapter 4-8, "Fire Temperature-Time Relations," in the *SFPE Handbook of Fire Protection Engineering* [12].

Decay and Extinction. Fires decay and eventually burn out with time. Decay can be attributed to depletion of fuel load, lack of ventilation, or manual or automatic suppression systems extinguishing the fire. Analysis and simulation techniques exist to predict the decay period for some scenarios [16]. During decay and extinction, the energy release is reduced substantially; however, production of smoke and toxic and corrosive products can continue or possibly increase. In extreme events, such as earthquakes and bombings, and situations where buildings or portions of buildings collapse, firefighting activities can be substantially delayed, and production of smoke may continue for many weeks, as occurred after the World Trade Center attack on September 11, 2001.

Fire Modeling

Various calculation methodologies and computer models are available to model a fire in a compartment or building. Such models can be used to predict the impact of a fire on the compartment, the entire building, and the building's occupants. Refer to Section 3 of the NFPA Fire Protection Handbook [14] for in-depth discussions of various calculation methodologies and models.

Fire Scenarios and Design Fire Scenarios

The shape of the HRR curve of a fire has been discussed in terms of energy release versus time. The effects of any one of these fires can

vary greatly depending on the characteristics of the confining building and its fire protection and mechanical systems, the fuels that are
burning, and the location of the fire within the building or facility, as
well as a number of other factors. For example, a fire by the main
exit in a large assembly occupancy would likely have a greater effect
on the life safety of the occupants than the same fire confined to a
small-compartmented area on a single floor. Because of the variable
nature of fire events and the myriad of different possible configurations and scenarios, risk-based methodologies, such as those outlined
in Chapters 2 and 4, are often more effective for designing tailored
protection strategies to meet the life safety, property protection, and
business continuity goals of a given building.

For design purposes, the fire characteristics described in the previous sections of this chapter must be completely and succinctly described for the credible scenarios associated with the building,
facility, or structure in question. These descriptions are known as *possible fire scenarios.* Possible fire scenarios, as detailed in the *SFPE Engineering Guide to Performance-Based Fire Protection Analysis and Design of
Buildings* [17], should include descriptions of the components that
can contribute to and/or control the way a fire affects a building, its
contents, and its occupants. Some of the components are as follows:

- Building characteristics
  Architectural features
  Structural components
  Fire protection systems
  Building services and processes
- Operational characteristics
  Fire department response details
  Environmental factors
- Fire characteristics
  Ignition sources
  Growth
  Flashover
  Full development
  Decay and extinction

A fire scenario should include the set of conditions that describes
the damage or personal injury potential. The location and damage
potential of building contents and critical operations or equipment is
also part of a fire scenario. Full fire scenario descriptions should also
include descriptions of occupant characteristics. The location and

number of exposed occupants and their physical capabilities should be part of the considerations of a fire scenario for fire safety design and emergency planning. This is discussed in detail in Chapter 12.

Identification of possible design fire scenarios can be accomplished through numerous means, including failure modes and effects analysis, failure analysis, "what if?" analysis, historical data, manuals and checklists, and statistical data. These methods are discussed in Chapters 2 and 4, and in the *SFPE Engineering Guide to Performance-Based Fire Protection Analysis and Design of Buildings* [17] and in *Introduction to Performance-Based Fire Safety* [18]. For any given building, hundreds of individual fire scenarios may be possible.

Once possible fire scenarios have been identified, they must generally be narrowed down to a limited set of design fire scenarios. These can then be used to evaluate potential design solutions. Design fire scenarios therefore should include detailed descriptions or building, occupant, and fire characteristics. The *SFPE Engineering Guide to Performance-Based Fire Protection Analysis and Design of Buildings* [17] provides a methodology for developing design fire scenarios that can be used to evaluate trial designs.

Identification of appropriate design fire scenarios can be accomplished through two approaches: probabilistic fire modeling or deterministic fire modeling. Probabilistic fire models use statistics, historical information, failure analysis, system reliability analyses, and risk analysis to define appropriate and critical design fire scenarios. The deterministic approach uses analysis or judgment based on scientific principles or correlations developed from physical testing to determine appropriate design fire scenarios. The method chosen will generally depend on the information available regarding the given building or occupancy type or the associated fire hazards. For instance, where statistical, historical, or failure data are not available for a given type of facility, a deterministic approach may be necessary.

SUMMARY

Fire can be a powerful destructive force. It is difficult to accurately predict, challenging to control, and physically and emotionally scarring. Therefore, it is a great concern for the general public, and a valuable tool for terrorists. Fire can cause extreme events such as explosions, or it may be caused by other extreme events, such as earthquakes, explosions, or lightning storms. Fire itself can be an extreme event; wildland fires and urban conflagrations are examples of this.

Because of its unpredictable nature and destructive potential, it is critical that fire be carefully considered in the rational design of built environments that may be exposed to extreme events.

Some fires can cause significant risks and consequences that approach those associated with large-scale events such as earthquakes, floods, and terrorist activities; therefore, designing and planning for fire-related extreme events requires an understanding of the basic causes of accidental, natural, and incendiary fires, as well as an understanding of the principles of fire spread and growth. This chapter has provided a brief overview of some of the factors that should be included when considering fire and its impact on buildings and structures and has outlined the process for developing scenarios against which mitigation strategies can be evaluated.

Protection strategies, such as controlling amounts and locations of fuels and combustible contents in buildings, providing structurally sound fire barriers and compartmentation, and planning for occupant evacuation or protection in place, can help control or limit the damage resulting from a fire-related extreme event. These strategies are discussed in detail in Chapter 11. Also, Chapter 9 is devoted to structural design for extreme events, and it includes discussion of structural fire protection. Evaluating candidate strategies requires development of realistic design fire scenarios that encompass worst-case conditions and rational decision-making techniques based on the risks and consequences of those scenarios. This process is critical, because it can help ensure that buildings are designed with attention to the actual fire hazards they may encounter in mind.

⎯ BIBLIOGRAPHY⎯⎯⎯⎯⎯⎯⎯⎯⎯⎯⎯⎯⎯⎯⎯⎯⎯⎯⎯⎯⎯⎯⎯⎯⎯

References Cited

1. NFPA, 1996. "Fire Investigation Report: Kobe Earthquake," National Fire Protection Association, Quincy, MA.
2. Borden, F. W., 1995. "Kobe Earthquake: Lessons for the United States," *Fire Engineering*, Vol. 148, No. 5, pp. 43–45, 48, 51–52.
3. NISTIR, 1997. *Fires Following the Northridge and Kobe Earthquakes*, NISTIR 6030, National Institute of Standards and Technology, Gaithersburg, MD.
4. Scawthorn, C., Eidinger, J., and Schiff, A. (Eds.), 2005. *Fire Following Earthquake*, Technical Council on Lifeline Earthquake Engineering, Monograph 26, American Society of Civil Engineers, Reston, VA.

5. Garrison, W. G. (Ed.), 1988. *100 Large Losses: A Thirty-Year Review of Property Damage Losses in the Hydrocarbon Chemical Industries,* M&M Protection Consultants, Chicago, IL.

6. Zalosh, R. G., 2003. *Industrial Fire Protection Engineering,* John Wiley & Sons, West Sussex, England.

7. Fleming, R. P., 1998. *Analysis of Fire Sprinkler Systems Performance in the Northridge Earthquake,* NIST GCR 98-736, National Institute of Standards and Technology, Gaithersburg, MD.

8. O'Rourke, T. K., Toprak, S., and Sano, Y., 1998. "Factors Affecting Water Supply Damage Caused by the Northridge Earthquake," *U.S./Japan Work on Earthquake Disaster Prevention for Lifeline Systems,* 7th Proceedings, November 4–7, 1997, Seattle, WA.

9. NIST, 1995. *Proceedings of the Post-Earthquake Fire and Lifelines Workshop,* NIST Special Publication 889, National Institute of Standards and Technology, Gaithersburg, MD.

10. FEMA, 2002. *World Trade Center Building Performance Study,* Publication 403, Federal Emergency Management Agency, Washington, DC.

11. Babrauskas, V., and Grayson, S. J. (Eds.), 1992. *Heat Release in Fires,* Elsevier Applied Science, New York.

12. SFPE, 2002. *The SFPE Handbook of Fire Protection Engineering,* 3rd ed. National Fire Protection Association, Quincy, MA.

13. Fitzgerald, R. W., 2004. *Building Fire Performance Analysis,* John Wiley & Sons, West Sussex, England.

14. Cote, A. (Ed.), 2003. *Fire Protection Handbook,* 19th ed., National Fire Protection Association, Quincy, MA.

15. Karlsson, B., and Quintiere, J. G., 2000. *Enclosure Fire Dynamics,* CRC Press, Boca Raton, FL.

16. Evans, D., 1993. *Sprinkler Fire Suppression Algorithm for HAZARD,* NISTIR 5254, National Institute of Standards and Technology, Gaithersburg, MD.

17. SFPE, 2000. *SFPE Engineering Guide to Performance-Based Fire Protection Analysis and Design of Buildings,* National Fire Protection Association, Quincy, MA.

18. Custer, R. L. P., and Meacham, B. J., 1997. *Introduction to Performance-Based Fire Safety,* Society of Fire Protection Engineers, Bethesda, MD.

NFPA Codes, Standards, and Recommended Practices

NFPA Publications.   The following NFPA guide is cited in this chapter. See the latest version of the *NFPA Catalog* for availability of the current edition of this document.

NFPA 921, *Guide for Fire and Explosion Investigations*

Additional Readings

Babrauskas, V., 2002. "Heat Release Rates," Chapter 3-1, *The SFPE Handbook of Fire Protection Engineering*, 3rd ed., National Fire Protection Association, Quincy, MA.

Bukowski, R., 2003. "Fire Hazard Analysis," Chapter 3.7, in Cote, A. (Ed.), *Fire Protection Handbook*, 19th ed., National Fire Protection Association, Quincy, MA.

Custer, R., 2003. "Dynamics of Compartment Fire Growth," Chapter 2.4, in Cote, A. (Ed.), *Fire Protection Handbook*, 19th ed., National Fire Protection Association, Quincy, MA.

Lie, T. T., 2002. "Fire Temperature-Time Relations," Chapter 4-8, *The SFPE Handbook of Fire Protection Engineering*, 3rd ed., National Fire Protection Association, Quincy, MA.

Walton, W. D., and Thomas, P., 2002. "Estimating Temperatures in Compartment Fires," Chapter 3-6, *The SFPE Handbook of Fire Protection Engineering*, 3rd ed., National Fire Protection Association, Quincy, MA.

9

Structural Design for Extreme Events

Faith Wainwright

Tony Jones

Chad McArthur

A s discussed in earlier chapters, building collapse can result from a number of extreme-event scenarios, including natural and man-made hazards. The goal of this chapter is to provide those involved in building design with a description of the concepts and strategies used by structural engineers to mitigate the consequences of such events. This discussion builds on descriptions of mitigation strategies outlined in previous chapters and provides details on current approaches for structural design to improve robustness and minimize progressive and disproportionate collapse. The codified or commonly accepted approaches to design vary from country to country and from project to project. Guidelines on robustness continue to change based on the occurrence of specific collapse events. This chapter discusses principles and key events that have contributed to current building-design guidelines.

__COLLAPSE EVENTS AND BUILDING DESIGN__

Before a building-design approach is selected, all parties should have an understanding of how buildings respond to local collapse and the concept of the robustness. In addition, before designing for robustness, all parties should understand the concepts of progressive and disproportionate collapse. This section addresses these concepts and provides a few illustrative case studies.

The structural design approach selected in mitigating against an extreme event depends on whether the event can be anticipated. In certain situations, a specific extreme event can be considered; for example, a facility storing explosive material can be designed to have a certain response should that material explode. However, in many cases it will be impossible to consider all types of extreme events or to foresee how these extreme events will change in the future. Therefore, a general approach for giving a structure the ability to withstand a certain amount of damage is needed. Such an approach will not prevent total collapse given a severe enough event, but it does give a basis for design that offers reasonable confidence in the performance of the structure for a range of extreme events.

Concepts of Progressive and Disproportionate Building Collapse

Progressive collapse and *disproportionate collapse* have distinct meanings. However, the two terms are often linked. Progressive collapse will generally be considered as disproportionate, because damage to a limited portion of the structure is not expected to spread uncontrollably.

Progressive. *Progressive collapse* describes the spreading of a collapse of one part of a structure to other areas that were initially not touched by the damage event, such as a fire or blast. Progressive collapse occurs when one part of the structure depends on the performance of other parts, which then become damaged, or when debris from damage overloads other parts of the structure, which then collapse under the abnormal load. Most of the damage that occurred in the April 1995 bombing of the Alfred P. Murrah Federal Building in Oklahoma City was caused by progressive collapse.

Disproportionate. *Disproportionate damage* occurs when the consequence of an event is far greater than expected. As such, there is a link between the event witnessed and the expectation of the damage it results in, even before the extent of that damage becomes known. This is about human perception, and it relates not only to buildings, but also to organizations. For buildings, "small" damage events would generally be expected to have "small" consequences (i.e., small amounts of damage). Similarly, "large" events are expected to cause large amounts of damage, particularly if the event is rare or unforeseen. A small event resulting in large amounts of damage would be considered disproportionate.

The collapse of the World Trade Center Towers raised much debate about whether the damage from the terrorist attacks was disproportionate. After the initial devastating astonishment that these towers could be toppled in such a short time, it was generally considered that the damage was not disproportionate, given the extreme loading from the event.

Robustness of Structures

Robustness is a fundamental concept in engineering design and one of the public's expectations for a building. Robustness implies a certain degree of reserve strength to deal with variations in loading that a building may see in its lifetime and that are not entirely predictable. The simplest and most common principles of robustness are to accomplish the following:

- Allow for strength of materials to be variable, taking a statistically justified approach to the design strength.
- Enable imposed loads to be greater than codified values, adopting a margin for error based on experience/historical precedence.
- Allow for a limited amount of damage or failure of part of the structure and design for the subsequent redistribution of loads to the remaining structure.

Case Study: Ronan Point

History. On May 16, 1968, a gas explosion occurred on the eighteenth floor of Ronan Point, a 22-story block of flats in Canning Town, Newham, East London [1]. The explosion was caused by a gas leak from the supply connection to a cooker on the eighteenth floor. The building was "system built"; large panels of precast concrete formed both walls and floor slabs. The explosion blew out a non-load-bearing story-height wall panel and a load-bearing story-height flank wall panel at the corner of the block. The floor slab immediately above this wall then collapsed, which was followed by the collapse of corresponding walls and slabs up to roof level. Falling debris dislodged the walls and slabs on the lower floors. The result was a progressive collapse that occurred over virtually the full height of one corner of the building, as shown in Figure 9.1. Four people were killed and 17 were injured.

Conclusions. A U.K. government inquiry concluded that the explosion itself was not of exceptional violence for such an event, having produced pressures ranging from 3 to 12 pounds per square inch

FIGURE 9.1   Ronan Point Following the Blast.

(*Source:* Arup.)

(21 to 83 kilometers per square meter), which are considered "normal" for domestic gas explosions [1]. The building's behavior in the explosion was judged to be an inherent consequence of its design, despite its compliance with building bylaws and relevant codes of practice, which did not call explicitly for a consideration of the possibility of progressive collapse.

Particular concern was expressed about the robustness of the joints between wall panels and floor slabs. The load-bearing external wall panel had been dislodged in the blast due to inadequate restraint from the floor slab above, which had no mechanical connection to the wall.

The government's report urged that such structures should have alternative load paths so that progressive collapse would not result should a local structural failure occur. The government recommended that building regulations embrace the issue of progressive collapse, that a code of practice be prepared explicitly for large-panel construction, that wind-loading code be updated, and that the Ministry of Housing and Local Government should ensure that building regulations and relevant codes of practice be kept up-to-date. Recommendations were related to buildings over six stories high and constructed with load-bearing precast concrete panels [2, 3, 4].

Subsequently, the Institution of Structural Engineers published paper RP/68/05 [5], which expressed the view that a fully framed structure with continuous columns would be adequate to resist progressive collapse so long as it met the following criteria:

- It was designed and constructed in accordance with the then-current relevant code of practice for steel or concrete (BS449, CP114, CP115, or CP116).
- It was provided with continuous horizontal ties of specified strength in two directions at right angles at each floor and roof level.
- It was built with floor and roof slabs effectively anchored to their supports, with continuity provided for over supports.

Influence on Design. How did Ronan Point influence today's structural designers? In the United Kingdom, its legacy is Building Regulation Requirement A3 [6, 7], together with clauses in codes of practice that urge "robustness" to be consciously incorporated into the design through positive measures. Typically, these measures include the following:

- Adopting a robust and stable structural form
- Ensuring interactions between components by connections or provision of ties
- Providing adequate stiffness and strength to resist "notional" lateral loads even when "actual" lateral loading to be resisted is minimal
- Identifying elements that are vulnerable to accidental damage and either protecting or strengthening them (if they cannot be "designed out")
- Having one party responsible for the overall stability of the structure (especially important for "hybrid" structures, whose components are often proprietary items fabricated off-site in various

materials; these components need to be assembled and connected so as to achieve overall robustness)

The experience of Ronan Point has resulted in explicit requirements for demonstrable robustness being incorporated in U.K. codes and, more recently, in Eurocodes, such as the new *Eurocode 2 for the Design of Concrete* [8]. Different countries are coming to grips with codifying their own robustness needs. However, the requirements that followed from Ronan Point embody principles that are relevant to most building construction.

Case Study: Murrah Building

History. The Murrah Federal Office Building in Oklahoma City was constructed between late 1974 and early 1976 [9]. It was formed of reinforced concrete frame with shear walls. Figure 9.2 shows the Alfred P. Murrah Federal Building prior to the 1995 blast.

In April 1995, the building was heavily damaged by a terrorist bomb blast equivalent to over 2 tons (1800 kilograms) of TNT. At the third floor, the nine-story building had a transfer beam on its perimeter such that the column spacing above the beam was half of that below. The large truck bomb completely destroyed one of the lower columns, which was approximately 15 feet (4.75 meters) away from it. Two adjacent columns failed in shear; however, it is not clear whether this shear was directly due to blast loading or due to shears developed in the columns due to the distortion resulting from the loss of the adjacent column. This left the perimeter transfer beam spanning approximately 165 feet (50 meters). Failure of this transfer beam led to a loss of approximately 50 percent of the floor area of the building [10]. It is estimated that the collapse took place within 3 seconds. Most of the damage, shown in Figure 9.3, was caused by progressive collapse rather than by the direct effects of the explosion.

Conclusions. The American Concrete Institute (ACI) Building Code [11] introduced a requirement for "structural integrity" reinforcement in 1989; however, the Murrah building was constructed before this requirement, and there was no continuity of bottom steel at the column locations. Studies showed that a small amount of additional hoop reinforcement could have prevented the failure of the two adjacent columns. Even if only the column adjacent to the explosion had been destroyed, the transfer beam would still have collapsed. By making the bottom bars effectively continuous over the columns, the

FIGURE 9.2 Murrah Federal Building Prior to the Blast.

(*Source:* AP/Wide World Photos.)

transfer beam would have been able to span the removed column. These same studies have shown that if British code requirements for notional horizontal loads had been designed for, the progressive collapse would not have occurred [12]. Logically, it seems improbable that this requirement, on its own, without the corresponding requirements for ties, would have prevented similar damage.

___STRUCTURAL DESIGN APPROACHES___

Mitigation approaches for extreme events include redundancy, the exploitation of alternative load mechanisms, the tying of elements, and increased ductility. In reality, any particular approach will rely on a combination of these provisions.

For example, for a catenary to form after a column is removed,

FIGURE 9.3   Damage to the North and East Sides of the Murrah Federal Building.

(*Source:* FEMA News Photo.)

the structure must have sufficient ductility, otherwise a brittle failure may occur before the catenary has found equilibrium. Proper tying is required so that the catenary forces can be distributed to the rest of the structure. Some redundancy in the remaining column capacities is required to carry the vertical load previously held in the removed column. It should be noted that none of the following approaches avoid local failure, and the emphasis is to limit the area of failure and to transfer forces into the remaining structure.

Key Point   If an event is reasonably predictable, then it is possible to design for that event such that no structural damage occurs. However, this may not be practical or economical. Therefore, the amount of damage that is reasonable for a given event must be defined.

Mitigation approaches will also vary based on differences in the designs for particular extreme events and knowledge of the impact of events, such as fire, on structural behavior.

Alternative Load Paths and Redundancy

Key Point   One key aspect of designing against the loss or damage of a structural element is to ensure that there are alternative ways to carry the load that was previously supported by the damaged element.

One way to design against loss or damage is through the provision of alternative load paths or through the provision of additional structure. An example of an alternative load path is a two-way spanning slab; loss of one support or damage to the slab causes the slab to span predominantly in the other direction. Capacity may be reduced in this direction, but it is logical to consider reduced loads (and load factors), and normally designed slabs are often adequate for the revised loads. Similarly, a column may go into tension and support the floor below it if the column below the floor is removed. This relies on the horizontal structure above the column being capable of transferring this new load to vertical load paths that continue to ground.

Redundancy can be provided either in the form of additional elements or by the over design of existing elements. In reality, it is normally a combination of the two. For example, a facade could be designed such that a beam has sufficient strength to span a removed column, in which case there are additional columns and an overdesign of the beam in the undamaged situation.

Although these approaches will improve the general robustness of a structure, they are most effective when the nature of the damage can be predicted so that the structure can be designed to bridge it. As the structure continues to carry load through normal flexural action, deformations, although increasing, may not be excessive. Limiting deformations under extreme events can be beneficial when the integrity of the elements supported on a structure is important; for example, fire partitions may be compromised if deformations are too large.

Alternative Resistance Mechanisms

A building can be designed so that when the capacity of a member is exceeded during an extreme event, partial failure may occur, but an alternative resistance mechanism is formed. The most obvious example of this is the formation of a catenary after a flexural failure. These alternative resistance mechanisms have their own boundary conditions. For example, for a catenary to form, significant horizontal reactions will be created at its ends. These horizontal forces will need to be resisted by the remaining structure. In Figure 9.4, a catenary force P is created, which is approximately the load per unit length of the beam (ω) multiplied by the length (l) squared, and divided by eight times the deformations (ϵ). As the deformation, ϵ, increases, the force, P, decreases. Provided the system has enough ductility, the beam will eventually find a new equilibrium in a sagging catenary. Because each floor will effectively look after itself, such a load path can be effective when the same column is lost on a number of floors.

Key Point   Structures can be designed such that when the capacity of a member is exceeded during an extreme event, partial failure may occur, but an alternative resistance mechanism is formed.

For two-way spanning structures, the same effect can occur, but in two dimensions. This is known as *tensile membrane action* and is shown in Figure 9.5. If the central column is removed, catenaries form in two dimensions. The resistance to the tensile forces can be provided by a compression ring in the slab.

Alternative resistance mechanisms, and in particular the development of catenaries, can be achieved simply, with little increase to the cost of the structure. Therefore, they can be provided as a general provision to improve robustness or be considered for specific events. As the mechanism in which the load is carried changes, large deformations will likely result. Catenaries may require significant deformations of span, and this may compromise the integrity of any fire protection of fire compartments supported by the slab.

Tying of Elements

The tying of elements is necessary if catenary action is to be developed, but it is also important from a general robustness point of view.

FIGURE 9.4   Catenary Action.

(*Source:* Arup.)

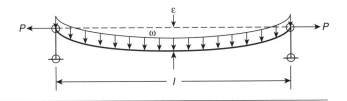

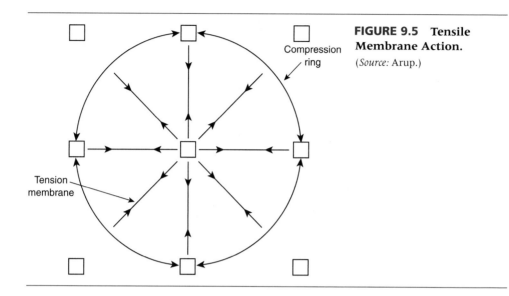

FIGURE 9.5 Tensile **Membrane Action.**
(*Source:* Arup.)

Compression ring

Tension membrane

Elements such as columns can experience lateral and tensile forces completely different from those experienced in their normal design conditions.

Premature failure can be prevented by ensuring that all structural elements are tied together at their joints. For example, if a wall panel is not tied adequately to adjacent floors, it may become dislodged well before its structural capacity is reached. Tying can also prevent shock loads. For example, tying a floor to the top of a column may prevent the floor from lifting off of the column and then impact loading the column during an explosion.

However, there is a counterargument to this. If a collapse is initiated in a properly tied building, then load will shed to the surrounding structure, which may then become overloaded, causing further collapse. In an untied structure, it may be possible for part of the building to collapse, leaving the remaining structure relatively intact. The benefits of this approach depend on the expected damage event. Generally, event-independent guidance advocates tying.

Deformation and Ductility

Many extreme events are associated with a dynamic load. Even when failure is caused by a static load, debris loading on the rest of the structure will have a dynamic component. Therefore, for extreme events and the avoidance of progressive collapse, the ability to resist dynamic loads is beneficial. Dynamic load can be quantified as an energy that the structure must absorb. The energy that the structure can absorb is a function of both the resistance it provides and the amount it deforms. Some energy can be absorbed during the elastic deformation of the structure. Indeed, if the structure is strong enough it may be able to absorb all of the energy. However, once the capacity of the element is reached, further energy can be absorbed in the plastic deformation. A ductile member with sufficient plastic-deformation capacity can absorb more energy than a stronger member with less deformation capacity. Figure 9.6 shows the force-deformation characteristics for two different elements. Although element 1 is stronger than element 2, the area under the force-deformation graph is smaller, and so it can absorb less energy.

Additional ductility often can be provided without adding cost. However, the quantification of ductility is relatively new for nonseismic design.

Key Point   Where large deformations are associated with energy absorption, fire protection or compartmentation materials may become compromised.

FIGURE 9.6 Force-Deformation Characteristics for Two Different Elements.
(*Source:* Arup.)

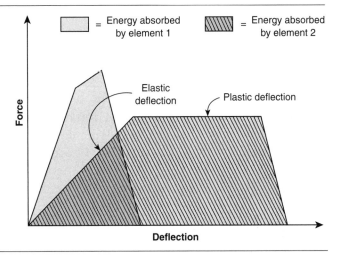

DESIGN ISSUES FOR PARTICULAR EVENTS

Seismic Activity

Seismic design shares many similarities with design for other extreme events, particularly those involving dynamic loading. However, key differences need to be considered when transferring knowledge from seismic design to that for other extreme events. In an earthquake, the forces induced are normally due to the mass of the building being accelerated by the ground movement. After the event, the forces acting on the members return broadly to their initial state. In addition, seismic events affect the whole building. With other extreme events, an external action is likely, and depending on its severity, it is possible that local collapse will occur and the remaining structure will be subject to debris loading, which will remain after the event. For these other extreme events, local failure may be acceptable, and the aim is to prevent it from affecting too much of the structure.

Fire Events

In the context of extreme events, the behavior of a damaged structure may also be affected by severe fire. The collapse of the World Trade Center Towers in New York in September 2001 has accelerated research and discussion on this topic. This chapter is not intended to present methodologies for design of structures to resist fire events; however, anyone designing structures to be robust in damage events should be mindful of the impact of fire on the postulated behavior of a damaged structure. They should also be aware of the role of structural design in improving the performance of structures in fire, regardless of whether the fire is accompanied by a blast or impact event that compromises the structural behavior.

Key Point Structural integrity requirements may be driven by needs such as safe evacuation routes and integrity of compartmentation, property protection, and business continuity.

Successful design requires the collaborative participation of all members of the design team in achieving the client's objectives.

—STRUCTURAL DESIGN ISSUES AND—————
BUILDING GUIDELINES

Two structural design issues are relevant to the prevention of dispro-portionate and progressive collapse, as outlined in this chapter. First, significant deformations of the structure, which will be anticipated in the structural design, are likely to compromise the effectiveness of fire protection and life safety measures. Second, simple tests of build-ing elements in furnaces do not indicate how a real structure will be-have in a fire. Such tests are only able to describe the expected performance of individual building elements.

Key Point   It is important that structural engineers work closely with other members of the project team in identifying objectives and determin-ing design priorities.

Structural design issues can be addressed by conventional miti-gation approaches, such as building codes and government guide-lines, or other mitigation approaches, such as risk assessment and modeling of structural behavior.

Conventional Mitigation Approaches

The key references that codify design to allow general application of the principles discussed earlier are addressed in this section.

U.S. Building Codes. In the United States, although building codes vary from state to state, many of these codes make reference to ASCE 7, *Minimum Design Loads for Buildings and Other Structures,* which provides provisions for structural robustness in Section 1.4, "General Structural Integrity" [13].

This section simply states that "Buildings and other structures shall be designed to sustain local damage with the structural system as a whole remaining stable and not being damaged to an extent dis-proportionate to the original local damage" [13]. This provision also makes reference to the use of continuity, redundancy, and ductility to achieve this performance, as has been explained in this chapter.

The commentary associated with Section 1.4 of ASCE 7 provides further information on the intended use of this provision, pointing out that that "ASCE does not intend, at this time, for this standard to establish specific events to be considered during design, or for this standard to provide specific design criteria to minimize the risk of progressive collapse" [10]. In addition, the commentary points out the "apparent lack of general awareness" among the design community that this issue "is important enough to be regularly considered in design" and qualitatively outlines acceptable design methodologies and provides general guidelines (again qualitative) for how improved robustness can be achieved [13].

In review of these provisions, it becomes clear that their general nature and qualitative guidelines may result not only in a wide variety of design approaches, but also in a widely varying degree of resilience in building construction. As such, there is no uniformly accepted U.S. standard as to how much resilience is necessary or how to quantify it.

U.S. Government Guidelines. To its credit, the General Services Administration (GSA) recognized the need for a prescriptive design requirement for their buildings following the events in Oklahoma City. These requirements are spelled out in the GSA's *Progressive Collapse Analysis and Design Guidelines for New Federal Office Buildings and Major Modernization Projects* [14].

Although the measures described in this document are mandatory for GSA buildings, much of the information could be applied to other building projects, if desired. However, it should be noted that these extensive guidelines are based on a threat-independent approach, and therefore may not always result in the most appropriate design for all facilities. Furthermore, caution should be taken in any instance where guidelines are adopted for any application other than their original intended use.

Although the GSA guidelines are extensive, they are not the only guidelines in use. In 2004, the Department of Defense (DoD) issued *Design of Buildings to Resist Progressive Collapse* for use with defense-related buildings [15]. This document shares similarities with both the U.K. and the GSA standards, depending on the type of building being considered, and also offers guidelines for timber and masonry structures, which are not covered in detail by the U.K. and GSA documents.

U.K. Building Regulations. In the United Kingdom, requirements are set out in the Building Regulations to help ensure that the extent of a collapse is not disproportionate to the initiating event. Until 2004, the requirements were entirely prescriptive and only applied to buildings of five or more stories. In some situations, this led to illogical conclusions. For example, a high-occupancy building with a high risk of damage could ignore the disproportionate collapse requirements of the Building Regulations if it were fewer than five stories. This was recently rectified, and beginning December 2004, the requirement applies to all buildings. However, the methods used to satisfy the regulations vary based on the use and size of the building. As shown in Table 9.1, U.K. Building Regulations divide structures into four classes [7].

The approach to satisfying the U.K. Building Regulations for each class can be summarized as follows:

- *Class 1.* It is acceptable to follow normal building practice.

- *Class 2A.* Horizontal ties within the floors or anchorage of the floors to the supporting walls are required.

- *Class 2B.* In addition to horizontal ties, vertical ties are also required. Alternatively, the removal of specified elements of supporting structure is considered and limits are placed on the amount of floor at risk from collapse. If it is not possible to limit the collapse area as required, the element must be designed as a "key element." Key elements are designed to resist a specified accidental load case.

- *Class 3.* A systematic risk assessment is required, taking into account both normal and abnormal hazards. The approach to buildings in this class will be building specific, but is likely to include the provisions of Class 2B.

The U.K. Building Regulations refer to the various material codes of practice for how to comply with the requirements [15, 16]. These codes specify the strength and location of the ties required, and they offer additional guidance on the approach to be taken on the removal of elements. In addition, each of the material codes referenced requires a minimum horizontal load to be designed for, which is related to the mass of the building. For many building configurations, this minimum horizontal load will exceed the horizontal design loads due to wind.

It can be seen that the principal approach in the United Kingdom is that of tying. This protects against the removal of individual elements and enables catenaries to form where elements become damaged. The deformations associated with these catenaries can be large, and in the case of concrete structures deformations in excess of one-tenth the span are required to justify the tying forces specified. The tying of vertical elements also enables load to be distributed up the

TABLE 9.1   Classes of Structure According to U.K. Building Regulations

Class	Building Type and Occupancy*
1	Houses not exceeding 4 stories Agricultural buildings Buildings into which people rarely go, provided no part of the building is closer to another building or area where people do go than a distance of 1.5 times the building height
2A	5-story single-occupancy houses Hotels not exceeding 4 stories Flats, apartments and other residential buildings not exceeding 4 stories Offices not exceeding 4 stories Industrial buildings not exceeding 3 stories Retailing premises not exceeding 3 stories of less than 2000 m^2 floor area per story Single-story educational buildings All buildings not exceeding 2 stories to which members of the public are admitted and which contain floor areas not exceeding 2000 m^2 at each story
2B	Hotels, flats, apartments, and other residential buildings greater than 4 stories but not exceeding 15 stories Educational buildings greater than 1 story but not exceeding 15 stories Retailing premises greater than 3 stories but not exceeding 15 stories Hospitals not exceeding 3 stories Offices greater than 4 stories but not exceeding 15 stories All buildings to which members of the public are admitted, and which contain floor areas exceeding 2000 m^2 but less than 5000 m^2 at each story Car parking not exceeding 6 stories
3	All buildings defined above as Class 2A and 2B that exceed the limits on area and/or number of stories Grandstands accommodating more than 5000 spectators Buildings containing hazardous substances and/or processes

* For buildings intended for more than one type of use, the class should be that pertaining to the most onerous type. In determining the number of stories in a building, basement stories may be excluded, provided such basement stories fulfill the robustness requirements of Class 2B buildings.
Source: HMSO, 2004. *Approved Document A: Structure,* The Building Regulations, Her Majesty's Stationery Office, London.

building in the event of the loss of a vertical support, and this may activate beneficial effects, such as moment frame action in the frames above. In the event that vertical tying is not possible, the regulations allow the loss of the vertical member to be considered. This solution enables alternative load paths to be utilized and allows for the provision of some redundancy to limit the failure, as required. Neither the regulations nor the material codes that implement them contain requirements for the ductility of ties, and ties are specified based on strength.

Developments in Mitigation Approaches

Application of the principles of robustness outlined thus far will result in buildings that have a certain level of resistance to extreme events and will encourage the engineer to have a clear approach to robustness. However, approaches to robustness should be developed for two main reasons:

- *Limitations to the approaches.* An example limitation would be the incompatibility between the desire for large deformations to maintain structural integrity and the need for fire protection and compartmentation to remain intact.
- *An increasing desire to understand a building's structural response.* It is necessary to understand just how much damage might be expected in an extreme-event scenario and how it would affect, for example, an evacuation.

Therefore, mitigation approaches are being researched and selectively adopted for certain buildings.

Risk Assessment. Typically, risk assessment, which was discussed in Chapter 4, plays a critical part in determining objectives and the design approach. This methodology allows a structured evaluation of where effort is most usefully expended in upgrading the robustness of a building. To this end, explicit damage scenarios may be developed and the performance of the structure evaluated. Various mitigation measures can be tested to determine the benefits of those measures in relation to their cost.

Explicit Modeling of Structural Behavior. The actual behavior of a structure can be examined through detailed modeling using finite-element techniques. This is not a standard approach, though, for good reason. Quite apart from the limitations of computing speed, a detailed model relies on detailed inputs, and because the loading scenario will not be determined exactly, approximations in modeling or the use of prescriptive requirements are usually appropriate.

Key Point   Detailed modeling is becoming more accessible as faster and cheaper computing resources become available. It is increasingly being used to understand the detailed behavior of components and local areas of a structure, such as a set of facade columns subjected to a blast.

In recent years, finite-element modeling of whole floors has been used to capture the real behavior of structures in a fire. This enables building designers to understand how much fire protection is required in order to significantly affect performance. Explicit modeling of steel beam-to-concrete core connections on the International Finance Center in Hong Kong led to savings in cost along with improved performance in fire. Powerful modeling tools exist, and in the hands of skilled engineers they can yield real value to the client. We will continue to see further developments in the modeling of the real behavior of structures in damage events.

SUMMARY

This chapter outlined the principles behind various design approaches for building robustness. The concepts of progressive collapse, disproportionate collapse, and robustness were outlined, and the influence of design on particular events was described through case studies.

The current regulatory environments in the United Kingdom and the United States were discussed. An introduction was provided on the use of non-code-based approaches, first principles, and approaches to design that are developing as a result of greater interest from owners and designers in the actual performance of buildings in extreme events.

BIBLIOGRAPHY

References Cited

1. Griffiths, H., et al., 1968. *Report of the Inquiry into the Collapse of Flats at Ronan Point, Canning Town,* Her Majesty's Stationery Office, London.

2. Ministry of Housing and Local Government, 1968. *Flats Constructed with Precast Concrete Panels. Appraisal and Strengthening of Existing High Blocks: Design of New Blocks,* Circular 62/68, London.

3. ISE, 1968. *Structural Stability and the Prevention of Progressive Collapse,* paper RP/68/01, Institution of Structural Engineers, London.

4. ISE, 1969. "The Implications of the Report of the Inquiry into the Collapse of Flats at Ronan Point, Canning Town," *The Structural Engineer,* Vol. 47, No. 7, pp. 255–284.

5. ISE, 1971. *The Resistance of Buildings to Accidental Damage,* paper RP/68/05, Institution of Structural Engineers, London.

6. HMSO, 1991. *Approved Document A: Structure,* The Building Regulations, Her Majesty's Stationery Office, London.

7. HMSO, 2004. *Approved Document A: Structure,* The Building Regulations, Her Majesty's Stationery Office, London.

8. BSI, 2004. *Eurocode 2 for the Design of Concrete BSEN 1992-1-1:2004 Eurocode 2: Design of Concrete Structures Part 101: General Rules and Rules for Building.* British Standards Institute, London.

9. Corley, W. G., et al., 1998. "The Oklahoma City Bombing: Summary and Recommendations for Multihazard Mitigation," *Journal of Performance of Constructed Facilities,* Vol. 12, No. 03, pp. 100–112.

10. Corley, W. G., et al., 2001. "Effects of Structural Integrity on Damage from the Oklahoma City, USA Bombing." In Neal B. S. (Ed.), *Forensic Engineering, the Investigation of Failures,* Thomas Telford, London.

11. ACI, 1989. *Building Code Requirements for Reinforced Concrete,* ACI 318-89, American Concrete Institute, Farmington Hills, MI.

12. Sozen, M. A., et al., 1998. "The Oklahoma City Bombing: Structure and Mechanisms of the Murrah Building," *Journal of Performance of Constructed Facilities,* Vol. 12, No. 03, pp. 120–136.

13. ASCE, 2002. *Minimum Design Loads for Buildings and Other Structures,* ASCE 7, American Society of Civil Engineers, Reston, VA.

14. GSA, 2003. *Progressive Collapse Analysis and Design Guidelines for New Federal Office Buildings and Major Modernization Projects,* General Services Administration, Washington, DC.

15. DoD, 2004. *Design of Buildings to Resist Progressive Collapse,* U.S. Department of Defense, Washington, DC.

16. BSI, 1997. *Structural Use of Concrete. Code of Practice for Design and Construction,* BS 8110-1:1997, British Standards Institute, London.

17. BSI, 2000. *Structural Use of Steelwork in Buildings. Code of Practice for Design,* BS 5959-1:2000, British Standards Institute, London.

Additional Reading

ENR, 1993. "Post-Andrew Changes Made," *Engineering News-Record,* Vol. 230, No. 11, p. 17.

10

HVAC System Design for Extreme Events

Fiona Cousins

This chapter describes typical building heating-ventilation-and air-conditioning (HVAC) systems and the types of risks associated with them. The behavior of the systems under different types of extreme events is also described.

OVERVIEW

Types of Mechanical Systems

Most modern buildings include mechanical systems that are used to maintain comfort and provide adequate ventilation during normal operation. This is accomplished through either air-based or mixed systems. Air-based systems use air to provide heating, cooling, and ventilation throughout the building. The air is often recirculated for energy-saving reasons. Mixed systems use pipes to distribute water to provide heating and/or cooling and air, usually much less than in all-air systems, for fresh air ventilation only. In most mixed systems, such as fan-coil or chilled-ceiling systems, all of the air is exhausted after use; it is not recirculated. Air-based systems generally require large ducts but do not need distribution piping. Mixed systems use smaller ducts and have distribution piping.

Under most emergency conditions, these mechanical systems are allowed to fail. Providing thermally comfortable conditions during emergency evacuation offers few apparent benefits, and the amount of oxygen available from the normal air in a building is more than adequate to support life during normal (or even extended) egress periods. The costs of maintaining thermal conditions or of providing fresh-air ventilation (for breathing purposes) during an emergency are usually high. These costs include emergency power systems, specialized ductwork and fan equipment that can resist high temperatures or large movements, and the associated space.

Of course, a few mechanical systems must operate during an emergency. These systems are put in place specifically for life safety reasons and include smoke management systems, generator cooling systems, generator fuel supply systems, sprinkler systems, standpipe systems, and, in a very few cases, cooling systems for structural elements. Elevators may also be required to operate in high-rise buildings.

System Design Issues

The nature of mechanical systems is to use networks of ducts and pipes that connect various parts of the building together. Even if the systems are off, these networks can provide routes through the building that allow the spread of fire, smoke, and biological or chemical compounds, causing the danger to spread beyond the hazard's origin. A number of building-design elements can limit the likelihood of such systems from spreading fire, smoke, or chemicals through a building. These elements include the following:

- Smoke and fire spread can be addressed through the use of automatic dampers that seal ducts at certain points in their routes.
- The spread of chemical or biological agents, smoke, or fire can be limited by designing separate duct networks for different parts of the building.
- The risk of introducing smoke or chemicals into the systems can be reduced by careful location of the air intakes, monitoring of the air intakes, and stringent filtration.

Most of the risks of spreading contaminants are associated with duct systems. These systems are large and open to the air at many locations. Piping systems for HVAC systems are generally closed loops; their contents do not come into contact with air, or people, at any point. The most common exceptions to this are domestic water systems and open-loop cooling tower systems. Many of the mitigation measures for ductwork are required by International Code Council (ICC) [1] and National Fire Protection Association (NFPA) building codes, including the following:

- *NFPA 5000®, Building Construction and Safety Code®*
- "Air-Conditioning and Ventilating Systems," *Fire Protection Handbook* [2]
- NFPA 90A, *Standard for the Installation of Air-Conditioning and Ventilating Systems*
- NFPA 90B, *Standard for the Installation of Warm Air-Heating and Air-Conditioning Systems*

For example, fire dampers and smoke dampers are required in most ductwork systems to maintain smoke and fire compartmentation. This is illustrated in Figure 10.1. Many of these measures are described in detail later in this chapter and in Chapter 11.

Similarly, building codes may require smoke detection in outside air ducts to prevent smoke outside the building from entering. Upon detection of smoke coming from outside, it is normal for the outside air damper to close. The air-handling unit may continue to provide cooling and heating using recirculated air, but it will not pull in smoky air from outside.

Other mitigation measures are not typically required by building codes. For example, air intakes are usually required to be located so that normal street-level pollutants, such as diesel exhaust particles, are not drawn into the systems. However, they are not required to be inaccessible to the public or to have video surveillance to minimize the risk of the introduction of toxic compounds into the buildings. Although such precautions may not be necessary for small, lightly occupied buildings, these measures should be carefully considered for densely occupied, public or high-profile buildings such as museums, concert halls, and government offices. Figure 10.2 shows an unprotected air intake.

The following sections of this chapter examine the behavior of mechanical systems under different types of extreme events.

FIRE EVENTS

During a fire, mechanical systems may be called upon in a number of ways. (Fire events are addressed in detail in Chapter 8.) These systems typically perform the following tasks:

- Prevention of smoke spread from source area to other areas
- Maintenance of clear exit pathways
- Maintenance of tenable conditions for fire fighting

FIGURE 10.1   Typical Building Duct Installations with Protected Openings.

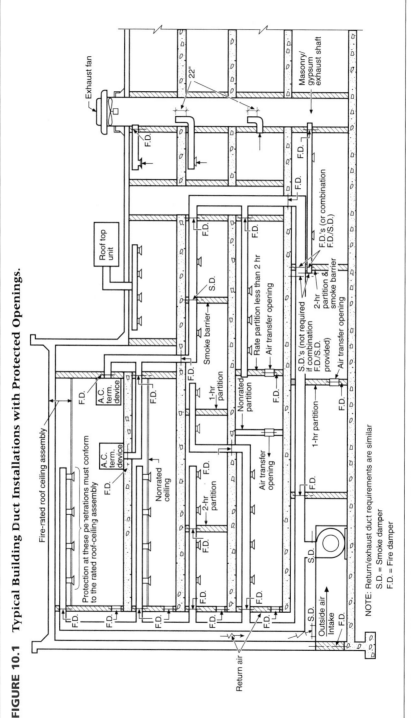

(Source: Cote, A. (Ed.), 2003. *Fire Protection Handbook,* National Fire Protection Association, Quincy, MA, Fig. 12.15.2.)

FIGURE 10.2 **Example of an Unprotected Building Air Intake at Ground Level.**

(*Source:* Photo by Marc Scrivener.)

Two major design strategies are used to fulfill these needs: physical separations and active smoke management. Information on these strategies can be found in several publications and in NFPA building codes, including the following:

- *Principles of Smoke Management*, American Society of Heating, Refrigerating, and Air-Conditioning Engineers, Inc. [3]
- "Air-Conditioning and Ventilating Systems," *Fire Protection Handbook* [2]
- NFPA 92A, *Standard for Smoke-Control Systems Utilizing Barriers and Pressure Differences*
- NFPA 92B, *Standard for Smoke Management Systems in Malls, Atria and Large Spaces*

After a fire, mechanical systems may also be used to help clear smoke from the building. The process of using a mechanical system to remove smoke after the fire is called *smoke purge*.

Physical Separations

Smoke and fire spread is usually prevented through the use of special dampers in the ducts to break the connections between different areas of the buildings. The types of dampers that can be used include fire dampers, smoke dampers, and combination fire and smoke dampers.

Fire Dampers. Fire dampers are used to maintain the integrity of fire compartmentation in case of a fire. As shown in Figure 10.3, the use of a fire damper in a rated partition can help stop the spread of fire. There are several types of these devices, but almost all fire dampers close through spring action. The damper is held open using

FIGURE 10.3   Diagram of How a Fire Damper Can Stop Fire Spread.
(*Source:* Arup.)

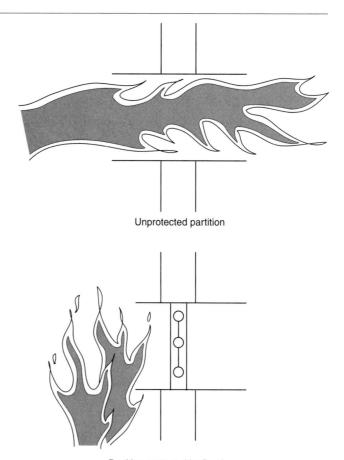

Unprotected partition

Partition protected by fire damper

a "fusible link." This link melts at a fairly low temperature (~165°F or ~739°C), and this link failure releases a spring that closes the damper. Most fire dampers cannot be reopened automatically; once the fusible link has failed, it must be reset manually.

Smoke Dampers. Smoke dampers are used to maintain smoke-proof enclosures, such as elevator lobbies. These dampers close when the fire alarm system detects smoke. Once it receives a signal from the fire alarm system, the damper closes using a motor or by releasing a spring. Smoke dampers can usually be reopened automatically by the fire alarm or building management system. Most smoke dampers "fail close," so that if the power to the motor is cut, the damper will close.

Combination Dampers. Combination fire and smoke dampers combine the ability to close automatically due to the heat of a fire with the ability to close on a command from the fire alarm system, as shown in Figure 10.4. A number of configurations are possible, but most combined fire and smoke dampers fail close on power failure. Fire-damper action is achieved through an in-duct heat detector that causes power to the damper motor to be cut on detection of heat so that the damper closes.

Special Areas. Some buildings have areas that need to be protected so that they can be used to assist in fire fighting. These areas will include fire command centers and other areas where fire fighters can control smoke management systems and monitor the operation of the fire alarm system.

Key Point Fire command centers and other areas from which fire fighters can control smoke management and fire alarm systems should be ventilated separately and cooling, heating, and ventilation should be powered from an emergency power system, if one is available.

Active Smoke Management

Smoke spread can also be limited through the movement of air. This can be achieved through a number of common strategies, such as floor-by-floor pressurization, stair pressurization, and atrium smoke exhaust, which are addressed in the following sections. These same

FIGURE 10.4 Typical Combination Fire and Smoke Damper.

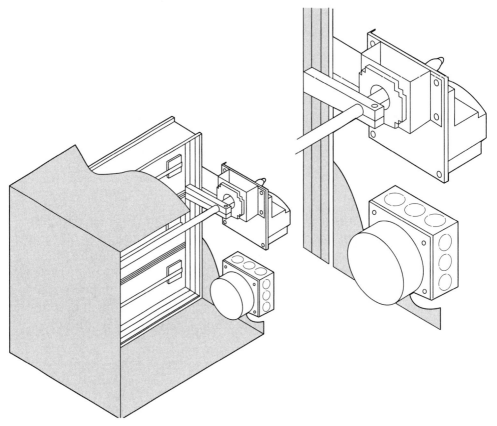

(*Source:* Arup.)

strategies are used to keep exit passageways as clear as possible. An active smoke management system is any strategy that uses the mechanical or natural supply or exhaust of air during a fire to control the spread of the fire. Additional information on active smoke management is available in the following publications and NFPA codes:

- NFPA 92A, *Standard for Smoke-Control Systems Utilizing Barriers and Pressure Differences*
- NFPA 92B, *Standard for Smoke Management Systems in Malls, Atria and Large Spaces*
- *Principles of Smoke Management*, American Society of Heating, Refrigerating, and Air-Conditioning Engineers, Inc. [3]
- "Smoke Control," *The SFPE Handbook of Fire Protection Engineering* [4]

- "Smoke Management in Covered Malls and Atria," *The SFPE Handbook of Fire Protection Engineering* [5]

Floor-by-Floor Pressurization. To prevent the spread of smoke from a fire floor to adjacent floors, a floor-by-floor pressurization system is often used. Once a fire has been detected by the fire alarm system, the supply-air ducts for the fire floor are turned off and the return-air ducts for the fire floor are switched to full flow. In some cases, this means that smoke dampers, previously closed by the fire alarm system, must be opened. At the same time, the supply-air ducts for the floors above and below the fire are switched to full flow and the return-air ducts are turned off. This course of events has the effect of building positive pressure in the nonfire floors, making it more difficult for smoke to migrate there, and of building negative pressure in the fire floor, helping to maintain the smoke within that floor. Figure 10.5 illustrates this type of a smoke-control system.

Stair Pressurization. A stair-pressurization strategy is generally used to help fire fighters and evacuees by keeping the egress paths free of smoke during the egress period. In most buildings taller than two stories, egress from upper levels is through smoke-proof and fire-rated stair enclosures. Once the highest occupied level is more than 75 feet above the level of fire department access, or as dictated by local building codes, the stairways may also be pressurized. Once a fire has been detected by the fire alarm system, a special dedicated stair-pressurization system is turned on. This system supplies a large volume of outside air into the staircase so that it will be smoke free.

Key Point   The design criterion for stair pressurization is that two or three full-size doors to the stair must be assumed to be open, while a particular velocity or pressure drop must be maintained across each of these door openings.

Atrium Smoke Exhaust. A smoke exhaust system is used in buildings that have large openings between more than two floors. If there is a fire in an atrium, people will be affected at a number of different levels. For all of these people to be kept safe, a smoke exhaust and make-up air system is usually installed. The system is usually designed to keep the bottom of the layer of smoke at least 10 feet above the highest surface on which there may be occupants, as shown in

FIGURE 10.5 Typical Zoned Smoke-Control System.

(*Source:* Arup.)

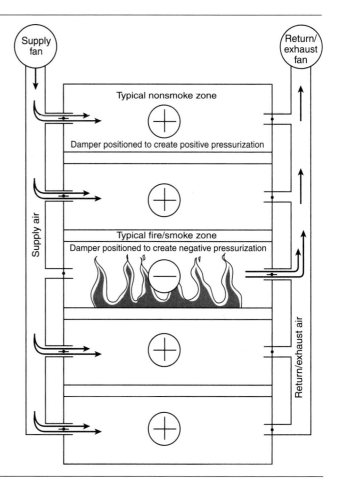

Figure 10.6. At the same time, make-up air is drawn into the atrium from openings to the outside, and, where necessary, supplied using a make-up air fan. It is also important to make sure that smoke exhaust fans do not discharge where they will affect people who have already escaped from the building. See Chapter 11 for additional discussion on fire protection issues.

Key Point With active smoke management systems, it is important to make sure that the smoke exhaust discharge points are kept well away from fresh-air, stair-pressurization, and make-up air intake points.

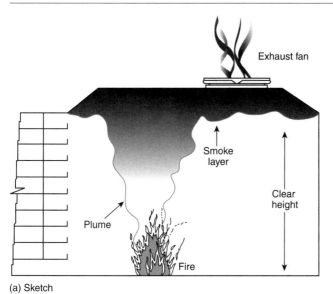

FIGURE 10.6 Atrium Fire.
(*Source:* Arup.)

Exhaust fan

Smoke layer

Clear height

Plume

Fire

(a) Sketch

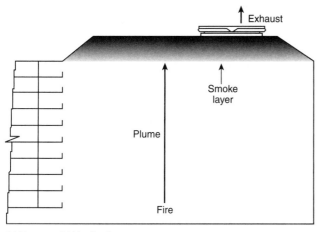

Exhaust

Smoke layer

Plume

Fire

(b) Zone model idealization

Smoke exhaust systems must be designed to ensure that smoke is drawn only from the smoke layer, and not from the clear layer beneath. This usually means that the velocity of air entering the smoke exhaust system must be limited. *"Plug holing"* occurs when air is drawn from the clear layer. When plug holing occurs, the effectiveness of the smoke-removal system is reduced. This phenomenon can be avoided by limiting the exhaust air velocity. Make-up air systems must be designed to ensure that the movement of air toward the fire does not "fan the flames." This usually means that air velocities must be limited.

Active smoke management systems also may be required by local codes for certain types of buildings. Typical examples include places of assembly and stages in performance arts buildings. In small, lightly occupied buildings, such systems are rarely required, but they should be considered for large, heavily occupied, high-profile buildings that have a higher threat risk.

Requirements for Smoke Management Systems

When ductwork systems are required for use in active smoke management systems, they must be built and designed to accommodate higher temperatures than are usually considered (i.e., higher than ambient temperature). The actual temperature requirements are usually determined through analysis or set by the local building codes. A typical requirement for an atrium smoke exhaust system would be for all of the components that handle hot smoke to be rated for operation at 482°F (250°C) for one hour.

Such a temperature requirement can have significant implications for the type of construction used to build the duct. For example, a typical HVAC duct is built from galvanized sheet metal with a gauge thickness of between 18 and 22 gauge. The sealants, mastics, or gaskets used to seal the joints are made from materials that typically have low melting points. At high temperatures, ducts will also expand significantly, which can lead to warping of the ducts and failure of the joints between the duct segments.

To resolve the issues of duct leakage through joint failure due to either melting or warping, ducts made to withstand high temperatures are typically built to incorporate additional, heat resistant, flexible joints to prevent warping of the ductwork. Where extremely high temperatures are expected or if a fire within the duct is likely then ¹/₈-inch (3.2 millimeters) black steel with welded flanged joints is used.

Key Point   Long runs of straight ductwork should be avoided. If long runs cannot be avoided, "soft" sections (achieved through appropriately rated flexible connections) may need to be included in order to accommodate thermal expansion of the ducts.

Fans, supports, and other components of the system must also be upgraded in order to withstand high temperatures. A number of national standards describe testing procedures for these components, and appropriate equipment is usually listed or rated.

Key Point Ducts that are expected to reach high temperatures must be located away from combustible materials so that the heat from the duct does not cause them to burn, and thus spread the fire to other zones.

Sometimes the ducts in a smoke management system must pass through a different fire zone. In this case, the designer must ensure that the compartmentation between the different fire zones is maintained. This compartmentation can be achieved through the design of the duct, through the construction of a shaft around the duct, or through the use of a fire-resistant wrap. Examples of different types of ducts are shown in Figure 10.7. Fire-resistant ducts should be designed to accommodate expected conditions. The Type A duct, shown in Figure 10.7(a), has been designed to pass through a fire compartment and prevent spread of fire from that compartment to other areas. This type of duct provides up to 4 hours of stability, integrity, and insulation, and it is typical for escape-lobby ventilation and staircase pressurization. The Type B duct, shown in Figure 10.7(b), has been designed to exhaust air from the fire zone, through another compartment, without allowing the fire to spread to the compartment that it passes through. This type of duct provides up to 3 hours of stability and integrity and 2 hours of insulation. It is typical for kitchen-extract, smoke-extract, and other fire-rated systems.

For smoke management systems to operate reliably during a fire, an emergency electrical system is required. Cabling must also maintain its integrity during a fire.

Sprinklers, fire pumps, and other components of the fire protection system are described in Chapter 11. Significant information regarding the details of design of smoke management systems is also available in the following literature:

- "Smoke Control," *The SFPE Handbook of Fire Protection Engineering* [4]
- "Smoke Management in Covered Malls and Atria," *The SFPE Handbook of Fire Protection Engineering* [5]
- *Principles of Smoke Management*, American Society of Heating, Refrigerating, and Air-Conditioning Engineers, Inc. [3]
- "Air-Conditioning and Ventilating Systems," *Fire Protection Handbook* [2]

FIGURE 10.7   Ducts Resisting Fire.
(*Source:* Arup.)

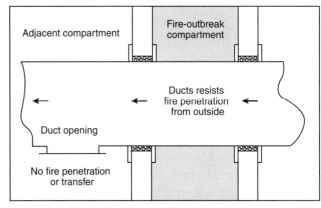

(a) Type A duct—Resisting Fire from the Outside

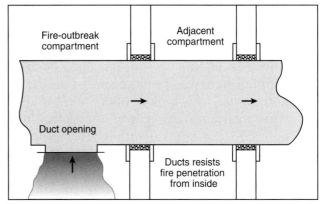

(b) Type B duct—Resisting Fire from the Inside

___CHEMICAL, BIOLOGICAL, AND___
RADIOLOGICAL EVENTS

Chemical, biological, and radiological (CBR) substances are addressed in detail in Chapter 6. The potential for an extreme event involving these substances exists whenever a CBR substance is present in a building. Chemical weapons include nerve, blood, blister, choking, and tear agents; incapacitants; psychochemicals; and industrial chemicals. Biological weapons include anthrax, botulism, plague, smallpox, tularemia, hemorrhagic fever, and toxins.

Chemical agents and toxins may be dispersed using open gas cylinders, evaporating open containers, aerosol generators, spray tanks, or explosive charges. Biological weapons are likely to be dispersed through infected powders. Agents can be delivered to buildings as packages, by intruders, through vehicles, and by projectiles. Each of these methods of delivery will require a different means of hardening the HVAC systems against an attack.

HVAC systems provide a network of pipes and ducts through which a contaminant could be dispersed through a building. It is unlikely that heating or cooling pipes would be used for dispersal, because the building occupants are not exposed to the contents of these systems. The most likely HVAC path for dispersal is the air-system ductwork.

Protection Inside the Building

One of the key issues with HVAC systems is that they link multiple parts of the building together through relatively large pathways. The size of the connection depends on the type of system selected and the way in which the building is normally operated.

If an agent is released within a building, then the HVAC systems will provide a path for dispersion to all areas connected to that HVAC system. The most effective way to prevent spreading of the agent is to isolate the systems serving the room in which the agent is released from those serving the rest of the building [6, 7, 8, 9]. In most buildings, it is not practical to do this for every room within the building, because this would mean providing extremely large equipment rooms and distribution shafts.

Key Point The best approach to protecting a building from an interior-agent release is to identify the rooms where an attack is likely to occur and to protect the rest of the building from that area.

Two scenarios that apply to most buildings, and for which mitigation measures are both inexpensive and effective, are the release of an agent in a delivery area and the release of an agent in a mechanical space.

Delivery Areas. If the agent is brought in through the delivery of a package, then the area where the package is most likely to be opened should be protected. In most commercial buildings, this means that independent HVAC systems should be provided in reception areas, the mailroom, and the loading dock and adjacent receiving areas.

These systems should be independent of other areas of the building. They should recirculate air within those rooms only, and all air leaving those rooms should be exhausted from the building. The exhaust outlet should be located well away from any air intakes. These measures will help to control the spread of any agent that is released.

Key Point   Exhaust systems should be sized to ensure that rooms are under negative pressure relative to the rest of the building so that all airflow from surrounding rooms is into the receiving area.

This will help control the spread of any agent that is released. An example of an independent exhaust system used in a reception area is shown in Figure 10.8. The figure shows a chemical and biological

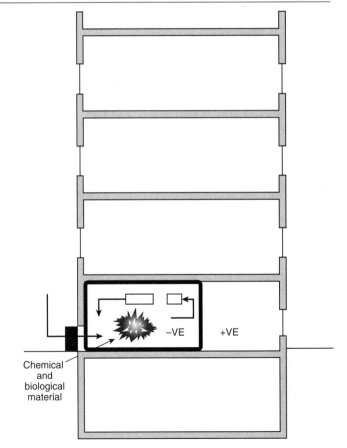

FIGURE 10.8   Example of an Independent Exhaust System.

(*Source:* Arup.)

Chemical and biological material

−VE   +VE

material released from the outside into the reception area. All air is recirculated within the room, and the room's system does not interface with any other building systems.

Of course, management procedures are also required to ensure that all packages are delivered and opened centrally. In the future, technology may become available to detect chemical and biological hazards and trigger smoke dampers to achieve emergency compartmentation.

Mechanical Rooms. Another area of high vulnerability is the mechanical room. If an agent is introduced within an air-handling unit, it will be dispersed around the building very quickly. In this case, the risk can best be reduced by controlling access to the mechanical room. The level of access control required will depend on the use of the building.

Protection Outside the Building

All buildings with mechanical ventilation have air intakes. In general, each air intake serves a large portion of the building. The air intake is more critical than the exhaust because it allows a contaminant to be drawn into the building. Air exhausts should also be protected, although to a lesser extent, because they provide weak points for contaminants to enter the building when the systems are off. Several strategies can be adopted to minimize the risk of a contaminant being drawn into the building, depending on the level of risk associated with the building.

A number of mitigation measures can be provided at minimal cost as part of good-practice HVAC design [6, 7, 8, 9]. These measures include the following, in order of ease of incorporation:

- Restrict access to building system plans.
- Locate air intakes away from public access areas.
- Install air intakes at high levels.
- Require security clearance for maintenance personnel.
- Locate air intakes away from horizontal surfaces.
- Provide physical protection of air intakes.
- Control the supply of air system components.
- Provide surveillance at air intakes.
- Provide multiple air intakes.
- Provide filtration at air intakes.

Restrict Access to Building System Plans. Controlling who has access to HVAC system plans prevents an attacker from determining where the intake locations are. It also prevents a would-be attacker from understanding the interconnection of the various areas of the building and knowing the levels of protection that have been put in place. This lack of information makes planning an attack more complicated and increases the likelihood of failure. Information that should be restricted includes: mechanical and electrical systems; elevators; fire, life safety, and security systems; and emergency operations procedures.

Locate Air Intakes Away from Public Access Areas. Air intakes should be located in nonpublic areas. Placement in nonpublic areas prevents an attacker from releasing an agent adjacent to the air intake without first obtaining access to the air intake. Access management practices can be implemented to reduce the risk of attack.

Install Air Intakes at High Levels. Most chemical and biological agents are heavier than air. Locating the air intakes at high levels, even if they are on a publicly accessible street, reduces the risk of the agent actually entering the building. Figure 10.9(a) shows an example of a vulnerable system; Figure 10.9(b) shows an example of a more protected system. Figure 10.9(c) shows a best-case scenario.

Require Security Clearance for Maintenance Personnel. The mechanical systems of any building are highly vulnerable. All maintenance personnel should be security screened upon employment. Maintenance workers on external contracts should be supervised at all times or subject to the same security clearances.

Locate Air Intakes Away from Horizontal Surfaces. If an intake is located at a high level, then the easiest way to release an agent into the system is to send a projectile up to the air intake. It is more difficult to do this if there is no horizontal surface on which the projectile can lodge and release the agent. Air intake and exhaust openings should therefore be sloped or vertical.

Provide Physical Protection of Air Intakes. Air intakes should be protected so that they cannot be penetrated by a projectile or other device. Air intakes are usually protected by steel louvers for weatherproofing and have a half-inch metal mesh to prevent birds and vermin from nesting within them. These physical barriers can be

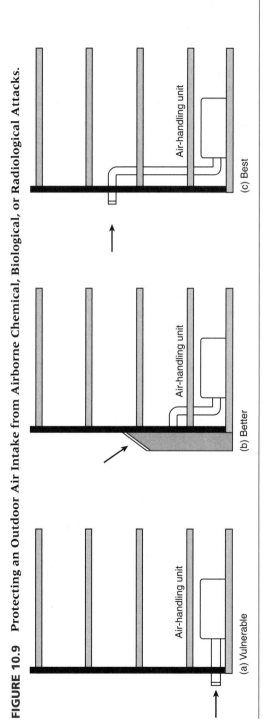

FIGURE 10.9   Protecting an Outdoor Air Intake from Airborne Chemical, Biological, or Radiological Attacks.

(a) Vulnerable

Air-handling unit

(b) Better

Air-handling unit

(c) Best

Air-handling unit

(*Source*: Arup.)

strengthened by using heavier gauge meshes and more protective louvers; however, these measures will also increase the required size of the air intake.

Control the Supply of Air System Components. Components that are to be introduced directly into the air system and that require frequent replacement, such as filters, should be bought from reputable manufacturers and inspected for tampering before being used within the system. Such supply management will prevent an agent from being introduced through system components.

Provide Surveillance at Air Intakes. It is sometimes not possible to locate air intakes away from horizontal surfaces or to protect them from projectile attack. Many building intakes are located at high levels of the building, set back from the edge of the roof. This situation has the advantage of making them invisible to a casual street-level observer and meets the requirement to put them out of a publicly accessible area, but it does not meet the requirement to locate them away from horizontal surfaces. In these cases, the most practical approach may be to provide camera surveillance or motion detection at the air intake. This type of surveillance will shut down the system if suspicious activity is observed.

Provide More Air Intakes. Another strategy is to provide more air intakes, as shown in Figure 10.10, so that the portion of the building impacted by an event is reduced. However, this approach may lead to more complex HVAC systems and additional surveillance requirements, and so it may not be a practical solution.

Provide Filtration at Air Intakes. If a chemical or biological agent is released, then it may be possible to prevent the spread of the agent using filtration [6, 7, 8, 9]. Such protection can be provided through physical filtration, which uses fibrous filters, or chemical filtration, which uses chemical reactions to eliminate gases, usually with activated carbon or through the use of UV light to denature bacteria and viruses.

Key Point   A filtration-protection strategy should only be used for high-risk buildings or for high-risk areas within buildings, because it can lead to significant energy use increases and maintenance impacts.

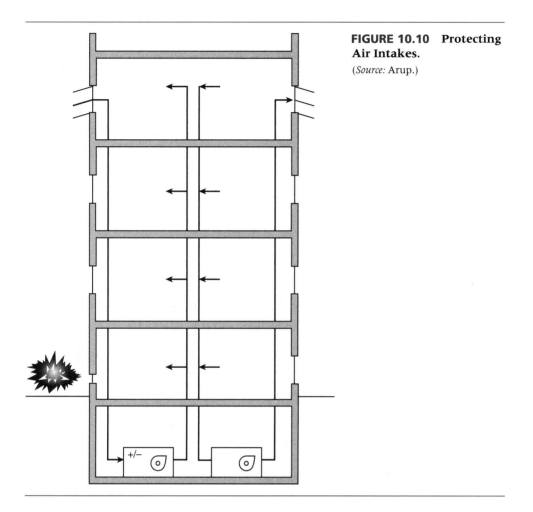

FIGURE 10.10 Protecting Air Intakes.

(*Source:* Arup.)

Energy use increases with the use of physical filters because the filters introduce a pressure drop that the fans within the mechanical systems must overcome. Filtration for chemical and biological agents should be suitable for particle sizes of 0.3 to 35 microns for bacteria and of 0.01 to 0.3 microns for viruses. These sizes are much smaller than the sizes usually filtered out using standard building filters. Filters are rated using the MERV system—a minimum efficiency reporting value. High efficiency particulate air (HEPA) filters are commonly used for this type of filtration.

Physical filters are of two main types. A low-efficiency filter consists of a mat of fibers contained in a cardboard or metal frame. High-efficiency filters consist of bags or folded sheets of fibrous material.

The folded sheets or bags serve to increase the surface area through which the air can pass, allowing large areas of closely woven or felted material to be used without creating a pressure drop that cannot be reasonably overcome by a fan.

HEPA filters were developed during World War II by the Atomic Energy Commission to remove radioactive dust particles from research spaces. They are used in nuclear facilities, asbestos abatement, surgical facilities, tuberculosis wards, clean rooms, and computer rooms. HEPA filters are composed of pleated glass microfiber paper supported by aluminum fins and housed in a cartridge. These filters are 99.97 percent efficient in capturing 0.3-micron diameter particles, as shown in Figure 10.11.

The initial pressure drop of a standard HEPA filter is approximately 1.0 inch (25 milimeters) at a flow velocity of 250 feet per minute (fpm) (1.25 meters per second [m/s]). High-capacity HEPA filters have an initial pressure drop of 1.4 inches (35 millimeters) at 500 fpm (2.5 m/s). The typical total pressure drop for an air handling system in a large commercial system is approximately 6 inches (152 millimeters), and a typical velocity for air through an air handling unit is approximately 500 fpm (2.5 m/s). The implications of the addition of HEPA filtration to a system are, therefore, an addition of 15 to 20 percent to the total fan energy use required, based on the increased pressure drop necessary. If standard filters are used, then there will also be a large increase in the cross-sectional area of the air-handling units to allow the air to pass slowly across the filter. Special attention also has to be paid to sealing around the filters to ensure that the air passes through the filter and not around it.

High-efficiency MERV filters have a similar construction to HEPA filters, but with a lower efficiency. The high-efficiency filters are 90

FIGURE 10.11 **Typical Performance of a HEPA Filter.**

(*Source:* Arup.)

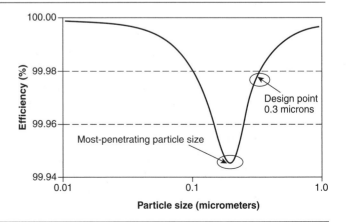

to 99 percent efficient for anthrax bacteria (1 micron), 100 percent for spore state (2 microns), but only 60 to 95 percent efficient for pathogenic bacteria (0.2 to 0.5 micron). The pressure drop for a high-efficiency filter is approximately 0.4 to 0.85 inches (10.2 to 21.6 millimeters) at 500 fpm (2.5 m/s).

Electrostatic filters are similar to particle filters except that polarized fibers are used to increase the collection efficiency. These filters typically have less packing density and consequently will have a much lower pressure drop than a mechanical filter of similar efficiency. Figure 10.12 summarizes the filtering mechanisms that are available.

Neither HEPA filters nor high-efficiency filters can be used to control chemical contaminants, because these contaminants are not usually in particulate form. Active chemical filters must be used for chemical contaminants. Active chemical filters require significant maintenance and usually require an additional physical filter to prevent the activated carbon from entering the system.

Activated carbon filters absorb airborne odors and vapors through chemical reactions. The filters are made through a carbonization process, whereby wool, coal, or coconut shells are subjected to high temperatures. Activated carbon filters are of two types: granular activated carbon and impregnated pads. Granular activated

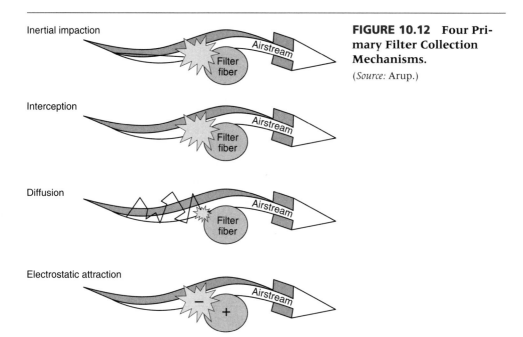

FIGURE 10.12 Four Primary Filter Collection Mechanisms.

(*Source:* Arup.)

Inertial impaction

Interception

Diffusion

Electrostatic attraction

carbon filters are more effective than impregnated carbon pads and require less frequent servicing. However, impregnated carbon pads are much simpler to change and do not require additional particle filtration to prevent carbon dust from entering the remainder of the system.

Ultraviolet systems are used in many water and air systems to kill bacteria and viruses. The systems use electricity to power the light, and therefore have energy consumption associated with them. The effectiveness of such systems depends both on the length of time for which the bacteria are exposed to the light and the intensity of the light. These systems have been used for about 50 years as a germicide in health care, food processing, and waste treatment.

Key Point   Be aware that the effectiveness of ultraviolet systems has not been researched for the types of bacteria used in biological weapons.

OTHER TYPES OF EXTREME EVENTS

Buildings can experience extreme events other than CBR releases and fire. In some cases, such events have a high risk of occurrence and are typically designed for. In other cases, the risk of the event is so small that for noncritical facilities the cost of designing and installing systems to withstand the events outweighs the potential benefits.

Seismic Events

In the event of an earthquake, the three most likely life safety hazards are falling debris, fire, and flood. Flood could be from inadvertent water discharge from pipe failures or rain as a result of facade failure. Fire and flood usually occur some time after the earthquake as a result of a secondary failure. It is generally not important to keep HVAC systems in operation following an earthquake.

In most U.S. jurisdictions, well-defined code requirements regulate the suspension of hanging mechanical equipment. These codes usually apply to anything weighing more than 75 pounds. A typical support detail for hanging equipment prevents horizontal movement through the addition of diagonal aircraft wires to a standard trapeze arrangement. These wires are slack under normal circumstances, but become taut in the event of excessive horizontal movement. The wires prevent deformation and failure of the primary support system.

Large, floor-mounted equipment that requires vibration isolation is protected through the use of snubbers. These devices prevent excessive lateral movement of the standard support system of vibration-isolation springs so that it does not deform and fail.

HVAC systems should be kept operational in a few types of high-risk buildings. These buildings include hospitals, air-traffic control facilities, and local emergency command centers. The systems can be braced against the building and flexible connections provided at zones where large movements are expected.

Key Point In high-risk buildings, the integrity of the HVAC system is best maintained through structural building design that restricts the movement of the building.

Extreme Wind Events

Extreme wind events include tornadoes and hurricanes. Wind speeds in a Category V storm are greater than 155 mph. High winds such as these, and even those in weaker storms, can cause major damage to buildings. The two major sources of damage are from the removal of loosely attached building components by wind and impact from windborne debris.

Hurricanes are generally predictable several hours, or even days, in advance, and this can lead to the evacuation of most building occupants to special shelters away from the direct path of the storm or to strengthened buildings within the path of the storm. Tornadoes are often not predictable, but they often have very localized areas of impact.

In the case of extreme wind events, the HVAC systems of most buildings do not need to be operational. However, openings for HVAC air intake/exhaust and windows are natural areas of weakness in the building. These openings should be fitted with metal shutters or plywood coverings.

Blast Events

HVAC systems do not need to operate during or after a blast event, unless there is a fire, in which case the response of the mechanical systems and level of protection required is the same as for a fire event. Openings for HVAC air intake/exhaust are a natural area of weakness in a building that could be exploited by someone seeking to cause maximum damage using a bomb located outside the building. As such, all air intake and exhaust points should be closed using tamper-proof fixings. See Chapter 5 for additional discussion on blast hazards.

The movies are rich with images of villains and heroes finding their way through buildings using the ducts as pathways. In most cases, ductwork doesn't provide as easy a route as shown in the movies, due to high air velocities, smooth duct interiors, and small dimensions. Wire mesh screens are usually installed at all exit/entry points to prevent birds and vermin from entering the system. In sensitive buildings, it may be necessary to install more robust mesh screens at the entry and exit points.

SUMMARY

A fundamental purpose of HVAC systems is to maintain comfort and to provide adequate ventilation during normal building operation. These systems can also be used to control the spread of contaminants, smoke, and other airborne materials within a building. As such, they serve a useful purpose in helping to mitigate the impact of extreme events, particularly fire and CBR type events.

However, because HVAC systems are often interconnected, adequate protection needs to be provided against extreme events as well. This protection includes provision of components such as fire and smoke dampers, filters, detectors, and the like. Holistic design of building HVAC systems for mitigating extreme events requires close cooperation with other building systems and disciplines, so as to achieve the overall life safety and property-protection goals as well as comfort and amenity goals to be achieved during normal building operations.

BIBLIOGRAPHY

References Cited

1. ICC, 2003. *International Building Code*, International Code Council, Falls Church, VA.
2. Webb, W. A., 2003. "Air-Conditioning and Ventilating Systems," Chapter 12.15, in Cote, A. (Ed.), *Fire Protection Handbook*, 19th ed., National Fire Protection Association, Quincy, MA.

3. Klote, J., and Milke, J. A., 2002. *Principles of Smoke Management*, American Society of Heating, Refrigerating, and Air-Conditioning Engineers, Atlanta, GA.

4. Klote, J. H., 2002. "Smoke Control," Chapter 4-12, *The SFPE Handbook of Fire Protection Engineering*, 3rd ed., National Fire Protection Association, Quincy, MA.

5. Milke, J. A., 2002. "Smoke Management in Covered Malls and Atria," Chapter 4-13, *The SFPE Handbook of Fire Protection Engineering*, 3rd ed., National Fire Protection Association, Quincy, MA.

6. USACE, 2001. *Protecting Buildings and Their Occupants from Airborne Hazards*, United States Army Core of Engineers, Washington, DC.

7. CDC, 2002. *Guidance for Protection Building Environments from Airborne Chemical, Biological, or Radiological Attacks*, Centers for Disease Control and Prevention, Atlanta, GA.

8. ASHRAE, 2003. *Report of the Presidential Ad Hoc Committee for Building Health and Safety under Extraordinary Events*, American Society of Heating, Refrigerating, and Air-Conditioning Engineers, Atlanta, GA.

9. FEMA, 2003. *Risk Management Series: Reference Manual to Mitigate Potential Terrorist Attacks Against Buildings*, Federal Emergency Management Agency, Washington, DC.

NFPA Codes, Standards, and Recommended Practices

NFPA Publications.   The following is a list of NFPA codes, standards and recommended practices cited in this chapter. See the latest version of the *NFPA Catalog* for availability of current editions of these documents.

NFPA 90A, *Standard for the Installation of Air-Conditioning and Ventilating Systems*
NFPA 90B, *Standard for Installation of Warm Air Heating and Air-Conditioning Systems*
NFPA 92A, *Standard for Smoke-Control Systems Utilizing Barriers and Pressure Differences*
NFPA 92B, *Standard for Smoke Management Systems in Malls, Atria and Large Spaces*
NFPA 5000®, *Building Construction and Safety Code®*

11

Design to Manage Fire and Its Impact

Chris Marrion

Richard Custer

This chapter examines design alternatives that can be implemented to help manage fire either by itself or as a direct or indirect result of an extreme event in order to limit a fire's impact on a building and its occupants. The topics addressed include preventing ignition, managing fire development and spread, and protecting occupants. In addition, the chapter also presents a variety of fire and life safety–related systems that can be used to further address these objectives. Such systems include detection and alarm systems, suppression systems, and smoke management systems. Emergency response issues are also addressed.

OVERVIEW

A number of possible goals and objectives are associated with managing fires related to extreme events. These goals and objectives can be achieved in multiple ways. For example, given a goal of providing life safety, one objective would be to prevent loss of life outside the compartment of origin. Fire protection alternatives to achieve this objective might be to limit the potential for flashover in the compartment of origin, to confine the fire and smoke to the compartment, or to maintain tenable conditions outside the compartment of origin by additional means.

When selecting a fire protection alternative, it is important to identify the goals and objectives that need to be achieved. From there, various fire protection strategies can be developed. These strategies may employ one or more design alternatives in order to meet the stated objective(s).

The content of this chapter is presented as a series of subsystems that comprise an overall approach to building fire and life safety. These subsystems are generally organized by the Fire Safety Concepts Tree found in the National Fire Protection Association (NFPA) document NFPA 550, *Guide to the Fire Safety Concepts Tree*. The discussion of each subsystem includes topics on general principles, as well as considerations for addressing extreme events.

THE FIRE SAFETY CONCEPTS TREE

NFPA 550, *Guide to the Fire Safety Concepts Tree*, can be used as a guide in developing fire strategies. The Fire Safety Concepts Tree presents numerous elements that may be considered in the development of a strategy to address specific objectives. The main branch of the Fire Safety Concepts Tree is shown in Figure 11.1.

The following discussion describes the details of the concepts and subsystems that should be considered when developing strategies to manage fires. Additional information is available in the following publications:

- *SFPE Engineering Guide to Performance-Based Fire Protection Analysis and Design in Buildings* [1]
- *The SFPE Code Official's Guide to Performance-Based Design Review* [2]
- "Design of Structures for Fire Loading and Understanding Fire/Life Safety System Interdependencies," *ASCE Structures Congress 2005 Proceedings* [3]

Design Strategies

Several different strategies should be considered when developing designs to manage a fire, whether one occurring accidentally or as the result of an extreme event. These strategies may include combinations of active systems, passive systems, and initiating systems, or they may involve taking no action at all.

Active systems are those that take direct action to limit the growth rate of a fire or to control the movement of smoke and fire. Examples of active systems include automatic sprinklers or the use of fans to exhaust or control the movement of smoke. *Passive systems* control the likelihood of ignition, as well as the growth and spread of fire

FIGURE 11.1   Main Branch of the Fire Safety Concepts Tree.

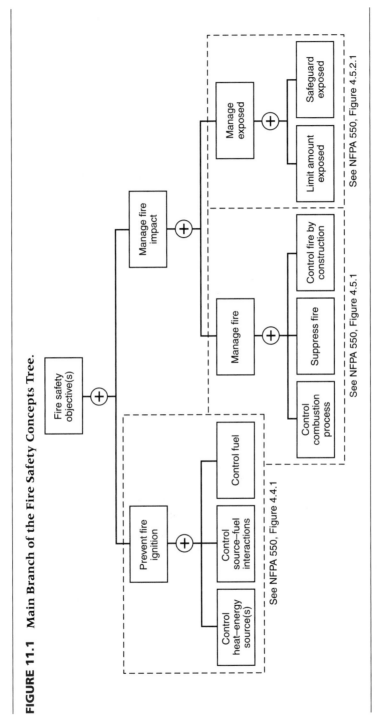

(*Source:* NFPA, 2002. NFPA 550. *Guide to the Fire Safety Concepts Tree,* National Fire Protection Association, Quincy, MA, Figure 4.3.)

and smoke once ignition has occurred. Passive systems can be used to control the spread of fire or smoke through the presence of physical barriers. *Initiating devices* activate suppression systems; release doors in passive systems, such as fire walls; set off smoke management systems; or trigger notification appliances. Examples of initiating devices include smoke and heat detectors.

___ PREVENTING IGNITION

The objective of the Prevent Fire Ignition subsystem in the Fire Safety Concepts Tree is to reduce the frequency of ignition and to assist in the development of fire prevention measures. The Prevent Fire Ignition subsystem is shown in Figure 11.2.

Principles of Ignition Prevention

Ignition sources can be controlled in a number of different ways, including removing them from the compartment if their presence is not required there, in order to limit the chance of ignition and fire. Ignition-prevention strategies are addressed in NFPA's *Fire Protection Handbook* [4], *SFPE Engineering Guide to Performance-Based Fire Protection Analysis and Design in Buildings* [1], and *The SFPE Code Official's Guide to Performance-Based Design Review* [2].

Contact between transient types of ignition sources (i.e., smoking materials, temporary wiring/lighting, etc.) and combustible materials should be limited. Such materials should be a sufficient distance away from each other to minimize ignition from various heat transfer means (i.e., radiation, conduction, or convection) [5]. Potential ignition sources and combustible materials may be separated by fire separations. Appliances or equipment within a compartment or building may have built-in ignition or heat sources inherent to their operation; such sources could potentially cause ignition of nearby combustible materials. Alternative equipment may be available that is designed to be intrinsically safe, thus limiting the potential for ignition.

Key Point   A fire separation is a horizontal or vertical assembly of fire resistance-rated material that is designed and tested to withstand the spread of fire for a given period of time.

FIGURE 11.2 **Prevent Fire Ignition Branch of the Fire Safety Concepts Tree.**

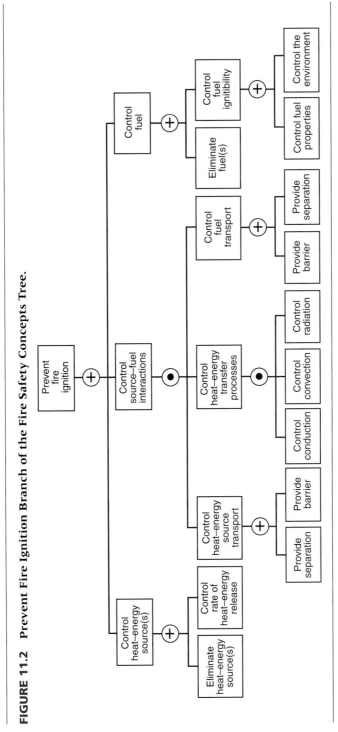

(*Source:* NFPA, 2002. NFPA 550, *Guide to the Fire Safety Concepts Tree*, National Fire Protection Association, Quincy, MA, Figure 4.4.1.)

Construction materials and structural elements, as well as contents, should be selected that resist ignition. Using such materials will reduce the risk of ignition in a building should an ignition source become present. Materials that use fire retardants or that have high thermal inertias may also be less likely to ignite. More guidance on this topic is available in "Conduction of Heat in Solids," in *The SFPE Handbook of Fire Protection Engineering* [6].

> **Key Point** The potential for ignition can be reduced by selecting construction materials and structural elements, as well as contents, that resist ignition.

In addition to controlling ignition sources, fuels, and their interaction, fire safety management and good housekeeping procedures can be developed and implemented to further assist in controlling ignition sources and the amount, location, and type of combustible materials. These concepts are discussed further in the Prevent Fire Ignition branch of the Fire Safety Concepts Tree, as shown in Figure 11.2. In addition, fire prevention codes such as NFPA 1, *Uniform Fire Code*™, and the ICC's *International Fire Code*®, contain information to help reduce fire ignition and control the development of fires.

Extreme Event Considerations

As discussed in previous chapters, extreme events can introduce unusual and challenging ignition sources (e.g., high energy blast, impacts). Depending on the type(s) of events that are deemed credible, consideration should be given as to what ignition sources may be present or introduced and the impact these may have on the building. Appropriate measures, including selecting and locating candidate materials in such a way as to limit ignition during or following an extreme event, should be developed to help isolate potential ignition sources from combustible materials.

MANAGING FIRE DEVELOPMENT AND SPREAD

The Manage Fire subsystem of the Fire Safety Concepts Tree, shown in Figure 11.3, is intended to reduce the rate of fire development and limit smoke and heat production.

Principles of Fire Management

Fire safety concepts that can be implemented to assist in controlling the development of a fire include selection and placement of con-

FIGURE 11.3   **Manage Fire Branch of the Fire Safety Concepts Tree.**

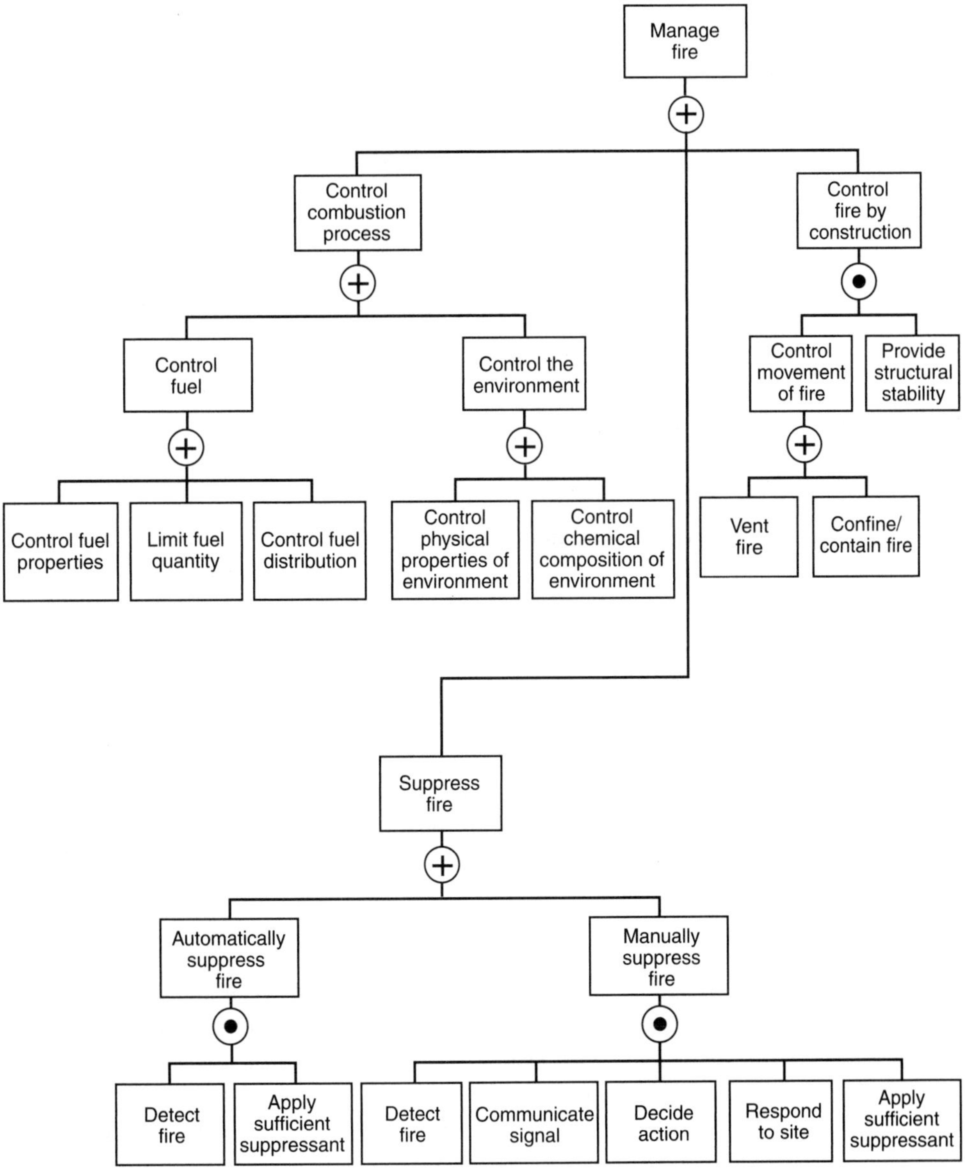

(*Source:* NFPA, 2002. NFPA 550, *Guide to the Fire Safety Concepts Tree*, National Fire Protection Association, Quincy, MA, Figure 4.5.1.)

tents, selection of interior finishes and construction materials, limiting the quantity of materials, and controlling the size, geometry, and ventilation of a compartment. More information on these topics can be found in *The SFPE Handbook of Fire Protection Engineering* [7]; NFPA's *Fire Protection Handbook* [4]; NFPA 550, *Guide to the Fire Safety Concepts Tree; SFPE Engineering Guide to Performance-Based Fire Protection Analysis and Design in Buildings* [1]; and *The SFPE Code Official's Guide to Performance-Based Design Review* [2].

Some materials, such as plastics and ignitible liquids, are more prone to rapid fire development, as well as higher rates of smoke production, as explained in Chapter 3-1, "Heat Release Rates," of *The SFPE Handbook of Fire Protection Engineering* [8]. In addition, some materials generate higher smoke rates than others on a per mass of consumed material basis [9]. Depending on the use and the degree of flexibility needed for a space to function as intended, materials that have lower fire growth and smoke production rates may be selected. In addition, by placing combustible materials far enough apart from each other, the potential for radiant ignition of adjacent fuel packages may be decreased, thus limiting the potential for further fire development and spread. Combustible interior finishes that are applied to vertical surfaces, and even more so to ceilings, can increase fire spread dramatically.

Key Point   The rate of fire development and its resultant spread can be controlled not only by the selection of materials, but also by the arrangement of contents in a space, including their placement in relation to each other, so as to limit radiant ignition.

Test methods are available to assist in determining flame-spread ratings (see ASTM International's *Standard Test Method for Surface Burning Characteristics of Building Materials* [10]). Heat release rates of candidate interior finishes are also available (see Chapter 3-1, "Heat Release Rates," and Chapter 3-3, "The Cone Calorimeter," in *The SFPE Handbook of Fire Protection Engineering* [8, 11]).

These tests may assist in the selection of materials. Tests such as the room-corner fire test can also help assess how materials may burn and may provide additional valuable information that cannot be obtained from other tests such as the ASTME-84 Steiner Tunnel Test. The overall construction and configuration of a compartment can also effect fire development. Combustible construction elements can add to the overall fuel load, as well as assist in spreading fire throughout a compartment and to adjacent compartments. Openings or limited compartmentation, as well as ventilation systems, can supply oxygen, contributing to the growth and duration of a fire. In contrast, larger compartments are better able to dissipate heat. Also, higher ceilings help reduce radiant feedback from the ceiling jet and upper layer to materials below.

Extreme Event Considerations

With respect to extreme events, various issues should be assessed regarding the management of fire growth and spread. These may include arson and impacts by vehicles, planes, missiles, or other projectiles. Arson-related fires frequently result in the introduction of accelerants that serve as substantial ignition sources. These can simultaneously ignite large amounts of fuel in the vicinity and potentially provide additional fuel. As discussed in Chapter 8, accelerants can ignite other combustible materials and significantly enhance fire growth and promote spread. Impacts by vehicles, planes, missiles, and other projectiles may introduce additional fuel and ignition sources into a building as well as redistribute the combustible materials within a compartment, which can lead to faster fire growth rates and longer fire durations. Depending on the type of extreme event(s) deemed credible, its impact on enhancing fire development and spread should be assessed.

PROTECTING OCCUPANTS

The Manage Exposed subsystem of the Fire Safety Concepts Tree, shown in Figure 11.4, addresses providing occupants with a safe means of access to a place of safety in the event of a fire.

Principles of Occupant Protection and Evacuation

The evacuation subsystem contains many components, including notification, access, egress capacity, and the protection of escape routes. More information on these topics is available in *The SFPE Handbook of Fire Protection Engineering* [7], NFPA's *Fire Protection Handbook* [4], *SFPE Engineering Guide to Performance-Based Fire Protection Analysis and Design in Buildings* [1], and *The SFPE Code Official's Guide to Performance-Based Design Review* [2].

An evacuation begins once an event has been detected and the occupants have been notified that an evacuation must occur. It is important that detection and notification occur promptly so that the building occupants have as much time as possible to respond.

FIGURE 11.4   Manage Exposed Branch of the Fire Safety Concepts Tree.

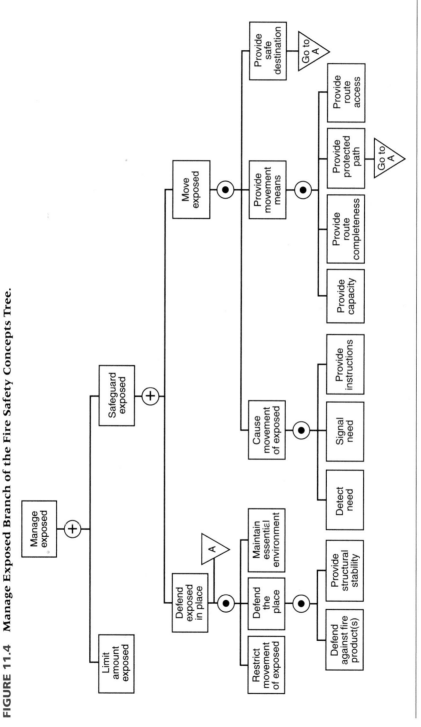

(*Source*: NFPA, 2002. NFPA 550, *Guide to the Fire Safety Concepts Tree*, National Fire Protection Association, Quincy, MA, Figure 4.5.2.1.)

Notification should include clear and intelligible directions to the occupants as to the situation and what they are supposed to do. Once notified, occupants will need to be able to access an exit. Chapter 12 of this book includes in-depth discussion of evacuation considerations and design approaches for occupant life safety.

Extreme Event Considerations

Extreme events may introduce special concerns with regards to evacuation and life safety, as well as introduce the need for specific evacuation scenarios and strategies that need to be considered. Chapter 12 examines evacuation considerations specific to extreme events.

DETECTION AND ALARM SYSTEMS

Other branches of the Fire Safety Concepts Tree are often reliant on detection and alarm systems in order to achieve their objectives. The intent of the fire detection and alarm system is to provide early detection of a fire or smoke condition so that occupants and emergency personnel can be notified. In addition, detection and alarm systems are often provided to activate fire protection systems, such as smoke management systems and release automatic doors.

Principles of Detection Systems

Detection of a fire can occur manually when a fire is sensed by occupants or automatically via initiating devices, such as smoke detectors, heat detectors, and sprinklers. It is important to have some type of detection system in order to help expedite detection of a fire. This is even more important in areas that are not typically occupied or accessible, where occupants are not awake, or that contain high hazards. Depending on the intent of the detection system (i.e., occupant notification, emergency responder notification, activation of another subsystem, etc.), different types of initiating devices may need to be provided, each with potentially different design parameters.

Detection systems typically sense a fire by detecting various fire signatures. Fire signatures are effects produced by a fire, such as smoke, heat, radiant emissions, or other by-products. The type of detection system used should be based on the type of fire signature(s) that will be produced during the phase of the fire when detection is intended to occur. For example, a fire may produce different fire signatures during the smoldering phase (e.g., smoke) than when it is more fully developed (e.g., heat, radiant emissions). The point at which a fire should be detected will impact the selection of the detector and its ability to perform as intended. Ambient conditions also need to be considered to limit the possibility of false or nuisance alarms.

In selecting an appropriate detection system, the location of the detector with respect to the potential fire also needs to be considered. The decision of where to locate a detector is often based on the configuration and geometry of the compartment (i.e., ceiling height, volume, etc.), the configuration of the ceiling (beams/joists, sloped, peaked, etc.), and the potential location of the fire or combustible materials. These factors may impact the ability of the fire signature(s) to reach the detector, and thus affect detection time. Zoning of the fire alarm system also needs to be coordinated with other fire and life safety systems, including egress, smoke management, and sprinkler system zones. It is critical that fire and life safety systems be coordinated.

Annex B of *NFPA 72®, National Fire Alarm Code®*, provides a performance-based guide to designing detection systems and details regarding the information that should be considered in selecting an appropriate detection system and locating initiating devices to meet the intended goals and objectives.

Principles of Notification Systems

Notification may be provided to building occupants either by audible and/or visual means. Audible notification appliances include voice alarm systems, horns, gongs, whereas visual notification is typically achieved through the installation of strobes. Notification may also be provided by pagers, email/computers, mass notification systems, and often recognized notification appliances. Notification systems can be initiated either manually or automatically via detection systems.

Notification may also include contacting emergency responders, either those on site or at the local fire service. Once responders are on site, the notification system can provide them with further information to assist them in determining the location and extent of the fire. When assessing fire detection and alarm systems, delays associated with sensing fire signatures, alarm verification and system processing times, and sending the signals to emergency responders (including via an intermediate monitoring facility) should be understood and factored into the assessment as needed.

Extreme Event Considerations

Detection and alarm systems are a critical component for responding to extreme events. Systems should therefore be designed for reliability and redundancy so that they are not adversely impacted by various threats.

Key Point System designers must understand credible threats and design detection and alarm systems to help provide early detection and proper notification with appropriate instructions and be robust to limit the effect of extreme events on their operation.

Designers should consider the benefits of providing multiple circuits to detection and notification systems, as well as to the systems that they control (i.e., smoke management, voice alarm, etc.). Such performance-based design may include redundant systems, local transponders, and running circuits in protected routes separated by sufficient distances such that if one is severed, the remaining one can still provide the needed function. The system should be designed in conjunction with a threat and risk assessment (TARA). TARA is discussed in depth in Chapter 4.

For additional guidance regarding performance-based designs of detection and alarm systems, see Annex B of *NFPA 72, National Fire Alarm Code,* and *The SFPE Handbook of Fire Protection Engineering* [7].

Detection. A significant amount of research is being devoted to chemical, biological and radiological (CBR) hazard detection. CBR detection/initiating devices should be supervised and monitored, by the fire alarm control panel. These types of initiating devices may assist in providing early detection of CBR events.

Notification. It is important to provide sufficient information to the occupants to direct them in an emergency. The information should be broadcast loudly enough (audibility) and be understandable (intelligibility) so that occupants can comprehend the message. Voice alarm systems should be provided that meet the intelligibility recommendations of *NFPA 72, National Fire Alarm Code.* In addition, consideration should be given to providing messages in multiple languages, depending on the occupant population.

As much information as possible should be provided to the people managing the incident, particularly if notification is via a live voice message. Those managing the incident should have sufficient information such that appropriate messages can be broadcast to the occupants. Consideration also should be given to mass notification systems (see *NFPA 72*).

Fire Alarm Control Panels. The fire alarm control panel (FACP) is critical, because it monitors the fire and life safety systems, controls for those various other systems, and can be used to notify occupants and emergency responders in the building. Care should be taken to locate the FACP in an area away from exposure to potential threats. If the FACP cannot be separated by a sufficient distance, then a hardened room, along with a robust and protected means to access the room from the exterior of the building, may provide the necessary protection.

It may be advantageous to provide redundant or remote FACPs, such that if one is impacted, others can be used to monitor and control the systems and communicate with occupants. It may also be necessary to provide a separate ventilation system for the command center or location of the FACP so that fresh air is provided, particularly if CBR threats are considered credible. Remote annunciators should also be available so that information regarding the incident can be provided to emergency responders prior to entering the area or building.

SUPPRESSION SYSTEMS

Fire suppression systems are provided to extinguish or at least control the further development of a fire.

Principles of Suppression Systems

Fire suppression can be by manual or automatic means, and suppression systems come in a variety of forms. Automatic suppression systems do not require human interaction for activation. Automatic systems typically include water, foam, or gaseous (i.e., FM200, Inergen, etc.) suppression systems. Depending on the type of fire and fuel involved, different types of suppression agents may be required. For example, some fires involve flammable liquids that are better suppressed by foam than by water or gaseous agents. When selecting a suppression system, it is important to understand the maximum accepted fire size in order to assess when suppression or extinguishment operations need to occur for different types of systems. For instance, in a space where there is a computer or electronic equipment with a high sensitivity to heat, smoke, and other products of combustion, a sensitive detection system activating a gaseous suppression system would typically provide earlier suppression/control of a fire than an automatic sprinkler system.

Key Point Some suppression systems require activation of a fire detection system in order to operate. When designing these systems, it is important to be able to assess detection time and determine when to discharge the suppressant.

The capabilities of these systems to activate in an acceptable amount of time and to discharge an appropriate quantity and type of suppressant need to be considered. Pertinent features that impact the effectiveness of such systems include the maximum fire size at detection, the maximum fire size at suppression, the type of fire signature being produced, the ability of the fire signature to get to the initiating device, and the effectiveness of the suppressant agent on the type of fire. Annex B to *NFPA 72, National Fire Alarm Code* provides additional details that should be considered in designing these systems.

When selecting a suppression system, the characteristics of the compartment should be considered, such as the overall geometry and size of the compartment being protected. For example, activation may be delayed for sprinklers on high ceilings. They may also have difficulty in providing adequate quantities of water onto the fire below due to the updraft of the plume once the fire has grown to a size sufficient to cause activation.

Key Point Natural or extreme event related ventilation or openings in a compartment may affect the ability of the suppression system, particularly for gaseous-type suppression systems, to maintain the design agent concentration in order to suppress a fire.

Manual suppression systems can also be provided to assist occupants, in-house fire brigades, or the local fire department in fighting fires. If provided, various aspects should be considered, including notification, response time to site, access to the area of origin, the number of emergency responders, and the fire-fighting equipment located at the building, including the water supply. First-aid fire-fighting equipment intended for use by building occupants, such as fire extinguishers, can also be provided so that occupants can begin fire suppression activities, if possible. However, unless this kind of suppression effort is initiated early on and the fire is small, these efforts may not be able to extinguish or control the fire. Additional types of suppression may therefore be needed and may be provided by automatic suppression systems or by the fire department.

Some types of suppression systems are used to control fires (i.e., standard sprinklers), whereas others are intended to extinguish fires (e.g., early suppression fast response sprinklers, gaseous systems, etc.). The objective of the suppression system should be clear. For instance, if the intent is only to control the fire, then the resultant ongoing conditions produced by a fire that is only being controlled should be analyzed to verify the achievement of the objective.

Key Point   It is critical that the zoning of the sprinkler systems be coordinated with other systems, including egress, smoke management, and fire alarm system zone systems.

Numerous guides and standards are available to assist in the design and assessment of suppression systems including the following:

- NFPA 13, *Standard for the Installation of Sprinkler Systems*
- NFPA 15, *Standard for Water Spray Fixed Systems for Fire Protection*
- *NFPA 72, National Fire Alarm Code,* Annex B
- NFPA 2001, *Standard on Clean Agent Fire Extinguishing Systems*

Extreme Event Considerations

Reliability and the need for redundancy of suppression systems should be assessed with respect to credible threats. Water supply system design may, for instance, include a looped supply, dual supply feeds, multiple fire pumps, or onsite water supply, for added robustness and redundancy.

Additional Fuel Load. When considering the type of suppression system, it is important to understand that additional fuels may be added to the compartment during an extreme event. This may change the type of fuel and the growth rate, peak heat release rate, and duration of the fire.

Multiple Suppressant Feeds. An assessment of the effectiveness and benefits of providing multiple feeds/risers to serve suppression systems and to bring the suppressant agent from the supply to the discharge nozzle should be developed in conjunction with the TARA and assessed against credible threats.

Additional Suppressant Supplies. The reliability and robustness of the suppressant agent supply should be assessed against credible threats in order to determine the potential effectiveness and benefits of providing multiple supplies to serve suppression systems. For example, a sprinkler system design may call for separation of inlets to the building, multiple fire pumps, multiple fire-pump rooms, on site water storage, looped supplies, dual water-supply feeds, and so on. This design should be developed in conjunction with the TARA.

SMOKE MANAGEMENT

The Smoke Management subsystem is intended to address the hazards resulting from the production and movement of smoke in a compartment.

Principles of Smoke Management

Smoke management systems address hazards resulting from smoke by limiting smoke production, controlling its movement, and/or reducing its amount. More guidance on this topic is available in *The SFPE Handbook of Fire Protection Engineering* [7], NFPA's *Fire Protection Handbook* [4], and *Principles of Smoke Management* [12].

One of the primary means of limiting smoke is to manage its production. Some building materials may produce large volumes of smoke.

Key Point   Materials in a building or compartment can sometimes be controlled in order to limit the quantities and rates of smoke production that can be expected from a fire involving those materials.

In addition to controlling the use of smoke-producing materials, suppression systems can be provided to limit fire development, and thus indirectly limit the quantity of smoke produced. Dependencies on other subsystems, including suppression, detection, and alarm systems, should be assessed in parallel with regards to their potential impact on fire size, smoke production and duration, and the activation time of the smoke management system.

If the use of certain building materials cannot be controlled, then the generation of smoke needs to be managed. Smoke can be removed from a compartment either by natural or mechanical means. Natural ventilation involves vents that are either automatically or manually opened upon detection of a fire so that smoke is vented from the building or compartment due to its natural buoyancy. Mechanical smoke exhaust systems can also be provided to exhaust smoke.

Several guides are available that provide additional information on smoke management, including NFPA 92A, *Standard for Smoke-Control Systems Utilizing Barriers and Pressure Differences*; NFPA 92B, *Standard for Smoke Management Systems in Malls, Atria, and Large Spaces*; *Principles of Smoke Management* [12]; and Chapter 4-9 of *The SFPE Handbook of Fire Protection Engineering* [13]. In addition, computer models can be used in assessing and designing smoke management systems. These range from simple zone models to more complex computational fluid dynamics models.

Smoke exhaust systems can be used to clear smoke from large-volume spaces, including atria. Such systems can maintain a clear layer so that occupants can exit during tenable conditions and fire fighters can undertake their operations.

If smoke cannot be exhausted from a space such as an atrium, then it may be possible to create pressure differentials to direct the movement of smoke from high-pressure areas to low-pressure ones. This is often done for pressurized stairways and other shafts in order to limit smoke movement into them.

In addition, smoke can be contained in the compartment of origin so that it does not spread. Such containment may include the use of smoke-control doors, smoke dampers, lobbies, and so on in a passive compartmentation/smoke management method.

The design of smoke management systems requires the incorporation of a number of design parameters. In assessing these systems, the following performance criteria should be evaluated: detector activation times, fan start-up times, fan ramp-up times, controls, interfaces with building management systems, supply air rates and locations, extract rates and locations, and ducting and fan design criteria, including temperature ratings.

Extreme Event Considerations

The overall potential effectiveness and benefit of additional smoke management measures should be assessed against credible threats. This assessment may identify additional requirements above code requirements for further limiting smoke spread and may include pressurized elevator lobbies and areas of refuge, as well as pressurized stairs with vestibules for fire department operations and emergency assistance.

Items that may need to be assessed with regard to various types of events include the following:

- Impact of an explosion or impact on ductwork and its ability to continue to function
- Larger than anticipated fire and smoke generation
- Temperature ratings of the fans and other equipment if fires are larger or longer than anticipated or if sprinkler system may be impaired
- Intakes provided at high level to limit introduction of agents
- Intakes located remote from exhaust to limit recirculation
- Damage to control equipment, including wiring and fans

The concept of using the smoke management system to also address CBR threats also should be reviewed in conjunction with a TARA.

The potential for multiple events should also be addressed, as should the possibility of air handling and smoke management systems to be used in an adverse manner. For instance, a CBR agent may be introduced in one area and a fire started simultaneously in an adjacent area such that the smoke control system pulls supply air from the area with the agent, in turn introducing it into the facility. The benefits of providing dedicated supply/exhaust equipment per zone may also have an additional advantage in addressing smoke as well as CBR isssues.

EMERGENCY RESPONDERS

The Emergency Responder subsystem is intended to identify features that should be provided in order to assist emergency responders in their rescue and fire control operations. Chapter 14 discusses emergency response in depth. This section presents several basic principles regarding the design of building components to assist emergency responders in performing their functions.

Emergency Response

Several features should be addressed to assist emergency responders in their work, including the following:

- Notification
- Site and building access
- Fire command center
- Equipment
- Water supply
- Smoke-purge systems
- Emergency response plans

Notification. Notification systems should be provided, preferably through automatic means, to give the fire department early and rapid notification of a fire. However, early detection and notification must be balanced with minimizing false alarms.

Site and Building Access. Easy access onto the site, into the building, and to the area of fire origin should be provided for the fire department and its equipment. Security gates, bollards, locked doors, and other security systems, which can help limit incidents, can also delay response to the area of origin.

Fire Command Center. A fire command center or area set aside as a control area should be provided. Depending on the building and its occupancy, susceptibility to various threats, and so on, it may also be beneficial to have a command center from which emergency responders can stage their operations. This area should contain appropriate equipment, including status indicators and controls for all appropriate fire protection equipment. The fire command center should be large enough to allow responders to undertake necessary operations.

Equipment. It may be necessary to provide equipment on site to assist fire fighters in their operations. This equipment may include hose reels, standpipes, communication systems, and so on. On site access to such equipment can reduce the amount of time it takes for emergency responders to get equipment to the area of origin, as well as assist them in undertaking their operations.

Water Supply. Adequate water supply should be provided on site. This includes not only a municipal supply, but also related equipment to access this supply, including fire hydrants and Siamese connections outside the building, as well as standpipes and hose reels within the building.

Smoke-Purge Systems. It may be necessary to provide means to clear the resultant smoke and heat during fire-fighting operations, as well as once the fire is out, to facilitate fire-fighting and search and rescue operations.

Emergency Response Plans. Emergency response plans should be developed to address the specific needs of the individual building. These plans are discussed further in Chapter 14.

Key Point Discussions with the fire department should be held early in the design process so that their concerns and requirements as they pertain to a building or facility can be incorporated.

Extreme Event Considerations

Issues including response location, fire command centers, and location of fire-fighting facilities should be discussed with respect to extreme events. Fire-fighting facilities should be in accordance with applicable codes, at a minimum, and reviewing the need for more resilient and robust designs as needed for systems such as standpipes, fire department access, and fire command centers. Additional provisions, such as fire department lockers on various floors, fire fighter elevators (including hardened elevators in separate shafts), water supplies, and air supplies, should also be considered and discussed with the fire department, if applicable. Also, the fire department should be consulted to ensure that communications will be sufficient throughout the building and site.

Training internally, as well as with emergency responders, will enable an incident to be managed more effectively. Such training may include pre-incident planning to assist emergency staff and building personnel in understanding the building, fire and life safety systems, particular hazards, key structural elements, and events that could impact critical equipment.

— STRUCTURAL PROTECTION —

Structural protection measures are intended to prevent or limit the premature collapse of part, or all, of a structure. This is indicated in the "Control Fire by Construction" branch.

Principles of Structural Protection

A structure should remain standing for a minimum duration in the event of a fire. The duration should provide sufficient time to allow occupants to evacuate and facilitate the ability of emergency responders to extinguish the fire [3]. Prevention of structural collapse limits potential adverse impacts on adjacent structures, including the possibility of disproportionate and progressive collapse. Structural protection also helps to achieve relevant fire and life safety goals and objectives, as well as performance criteria. In designing structures for fire, performance criteria may include the following:

- Limit damage to structural elements
- Prevent local collapse
- Prevent/limit deformation of structural elements
- Limit elongation of structural elements (i.e., so as not to impact integrated compartmentation walls, etc.)
- Prevent progressive collapse
- Prevent disproportionate collapse

Building codes typically require fire ratings of various durations for structural elements. These ratings depend on the size of the building and its occupancy type [14, 20, *NFPA 5000*, IBC 2006]. The fire ratings are developed via standardized tests. These tests typically assess a structural element's response over a time–temperature curve in a standardized furnace [15]. Note that structural elements and fireproofing materials do not always respond as predicted by small-scale tests. Such elements and materials may behave differently when the structural design is complicated or unusual connections exist and when interactions with other structural elements, load paths, and redistribution or varying fireloads are considered. Detailed analyses of proposed structural systems should be considered in order to provide a more accurate assessment of a structure's ability to maintain its integrity during a fire as compared to the standard time–temperature curve, as well as when compared to expected design fires that may differ from those in the tests, particularly in terms of growth rate and duration.

A number of factors should be considered when assessing the response of a structure to fire including the following:

- Design fire(s)
- Fire-induced environment
- Transfer of heat to structural elements
- Response of the structure to temperature changes

For the design fire(s), it is important that the fire growth rate, peak heat release rate, and duration are assessed, as well as the location of the structural element(s) relative to the fire. The building geometry and compartment size also have an effect on fire development, particularly with regards to temperature. For example, using the same design fire, temperatures increase faster in a smaller compartment than in a larger compartment, assuming all other variables are the same. In addition, if a fire is adjacent to or under a structural element, then consideration needs to be given to direct flame impingement, radiation, and plume temperatures.

The fire, and hence the fire-induced environment, may be affected by such systems as suppression systems, smoke management systems, and ventilation systems. The impact of these systems should also be considered when assessing the performance of the structural elements and the type/degree of structural fire protection needed. The analysis should then consider the transfer of heat into the structural elements. Heat transfer may be affected by the presence of fireproofing. Large structural elements may be inherently resistant to reaching high temperatures rapidly. This is because of their large thermal mass. Structural elements can also be specifically designed to withstand fires of varying severity, for example, by increasing their size, providing redundancy, and locating them away from fuel loads.

Structures that do not have an inherent resistance to high temperatures can be fireproofed. The typical intent of fireproofing is to limit the transfer of heat to the structural element. Fireproofing is available in many different forms such as the following [14, 16, 17]:

- Direct application (spray on)
- Filling (i.e., concrete, water, etc.)
- Membrane protection (i.e., gypsum board, etc.)

- Intumescent paints
- Water spray
- Radiation blocking
- Ablative coatings
- Subliming compounds

Underwriters Laboratories (UL) produces directories of various fireproofing methods and their associated fire ratings [17]. Recent advancements have also been made using fire-resistant steel that may have advantages in certain instances [16].

As temperatures increase, the heat begins to affect the structure's load-bearing capacity. It is therefore important to understand how high temperatures affect the various structural elements and their performance, as well as their ability to support their load and limit deformations/elongations. Care should also be taken to check whether changes to structural elements may impact other building systems, such as sprinkler piping, HVAC/smoke management equipment, and so on. Several factors should be considered when assessing a structure's response to thermal impacts. These include loading of the structural elements, potential transfer of loads, composite action of floor slabs/frames, stability and performance of connections, susceptibility to progressive collapse and/or disproportionate collapse, and so on. Several resources are available to assist in such assessments [13, 14, 16, 19].

Extreme Event Considerations

If blasts/explosions/impacts are considered credible hazards by the TARA, then the impact of such events on the structure and the resiliency of the fireproofing material, as well as the ability of the structure to redistribute and continue to carry loads, should be assessed. Their effects on egress components should also be considered. In addition, potential changes (i.e., location, growth rate, peak heat release rate, duration, etc.) to the design fire due to these extreme events should also be assessed to determine its potential impact on the response of the fireproofing and the structure.

Building codes require different fire ratings for structural elements based on the size of the building and its occupancy. These fire ratings are based on standardized tests [15] and typically assess a single structural element's response to a fire in a standardized furnace. Detailed assessments should look at the response of the actual structural elements and their response to threats and hazards deemed credible and appropriate hazard reduction/mitigation options developed and implemented to meet the desired objectives.

Key Point Structures do not generally respond to fire hazards as predicted by small-scale tests. Other factors may impact a structure's response to fire hazards, including complicated or unusual connections, design fire differences, and/or the interaction with other structural elements.

A detailed analysis of the proposed structural elements should be conducted to determine how the structure will respond in the event of a fire. Chapter 9 provides further discussion of structural protection for extreme events and should be referred to for additional information.

LIMITING FIRE SPREAD THROUGH PASSIVE MEASURES

Compartmentation is intended to provide various means to limit the extent of fire and smoke spreading from the compartment of fire origin to other areas or compartments of the building. This is indicated in the "Control Fire by Construction" subbranch.

Principles of Limiting Fire Spread Through Passive Measures

Compartmentation is intended to limit fire and smoke spread through passive means. It includes alternative concepts that can either be implemented on their own or that can be integrated with others to limit fire and smoke spread in a compartment. These alternative concepts include compartmentation, fire barriers, protection of openings, prevention of external fire spread, and control of the fire by automatic or manual suppression. More guidance on compartmentation is found in NFPA's *Fire Protection Handbook* [4] and *SFPE Engineering Guide to Performance-Based Fire Protection Analysis and Design in Buildings* [1].

Compartmentation and Fire Barriers. Compartmentation is a form of passive fire protection. It involves dividing buildings or spaces with fire-rated separations in order to isolate compartments from the compartment of fire origin, thus limiting fire spread both horizontally and vertically. Fire-rated separations are designed to resist the passage of heat and smoke for a specific amount of time when exposed to specific time–temperature curves. Reducing the size of compartments can also help limit the area involved in fire so that it does not become too large for emergency responders to extinguish [2].

Compartmentation should be provided in accordance with codes, at a minimum. Compartmentation should include appropriate separations between floors. High-hazard areas should be separated from adjacent areas as well.

The fire endurance of compartmentation components is determined by exposing them to a standard time–temperature exposure in a test furnace under fixed laboratory conditions [15]. Once these elements are installed in the field and exposed to installation conditions and fire exposures that vary from the laboratory conditions, their performance may vary from that predicted by the tests. These variations are due to a number of factors, including temperature conditions that differ from those of the test furnaces.

Key Point Changes in the characteristics of the compartment will affect the thermal impact of the fire on structural or compartment components and their ability to perform according to their listed or approved fire rating.

When fire protection systems and/or elements are connected with other structural components or building systems, system performance may be affected by the response of these interconnected components/systems. For instance, if a fire-rated wall is interconnected with a structural element that will expand during a fire, this expansion may adversely impact the performance of the fire wall during the fire.

Opening Protection. Openings in compartmentation and fire-rated separations can provide an easy path for the spread of fire and smoke. More information on this topic is available in NFPA's *Fire Protection Handbook* [4] and *SFPE Engineering Guide to Performance-Based Fire Protection Analysis and Design in Buildings* [1]. Openings exist in the form of doors or unrated windows. They can also be present other elements where wiring, piping, ductwork, and other elements penetrate a fire-rated separation and in areas where walls have been breached for various reasons. It is important, therefore, to not only provide fire-rated separations, but also to ensure that all openings are protected. Such protection may include automatic closing fire-rated doors, fire shutters, fire/smoke dampers, and fire stopping for wiring, pipes, ductwork, and so on. Automatic operating devices (door openers, fire shutters, fire dampers, etc.) should be properly installed and maintained so that they do not become blocked and stay open. Maintenance is also important to ensure that fire-rated walls that have been penetrated for the installation of building systems (i.e., heating, ventilation, and air conditioning (HVAC) equipment, wiring, etc.) or other purposes have been appropriately repaired to maintain their integrity and fire rating.

External Spread. Fires can also spread via the exterior of a building. Flames extending from windows can impinge on the floors above or provide sufficient radiant energy outside to ignite the contents on the floors above. Appropriate protection should be provided to limit this from occurring. Such protection may include sprinklers on the interior, spandrel walls of sufficient height, or ledges to push the flame away from the building.

Extreme Event Considerations

In considering extreme events, it is important to assess the physical impact of blasts, impacts, and other events on compartmentation. It is also important to note that such events may add additional fuel loads to the building, which may lead to fires that exceed the duration of the compartmentation fire rating.

FIRE AND LIFE SAFETY MANAGEMENT

A fire and life safety management program should be developed. This program should include maintenance, inspection, and testing of all fire and life safety systems, as well as good housekeeping and fire prevention procedures, hot-work permits, evacuation drills, and training. The overall fire and life safety strategy should be well documented. More guidance on program development is available in NFPA's *Fire Protection Handbook* [4], *SFPE Engineering Guide to Performance-Based Fire Protection Analysis and Design in Buildings* [1], and *The SFPE Code Official's Guide to Performance-Based Design Review* [2]. The fire and life safety strategy should be periodically reviewed to ensure that the systems and features continue to operate as intended, and that any changes made over time are appropriately incorporated. It may also be of interest to periodically review threats deemed credible, and if they change, to reassess the strategy and systems in order to address these new threats.

SUMMARY

Multiple systems must be considered concurrently in order to assess the overall fire and life safety level of a building or facility. These include egress, detection and alarm, suppression, compartmentation, smoke management, and fire-fighting facilities. Additional details regarding egress systems and structural systems and details that need to be assessed for extreme events are contained in other chapters and should be reviewed. A comprehensive assessment of these components and systems can result in a building design that will limit the potential for the development of significant fires and other emergency events as well as the impact of an extreme event on the building and its occupants. It will also help in developing a building design that will enable emergency responders to effectively manage an event, thus creating a safer built environment.

BIBLIOGRAPHY

References Cited

1. SFPE, 2000. *SFPE Engineering Guide to Performance-Based Fire Protection Analysis and Design of Buildings,* National Fire Protection Association, Quincy, MA.

2. SFPE, 2004. *The SFPE Code Official's Guide to Performance-Based Design Review*, Society of Fire Protection Engineers and National Fire Protection Association, Quincy, MA.

3. Marrion, C., 2005. "Design of Structures for Fire Loading and Understanding Fire/Life Safety System Interdependencies," *ASCE Structures Congress 2005 Proceedings,* American Society of Civil Engineers, Reston, VA.

4. Cote, A. (Ed.), 2003. *Fire Protection Handbook,* 19th ed., National Fire Protection Association, Quincy, MA.

5. Drysdale, D. D., 1999. *Introduction to Fire Dynamics.* John Wiley & Sons, New York.

6. Rockett, J. A., and Milke, J. A., 2002. "Conduction of Heat in Solids," Chapter 1-2, *The SFPE Handbook of Fire Protection Engineering,* 3rd ed., National Fire Protection Association, Quincy, MA.

7. SFPE, 2002, *The SFPE Handbook of Fire Protection Engineering,* 3rd ed., National Fire Protection Association, Quincy, MA.

8. Babrauskas, V., 2002. "Heat Release Rates," Chapter 3-1, *The SFPE Handbook of Fire Protection Engineering*, 3rd ed., National Fire Protection Association, Quincy, MA.

9. Babrauskas, V., and Grayson, S. J., 1992. *Heat Release in Fires*, Elsevier Applied Science, New York.

10. ASTM, 2004. *Standard Test Method for Surface Burning Characteristics of Building Materials*, ASTM E-84, ASTM International, West Conshohocken, PA.

11. Babrauskas, V., 2002. "The Cone Calorimeter," Chapter 3-3, *The SFPE Handbook of Fire Protection Engineering*, 3rd ed., National Fire Protection Association, Quincy, MA.

12. Klote, J., and Milke, J. A., 2002. *Principles of Smoke Management*, American Society of Heating, Refrigerating, and Air-Conditioning Engineers, Atlanta, GA.

13. Milke, J. A., 2002. "Analytical Methods for Determining Fire Resistance of Steel Members," Chapter 4-9, *The SFPE Handbook of Fire Protection Engineering*, 3rd ed., National Fire Protection Association, Quincy, MA.

14. Marrion, C., et al., 2004. *Fire Safety Protection of Structural Steel in High-Rise Building Materials*, Civil Engineering and Research Foundation, Reston, VA.

15. ASTM, 2000. *Standard Test Methods for Fire Tests of Building Construction and Materials*, ASTM E-119, ASTM International, West Conshohocken, PA.

16. Buchanan, A. H., 2001. *Structural Design for Fire Safety*, John Wiley & Sons, New York.

17. UL, 2003. *Fire Resistance Directory* (Vol. 1), Underwriters Laboratories, Inc., Northbrook, IL.

18. ThyssenKrup Steel (TKS), 2001. *Fire Resistant Structural Steel FR 30 from TKS*, ThyssenKrup Steel, Duisberg, Germany.

19. ASCE, 2003. *Standard Calculation Methods for Structural Fire Protection*, American Society of Civil Engineers and Society of Fire Protection Engineers, Reston, VA.

20. ICC, 2006. *International Building Code*. International Code Council, Falls Church, VA.

NFPA Codes, Standards, and Recommended Practices

NFPA Publications.   The following is a list of NFPA codes, standards and recommended practices cited in this chapter. See the latest version of the *NFPA Catalog* for availability of current editions of these documents.

NFPA 1, *Uniform Fire Code*™
NFPA 13, *Standard for the Installation of Sprinkler Systems*
NFPA 15, *Standard for Water Spray Fixed Systems for Fire Protection*
NFPA 72®, *National Fire Alarm Code*®
NFPA 92A, *Standard for Smoke-Control Systems Utilizing Barrier and Pressure Differences*
NFPA 92B, *Standard for Smoke Management Systems in Malls, Atria, and Large Spaces*
NFPA 550, *Guide to the Fire Safety Concepts Tree*
NFPA 2001, *Standard on Clean Agent Fire Extinguishing Systems*
NFPA 5000®, *Building Construction and Safety Code*®

Additional Readings

ASME, 2004. *Workshop on Use of Elevators in Fires and Other Emergencies*, American Society of Mechanical Engineers International, Atlanta, GA.

FEMA/ASCE, 2002. *World Trade Center Building Performance Study: Data Collection, Preliminary Observations and Recommendations*, Publication 403, American Society of Civil Engineers, Reston, VA, and Federal Emergency Management Agency, Washington, DC.

ICC, 2003. *International Building Code*, International Code Council, Falls Church, VA.

Milke, J. A., 2002. "Smoke Management in Covered Malls and Atria," Chapter 4-13, *The SFPE Handbook of Fire Protection Engineering*, 3rd ed., National Fire Protection Association, Quincy, MA.

Schifiliti, R., Meacham, B., and Custer, R., 2002. "Design of Detection Systems," Chapter 4-1, *The SFPE Handbook of Fire Protection Engineering*, 3rd ed., National Fire Protection Association, Quincy, MA.

12

Evacuation Planning and Modeling for Extreme Events

Jeffrey S. Tubbs
David Jacoby

Well-planned, effectively implemented evacuation strategies can provide occupants with the time necessary to safely evacuate buildings under a variety of conditions, including extreme events. This chapter presents evacuation-planning and design concepts as well as information regarding prescriptive egress components and strategies, performance egress approaches, dynamic or timed egress methodologies, and emergency action plans in the context of developing strategies for extreme events.

__OVERVIEW__

Prescriptive building codes have long-established approaches to the design of egress systems within buildings subject to "traditional" building threats. "Traditional" building threats, as used in this context, include events such as sprinkler-controlled fires, fires limited to a single compartment, power outages, limited nontoxic hazardous materials releases, or similar incidents. Before September 11, 2001, egress strategies and evacuation plans were typically developed to address such "traditional" threats. These strategies and plans relied on specific maximum and minimum limits for egress features to develop "safe" egress designs. For example, limits were set for minimum stair and door widths, as well as for maximum travel distances to exits—evacuation solutions incorporated time-tested concepts, such as evacuating one or several floors above and below the floor affected by fire in a conventional high-rise building. After the World

Trade Center and Pentagon attacks in 2001, new approaches and strategies were needed to address "nontraditional" events.

Egress strategies for extreme events typically use prescriptive-code-compliant fire and life safety components and features; however, the overall strategies incorporate different approaches than those used in prescriptive designs. To implement these strategies, dynamic or timed egress analyses are often necessary. Timed egress analyses enable comparison of evacuation times with times to hazardous conditions, such as the time to untenable conditions. These types of analyses enable the design to address the actual hazards for a facility, rather than simply applying a set of universally prescriptive provisions.

HISTORICAL EVENTS

Historically, building code development has been influenced by the results of tragic events that were deemed unacceptable by society. In response to a particularly tragic event, new requirements are often layered onto existing codes in an attempt to prevent a similar result from occurring in the future. The following sections discuss some historical events that have shaped current life safety and egress design strategies for high-rise buildings and large assembly spaces.

High-Rise Facilities

Case History: Triangle Shirtwaist Factory. The Triangle Shirtwaist Factory fire in New York City in 1911 resulted in 146 deaths [1]; this was one of the first tragic events to shape U.S. building codes. The fire started in the upper floors of the 10-story factory. These floors were used for cutting and sewing garments—processes that resulted in the accumulation of large quantities of cloth scraps. The fire started within a bin of cloth scraps and rapidly grew out of control. Three exits were provided; however, due to the severity of the fire, some of these exits became unavailable. Figure 12.1 depicts the condition of the fire escape (the fire escape failure was reportedly the result of fire impingement and inadequate design), another enclosed exit was locked to prevent theft, and the fire quickly blocked the final exit [1].

Conclusions. Because of the magnitude of this incident, the National Fire Protection Association (NFPA) created the Life Safety Committee, which is discussed in detail in "Case Histories: Fires Influencing

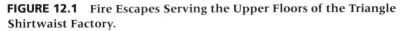

FIGURE 12.1   Fire Escapes Serving the Upper Floors of the Triangle Shirtwaist Factory.

(*Source:* Courtesy of the New York Board of Fire Underwriters.)

the Life Safety Code," in NFPA's *Life Safety Code® Handbook*. This committee produced several documents; the first was published in 1913 and dealt with exit drills in factories, schools, department stores, and theaters. In 1927, the Life Safety Committee published the *Building Exits Code*, which included requirements for the number and size of exits, as well as requirements for keeping exits unlocked and available to occupants. The *Building Exits Code* ultimately developed into the current edition of the NFPA *101®, Life Safety Code®*.

Relocation and Phased Evacuations. As buildings have grown in height, it has become more and more difficult to quickly evacuate occupants. With the advent of the elevator, high-rise buildings were built in many major cities within the United States and around the world. The cost of construction, limitations of available property area, and the codes at the time resulted in structures with limited footprints, such that the tallest part of the building would often have limited space and therefore limited width for egress.

Conclusions. As a result of fires in several high-rise buildings, such as the One New York Plaza fire in 1970, New York City passed a major revision to the city code to address fires in high-rise buildings. This change, Local Law 5 [2], provided for relocation, as opposed to complete evacuation, of occupants in high-rise buildings. The overall concept was for occupants on the affected floor and the floor above to exit to the stairwells, leaving the affected floor and reentering at a floor at least two levels below. A modified version of this concept has been the basis for evacuation of high-rise buildings in the United States since the 1970s. This strategy is typically referred to as a *phased evacuation* or *relocation approach* and includes evacuating the fire floor and one or several floors above and below it. Phased-evacuation approaches are discussed further in the evacuation strategies section of this chapter.

Case History: World Trade Center Bombing. Complete evacuations can be a lengthy process in high-rise buildings designed for a phased-evacuation approach. For instance, in the 1993 bombing of the World Trade Center in New York, it took up to six hours for occupants to evacuate the entire complex [3]. The bombing resulted in power failure, loss of communication, and smoke filling the stairs and spreading throughout the tower. Many occupants remained on their floors until reached by emergency workers. Six people died and thousands were injured during this event.

Conclusions. Extended evacuation times during the 1993 bombing of the World Trade Center prompted the Port Authority of New York and New Jersey to institute a significantly more rigorous evacuation plan and more robust emergency systems. Within the new evacuation plan, the strategy still centered on relocating occupants to lower floors, but more in-depth occupant training was performed, including actual evacuation drills.

Infrastructure improvements included more robust emergency power, local battery-powered lights, and an enhanced fire alarm and voice communication system [4]. On September 11, 2001, these additional features and training proved to be valuable when almost all occupants below the impact floors were able to safely evacuate the buildings.

Even with these enhancements, the new threat of terrorism has shown that current egress requirements need to be reevaluated. For some buildings, building owners, developers, designers, and managers must now consider events that will affect the entire building instead of designing for localized events.

Assembly Facilities

Large assembly and retail occupancies, such as stadium facilities, arenas, convention centers, nightclubs, malls, and other similar spaces, are designed for large numbers of occupants to simultaneously enter and exit as part of normal operations. Further, these types of spaces tend to have large open spaces connecting multiple floors. As a result of these design features, assembly spaces have historically incorporated complete evacuation strategies. Unlike high-rise facilities, large numbers of occupants can typically exit a stadium or other large assembly facility relatively quickly, because they do not need to travel down many flights of stairs. However, even with these comparatively large exit capacities, large fires and other tragic incidents have resulted in many deaths and injuries within sport stadia and nightclubs.

Fire Disasters. Evacuation strategies will always depend on owners and managers complying with code and implementing egress plans. Unfortunately, even with a good plan and adequate egress, ineffective maintenance procedures can lead to tragic results; the 2004 catastrophic fire in Paraguay is an example. A fire initiated in a large retail establishment after several reported explosions. Early reports from the fire scene indicated that egress doors were locked or blocked by employees in an attempt to prevent theft. The high fuel load and blocked exits resulted in the staggering consequence of more than 400 deaths. More information on this catastrophic fire is available in "Tragic Fire in Paraguay" in the September/October 2004 issue of *NFPA Journal* [5].

Another tragic example was the February 20, 2003, fire at The Station nightclub in West Warwick, Rhode Island. On this evening, a rock concert began with a flash of pyrotechnics; the pyrotechnics ignited foam installed on portions of the interior walls of the club. Within minutes, the entire club was engulfed in flames. This disastrous incident ultimately claimed the lives of 100 building occupants [6].

Crowd Disasters. Catastrophic crowd-crush incidents have occurred from circumstances unrelated to fire. "The Causes and

Prevention of Crowd Disasters" by J. Fruin [7] lists a number of such incidents.

A deadly crowd-crush incident occurred in 1913 during a second-floor Christmas party at the Italian Hall in Calumet, Michigan. Newspaper reports indicate that intoxicated, disgruntled workers yelled "Fire!" at the base of the stairs [8]. For this reason, or perhaps for another unknown reason, occupants rushed down the main stairway. The door at the bottom of the main exit stairway had a swing opposite to the egress path direction; this door ultimately became blocked. The resulting crush within the stairwell led to 72 fatalities; all of these people were either crushed or suffocated [8].

The Qutab tower in New Delhi, India, was built in the late twelfth to early thirteenth century and stands approximately 256 feet tall. Fruin [7] reports that a 1981 power failure ultimately caused a tragic crowd crush that resulted in 45 fatalities. Witnesses said that they heard cries that the tower was falling during the blackout, prompting 300 to 400 people to attempt to evacuate. The sudden rush of evacuees likely caused the ensuing crowd crush.

In 1988, a "sudden, violent hailstorm caused 30,000 spectators to [attempt to] evacuate the open grandstand" [7] of the Nepal National Stadium in Katmandu. These occupants encountered locked exit gates. More than 100 occupants died and more than 700 were injured due to the resulting crowd crush.

More recently, in 2003, a deadly crowd crush at the E2 club in Chicago resulted in 21 fatalities; 57 were injured. This incident was reportedly initiated when a security guard sprayed mace to break up a fight. The mace apparently caused occupants on the overcrowded second floor to rush to the main entrance stair. All of the fatalities were found on this stair [9].

Conclusions. These crowd disasters emphasize the need for owners and managers to develop evacuation plans, maintenance procedures, and training policies for fires and other emergency incidents. The goal is for the critical life safety systems, as well as properly trained staff, to be adequate and available when needed.

— EVACUATION PLANNING AND DESIGN

When developing an evacuation strategy for a specific building, stakeholders need to understand how the facility will normally be used and how the building will respond to the various anticipated threats. These concepts may lead to further questions, such as the following:

- What events will be considered?
- What paths will occupants use to normally exit the building versus during an emergency?
- What training have the building occupants been given?
- What training is necessary?
- What assistance do occupants need to evacuate?
- Will occupants need to use different exit routes or paths under specific circumstances?

This section describes evacuation strategies and egress components used to carry out these strategies. Egress systems for extreme events typically follow performance approaches. However, many of the egress components in these systems are based on prescriptive means and methods. The first portion of this section provides some background by defining some of the basic prescriptive egress concepts. Next, life safety goals and performance egress concepts are discussed. Finally, evacuation strategies, specific extreme event issues, and the overall systems approach are discussed.

Prescriptive Means of Egress

Prescriptive egress provisions can be separated into three components: exit access, exit, and exit discharge. More guidance on prescriptive egress is available in the following references:

- NFPA *101*, *Life Safety Code*
- *NFPA 5000®, Building Construction and Safety Code®*
- *International Building Code* [10]

Exit access can be defined as the pathways from all areas of the building that lead to exits, including all open exit stairwells, corridors, and ramps. Within all building spaces, including occupied roofs, it is essential to provide an appropriate number of exit-access pathways. Egress paths may need to be protected and provided with pathway marking and lighting, as appropriate to the number of occupants and the hazard. Egress pathways and components (e.g., aisles, doors, etc.) should be properly maintained and kept free of materials that block access.

Exits include exterior exit doors to grade, enclosed stairs, exit passageways, and horizontal exits. Exit passageways are typically separated from other areas of the building by fire-rated construction, similar to stairways. Exit passageways may be extensions of stairways. A horizontal exit divides a floor into separated areas of refuge, allowing relocation to a protected area of the building.

Each floor of a building must be provided with an appropriate number of exits. Exits should be sized and protected appropriate to expected hazards and the number of occupants. Travel distance to exits and separation of exits also should be appropriate to the number of occupants and the expected hazards. The widths of exit components should not decrease in the direction of travel.

The *exit discharge* includes the pathways from where the exit components leave the building and provide access to the public way. It is essential for exit-discharge paths to be continuous and unobstructed.

Key Point Horizontal exits differ from other types of exits; horizontal exits do not provide immediate access to a public way. Rather, occupants are directed to a safe area, where more time for egress is available.

Prescriptive exit provisions provide a set of maximum or minimum limits for each of these components.

Performance-Based Means of Egress

Performance-based concepts are typically used when developing egress systems for extreme events.

Key Point In contrast to prescriptive means of egress, performance-based systems are designed according to specific goals and objectives, rather than prescribed maximum or minimum conditions for the various design components.

The general intent of performance-based egress is to provide appropriate life safety features to allow time for occupants to safely exit buildings or to relocate to a safe place within a building. This concept relies on providing egress measures appropriate to the actual hazards or risks. Goals and objectives are discussed in more detail later in the text.

Performance systems will likely rely on conventional egress components and principles, but they may also use "unconventional" egress methods, such as elevators for general evacuation, relocation without the use of horizontal exits, and the use of open stairs and escalators for general evacuation. If unconventional components are used, special training or occupant instructions may be necessary, because use of these components may be contrary to conventional life safety messages and training. For example, many high-rise facilities in the United States provide signage to discourage the use of elevators in an emergency. Therefore, specific training would be necessary to incorporate elevators into an evacuation plan.

These unconventional components will also need to be coordinated with other systems. For example, if elevators are to be used during a fire emergency, then smoke management systems, controls, and other supporting systems should be coordinated with the elevators. System details, as well as component and system coordination requirements, are discussed later in this chapter.

Life safety Goals and Objectives. One of the first steps in developing a comprehensive evacuation approach is to determine specific life safety goals and objectives for the facility (see Chapter 2 for details of goals and objectives). Goals and objectives must be understood and agreed on by the stakeholders. Developing and agreeing on goals and objectives means that the evacuation strategy will be based on a common understanding of the underlying purpose of the life safety systems.

The 2000 edition of NFPA *101, Life Safety Code,* was the first edition of that code to explicitly state goals and objectives. Section 4.1.1 of the 2003 edition stated that the "goal of the Code is to provide an environment for the occupants that is reasonably safe from fire and similar emergencies by the following means: (1) Protection of occupants not intimate with the initial fire development; (2) Improvement of the survivability of occupants intimate with the initial fire development."

Similar goals and objectives are defined in a number of resources, including:

- *NFPA 5000, Building Construction and Safety Code*
- *SFPE Engineering Guide to Performance-Based Fire Protection Analysis and Design of Buildings* [11]
- *The SFPE Code Official's Guide to Performance-Based Design Review* [12]
- *CIBSE Guide E: Fire Engineering* [13]
- *Fire Engineering Design Guide* [14]
- *International Code Council Performance Code* [15]

Performance Criteria. As discussed in Chapter 2, goals and objectives are further refined into performance criteria. In practice, performance criteria are typically quantified in terms of providing a tenable environment within the building spaces and egress paths. *Tenability,* as used in this context, can generally be defined as providing an environment that permits self reserve of occupants for a specific period of time, according to NFPA 130, *Standard for Fixed Guideway Transit and Passenger Rail Systems.*

Acceptable limits for tenable conditions may vary based on the overall life safety goals and specific event considered, as well as the facility's size, configuration, and use. For example, tenability for fire events may need to be defined in terms of smoke toxicity, visibility, or thermal effects, whereas tenability for blast events may need to be defined in terms of structural stability or protection from falling objects.

Tenability Criteria

The next section provides information regarding tenability criteria [16]. The following sources provide additional information regarding tenability criteria:

- *Fire Engineering Design Guide* [14]
- *CIBSE Guide E: Fire Engineering* [13]
- "Visibility and Human Behavior in Smoke" in *The SFPE Handbook of Fire Protection Engineering* [17]
- "Toxicity Assessment of Combustion Products" in *The SFPE Handbook of Fire Protection Engineering* [18]
- NFPA *101, Life Safety Code*
- NFPA 130, *Standard for Fixed Guideway Transit and Passenger Rail Systems*

Note that some tenability criteria are based on infinite exposure limits, whereas others limit exposure over a specified time. This introduces the concept of Fractional Effective Dose or FED. FED concepts are discussed in more detail later in the chapter.

Because tenability is a complex and evolving subject, readers are urged to consult the references cited in this section for details regarding application of tenability criteria. Further, some occupants, such as the young or ill or elderly persons, are more susceptible to exposure; therefore, special care must be taken when choosing tenability limits for these particularly vulnerable populations.

Key Point   It is important for designers to understand tenability limits. It is equally important for these limits to be defined, understood, and agreed on by the owners, designers, managers, approving authorities, and other stakeholders for the conditions, uses, and building considered.

Before discussing tenability concepts, it is useful to define scenarios in which these criteria are needed. The *Life Safety Code* provides four methods of assessing tenability when performance approaches are used to address fire events:

1. With some performance approaches, systems may be designed such that the egress paths are expected to become contaminated with heat, smoke, and other toxic or damaging products of combustion. Designs that address occupant egress through contaminated conditions may need to rely on the FED concepts, as detailed in "Toxicity Assessment of Combustion Products" in *The SPFE Handbook of Fire Protection Engineering* [18] and the *The SFPE Code Official's Guide to Performance-Based Design Review* [12]. FED provides a method for accounting for the fact that, in some cases, exposure to low doses over a long period of time may be as severe as higher doses over a shorter exposure.

2. The second method uses timed egress methods as well as smoke movement modeling techniques to determine whether occupants are able to evacuate a building or space before the predicted smoke layer contaminates the egress paths. Timed egress and smoke-movement modeling is discussed in more detail later in this chapter.

3. The third method requires the maintenance of a calculated smoke layer 6 feet or higher above all egress paths throughout the entire egress time (rather than only the time to exit a given component as in the second method). This can be accomplished through the use of smoke reservoirs or other similar smoke management features.

4. In some cases, heat, smoke, and other toxic or damaging products of combustion movement is limited through passive or

active systems; thus smoke may not reach specific occupied rooms or spaces.

The following section discusses concepts to consider when developing tenability criteria.

Thermal Effects. Thermal effects can be evaluated in terms of the temperature of heated gases or flames where occupants are directly exposed or through radiation from heated gases or flames where occupants are not directly exposed. Radiant and convective exposures may need to be combined.

Visibility. Visibility is a measure of the distance that occupants can see through smoke. Visibility depends on the density of the smoke, the illumination, and the physiological affects of smoke on the eyes. Visibility is typically evaluated in terms of the distance at which an occupant can read an illuminated exit sign or distinguish an exit path. Note that physiological effects can reduce visibility over time due to exposure to irritating smoke.

Smoke Toxicity. Products of combustion can be toxic. The inhalation of products of combustion can lead to reduced decision-making capacitation and impaired motor activity, which can lead to incapacitation or death. Tenability criteria for toxic combustion products are given as parts per million (ppm), grams per cubic meter (g/m^3), or as percentage concentration for a period of time.

Occupant Impact with Objects or Building Materials. Falling objects, airborne building materials, or structural collapse resulting from blasts, seismic incidents, or other events can cause injury. Additional information regarding injury due to impact with objects or building materials is provided in Chapter 5, "Bomb Blast Hazard Mitigation"; Chapter 7, "Natural Hazards"; and Chapter 9, "Structural Design for Extreme Events."

Sublethal Effects. The sublethal effects of heat, smoke, and other toxic products of combustion are another important consideration. Sublethal exposures can lead to severe injury and incapacitation. "Characteristics of Fire Scenarios in Which Sub-Lethal Effects of Smoke are Important," in the NFPA reference *Fire Technology* [20], suggests that production of toxic products is likely to vary inversely with ventilation and concludes that sublethal effects may affect egress within "multi-room residences, medical facilities, schools, and correctional facilities."

Evacuation Strategies

Historically, egress designs followed one of five typical egress approaches, including the following:

- Full building evacuation for small buildings
- Phased or partial evacuation
- Smoke-protected assembly seating egress
- Relocation to a safe place
- Defending in place

In the post–September 11 environment, these conventional philosophies have been questioned; building owners and designers are now considering designs that specifically address the possibility of extreme events. New egress system approaches have been developed to address the very different and more challenging threats posed by extreme events. These new views amount to a shift in egress concepts for at-risk buildings, incorporating significantly different evacuation solutions [21], including the following:

- Full-building evacuation for large or tall buildings
- Event-specific evacuation strategies
- Evacuation strategies for events outside the building of interest
- The possibility of using protected elevators or other nonprotected elements (i.e., open stairs, open escalators, etc.) during emergency events

The following sections discuss these concepts in detail. It is important to note that regardless of the specific strategy used, well-marked, intuitive egress systems tend to enable occupants to efficiently use the system, whereas complicated systems tend to confuse occupants, hinder egress, and increase the time needed for occupants to exit a building or facility. Further, the use of normal circulation paths enhances occupant awareness of egress paths and the ability to use these paths during emergency events.

Full-Building Evacuation. Typically, most small or uncomplicated facilities evacuate the entire building upon any alarm signal. The September 11, 2001, attacks on the World Trade Center Towers in New York City presented the need to consider employing a full-building evacuation strategy for many different types of facilities.

Full-building evacuation may require greater egress capacities than commonly required by current codes. However, since there are no universally accepted maximum evacuation times, performance strategies are typically necessary. Using performance-based design strategies, a hazard can be analyzed to determine time to the onset of hazardous conditions. This information can then be used to determine the maximum amount of time available for occupants to exit a facility.

Key Point   The egress system should be designed to minimize "choke points," areas that cause large lines of occupants to form.

Consideration should be given to areas to which occupants move to after leaving the building. High-rise facilities and large assembly facilities may have a large number of occupants who need a clear path away from the building during an event. The egress plan should include one or more rally points where occupants can go and be accounted for out of harms way. In urban settings, it is important to coordinate with neighboring buildings. Because certain events may result in several buildings being evacuated at the same time, multiple facilities could attempt to utilize the same park area as a rally point. Multiple building evacuations could result in confusion or congestion on the way to the rally point. Given the possibility of these conditions, alternate rally points may need to be designated.

Phased or Partial Evacuation. Traditional evacuation strategies for large or tall buildings, can include partial or phased evacuation. For tall buildings, phased strategies typically include evacuation of occupants on the affected floor as well as those occupants one to two floors above and below the fire. More floors may be evacuated within multistory or atrium spaces. In very large buildings, only the affected areas may be evacuated; occupants in areas remote from the incident may remain in place. Because a smaller number of occupants use the egress systems, occupants within the affected floors (or areas for partial evacuation of a single floor) can exit more quickly.

Occupants on the unaffected floors (or unaffected areas) can exit after the affected occupants, if necessary, or simply remain in place, if appropriate. The base assumption of this strategy is that the expected events will not affect occupants above the fire floor in tall buildings or occupants in remote areas of the building in very large buildings.

Smoke-protected assembly seating is a specific application of phased or partial evacuation strategies. This strategy permits the limited use of performance-based egress concepts and allows reduced egress capacities for facilities with large assembly seating areas (e.g., large arenas and stadia), when events only affect a portion of the overall space. If anticipated events affect only a portion of the facility, occupants sufficiently remote from the incident may not be in immediate danger. Thus, remote occupants may be able to safely evacuate with longer evacuation times, as compared to those within the affected areas. Codes require an engineering analysis to demonstrate that all occupants can safely evacuate, given the range of expected scenarios. The *Life Safety Code Handbook* discusses engineering analysis for smoke-protected assembly seating concepts in more detail.

Elevator-Assisted Evacuation. Some high-rise buildings are more than 80 stories tall. Elderly, disabled, or injured occupants, or occupants with other medical issues, such as heart conditions or foot or leg injuries, may have difficulty negotiating or may be incapable of descending stairs in a very tall building. Elevators can provide a safe and effective alternative to the difficult and time-consuming task of maneuvering down the stairs from the upper levels of a tall building. The *Emergency Evacuation Elevator Systems Guide* published by the Council on Tall Buildings in Urban Habitat [22] defines and discusses considerations for standard, enhanced, and protected elevators. Elevator evacuation methods are being considered by various code bodies.

Since the 1980s, a number of groups have conducted research on the use of elevators for emergency evacuation. The authors of "Fire Evacuation by Elevators" [23] suggest that if enhancements are provided to the elevator system, then elevators can be used for evacuation during emergency situations. Current recommended enhancements for elevators include smoke and heat protection, CBR and other contaminant protection, water protection, earthquake protection, and overheating protection, as well as emergency power. Other considerations include emergency communications, special control strategies, and occupant training. These specific enhancements are discussed in the "Use of Elevators" section of this chapter, but are mentioned here because it is critical that these enhancements be considered if elevators are to be used for egress.

The use of elevators can speed evacuation within tall buildings; during the 2001 collapse, many occupants of tower 2 of the World Trade Center used elevators to escape before the second airplane struck this building. Advantages of using elevators as part of the overall evacuation plan include the following [24]:

- Research described in the "Occupant Response to Fire Alarm Signals" [25] section of the *National Fire Alarm Code® Handbook* and other resources suggest that occupants tend to exit through the path that they used to enter; this pattern may hold true even if this entrance path involves the elevator. For tall buildings, the primary entrance path is typically through the elevator system. Some occupants may attempt to use the elevators even though specific signage stating "in case of fire, do not use elevators, use stairs" is provided.

- It is not uncommon for full evacuation of tall high-rise facilities to require more than 30 to 60 minutes. After the 1993 World Trade Center bombing, some occupants took as long as 3 hours or more to evacuate after they decided to exit [26]. Lengthy egress times can be very dangerous, particularly when occupants lack information regarding the incident. When elevators are used as part of the overall evacuation plan, it is possible to develop strategies that will reduce facility evacuation time.

- It may be impossible for elderly, disabled, or injured occupants and other occupants with medical conditions to use the stairway systems in a tall building. Elevators can be used to evacuate such occupants.

Emergency responders may need to use the elevators. Therefore, evacuation plans will need to address the dual use of protected elevators by both occupants and responders. Specific solutions may include dedicated elevators for responder use during an emergency or the use of special elevator controls.

Note that a number of buildings both within the United States and internationally have used elevators to assist with evacuation. The Stratosphere in Las Vegas provides an example. The 900-foot tall Stratosphere tower includes 10 levels located at the top of the tower;

the lowest occupied tower floor is 795 feet above grade. The upper levels of the tower include eight occupied levels and amusement rides. The principal method of evacuation includes protected egress stairs that discharge into dedicated open-air areas of refuge on the lower two floors of the upper levels. A single stair is provided from the areas of refuge. However, the main evacuation route from the areas of refuge is through four two-level elevators. The occupant load is limited by the number of serviceable elevators. Specific features have been provided by the owner to monitor and limit the number occupants within the tower. More information on these features is available in "Supplement 7—The Application of Performance-Based Design Concepts for Fire and Life Safety" [27] of NFPA's *Life Safety Code Handbook.*

Relocating. Relocating occupants to an area of refuge or other safe place can be an effective means of moving occupants from the affected area or floor. This strategy requires special attention to management procedures and may require specialized detection systems or other life safety features and procedures. Examples of facilities that may incorporate these concepts include hospitals; nursing homes; detention, correctional, or institutional facilities; and any facility employing horizontal exits as part of the egress design.

A relocation strategy assumes that occupants can be brought to a safe area during an event and may be used for events exterior to the building, smaller events within a building, or quick-acting events. For example, a hurricane in a major metropolitan area is an exterior event in which relocation within a building may be effective. Newer high-rise buildings often have a glass-curtain wall that may shatter if struck by debris, resulting in sharp projectiles. Occupants may be able to be relocated from the external walls to the core of the building to help provide protection from the high winds and the resulting projectiles. Assuming that the overall structure was designed to survive such an event and assuming that the safe area is adequately protected and sized, this strategy could then protect the occupants of the building even though the exterior of the building may be damaged.

Another example comes from the City of Hong Kong's General Provisions of Means of Escape in Case of Fire [28]. This code requires that area of refuge floors be provided for tall buildings at intervals of not more than 20 stories. Stairs are required to be interrupted on these refuge floors. The intent of refuge floors is to provide the following:

- A safe place for people to rest before continuing downward
- Safe passage for people using one staircase to move to an alternative staircase if they encounter smoke, fire, or other obstruction
- A safe place for people to wait for rescue in case the stairwells are not available

In the Hong Kong code, refuge areas are generally required to be 50 percent open on two sides; these openings may be required to be protected by water curtains. Elevators are normally programmed to bypass these floors; however, fire fighter controls can override this programming to assist in evacuating refuge floors [28].

Defend in Place. Defending or sheltering in place involves providing adequate life safety measures so that occupants can remain in place during an event. This strategy is often seen in institutional occupancies, such as hospitals and detention facilities, as well as in certain residential occupancies. In hospitals, occupants are often not ambulatory, and it may be very difficult, and perhaps more threatening to move a patient on life support or in surgery. In detention facilities, occupants are restricted to their cells and cannot self-evacuate. Detention facilities are typically designed using defend-in-place strategies.

Residential high-rise buildings are often highly compartmented; this level of compartmentation can also facilitate the use of defend-in-place strategies. Several fires in high-rise buildings have resulted in occupant deaths in areas remote from the fire. In some of these incidents, occupants attempting to exit died, whereas occupants in the compartments immediately adjacent to the fire compartment survived. One example of this is the 1998 fire in a New York City residential facility in which four evacuees died, whereas tenants who remained in their residences were uninjured [29].

Defend-in-place strategies usually rely on a combination of active and passive protection features. Typically, buildings are fully protected with automatic sprinklers, and each room or area is provided with passive compartmentation to prevent smoke and fire spread between compartments. In hospitals, jails, and similar spaces, detection may be provided such that staff or occupants can respond to the emergency. For example, nurses may be instructed to close all patient doors upon activation of the fire alarm system.

Additional mitigation features may be necessary when considering events other than fire; however, it may be impossible or cost prohibitive to use these strategies for all events. For blast events, blast relief, structural hardening, or other blast-resiliency measures to address a bomb blast, can be provided. Protection for a chemical, biological, or radiological event may require additional shielding or filtration.

It should be noted that given the results of September 11, 2001, defend-in-place strategies may be difficult to implement. In urban areas in the United States, an occupant's first instinct may be to evacuate the building if he or she notices people evacuating from adjacent buildings. However, if the event is outside, remaining within the building may be the safest option. In order for these strategies to work, communication and training will be essential to convince occupants to remain within the building. The immediate flight response of some individuals, or perhaps large groups of occupants, may need to be considered in the evacuation plan as well as in the overall egress design.

Event-Specific Evacuation. If decision makers can be given information regarding a specific threat, simple rules can be developed to vary the evacuation response based on that threat. This type of strategy is particularly useful for buildings that may be exposed to a variety of events. In these buildings, events occurring outside the building may require a different response than those occurring inside the building.

For instance, in a building with blast-resistant windows and walls, if information is known regarding an impending external blast, relocation or defend-in-place strategies may be appropriate. For interior localized fires in a tall building, evacuating only occupants on the fire floor and other threatened floors may be appropriate. These responses are in contrast to the need for some buildings to fully evacuate buildings due to an impending large-scale natural or man-made disaster or interior chemical event.

As another example, consider a high-rise building with a hardened facade that is fully protected with automatic sprinklers and that has HVAC systems designed to isolate the building from exterior CBR events. An event-specific evacuation strategy may be designed as follows:

- Exterior bomb threat: Defend in place
- Exterior chemical or biological event: Defend in place

- Nondeliberate fire event: Evacuate specific floors
- Significant earthquake event: Evacuate the entire building

When using these concepts, it is imperative to create appropriate methods for obtaining information quickly and for empowering decision makers with the appropriate authority to make decisions. This is particularly important in tall high-rise facilities or other sensitive facilities, where the significant costs associated with full evacuation may delay or alter the decision to fully evacuate a facility.

__EGRESS FOR EXTREME EVENTS__

Evacuation systems designed for extreme events will likely require features not typically provided within traditional egress systems, such as hardened elevators or egress paths, egress pathway marking, enhanced detection systems, or special shelter-in-place rooms. This section discusses specific enhancements for egress and life safety systems to consider when addressing various threats. Next, the use of elevators is discussed. Finally, the concept of defense in depth is discussed.

Features of Extreme Event Egress Systems

Emergency Plans. FEMA recommends the establishment of written emergency plans for evacuation and defending in place [30]. The Occupational Safety and Health Administration (OSHA) requires plans for specific commercial buildings; local fire departments have additional requirements for emergency plans. Emergency plans are discussed further in the "Evacuation Planning" section of this chapter.

Exit Pathways. FEMA recommends that the use of false ceilings in exit hallways be avoided, because they can fall and interfere with evacuation or responder actions [30]. For some facilities, protected enclosures extending to the exterior may be appropriate. All facilities should provide clear, obvious, and well-maintained paths to the exterior.

Occupant Loads. A list of typical prescriptive code–based occupant loads can be found later in this chapter. Actual occupant loads may differ from these prescribed loads.

Key Point   It is important for building designers to anticipate severe-case use when determining design occupant loads.

Width of Exit Stairs. Prescriptive code egress widths are based on a specific width per person. This methodology does not account for the actual time needed for occupants to exit a tall facility, nor does it account for counterflows. Counterflow occurs when fire fighters travel up the stairs at the same time occupants are exiting down the stairs. Performance-based egress design methods may need to be employed to determine the overall evacuation time as well as the effect of counterflows during extreme events.

Exit Stair Protection. Prescriptive codes require stairs to be separated by 50 percent of the overall diagonal distance of the space served. Exit separation can be reduced to 33 percent of the diagonal distance in buildings that are fully protected with automatic sprinklers. A given incident may affect more than one exit stair in buildings designed to code-minimum specifications; therefore, performance-based methods may be necessary to review exit separation.

FEMA recommends creating "safe havens" within the protected core area of the building. Safe havens are recommended to be within fire-rated, tightly constructed, pressurized stairwells or elevator lobbies [30]. Blast protection may also be a consideration for such areas.

Exit Discharge. The exit discharge is an important component in the egress system. FEMA recommends the following enhancements for exit discharges [30]:

- Provide exterior egress doors that open outward.
- Avoid stairs that discharge into lobbies or parking or loading areas (where possible).
- Provide emergency exits that are easily accessible to emergency vehicles.
- Allow for space adjacent to emergency exits to accommodate rescue workers entering the building as well as injured persons exiting the building.
- Avoid canopies, overhanging balconies, or other ornamentation that may fall and block emergency exits.

Exit Stair Discharge Doors. Many traditional high-rise stairs have a single door at the bottom. This single exit may become a significant bottleneck within the egress system, because the flow on the stairs may exceed the flow capacity of the door. Therefore, it is suggested that two doors be used for stair discharges from typical 44- or 48-inch stairs. A performance analysis of the egress system can better determine the appropriate number of doors from the stairs.

Reentry Doors. A fire at the 35-story Cook County Building in Chicago resulted in the fatalities of six office workers on October 17, 2003. According to the investigation report [31] for this incident, all of the exit stairwell doors at the Cook County Building were locked from the stairwell side, which prevented these workers from reentering. Prescriptive codes typically require reentry doors on every three or five floors; reentry doors automatically unlock upon actuation of the fire alarm. Given the need for multiple evacuation routes during extreme events, consideration should be given to utilizing additional reentry doors.

Emergency Exit Lighting. Emergency power typically needs to be provided to supply adequate lighting throughout all egress paths. In buildings designed for extreme events, FEMA recommends that emergency lighting systems be extended to all areas of the building, including restrooms and other similar spaces to enable occupants to exit safely [30].

Emergency Pathway Marking. Photo-luminescent striping was applied to the stairwells in the World Trade Center after the 1993 bombing [32]. This pathway marking ultimately assisted occupants who had to navigate the stairwell system during the World Trade Center event in 2001 [33].

Shelter-in-Place Rooms. For some incidents, occupants can wait for rescue or for the incident to be mitigated in areas of refuge or in shelter-in-place rooms. Examples of rooms used to shelter occupants in place range from a vestibule within a stair designed specifically to accommodate mobility-impaired occupants, as shown in Figure 12.2, to a horizontal exit that separates the floor into two areas of refuge to a nuclear reactor control room that is designed to withstand fires and other incidents.

Defense in Depth

In some cases, redundancies are necessary as part of an overall egress strategy. The overall concept for defense in depth is to provide multi-

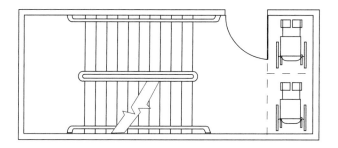

FIGURE 12.2 Exit Stair Used as an Area of Refuge. (*Source:* NFPA, 2003. NFPA *101*®, *Life Safety Code*®, National Fire Protection Association, Quincy, MA, Figure A.7.2.12.3.1.)

ple protection features to account for the possibility of unexpected events or system failures. This redundancy helps to provide a robust system. A common example of the defense-in-depth concept includes the prescriptive code–concurrent requirements for both 3-hour fire protection for structural members and automatic sprinkler protection. Protected structural members are tested in conditions similar to flashover or full-room involvement. Automatic sprinklers are designed to control, suppress, or extinguish fire. In theory, spaces that are fully protected with sprinklers should not reach flashover. However, because structural failure is intolerable, the cost associated with multiple protection features has been deemed acceptable.

Supporting Systems

Traditional egress approaches contain interactions between the various fire and life safety systems. Some of these interactions are complex, and perhaps not readily apparent, because some design components may rely on other components to function. A simple example can be seen within atrium egress requirements; the prescriptive approach assumes that smoke management is provided. Based on these and similar complex interactions, egress systems should be reviewed as part of an overall systems approach, rather than as a stand-alone design element. This is particularly important for systems provided to mitigate extreme events. This section provides a representative list and discussion of systems that may need to be reviewed when developing egress systems to respond to extreme events.

Fire Detection. A variety of automatic or manual devices are available for fire detection. Occupants who are not sleeping, disabled, ill, incapacitated, distracted, or otherwise unable to effectively see or smell are usually quite capable of detecting fires. Manual alarm devices can be strategically located to allow occupants to manually alert others after detecting a fire. Selection of detection methods should be based upon the life safety goals. For more guidance fire detection, see "Design of Detection Systems" in *The SFPE Handbook of Fire Protection Engineering* [36].

CBR Contaminant and Hazardous Material Dispersal Detection. Although gas and vapor detection systems are available to detect common vapors and gases (e.g., hydrogen, propane, acetone, benzene, etc.) found in chemical processing equipment, reliable, commercially available means for CBR contaminant detection are rare. CBR detection systems are currently being developed and will become more readily available in the near future. Even without detection, specific means, such as ventilation, exhaust, pressurization, and compartmentation systems, can be employed to minimize the risk of contaminant dispersal within a building. See Chapter 6 for additional information regarding CBR contaminants.

Occupant Notification. Notification is a critical component of extreme events evacuation for tall and large facilities. Research indicates that occupants tend to respond more effectively to live voice communication than to standard alarm tones [34]. If voice notification is necessary as part of the plan or design, both audibility and intelligibility need to be considered. *Audibility* refers to the ability of occupants to hear the alarm signal, whereas *intelligibility* refers to the ability of occupants to understand the alarm signal. A number of standards and engineering guides are available to provide guidance for location and distribution of audible and visible devices to achieve audibility. These include the following:

- "Americans with Disabilities Act Accessibility Guidelines" [35]
- "Design of Detection Systems," in *The SFPE Handbook of Fire Protection Engineering* [36]
- *Architectural Acoustics* [37]
- "Voice Intelligibility for Emergency Voice/Alarm Communication Systems" [38] in the *National Fire Alarm Code® Handbook*

The *National Fire Alarm Code® Handbook* addresses intelligibility in the appendix and supplemental materials. In particular, a detailed discussion of voice intelligibility is provided in Supplement 5, "Voice Intelligibility for Emergency Voice/Alarm Communication Systems," of that handbook [38]. Intelligibility is affected by the quality of equipment as well as the acoustic properties of the space. Because the intelligibility can be affected by acoustic properties, complex spaces benefit from the services of an acoustician.

The appendix to *NFPA 72®, National Fire Alarm Code®*, Section 4-3.1.5 discusses the Common Intelligibility Scale (CIS) and states that systems with CIS values of 0.70 or better are intelligible; other methods are also available to assess intelligibility.

Structural Integrity. A robust structure is essential to allow time for occupants to evacuate and responders to assist people with disabilities or other occupants needing assistance. Time is also needed for responders to mitigate the event, if possible. Chapter 9 of this text provides additional information regarding structural protection.

Facade and Interior-Partition Blast Protection. The type of facade and interior-partition blast protection, as well as the nature of the blast or impact threats, will influence evacuation strategies for some egress scenarios. Unprotected glass walls can shatter, dispersing glass-shard projectiles into the building. Specific protection should be considered for glass walls susceptible to blast loads. Chapter 5 provides additional information regarding facade protection.

Compartmentation. Compartmentation may need to be provided for stair shafts, floor and occupancy separations, areas of refuge, shelter-in-place rooms, and other critical areas, such as mail rooms, loading docks, public drop-off locations, fire command rooms, and security command rooms. Fire-rated partitions may be needed between occupied areas and construction areas, as well as between secure and non-secure areas. Partitions may also need to be hardened and coordinated with smoke partitions.

Fire Suppression and Standpipe Systems. Automatic fire-suppression systems, such as sprinkler systems and other special equipment, can be used to extinguish fires in the very early stages or to control fires at a given size. Standpipe hose valves can be provided for use in manual suppression activities. Design of automatic and manual fire suppression systems for extreme events may need to consider multiple supply risers and redundant supply systems to decrease the risk of an initial event rendering the systems incapable of extinguishing an ensuing fire. NFPA's *Automatic Sprinkler Systems Handbook* [39], as well as other sources, such as chapters on automatic sprinklers and automatic sprinkler systems [40] in NFPA's *Fire Protection Handbook* provide additional information regarding automatic fire suppression.

Fire Department Communication Systems. Fire department communication systems should be provided for tall or large facilities. Current codes require fire fighter outlet jacks with compatible fire fighter phones located within the central control station; however, strategically located repeater devices compatible with the fire fighter radios provide a more usable system. Regardless of the system, fire fighters and responding emergency personnel need to be able to effectively communicate from strategic locations in the facility. Typically communication is provided for the central control station, elevators, elevator lobbies, emergency power rooms, fire pump rooms, areas of refuge, and stairwells.

Smoke Management Systems. Active ventilation or passive compartmentation systems can reduce or mitigate smoke movement and dispersion within facilities. Chapter 8 of this text, as well as a number of other references such as NFPA 92A, *Standard for Smoke Control Systems Utilizing Barriers and Pressure Differences;* NFPA 92B, *Standard for Smoke Management Systems in Malls, Atria and Large Spaces;* and *Principles of Smoke Management* [41], provide information regarding smoke management within buildings. Compartmentation, pressurization, and exhaust systems used to inhibit smoke movement can also be effective for containing or reducing CBR dispersal or accidental chemical release.

In general, four smoke management methods are available: passive systems, pressurization systems, exhaust systems, and air flow systems.

- *Passive smoke management systems* include smoke-rated partition walls to inhibit smoke movement or contaminant flow across barriers.
- *Pressurization systems* enhance passive walls by inducing a positive or negative pressure across the smoke barrier. The goal is to maintain the contaminated compartment at a lower pressure relative to adjacent zones, thus further inhibiting contaminant flow into surrounding compartments.

- *Exhaust systems* mechanically extract sufficient quantities of smoke to maintain smoke layers at acceptable elevations above egress paths. This method is typically used to control smoke in large or tall spaces; exhaust can also be used to purge contaminants from spaces.
- *Air flow systems* supply or exhaust air at specific velocities through openings between compartments. Airflow systems are typically used in combination with other methods.

Normal HVAC systems can have a substantial effect on smoke and contaminant movement within facilities. These systems may need to be shut down to minimize dispersion during an event. Chapter 10 of this text provides additional information regarding smoke management and HVAC systems.

Emergency and Standby Power. Emergency or standby power is necessary for essential equipment for situations that may cause the normal power to become unavailable. NFPA 70, *National Electrical Code®*, requires emergency systems to be available within the time necessary for the application, but not more than 10 seconds; similarly, standby systems are required to be available within the time necessary for the application, but not more than 60 seconds. Emergency power is generally required to automatically supply essential systems, such as emergency lighting, fire and life safety systems, and systems for industrial processes "where current interruption would produce serious life safety or health hazards," as stated in NFPA 110, *Standard for Emergency and Standby Power Systems*. According to NFPA 110, standby power systems are typically installed to serve equipment that "when stopped could create hazards or hamper fire fighting operations." Standby power is typically required by code for smoke management; it may also be necessary for heating and refrigeration loads, communication systems, hazardous material ventilation systems, sewerage disposal systems, security systems, and industrial processes.

Security Interface. Security systems can provide a wide range of protection, including common security measures, such as stair doors that are locked from the stair side to secure floors in high-rise facilities or sports/entertainment venues, or very complex systems designed to provide highly secure areas for portions or all of a facility. Systems may be in place for institutional or correctional considerations, or they may be provided as part of an airport or similar facility.

Some of these systems may be as important as the life safety systems; however, in all but extreme cases life safety must take precedence over security concerns. This is especially important during an incident. The life safety systems, egress components, and evacuation procedures must be carefully coordinated with the security systems to ensure proper operation during an emergency.

Use of Elevators

Elevators can provide safe and effective evacuation alternatives, particularly in tall buildings. However, enhancements may be necessary, because standard elevators in compliance with current prescriptive codes may not provide adequate protection. The level of protection necessary will depend on the design scenarios. Various levels of elevator protection may be appropriate. These include standard, enhanced, and protected elevators [22].

Note that elevators are typically equipped with fire fighter recall features. Elevator recall automatically sends elevator cars to a "recall floor" upon detection of smoke within the shaft or vestibule.

Standard Elevators. Standard passenger elevators typically open into unprotected vestibules and may or may not be located within a protected shaft. Such elevators can be used as part of a building evacuation plan where occupants would not be threatened by using the elevators. Conditions where standard elevators may be appropriate range from could be related to weather scenarios, power failure (where standby or emergency power is provided), bomb threat, or other non-fire scenarios [22].

Enhanced Elevators. Enhanced elevators can be used for full building evacuation and phased evacuation for both fire and non-fire scenarios in which elevator damage is not expected. Protection features for enhanced elevators could include smoke- and heat-protected vestibules, smoke and heat sensors for recall, elevator recall function, and fire fighter operation modes. Elevator vestibules can be provided to separate the adjoining space by a smoke barrier and smoke stop doors to prevent smoke spread via the elevator hoistway due to stack effect and natural smoke buoyancy [22].

Protected Elevators. Specific enhancements that may need to be considered for elevators to be used for egress during a wide range of extreme events include: protection from fire and smoke, protection from CBR contaminants, protection from water, emergency power supplies, overheating protection, and earthquake protection [23, 42]. Additionally, emergency communication and special control strategies may be necessary. The following list discusses these enhancements [23, 42]:

- *Smoke and heat protection.* Elevator shafts and associated machine and control rooms open to the shafts should be protected from smoke and fire. Protection can be provided through a combination of fire-rated smoke barriers and positive-pressure systems. Elevators are typically open to ground floor lobbies. Ground floors can be a particularly vulnerable point in the system; these areas may need protected lobbies. Additionally, FEMA [30] suggests that elevators be placed within a protected core to mitigate blast and impact issues.

- *CBR contaminant protection.* If CBR threats are being considered, elevator shafts and machine rooms open to the shaft should be protected from CBR attacks. Compartmentation and pressurization systems may need to be considered to limit the potential for elevator contamination. See Chapter 8 of this text for additional information.

- *Water protection.* Elevators should be designed to function when compromised by water from sprinkler or firefighter operations or drainage and containment should be provided to prevent water from entering elevator shafts.

- *Emergency power.* Components and controls should be provided with emergency power. Conduits for emergency power should be located within the protected shaft or otherwise protected.

- *Overheating protection.* Components will need to be protected from overheating. This protection is particularly important when considering the possibility of large fires.

- *Earthquake protection.* All components should be designed to accommodate expected earthquake loads.

- *Emergency communication.* Two-way communication is necessary to all floors and within the elevator cab. A communication plan should be developed to keep waiting occupants informed.

- *Controls.* Special controls are necessary to determine the order in which floors are evacuated.

Additional elevator enhancements, such as stairs within the protected elevator shaft and additional fire fighter equipment, should also be considered [22]. During events that may cause elevators to be untenable or unusable (e.g., interior fire events or similar hazards), elevators should not be used as part of the able-bodied evacuation strategy unless enhancements are provided.

Training and Communication. Training and communication are critical when elevators are used for evacuation, because the general population has been trained to not use elevators in a fire. Occupants may be confused, as they may not know whether elevators should be used during a particular event. Another concern is that occupants may become impatient and overcrowd an elevator; overcrowding can lead to the complete loss of elevator function and substantial delays in evacuation [24].

EVACUATION MODELING

The time for a building or portion of a building to evacuate may be needed as part of an overall performance design for extreme events. Estimates of building evacuation time can be developed through timed or dynamic egress studies. A number of methods can be used to develop evacuation analyses, including those discussed in the following:

- "The Movement of People in Buildings and Design Solutions for Means of Egress," [43] in NFPA's *Fire Technology*
- *Pedestrian Planning and Design* [44]
- "Behavioral Response to Fire and Smoke" in *The SFPE Handbook of Fire Protection Engineering* [45]
- "Movement of People: The Evacuation Timing" in *The SFPE Handbook of Fire Protection Engineering* [34]
- "Emergency Movement" in *The SFPE Handbook of Fire Protection Engineering* [46]
- NFPA 130, *Standard for Fixed Guideway Transit and Passenger Rail Systems*

These methods typically account for the number of occupants, occupant characteristics, relevant building features, and safety systems provided. As noted in Figure 12.3, egress calculation estimates are divided into three components: notification, movement decision time, and movement times. These egress components, as well as occupant loads and occupant characteristics, are discussed in this section.

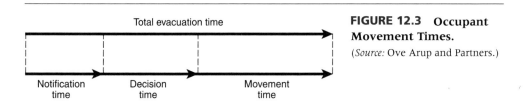

FIGURE 12.3   Occupant Movement Times.
(*Source:* Ove Arup and Partners.)

Occupant Loads

Occupant loads can be determined through specific knowledge of the expected number of occupants or, more often, through application of a set of factors. NFPA *101, Life Safety Code*; *NFPA 5000, Building Construction and Safety Code*; and the International Building Code [10] include occupant load requirements based on square footage or the number of fixed seats or, in some cases, on actual use. Table 12.1 lists occupant load factors from the *Life Safety Code*; these load requirements are based on average square feet per occupant for various uses. Actual occupant loads may differ from code-based loads; therefore, it is important to consider anticipated use to determine actual loads.

Key Point   The larger of the two occupant loads—either the code-based load requirement or the actual load—should be considered within the design.

Maximum expected occupant loads may vary based on the event considered, because different load conditions may lead to varying levels of safety. Hazards associated with high–occupant load events may differ from those for low–occupant load events; therefore, the overall relative hazard to occupants may not be intuitive. Egress systems and evacuation plans may need to consider the various expected hazard and occupant load conditions to be sure that those scenarios presenting the greatest challenges for life safety are addressed.

Occupant Characteristics

Occupants can be completely ambulatory, partially mobile, or incapable of self-preservation. These and other occupancy characteristics influence egress decisions and movement times and should be ac-

TABLE 12.1 Occupant Load Factor

Use	(ft² per person)	(m² per person)
Assembly Use		
Concentrated use, without fixed seating	7 net	0.65 net
Less concentrated use, without fixed seating	15 net	1.4 net
Bench-type seating	1 person/18 linear in.	1 person/455 linear mm
Fixed seating	Number of fixed seats	Number of fixed seats
Waiting spaces	See note	See note
Kitchens	100	9.3
Library stack areas	100	9.3
Library reading rooms	50 net	4.6 net
Swimming pools	50 (water surface)	4.6 (water surface)
Swimming pool decks	30	2.8
Exercise rooms with equipment	50	4.6
Exercise rooms without equipment	15	1.4
Stages	15 net	1.4 net
Lighting and access catwalks, galleries, gridirons	100 net	9.3 net
Casinos and similar gaming areas	11	1
Skating rinks	50	4.6
Educational Use		
Classrooms	20 net	1.9 net
Shops, laboratories, vocational rooms	50 net	4.6 net
Day-Care Use	35 net	3.3 net
Health Care Use		
Inpatient treatment departments	240	22.3
Sleeping departments	120	11.1
Ambulatory health care	100	9.3
Detention and Correctional Use	120	11.1
Residential Use		
Hotels and dormitories	200	18.6
Apartment buildings	200	18.6
Board and care, large	200	18.6
Industrial Use		
General and high-hazard industrial	100	9.3
Special-purpose industrial	NA	NA

TABLE 12.1 *Continued*

Use	(ft² per person)	(m² per person)
Business Use	100	9.3
Storage Use		
In storage occupancies	NA	NA
In mercantile occupancies	300	27.9
In other than storage and mercantile occupancies	500	46.5
Mercantile Use		
Sales area on street floor	30	2.8
Sales area on two or more street floors	40	3.7
Sales area on floor below street floor	30	2.8
Sales area on floors above street floor	60	5.6
Floors or portions of floors used only for offices	See business use.	See business use.
Floors or portions of floors used only for storage, receiving, and shipping, and not open to general public	300	27.9
Mall buildings	See note	See note

NA: Not applicable. The occupant load is the maximum probable number of occupants present at any time.
Note: There are various exceptions and qualifications for this table within the *Life Safety Code®*. Refer to it for additional quidance.
Source: NFPA, 2003. NFPA *101®, Life Safety Code®*, National Fire Protection Association, Quincy, MA, Table 7.3.1.2.

counted for when developing evacuation plans. "Occupant Response to Fire Alarm Signals" [25] in NFPA's *National Fire Alarm Code Handbook* and *SFPE Engineering Guide: Human Behavior in Fire* [47] suggest that specific occupant characteristics, such as responsiveness, alertness, commitment, physical and cognitive capabilities, roles, familiarity, social affiliation, condition, and gender and age, and the design of the building should be evaluated when assessing egress times. For more information on these subjects, consult these references.

Building Design. The layout of a building and the activities that take place inside the building directly affect the evacuation time. If the layout of a building makes it difficult for occupants to find their way, evacuation times will be longer than in a building with obvious evacuation routes. The evacuation time can be very different depending on whether the building population is evenly distributed, such as in an office building, or if people are concentrated in certain areas, such as in a movie theater. The distribution of occupants in a space affects the flow of people through egress components, as well as walking speeds.

A special characteristic in some spaces is focal points. In buildings where occupants focus their attention on a certain point, such as a stage or a podium, the occupants may look to that point for guidance. A focal point can be used effectively to deliver instructions to occupants, as described in "Occupant Response to Fire Alarm Signals" [25] in NFPA's *National Fire Alarm Code Handbook* and other sources [47].

Other building characteristics that can affect the evacuation time are visual access. The way a building is designed may prevent occupants from having visual access to the behavior of others. The presence of other occupants may increase the chances of being notified of an emergency, but occupants who are alone tend to respond more rapidly to ambiguous fire cues [25, 47].

Responsiveness. The type of warning system in a building directly affects how occupants will respond. Occupants respond slowest to basic fire alarm signals; the use of live messages over a voice communication system is the best way to initiate a quick response. Prerecorded messages are rarely as effective as live messages and are less informative. In either case, these systems need to be designed to provide audible and intelligible messages to building occupants.

Additionally, if a building warning system has frequent false alarms, it loses its efficiency to warn occupants. A large number of false alarms is three or more false alarms over a six-month period [25].

Alertness. The alertness of occupants may affect their awareness of the surroundings. An activity that directly affects alertness is sleeping. In addition, occupants may have limitations that could affect their egress time. Limitations may be perceptual, physical, or intellectual, or they may be due to consumption of alcohol, drugs, or medication [25, 47].

Commitment. People who are committed to their activities will be less likely to respond to an alarm signal. Activities that occupants may be committed to include waiting in line, eating at a restaurant, or gambling. However, if there is a change of environment, such as stopping a movie at a cinema, an occupant's attention will be captured quickly.

Physical and Cognitive Capabilities. The movement of occupants with disabilities is influenced by the nature of their disability and the egress elements of a building, such as doors, ramps, and stairs. The initial response of occupants with disabilities may involve considerable preparation time. In addition, people with hearing impairments may require special means of notification; those with visual impairments may need assistance finding an evacuation route [47].

Roles. In single-family homes, occupants tend to respond quickly to smoke alarms, because they are responsible for these alarms. However, people in public buildings do not respond quickly to alarms, because they do not feel responsible and assume they will be told further instructions. Instructions that come from well-trained staff or wardens will shorten premovement times. Staff must also be easily recognizable with distinctive uniforms. Training of occupants can also help provide a fast response, but training of occupants is only possible in buildings with a consistent population, such as an office building or school.

Familiarity. Occupants who are familiar with a building, who have participated in evacuation drills and who know the evacuation procedure are more likely to begin evacuation quickly [25]. However, infrequent users of the building will depend on staff and signs. Infrequent users are also more likely to leave by the route they entered the building and tend to rely on exit signs if their familiar route is impassable due to smoke or crowding.

Social Affiliation. The behavior of occupants is affected by whether they are alone or in a group. Occupants are more likely to attempt to gather with people with whom they have emotional ties to before starting evacuation, such as a family group. This characteristic could result in delay if the group is not together at the start of the incident [25, 47]. In addition, the walking speed of the group will be dictated by the slowest group member [47].

Condition. The condition of the occupants after exposure to fire and the products of combustion may affect their condition and ability to evacuate [47].

Gender and Age. Older studies have shown that females are more likely to alert or warn others and evacuate in response to fire cues and that males are more likely to fight the fire. However, many of these studies were completed over 20 years ago; rigid gender roles may have impacted these results, and further studies are needed [47].

Age has an impact on an occupant's ability to evacuate. Three categories of performance differences among age groups that could be expected to influence evacuation are sensory skills, decision making, and action [47].

Notification Times

Egress designs and evacuation plans may rely on manual or automatic notification schemes. Manual notification may consist of manual alarm stations (e.g., manual "pull" devices that activate audio/visual systems to notify building occupants). It may also rely on the use of building occupants or staff to notify others. Evacuation systems that rely on manual notification should account for the time for occupants to notice and understand an incident, the time for occupants to take action and notify others, and the time for other occupants to receive notification messages.

In general, the time required for automatic notification includes detector-actuation times and system-processing times. A number of references discuss automatic detection in more detail:

- *NFPA 72, National Fire Alarm Code*
- "Design of Detection Systems" in *The SFPE Handbook of Fire Protection Engineering* [36]
- "Performance-Based Design of Fire Protection Systems—New Methods and Old Gaps" in *International Conference on Engineered Fire Protection Design* [48]
- "Fire Detection Modeling: State of the Art" by the Fire Detection Institute [49]
- "Designing Fire Alarm Audibility" in NFPA's *Fire Technology* [38]

Chapter 8 of this book includes additional information regarding fire detection.

Delay Times

In the context of this chapter, *delay time* is defined as the time for an occupant to receive and understand evacuation cues plus the time to initiate the exiting process. During this time, occupants can perform a wide range of tasks, or they may simply decide to leave. Often, an occupant's premovement actions are linked to the specific activity in which he or she is engaged, and these actions can be significantly influenced by occupant characteristics. For instance, a mother of a small child who is awoken by the sound of a smoke detector will likely locate her child before deciding to leave her home. Occupants in a building with a history of nuisance alarms may investigate to determine if an actual fire is present or may not respond to an alarm at all. A list of the first actions undertaken by occupants during fire emergencies is given in "Behavioral Response to Fire and Smoke" in *The SFPE Handbook of Fire Protection Engineering* [45]. A partial list of these actions includes notifying others, searching for the fire, notifying the fire department, getting dressed, gathering family, and fighting the fire.

Various factors, such as occupant training and frequency of false alarms, may influence occupant decisions, and thus delay time. Evacuation may also be delayed while occupants determine the most appropriate pathway for exiting. Complicated or nonintuitive egress systems can significantly influence egress delay times.

A set of conditions that can be used to characterize occupant premovement or delay times is provided in "Occupant Response to Fire Alarm Systems" [25] in the *National Fire Alarm Code Handbook* and other resources [13, 50]. These conditions are also listed in Table 12.2. In some situations, occupant delay time may exceed evacua-

TABLE 12.2   **Estimated Occupant Delay Times**

Occupancy Type	Occupancy Characteristics	Recognition Time (min)		
		Live Voice Directives	Nondirective Voice or Visual Display	Alarm Bell, Siren, or Similar Display
Offices, commercial and industrial premises, colleges, and schools	Occupants awake and familiar with the building, alarm systems, and evacuation procedures.	<1	3	>4
Shops, exhibitions, museums, leisure centers, and other assembly buildings	Occupants awake, but may be unfamiliar with the building, alarm systems, and evacuation procedures.	<2	3	>6
Dormitories, boarding schools, and apartment buildings	Occupants may be asleep, but are familiar with the building, alarm systems, and evacuation procedures.	<2	4	<5
Hotels and boarding houses	Occupants may be asleep and unfamiliar with the building, alarm systems, and evacuation procedures.	<2	4	>6
Hospitals, nursing homes, and other institutional establishments	A significant number of occupants may require assistance.	<3	5	>8

Source: Adapted from SFPE, 2002, *The SFPE Handbook for Fire Protection Engineering*, 3rd ed., National Fire Protection Association, Quincy, MA, Table 3-13.1.

tion movement times. A report presented at the Second International Symposium on Human Behavior in Fire provides occupant delay times for a variety of fire incidents and fire drills [3]. As noted in the report, premovement delay times varied widely. Delay times for occupants within the MGM Grand Hotel fire ranged from one minute to almost five hours; delay times for occupants who were given instructions to remain in place during the 1993 World Trade Center bombing were more than 3 hours.

Note that recent thought suggests that the fire safety management system and occupant characteristics may be more important than the type of notification provided [51]; therefore, the values in Table 12.2 should be used with specific knowledge of expected management procedures along with occupant characteristics.

MOVEMENT TIME CALCULATIONS

Pedestrian movement times can be estimated through engineering calculation methods or through computer egress models. Designs may use conventional egress components, such as stairs, hallways, and doors, or unconventional components, such as elevators and escalators.

Engineering Calculation Methods

This section provides an overview of engineering calculation methods for egress. For further detail, consult the following references:

- *Planning for Foot Traffic Flow in Buildings* [52]
- "The Movement of People in Buildings and Design Solutions for Means of Egress" in NFPA's *Fire Technology* [43]
- *Pedestrian Planning and Design* [44]
- "Behavioral Response to Fire and Smoke" in *The SFPE Handbook of Fire Protection Engineering* [45]
- "Movement of People: The Evacuation Timing" in *The SFPE Handbook of Fire Protection Engineering* [34]
- "Emergency Movement" in *The SFPE Handbook of Fire Protection Engineering* [46]
- *The Application Fire Safety Engineering Principles to Fire Safety Design of Buildings—Part 6: Human Factors* [51]
- *SFPE Engineering Guide to Performance-Based Fire Protection Analysis and Design in Buildings* [19]
- *Engineering Guide: Human Behavior in Fire* [47]
- NFPA *101, Life Safety Code*
- NFPA 130, *Standard for Fixed Guideway Transit and Passenger Rail Systems*
- *NFPA 5000, Building Construction and Safety Code*

Occupants with Disabilities. Occupants with disabilities or special needs should be considered when assessing egress movement speeds. Note that several references provide information regarding travel for occupants with disabilities:

- "Americans with Disabilities Act Accessibility Guidelines" [35]
- "Occupant Response to Fire Alarm Signals" in NFPA *National Fire Alarm Code Handbook* [25]
- "Evacuating People with Disabilities" in NFPA's *Fire Engineering* [53]
- "Toward the Characterization of Building Occupancies for Fire Safety Engineering: Prevalence, Type, and Mobility of Disabled People" in NFPA's *Fire Technology* [54]
- "Toward the Characterization of Building Occupancies for Fire Safety Engineering: Capabilities of Disabled People Moving Horizontally and on an Incline Plane" in NFPA's *Fire Technology* [55]
- "Toward the Characterization of Building Occupancies for Fire Safety Engineering: Capabilities of Disabled People to Negotiate Doors" in NFPA's *Fire Technology* [56]
- "Toward the Characterization of Building Occupancies for Fire Safety Engineering: Characteristics of People with Disabilities to Read and Locate Exit Signs" in NFPA's *Fire Technology* [57]

Determining Travel Times. In general, developing engineering estimates of occupant movement times involves dividing egress paths into segments and determining the travel distances and occupant densities for each segment. Ranges of occupant flow through doors, corridors, and other similar features and travel speeds for various occupant densities on level surfaces and stairs vary with occupant density and are listed in Table 12.3. These simplified movement characteristics are taken from "Movement of People: the Evacuation Timing" in *The SFPE Handbook of Fire Protection Engineering* [34], *SFPE Engineering Guide to Human Behavior in Fire* [47], *CISBE Guide E: Fire Engineering* [13], and *Fire Engineering Design Guide* [14].

When estimating travel times to egress doors within a compartment or a group of compartments, it is important to consider that occupants may not necessarily start out adjacent to egress doors. Therefore, the time for the first occupant to reach a given door needs to be added to the flow time through the door. The total movement time for a compartment or group of compartments is the greater of the travel time for the furthest occupant to reach the exit openings or the travel time for the first occupant to reach the door added to the flow time through the openings. This relationship is depicted in the following equations:

Movement Time

$$= \textit{Travel time for first occupant to reach door} \qquad (1)$$
$$+ \textit{Occupant flow yime}$$

or

Movement time = Travel time for last occupant to reach door

Segments may be defined by doors, points where two occupant streams merge or diverge, or other egress components, such as stairwells, elevators, or escalators. Again, Table 12.3 lists estimates for occupant movement times.

A typical assumption is that occupants will use exits uniformly (within rooms with more than one exit); however, this assumption is not valid if a significant portion of occupants attempt to exit from the direction they entered. Another caution is that some of the exits may not be usable. The uneven use of exits was particularly evident in the February 20, 2003, fire at The Station nightclub [6, 58].

Calculating Flow Time. Figure 12.4 illustrates a simple calculation of occupant movement time. Assume the room depicted is a retail store with an occupant density of 30 square feet per person (2.8 square meters per person), with each of the exits being a set of double doors, each with two 39.4 inch (1000 millimeters) leaves. The maximum travel distance in the room is 197 feet (60 meters) as shown in the figure.

In this example, the code-dictated occupant load is 1286 occupants (60 × 60÷2.8). Assuming travel speeds of 150 feet per minute (0.762 meters per second), door flows of 40 occupants per minute per door leaf, and normally occupants would be 32.8 feet (10 meters) from the nearest exit, the occupant movement time could be estimated as 4.2 minutes:

- Travel time for occupants to exit the room is approximately 1.4 minutes (i.e., 60 meters ÷ 0.762 meters per second ÷ 60 seconds per minute).

TABLE 12.3   Occupant Movement

Egress Component	Density person/m² (person/ft²)	Speed m/min (ft/min)	Specific Flow people/min/m (people/min/ft)
Stair	Minimum 0.5 (0.05)	45.7 (150)[a] 55.1 (181)[b] 66 (217)[c]	<16.4 (<5)[a] 27.5 (8.38)[b]
	Moderate 1.1 (0.10)	36.6 (120)[a] 45.8 (150)[b] 45.9 (151)[d]	45.9 (14)[a] 50.4 (15.4)[b] 50.5 (15.4)[d]
	Optimum 2.0 (0.19)	29 (95)[a] 30.3 (99.4)[b] 30.4 (99.7)[d]	59.1 (18)[a] 60.6 (18.5)[b] 72 (21.9)*[c] 60.8 (18.5)[d]
	Crush 3.2 (0.30)	<12.2 (<40)[a] 9.64 (31.6)[b] 9.66 (31.7)[d]	<39.4 (<12)[a] 30.8 (9.39)[b] 30.9 (9.42)[d]
Corridor	Minimum 0.5 (0.05)	76.2 (250)[a] 71.4 (234)[b] 72 (236)[c] 73 (240)[d]	<39.4 (<12)[a] 35.7 (10.9)[b] 36.5 (11.1)[d]
	Moderate 1.1 (0.10)	61 (200)[a] 59.4 (195)[b] 59.4 (195)[d]	65.6 (20)[a] 65.3 (19.9)[b] 65.3 (19.9)[d]
	Optimum 2.2 (0.20)	36.6 (120)[a] 34.8 (114)[b] 34.8 (114)[d]	78.7 (24)[a] 76.6 (23.3)[b] 79.8 (24.3)[c] 76.6 (23.3)[d]
	Crush 3.2 (0.30)	<18.3 (<60)[a] 12.5 (41)[b] 12.5 (41)[d]	<59.1 (<18)[a] 40 (12.2)[b] 40 (12.2)[d]
Doorway	Moderate 1.1 (0.10)	51.8 (170)[a] 59.4 (195)[b] 59 (195)[d]	65.3 (19.9)[b] 64.9 (19.8)[d]
	Optimum 2.4 (0.22)	36.6 (120)[a] 30.4 (99.7)[b] 30.4 (99.7)[d]	73 (22.3)[b] 79.8 (24.3)[c] 73 (22.2)[d]
	Crush 3.2 (0.30)	15.2 (<50)[a] 12.5 (41.0)[b] 12.5 (41)[d]	40 (12.2)[b] 40 (12.2)[d]

*Flow for effective width.

Sources: [a]Proulx, G., 2002. "Occupant Response to Fire Alarm Signals," *National Fire Alarm Code® Handbook,* National Fire Protection Association, Quincy, MA; [b]SFPE, 2003. *Engineering Guide: Human Behavior in Fire,* Society of Fire Protection Engineering, Bethesda, MD; [c]Butcher, K., 1997. *CIBSE Guide E: Fire Engineering,* The Chartered Institution of Building Services Engineers, London; [d]Buchanan, A., 1994. *Fire Engineering Design Guide,* Centre for Advanced Engineering, Christchurch, New Zealand.

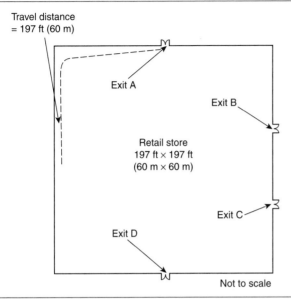

Travel distance
= 197 ft (60 m)

Exit A

Exit B

Retail store
197 ft × 197 ft
(60 m × 60 m)

Exit C

Exit D

Not to scale

FIGURE 12.4 Occupant Movement Example.

(*Source:* Arup.)

- Flow time is approximately 4.1 minutes (1286 occupants ÷ 4 doors ÷ 2 leaves per door ÷ 40 occupants per leaf, rounded up).
- Time for first occupant to reach the door is approximately 0.3 minutes (10 meters ÷ 0.762 meters per second, rounded up).

The flow time added to the time for the first occupant to reach the door is approximately 4.4 minutes, which is greater than the occupant travel time. This example does not consider the possibility of disabled occupants, nor does it consider premovement or detection times.

Computer Egress Models

A number of computer egress models are available to estimate egress movement times. Generally, these models fall into two categories: optimization models and simulation models. Optimization models provide estimates of the best possible movement time, whereas simulation models attempt to estimate actual movement times. Optimization models typically follow an approach similar to engineering calculations, providing a means to automate and optimize the process. Simulation models vary in sophistication; some models account for varying occupant movement speeds and provide movies of predicted movement.

Key Point   It is important to note that because a computer egress model simulation depicts only a single set of conditions; the overall evacuation analysis may need to simulate a range of inputs, varying occupant characteristics, available exits, and other necessary parameters in order to adequately simulate the estimated movement time for a given threat scenario.

Simulating a range of conditions can provide more confidence in movement estimates, because some of the inputs may have some degree of uncertainty. Sensitivity analyses can provide additional insight into the effects of the various uncertainties and help to bound results.

Several resources provide detailed listings of egress models and related references [46, 72]. A partial listing of evacuation models follows.

Evacnet 4. Evacnet 4 is an arc/node model [59]. Simulated occupants reside within nodes and can move through arcs to other nodes. A single set of occupant characteristics is applied to the entire population. Tabular data output, by node, can be developed.

STEPS. STEPS divides the domain into a grid [60]. Simulated occupants occupy grid cells and can move to adjacent grid cells when the cell is empty. Individual occupant characteristics can be applied. Occupants can "choose" exits based on travel distance to the exit, familiarity with the exit, crowding at the exit, and number of exit lanes at the exit; alternatively, occupants can be mapped to a specific exit. Tabular data output and simulation videos can be developed.

Simulex. Simulex divides the domain into a grid and creates distance maps to determine the closest exit from all areas [61]. The distance mapping results in concentric circles guiding occupants to exits. Occupants are tracked within the domain. Data are output in a tabular format, and simulation videos can be developed.

Exit 89. Exit 89 is an arc/node model, but it applies occupant travel speeds and flow characteristics based on local conditions [62]. Occupants are tracked individually and tenability data from fire models can be applied to individual occupants. Tabular data on individually simulated occupants are provided.

EXODUS. EXODUS divides the domain into a grid and develops arcs and nodes for simulated occupants to navigate the domain [63]. Occupants' positions are tracked and fractional effective doses can be calculated based on exposure to combustion products. A wide range of data is available, and simulation videos can be developed.

Summary

Additional guidance on the use of computer models is provided in ASTM E1895, *Standard Guide for Determining Uses and Limitations of Deterministic Fire Models* [64]. While these models tend to predict movement times better than engineering calculations, these methods do not account for phenomena such as merging conflicts (i.e., occupants entering a stair in the middle of its run) and counterflows (i.e., occupants or responders moving opposite of the general flow direction). In some cases, these limitations can underpredict movement times and should be accounted for in the overall analysis.

▬ ELEVATOR EVACUATION ▬▬▬▬▬▬▬▬▬▬▬▬▬

Historically, elevators are used infrequently during emergency events. During emergencies, elevators are generally taken out of service, with evacuation taking place through stairs. However, for very tall buildings, small-footprint towers, deep underground train stations; hospitals, or other occupancies where occupants may not be ambulatory, elevators may be the most practical means of evacuation. The *Life Safety Code* recognizes elevators as an acceptable second means of egress in some tower buildings.

> **Key Point**   Designers may consider using elevators to assist in the evacuation of large buildings or buildings that have occupants with disabilities or people who are not ambulatory.

The most common scheme for elevator evacuation considers all elevators moving to a designated discharge floor and discharging any existing occupants upon activation of an alarm within the building. The discharge floor should lead either directly to the outside of the building or to a designated area of refuge. From this point, the elevators begin a series of roundtrips to evacuate waiting occupants. Depending on the design of the elevator system within a given building, the elevators may act automatically during an emergency or they may require manual control by either the fire department or designated and trained building staff. Methods exist for estimating the time for evacuation with elevators; the basic concepts for this analysis are discussed in this section.

Calculating Elevator Evacuation Times

A comprehensive discussion of calculating elevator evacuation times for buildings is included in the American Society of Heating, Refrigeration, and Air-Conditioning Engineers' (ASHRAE's) *Principles of Smoke Management* [41]. The ASHRAE methodology was developed as part of a research project sponsored by the U.S. General Services Administration (GSA) to study the use of elevators for evacuation purposes. This methodology builds upon work by others [65, 66, 67].

Note that the operation of elevators during an emergency event can be complicated and varied. For example, it is difficult to predict where elevators will be needed for a given event and how many occupants will use the elevators for evacuation, thus an elevator evacuation analysis must consider such uncertainties and design for the most onerous situations. Other considerations include inefficiencies in the mechanical systems of the elevators; the possibility of individual elevators being out of service; and inefficiencies associated with the layout and design of elevators, elevator lobbies, and other building-egress components.

An elevator evacuation time analysis consists of the following components:

- *Startup time.* The time from activation of a building alarm to the commencement of elevator roundtrips to evacuate occupants.
- *Roundtrip time.* The time required for an elevator that starts at a discharge floor to reach the floor being evacuated, load occupants, return to the discharge floor, and discharge the occupants.
- *Standing time.* A component of the roundtrip time that includes the time needed to open and close the doors and the time needed for people to enter and leave the elevator.
- *Travel time.* A component of roundtrip time that occurs when the elevator is in motion; it includes acceleration, constant motion, and deceleration.

These components can be combined into a single mathematical expression that represents the total evacuation time. Essentially, this expression consists of startup time plus the time needed for occupants leaving an elevator to reach the outside or a safe area, plus the sum of the roundtrip times needed to evacuate the required occupants multiplied by an efficiency factor and divided by the number of operating elevators. This total evacuation time is represented by Equation 2.

$$
\begin{aligned}
\textit{Total} \quad &= \textit{Startup time} + \textit{Occupant travel time to exit} \quad (2) \\
\textit{evacuation} \quad &+ \textit{(Sum of all required roundtrip times} \\
\textit{time} \quad &\times \textit{Efficiency factor/number of} \\
&\quad \textit{evacuation elevators)}
\end{aligned}
$$

Using Computer-Aided Elevator Evacuation Models

Hand calculation of elevator evacuation time for a large building with multiple elevators or groups of elevators can be a time-consuming, repetitive process. Automated algorithms available for calculating elevator evacuation time can greatly increase the efficienct of this analysis. However, few commercially available elevator evacuation models exist. One such model, ELVAC, can be obtained for no charge from the Building and Fire Research Laboratory (BFRL) of the National Institute of Standards and Technology (NIST) at their Web site, www.bfrl.nist.gov. Another tool is ELEVATE, which can be obtained from Peters Research at www.elevate.peters-research.com.

___ EMERGENCY ACTION PLANNING___

A critical component in the development of egress systems for extreme events is emergency action planning. OHSA standards 29 CFR 1910.38, "Emergency Action Plans," and 29 CFR 1910.39, "Fire Prevention Plans," require emergency plans for workplaces. Seven weeks after the events of September 11, 2001, the City of Chicago passed an ordinance that mandates and regulates high-rise evacuation planning and training. In the summer of 2004, New York City enacted a new Emergency Action Plan law. Many other city and state fire departments throughout the United States have requirements for Emergency Action Plans (EAPs). These governmental mandates have resulted in a wide range of requirements for EAPs, evacuation plans, and fire prevention plans; the following section provides generalized requirements for EAPs.

Case Study: EAP Requirements in New York City

One of the recommendations made for buildings by the New York City Mayor's World Trade Center Building Code Task Force Recommendations on Improving Building Safety is the requirement for the development of a building EAP. The EAP is an enhanced version of the required fire safety plan that also takes into account scenarios other than fire. EAP requirements are still being developed at the time of publication; however, a brief overview of some of the proposed requirements follows.

The purpose of the EAP is to address incidents other than fire. Response to fires in a building should still follow the requirements of Local Law 5, which is to evacuate the floor of origin and the floor above, and evacuating down at least two floors below the floor of origin. The EAP should provide direction on how to safely and expeditiously remove or relocate occupants from a building, how to move people from endangered areas in the building to safe areas, and how to shelter in place.

The proposed requirements include similar requirements for a fire safety director, floor wardens, deputy fire wardens, and searchers, but with slightly different duties and different titles, referred collectively to as the EAP staff. The requirements for documentation are very similar to those for the fire safety plan, in that a written document must be developed identifying the EAP staff and the actions that need to be taken for each specific scenario.

The proposed legislation does not provide a list of scenarios that the EAP should address other than the three basic concepts of complete evacuation, movement to safe areas, and defend in place, however the rules developed by the fire department may. It does, however, require a system to be developed to account for all building occupants following implementation of the EAP. It also requires that the plan address street management, especially for complete evacuation scenarios. Occupants must be able to move safely away from the building without hindering or delaying emergency-service access to the site. Remote assembly points should be established and coordinated with surrounding buildings, in case several buildings need to be evacuated at once. The proposed EAP requirements also introduce the concept of using elevators for evacuation in emergencies other than fire and require this to be documented in the EAP if elevator use is planned.

Developing EAPs

OSHA Standard 29 CFR 1910.38, "Emergency Action Plans," details EAP requirements. Many local and state fire departments have additional requirements and require approval of these plans. Thus, EAP requirements, which may include evacuation plans and fire prevention plans, vary from state to state and, in many cases, city to city.

The EAP may include several documents, because information may need to be packaged or tailored to the various groups using the plan. For example, typical occupants may be provided with a small, simple brochure, whereas key personnel are given a larger document that explains the specific duties for each position [68].

The number and type of scenarios to be considered will depend on the building, building location, and the relationship to adjacent structures. As discussed in subsequent sections, scenarios can be grouped into those events occurring inside the building and those occurring outside the building. Building and fire codes typically address only accidental interior events, such as an unintentional fire. Plans that are developed to address extreme events would likely need to address a wide range of interior and exterior events.

A number of references describe topics that should be considered within an EAP. The checklist in Figure 12.5 consolidates information from several sources.

Communicating the EAP

Communication plays an important role for any emergency egress scenario. Notification is the first step in an active evacuation plan after detection of an event. It is possible, and perhaps likely in many tall or very large facilities, that occupants would not even know an event is occurring within the building.

NFPA 72, National Fire Alarm Code, has attempted to standardize the evacuation signal so occupants throughout a facility would be able to recognize this signal. The temporally coded signal required by *NFPA 72* is still relatively new and is not yet universally acknowledged. Older facilities generally have bells, whereas hospitals and areas with private notification systems may have chimes; modern voice alarm systems typically use the slow whoop. Some areas also use coded systems in which a tone, bell, or horn is used to indicate a code that corresponds to a location or a specific action. Live voice communication is the most effective means of communicating emergency conditions; voice communication is further discussed later in this section.

Evacuation plans that include relocation, defending in place, or complete evacuation based on specific events require a means to distinguish the required action. The easiest way to provide this information is through voice communication systems. For facilities that have

FIGURE 12.5   EAP Topic Checklist.

EAP Checklist

- ❏ Purpose of the plan
- ❏ List of events considered and major hazards within the building
- ❏ Procedures for accounting for employees and/or visitors and guests
- ❏ Procedures for reporting emergencies
- ❏ Assignment of the Fire Safety Director (FSD) or Emergency Coordinator (EC) with contact details
- ❏ Assignment of one or more deputy or Alternate Fire Safety Directors (AFSD) or Alternate Emergency Coordinators (AEC) with contact details
- ❏ Assignment of Floor Wardens, Deputy Floor Wardens, Area Wardens, Stairway Monitors and Elevator Monitors, as necessary, with contact detail
- ❏ Assignment of Crowd Managers, Emergency Evacuation Teams, Publicity Director, Utilities Superintendent, First Aid Officers, Fire Response Team or Fire Wardens, as necessary, with contact details
- ❏ Responsibilities matrix, including specific information on who is authorized to initiate evacuations, who is responsible for notifying the fire department, who is responsible for accounting for employees and/or visitors and guests, who is responsible for housekeeping, etc.
- ❏ Preferred means of building emergency notification
- ❏ Policies and procedures for those left behind to operate critical equipment, if any
- ❏ Procedures for critical operations shutdown
- ❏ Requirements and responsibilities for assisting persons with disabilities. This may include a confidential list of those with disabilities.
- ❏ Rescue and medical duties
- ❏ Essential fire and life safety features provided within the facility
- ❏ Fire and life safety system interfaces with the security measures
- ❏ Escape procedures, methods, and preferred evacuation routes for each event, including the appropriateness for use of elevators
- ❏ Post-emergency exit plans, minimally indicating exits, exit paths, and evacuation signs (emergency exit plans and posted locaitons for the plans should be included within the EAP, perhaps as an Appendix to the EAP)
- ❏ Responsibilities for in-house fire brigades
- ❏ Required frequency of fire drills
- ❏ Training requirements for occupants and key personnel (periodic training should be conducted This may include evacuation drills. The plan should keep records of all training and drills.)
- ❏ Maintenance requirements for fire and life safety systems and features
- ❏ Procedures for control of housekeeping (this might include proper clean up, maintenance of egress paths, etc.)
- ❏ Procedures for control of hazards and fuel sources (this might include control of welding permits, smoking, proper storage, etc.)
- ❏ Means to update the plan as necessary
- ❏ Names or job titles of persons who can be contacted for further information or explanation of duties under the plan

(*Sources:* Adapted from BOMA, 2002. *Emergency Preparedness, Building Owners and Managers Association International,* Washington, DC; OSHA, 2001. "How to Plan for Workplace Emergencies and Evacuations," Occupational Health and Safety Administration, Washington, DC; NFPA, 2001. *Introduction to Employee Fire and Life Safety,* National Fire Protection Association, Quincy, MA.)

a workforce that does not change frequently or that have multiple long-term tenants, it may be possible to train the occupants to recognize different signals, but in standard office buildings and other similar facilities turnover of employees and tenants could prevent signals from being properly understood.

In New York City, an inquiry signal must be sent throughout a building, to notify building personnel that there is an event in the building. Unfortunately, without continuous training, staff may not even be aware of the signal, and occupants could confuse it with the evacuation signal. Thus, for complex evacuation plans, it is very important to be able to communicate the desired response to the occupants.

If the evacuation plan includes several different responses, it is even more important that the notification system be audible and intelligible, so that occupants know the proper response. In order to provide intelligible messages, both prerecorded and live announcements can be used. Consideration must be given to the location where live announcements will be made. In newer buildings that have a separate fire command center, background noise should not be an issue; however, if the fire command station is open, for example, in the lobby, background noise may interfere with the intelligibility of the message. If live voice messages are being used, several messages for each scenario should be prepared in advance allowing the operator to be able to read the messages and provide concise, clear directions to the occupants. With newer fire alarm technology, it is possible to prerecord several messages and then select the proper messages based on the event. Intelligibility is discussed further in the "Occupant Notification" section of this chapter.

Assembling an Evacuation Team

As required in the EAP legislation in New York City and guidance from various cities, including Los Angeles, Minneapolis, and others, an emergency evacuation team should be assembled. The titles of each position on the team may change from area to area, but the general responsibilities are similar. The evacuation team should be led by a fire safety director (FSD).

Fire Safety Director. The FSD is the lead person in implementing an evacuation plan. In many locations, this person also is responsible for the readiness of the emergency team and the life safety systems in the building. The FSD is often a certified position. Whether or not certification is required, the FSD must be empowered to make decisions and to direct the implementation of these decisions. A deputy or an assistant director can be assigned to assist with FSD tasks. The FSD's responsibilities during an event include the following:

- Notification of emergency responders (fire department, police department, etc.)
- Initiation of the appropriate evacuation response
- Communication with other members of the evacuation team and the tenants to gain information and direct the evacuation
- Interface with the emergency responders
- Continual assessment of the conditions and response to changes

A building evacuation coordinator, evacuation supervisors, and a chief of exit drills may be appointed to assist the FSD and deputy FSD with some of these duties. In large campus settings, it is possible that an evacuation coordinator or supervisor may each be responsible for individual buildings, with the FSD having the overall responsibility for the campus. The FSD may also appoint a publicity director, a utilities superintendent, or a first-aid officer.

Floor Warden. The second level of the evacuation team includes floor wardens. Based on the size of the facility, floor wardens may be assisted by deputy floor wardens or area wardens. Floor wardens are responsible for directing occupants on a floor in accordance with instructions being given by the FSD or in accordance with the EAP. The floor warden should be able to be in contact with the FSD in order to provide information about conditions on the floor and to receive information to give to the occupants of the floor. The floor warden will often report when a floor is clear and when the occupants have arrived at their designated evacuation or relocation point.

Searchers and Emergency Evacuation Teams. Searchers or emergency evacuation teams can be assigned to assist floor wardens. Searchers help verify that all occupants on a floor have been notified and are responding to the directions that have been provided. Searchers often work in teams of two people, one male and one female, so that all areas of the floor, including bathrooms, can be searched quickly. Searchers report to the floor wardens and assist in directing occupants with the proper response. Stairwell monitors and elevator monitors may also be appointed to assist with some of these duties. It is important for these teams to be trained to understand unsafe conditions where they must immediately cease searching activities and exit the facility.

In-House Fire Brigade. Depending on the size of a facility, as well as the overall level of training and type of equipment provided (including Self-Contained Breathing Apparatus) for the in-house fire brigades, team members may be responsible for the following tasks, as addressed in NFPA's *Introduction to Employee Fire and Life Safety*:

• Use of fire extinguishers
• First aid
• Chemical spill procedures
• Search and rescue operations
• Firefighting operations

In-house fire brigade teams must be provided with proper training and equipment. Adequate time and budgets must be allotted for training and equipment maintenance. As with searchers, it is important for these teams to be trained to understand unsafe conditions where they must immediately cease searching activities and exit the facility.

Crowd Management Team. Evacuation plans may need to incorporate crowd management plans. The International Association of Auditorium Managers (IAAM) Crowd Management Curriculum Project Report [69] lists crowd management team members. Such a team may include a crowd management instructor, a crowd management administrator, a crowd assembly supervisor, and a crowd assembly facilitator. IAAM defines these roles as follows:

• *Crowd management instructor:* IAAM-trained instructors who train the facility team
• *Crowd management administrator:* Professional staff with experience and knowledge to develop and implement facility security, crowd management, and EAP activities
• *Crowd assembly supervisor:* Staff who direct and oversee crowd-assembly-facilitator activities
• *Crowd assembly facilitator:* Event staff providing services directly to guests; may include ushers, parking attendants, and security staff

Additional details regarding crowd management principles are provided in various publications [69, 70].

Other Team Members. Truly effective EAPs often involve a larger emergency action team. For example, some EAPs may include high-level company executives who can make decisions. A larger team may also include building engineers and other staff to operate equipment and to keep certain systems functioning during an event.

Management Support. It is extremely important that such teams have the full support of upper management and the tenants if it is a multi-tenant facility. Without the direct and obvious support or involvement of the management, occupants may be more likely to ignore the directions given by the emergency action team.

Training

An overall training plan needs to be developed that is appropriate to the size, function, and complexity of the facility. Occupants, employees, and staff need to understand the key personnel in charge during an emergency. OSHA [71] provides detailed training requirements; the following lists training concepts for staff and building occupants:

- Individual roles and responsibilities (staff and occupants)
- Types of threats, hazards, and emergencies (staff and occupants)
- Notification, warning, and communications procedures (staff and occupants)
- Means for locating family members in an emergency (occupants)
- Emergency response procedures (staff)
- Evacuation, shelter, and accountability procedures (staff)
- Location and use of common emergency equipment (staff)
- Emergency shutdown procedures (staff)

Specific facilities will need to modify this list, as appropriate. OSHA suggests that training should be provided when the initial plan is developed, when the plan is updated, when building layouts change, as well as when new employees are hired and when new equipment, materials, or processes are introduced [71].

MAINTENANCE

As discussed throughout this chapter, egress systems rely on the proper operation of a wide range of emergency, fire, and life safety systems. Therefore, it is critical for these systems to operate and function correctly. A regular preventative maintenance schedule should be developed for all fire and life safety systems that will be relied upon during an emergency evacuation.

The following references contain specific information regarding maintenance:

- NFPA 25, *Standard for the Inspection, Testing, and Maintenance of Water-Based Fire Protection Systems*
- NFPA 70B, *Recommended Practice for Electrical Equipment Maintenance*
- *NFPA 72, National Fire Alarm Code*
- NFPA 92A, *Standard for Smoke-Control Systems Utilizing Barriers and Pressure Differences*
- NFPA 92B, *Standard for Smoke Management Systems in Malls, Atria, and Large Spaces*
- NFPA 110, *Standard for Emergency and Standby Power Systems*

Additionally, *NFPA 101®, Life Safety Code®,* provides guidance on up-keep and maintenance of exits.

__SUMMARY

In summary, egress systems for extreme events may require enhancements that are not required for egress systems designed for traditional building threats. It is important that the overall egress strategy match the specific fire and life safety features provided. Special techniques, such as dynamic or timed egress analysis and overall performance techniques may be necessary to address a wide range of egress scenarios and support the overall strategy. Additionally, for egress systems addressing an extreme event, it is especially important that an EAP be developed; these plans may include specific evacuation techniques and a range of evacuation scenarios. Lastly it needs to be stressed that maintenance procedures are necessary for these systems to work as designed.

__BIBLIOGRAPHY

References Cited

1. Stein, L., 2001. *The Triangle Fire,* Cornell University Press, Ithaca, NY.
2. NYCDB, 1973. "Local Law 5," New York City Department of

Buildings, New York.

3. Fahy, R., and Proulx, G., 2001. "Toward Creating a Database on Delay Times to Start Evacuation and Walking Speeds for Use in Evacuation Modeling," *2nd International Symposium on Human Behavior in Fire: Conference Proceedings*, Interscience Communications Limited, London.

4. FEMA/ASCE, 2004. "World Trade Center Building Performance Study: Data Collection, Preliminary Observations and Recommendations," Publication 403, Federal Emergency Management Agency, Washington, DC.

5. Alvarez, E., and Moncada, J., 2004. "Tragic Fire in Paraguay," *NFPA Journal*, September–October, p. 24.

6. Tubbs, J., Meacham, B., Moore, A., McLaughlin, B., Johann, M., Woodward, A., 2004. "Fire and Life Safety Assessment of U.S. Egress and Sprinkler Requirements Within Nightclubs—A Preliminary Update," *Conference Proceedings of the Tenth International Interflam Conference 2004*, Interscience Communications Limited, London.

7. Fruin, J., 1993. "The Causes and Prevention of Crowd Disasters," *Proceedings of the International Conference on Engineering for Crowd Safety*, Elsevier Science Publishers, London.

8. Thurner, A., 1984. *Rebels on the Range—The Michigan Copper Miners' Strike of 1913–1914*, John H. Forster Press, Lake Linden, MI.

9. Johnson, M., 2003. "Chicago Club Had Been Told to Close," *Milwaukee Journal Sentinel*, February 18, 2003.

10. ICC, 2003. *International Building Code*, International Code Council, Falls Church, VA.

11. SFPE, 2004. *SFPE Engineering Guide to Performance-Based Fire Protection Analysis and Design in Buildings*, National Fire Protection Association, Quincy, MA.

12. SFPE, 2004. *The SFPE Code Official's Guide to Performance-Based Design Review*, Society of Fire Protection Engineering and International Code Council, Falls Church, VA.

13. Butcher, K., 1997. *CIBSE Guide E: Fire Engineering*, The Chartered Institution of Building Services Engineers, London.

14. Buchanan, A., 1994. *Fire Engineering Design Guide*, Centre for Advanced Engineering, Christchurch, New Zealand.

15. ICC, 2003. *International Code Council Performance Code*, International Code Council, Falls Church, VA.

16. Tubbs, J., and Moore, A., 2004. *Client Memo—Tenability Criteria*

Overview (Confidential Client), Ove Arup and Partners Massachusetts Inc., Westborough, MA.

17. Purser, D., 2002. "Visibility and Human Behavior in Smoke," *The SFPE Handbook of Fire Protection Engineering*, 3rd ed., National Fire Protection Association, Quincy, MA.

18. Purser, D., 2002. "Toxicity Assessment of Combustion Products," *The SFPE Handbook of Fire Protection Engineering*, 3rd ed., National Fire Protection Association, Quincy, MA.

19. SFPE, 2000. *SFPE Engineering Guide to Performance-Based Fire Protection Analysis and Design in Buildings*, National Fire Protection Association, Quincy, MA.

20. Peacock, R., Averill, J., Reneke, P., and Jones, W., 2004. "Characteristics of Fire Scenarios in Which Sublethal Effects of Smoke Are Important," *Fire Technology*, National Fire Protection Association, Quincy, MA.

21. Tubbs, J., and Meacham, B., 2004. *Egress Design Solutions—Draft*, John Wiley & Sons, Inc., Hoboken, NJ.

22. CTBUH, 2004. *Emergency Evacuation Elevator Systems Guide*, Council on Tall Buildings in Urban Habitat, Chicago, IL.

23. Klote, J. H., Deal, S., Donoghue, E. A., Levin, B. M., and Groner, N. E., 1993. "Fire Evacuation by Elevators," *Elevator World*, Vol. 41, No. 6, pp. 66, 70, 72, 75.

24. Kuligowski, E., 2003. "Elevators for Occupant Evacuation and Fire Department Access," *Proceedings of the CIB-CTBUH International Conference on Tall Buildings*, Council on Tall Buildings and Urban Habitat, Chicago, IL.

25. Proulx, G., 2002. "Occupant Response to Fire Alarm Signals," *National Fire Alarm Code® Handbook*, National Fire Protection Association, Quincy, MA.

26. Fahy, R., and Proulx, G., 2002. "A Comparison of the 1993 and 2001 Evacuations of the World Trade Center," *Proceedings—Fire Risk and Hazard Assessment Symposium*, National Fire Protection Research Foundation, Baltimore, MD.

27. Puchovsky, M., and Quiter, J., 2003. "Supplement 7—The Application of Performance-Based Design Concepts for Fire and Life Safety," *Life Safety Code® Handbook*, National Fire Protection Association, Quincy, MA.

28. Hong Kong Buildings Department, 1996. "The Provisions of Means of Escape in Case of Fire—1996," Hong Kong, China, www.info.gov.hk/bd/english/documents/index_crlist.html.

29. Proulx, G., 2001. "High-Rise Evacuation: A Questionable Concept," *2nd International Symposium on Human Behaviour in Fire: Conference Proceedings*, Interscience Communications Limited, London.

30. FEMA, 2003. "Risk Management Series: Primer for the Design of Commercial Buildings to Mitigate Terrorist Attacks," Publication 427, Federal Emergency Management Agency, Washington, DC.

31. Independent Commission, 2003. "Report of Cook County Commission Investigating 69 West Washington Fire of October 17, 2003," Chicago, IL, www.co.cook.il.us.

32. FEMA, 2002. "Risk Management Series: Reference Manual to Mitigate Potential Terrorist Attacks Against Buildings," Publication 426, Federal Emergency Management Agency, Washington, DC.

33. Proulx, G., and Fahy, R., 2004. "Account Analysis of WTC Survivors," *Human Behavior in Fire Symposium 2004*, Interscience Communications Limited, London.

34. Proulx, G., 2002. "Movement of People: The Evacuation Timing," *The SFPE Handbook of Fire Protection Engineering*, 3rd ed., Society of Fire Protection Engineering, Bethesda, MD.

35. Access Board, 2003. "Americans with Disabilities Act Accessibility Guidelines," Access Board, Washington, DC, www.accessboard.gov.

36. Schifiliti, R. P., Meachan, B., and Custer, R. L. P., 2002. "Design of Detection Systems," *The SFPE Handbook of Fire Protection Engineering*, 3rd ed., National Fire Protection Association, Quincy, MA.

37. Ginn, K., 1988. *Architectural Acoustics*, McGraw-Hill, New York.

38. Schifiliti, R., 2002. "Supplement 5—Voice Intelligibility for Emergency Voice/Alarm Communication Systems," *National Fire Alarm Code® Handbook*, National Fire Protection Association, Quincy, MA.

39. Puchovsky, M., 1999. *Automatic Sprinkler Systems Handbook*, National Fire Protection Association, Quincy, MA.

40. Isman, K., 2003. "Automatic Sprinklers," in Cote, A. (Ed.), *Fire Protection Handbook*, National Fire Protection Association, Quincy, MA.

41. Klote, J., and Milke, J., 2002. *Principles of Smoke Management*, American Society of Heating, Refrigerating, and Air-Conditioning Engineers, Inc., Atlanta, GA.

42. Kuligowski, E., and Bukowski, R., 2004. "Design of Occupant

Egress Systems for Tall Buildings," *CIB World Building Congress, 2004*, National Research Council Canada, Ottawa, Canada.

43. Pauls, J., 1984. "The Movement of People in Buildings and Design Solutions for Means of Egress," *Fire Technology*, National Fire Protection Association, Quincy, MA.

44. Fruin, J., 1987. *Pedestrian Planning and Design*, Elevator World, Inc., Mobile, AL.

45. Bryan, J., 2002. "Behavioral Response to Fire and Smoke," *The SFPE Handbook of Fire Protection Engineering*, 3rd ed., Society of Fire Protection Engineering, Bethesda, MD.

46. Nelson, H., and Mowrer, F., 2002. "Emergency Movement," *The SFPE Handbook of Fire Protection Engineering*, 3rd ed., National Fire Protection Association, Quincy, MA.

47. SFPE, 2003. *Engineering Guide: Human Behavior in Fire*, National Fire Protection Association, Quincy, MA.

48. Marrion, C., and Cholin, J., 2001. "Performance-Based Design of Fire Detection Systems—New Methods and Old Gaps," *International Conference on Engineered Fire Protection Design*, Society of Fire Protection Engineers, San Francisco, CA.

49. Schifiliti, R., and Pucci, W., 1996. "Fire Detection Modeling: State of the Art," Fire Detection Institute, Bloomfield, CT.

50. BSI, 1997. *Fire Safety Engineering in Buildings—Part 1: Guide to the Application of Fire Safety Engineering in Buildings* (DD 240), British Standards Institute, London.

51. BSI, 2004. *The Application Fire Safety Engineering Principles to Fire Safety Design of—6: Human Factors* (PD 7974-6), British Standards Institute, London.

52. Predtechenskii, V. M., and Milinskii, A. I., 1978. *Planning for Foot Traffic Flow in Buildings*, Amerind Publishing Co., New Delhi, India.

53. Juillet, E., 1993. "Evacuating People with Disabilities," *Fire Engineering*, National Fire Protection Association, Quincy, MA.

54. Boyce, K. E., Shields, T. J., and Silcosk, G. W. H., 1999. "Toward the Characterization of Building Occupancies for Fire Safety Engineering: Prevalence, Type, and Mobility of Disabled People," *Fire Technology*, National Fire Protection Association, Quincy, MA.

55. Boyce, K. E., Shields, T. J., and Silcosk, G. W. H., 1999. "Toward the Characterization of Building Occupancies for Fire Safety Engineering: Capabilities of Disabled People Moving Horizontally

and on an Incline Plane," *Fire Technology,* National Fire Protection Association, Quincy, MA.

56. Boyce, K. E., Shields, T. J., and Silcosk, G. W. H., 1999. "Toward the Characterization of Building Occupancies for Fire Safety Engineering: Capabilities of Disabled People to Negotiate Doors," *Fire Technology,* National Fire Protection Association, Quincy, MA.

57. Boyce, K. E., Shields, T. J., and Silcosk, G. W. H., 1999. "Toward the Characterization of Building Occupancies for Fire Safety Engineering: Characteristics of People with Disabilities to Read and Locate Exit Signs," *Fire Technology,* National Fire Protection Association, Quincy, MA.

58. Grosshandler, W., Bryner, N., and Madrzykowski, D., 2004. "Final Report of the National Construction Safety Team Investigation of the Station Nightclub Fire," National Institute of Standards and Technology, Gaithersburg, MD.

59. Kisko, T. M., Francis, R. L., 1986. "Evacnet+, A Building Evacuation Computer Program," *Fire Technology,* National Fire Protection Association, Quincy, MA.

60. Mott MacDonald Simulation Group, 2004. "Simulation of Transient Evacuation and Pedestrian Movements (STEPS)," Version 2, Mott MacDonald, Surrey, UK.

61. IES, 2001. "Simulex User Manual, Evacuation Modeling Software," Integrated Environmental Solutions, Inc., Glasgow, UK.

62. Fahy, R., 1996. "EXIT89—High-Rise Evacuation Model—Recent Enhancements and Example Applications," *Conference Proceedings of the Seventh International Interflam Conference,* Interscience Communications Limited, London.

63. Gwynne S., Galea, E., Lawrence, P., and Owen, M., 2001. "Simulating Occupant Interaction with Smoke Using Building EXODUS," *2nd International Symposium on Human Behaviour in Fire: Conference Proceedings,* Interscience Communications, Limited, London.

64. ASTM, 1997. Standard Guide for Determining Uses and Limitations of Deterministic Fire Models, E1895-97, ASTM International, West Conshohocken, PA.

65. Strakosch, G., 1983. *Vertical Transportation: Elevators and Escalators,* 2nd ed., John Wiley & Sons, New York.

66. Bazjanac, V., 1977. *Simulation of Elevator Performance in High-Rise Buildings Under Conditions of Emergency, Human Response to Tall Buildings,* Dowden, Hutchinson & Ross, Stroudsburg, PA.

67. Pauls, J., 1977. "Management and Movement of Building Occupants in Emergencies," DBR Paper No. 788, National Research Council, Ottawa, Canada.

68. BOMA, 2002. *Emergency Preparedness,* Building Owners and Managers Association International, Washington, DC.

69. IAAM, 1998. "IAAM Crowd Management Curriculum Project Report, February 22, 1998," Center for Venue Management Studies, International Association of Auditorium Managers, Irving, TX.

70. Fruin, J., 1984. "Crowd Dynamics and Auditorium Management." *Auditorium News,* International Association of Auditorium Managers, Irving, TX.

71. OSHA, 2001. "How to Plan for Workplace Emergencies and Evacuations," Occupational Health and Safety Administration, Washington, DC.

72. Kuligowski, E., Peacock, R., 2005. Technical note 1471. A Review of Building Evacuation Models. National Institute of Standards and Technology, Gaithersburg, MD.

NFPA Codes, Standards, and Recommended Practices

NFPA Publications.   The following is a list of NFPA codes, standards and recommended practices cited in this chapter. See the latest version of the *NFPA Catalog* for availability of current editions of these documents.

NFPA 25, *Standard for the Inspection, Testing, and Maintenance of Water-Based Fire Protection Systems*

NFPA 70®, *National Electrical Code*®

NFPA 70B, *Recommended Practice for Electrical Equipment Maintenance*

NFPA 72®, *National Fire Alarm Code*®

NFPA 92A, *Standard for Smoke-Control Systems Utilizing Barriers and Pressure Differences*

NFPA 92B, *Standard for Smoke Management Systems in Malls, Atria, and Large Spaces*

NFPA 101®, *Life Safety Code*®

NFPA 110, *Standard for Emergency and Standby Power Systems*

NFPA 130, *Standard for Fixed Guideway Transit and Passenger Rail Systems*

NFPA 550, *Guide to the Fire Safety Concepts Tree*

NFPA 5000®, *Building Construction and Safety Code*®

Additional Readings

Jin, T., 2002. "Visibility and Human Behavior in Smoke," *The SFPE Handbook of Fire Protection Engineering*, 3rd ed., National Fire Protection Association, Quincy, MA.

Schifiliti, R., 1988. "Designing Fire Alarm Audibility," *Fire Technology*, National Fire Protection Association, Quincy, MA.

Teague, P., 2003. "Supplement 1—Case Histories: Fires Influencing the *Life Safety Code*," *Life Safety Code® Handbook*, National Fire Protection Association, Quincy, MA.

Title 29, Code of Federal Regulations, part 1910.38, "Emergency Action Plans," U.S. Government Printing Office, Washington, DC.

Title 29, Code of Federal Regulations, part 1910.39, "Fire Prevention Plans," U.S. Government Printing Office, Washington, DC.

13

Information Technology and Telecommunications Design

Al Lyons

Clear, robust, and reliable internal and external communications are critical to an organization's ability to mitigate, manage, and recover from extreme events. Today, information technology and telecommunications (IT&T) systems and services are usually required to support both normal and emergency communications.

This chapter discusses IT&T design requirements as well as the policies and procedures necessary to ensure performance during both normal operations and extreme events. Two important issues are the roles that IT&T systems and services play in mitigating the likelihood that an extreme event will occur at a facility and in facilitating recovery if an extreme event does occur. IT&T systems include the following:

- Voice and data communications systems, such as telephones, local area networks (LANs), and wide area networks (WANs)
- Wireless communications systems, such as wireless LANs (WLANs), cellular phones, and 2-way private mobile and first responder (e.g., emergence service, police, fire department) radios
- Data and information processing and storage systems

ROLE OF IT&T SYSTEMS

Normal Operations

During normal operations, the role of communications and IT&T systems and services is to support the ongoing operation of the facility and the businesses and/or organizations it houses. Typically, this support means that the IT&T systems and services must include the following:

- Facilitate communication among staff (internal and external) and between the organization and clients and suppliers as well as government or regulatory agencies
- Process information so that it is useable
- Store and archive information
- Recover information from archives

During normal operations, IT&T systems and services play a critical role in mitigating the impact of extraordinary events on businesses and organizations. Extraordinary events are unplanned events that have the potential to become extreme events but do not become such events because the systems, policies, and procedures in place work as designed, mitigating the impact of the event on the organization or facility. Examples of extraordinary events include power outages and communication-carrier failures that do not impact a business or facility because staff is well trained, policies and procedures work, and emergency power and redundant communications links function as designed. Such mitigation is achieved by the following measures:

- Sharing information and policies throughout the organization so that extraordinary events are detected quickly
- Quickly detecting, deterring, and responding proactively to extraordinary events so that they do not become extreme
- Failing deterrence, minimizing the consequences of an extreme event by facilitating communications during and following the event

When organizations and facilities do not have adequate systems, policies, procedures, training, and staff in place, it is more likely that an extraordinary event will become an extreme one that will have an adverse impact on the organization or facility.

From a communications perspective, successful mitigation requires that policies and procedures be developed to facilitate response to extraordinary and extreme events. These policies and procedures may include developing programs to ensure that staff, suppliers, customers, and others impacted by the organization all know how to respond to potentially extreme events. As part of normal operations, these policies and procedures must be communicated to all constituents and necessary updates and training provided. Although it is impossible to anticipate all possible extraordinary and extreme events, organizations should conduct simulations and desktop exercises to test and fine-tune policies and procedures to confirm that they work as expected.

Although IT&T systems and services play a critical role in the normal operations of most businesses and organizations, they play an equal, and perhaps more important, role in responding to and recovering from extraordinary and extreme events. From an IT&T perspective, creating facilities and organizations with robust IT&T systems and services begins with tailoring the network design to the unique needs of the facility and integrating the IT&T infrastructure into the design of the facility, business, or organization. What makes sense for one facility, business, or organization may not make sense for others.

Figure 13.1 depicts the impact of the East Coast power failure of August 2003. Figure 13.1(a) shows an image taken at 9:29 P.M. on August 14, 2003, approximately 20 hours before the blackout. Figure 13.1(b) shows an image taken at 9:14 P.M. on August 14, 2003, about 7 hours after the blackout. For most organizations and facilities, this extraordinary event became an extreme event. But for some, such as the International Arrivals Building at JFK Airport in New York City, it was merely an extraordinary event: emergency power systems, redundant communications systems/services, policies, and procedures all worked as planned, and, unlike other terminals, the terminal was able to continue operating.

Extreme Event Operations

The role of IT&T systems and services during extreme events is similar to their function during normal operations, but the constituents for whom communications must be supported and information processed and archived are different. During extreme events, normal operations of an organization or a business are interrupted. Although it is critical to support communications with all of the organization's normal constituents, during extreme events it becomes equally, if not more, critical to support communications with emergency responders, government agencies, and others who become involved.

FIGURE 13.1   Impact of the August 14, 2003, Power Failure on the East Coast of the United States.

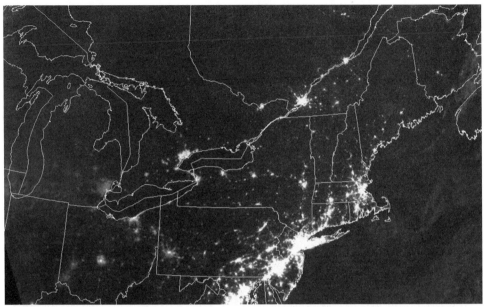

(a) Satellite Image Taken 20 Hours Before the Blackout.

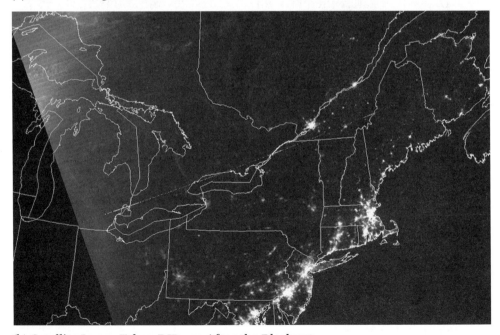

(b) Satellite Image Taken 7 Hours After the Blackout.

(*Source:* Image courtesy of Chris Elvidge, U.S. Air Force.)

For most organizations and businesses, mission-critical IT&T systems are generally hard wired (physically connected) to fixed positions, such as desks or workstations. This facilitates reliable (high-availability) high-bandwidth, secure communications links. *Bandwidth* is a measure of the rate at which data are sent and received. It is typically measured in thousands of bits of information per second (kilobits), millions of bits (megabits), billions of bits (gigabits), or trillions of bits (terabits).

During extreme events, the nature of IT&T requirements changes. Low-bandwidth links to mobile locations become much more important than high-bandwidth secure links to fixed locations. Thus, wireless services and infrastructure become much more important, because first responders and others involved with responding to extreme events must generally be mobile.

Although the IT&T systems and services needed by organizations and businesses during normal operations are very different, their communications needs during and following extraordinary and extreme events are very similar. These requirements include support of communications among first responders, fire safety personnel, management, security and facilities staff, and building or staff occupants. This communication is often achieved via public address systems associated with the fire detection and alarm systems installed in most buildings. Many of these voice communications are now being augmented by e-mail and other text-based messages sent to workstations and wireless communications devices and/or displayed on dynamic signage elements. Communication among first responders, fire safety personnel, security, facilities staff, and management is often achieved via fire fighter telephones or floor-warden phones, radios, and text messaging.

Identifying who is still in a facility and who has been safely evacuated is vital to determining how to respond during an extreme event. Analyzing information from security/access control and time clock systems is useful in determining who was in a facility at the time of the event, but it may not be useful in determining who has been safely evacuated. To determine the whereabouts of building occupants, it is critical that organizations establish policies for staff to assemble at mustering points or call in, text message, or e-mail when they have reached safety.

Communicating with staff, customers, suppliers, and others who will be impacted by the extraordinary or extreme event is important to mitigating its impact and facilitating recovery. The media often plays a role in disseminating information; therefore, press releases must be clear and accurate. To ensure that the organization gets the right message out, press conferences and press releases should be augmented with e-mails or phone calls to vital constituents and the most current information should be posted on the business or organization's Web site.

For example, during the July 7, 2005, subway and bus terrorist bombings in London, Arup (a leading international consulting firm) was able to account for all local and visiting staff in a short period of time due to the robust communications policies it implemented following the 2001 terrorist attacks in New York City. This enabled the organization to implement a staged return to normal operations on the following day.

Figure 13.2 shows a copy of the Arup Emergency web page. It facilitates locating staff and provides an easily accessible means of archiving and downloading emergency procedures.

Although response details vary depending on the type of extreme event, all responses do have some common features. For example, people must be contacted. Additionally, it is impossible to identify all possible extraordinary and extreme events. Hence, it is recommended that organizations develop a comprehensive, holistic approach to the creation of plans to respond to extraordinary and extreme events.

One aspect of proactive planning for extreme events is reaching out to the communities where offices are located to identify and leverage community resources. Recently, many municipalities have established and participate in the Corporate Emergency Access System (CEAS). More information about CEAS can be found on its web site [1]. Many organizations participate in CEAS to facilitate the maintenance or recovery of IT&T systems following an extreme or extraordinary event. During extreme events, access to the areas involved is generally restricted. CEAS enables organizations to identify critical staff (typically less than 10 percent) who will be allowed into areas that are involved in extreme events to maintain or recover IT&T (business) systems operations. CEAS is one of the many resources available through the Business Network of Emergency Resources (BNER). More information about BNER can be found on its web site [2].

According to BNER, most businesses do not have an emergency plan in place, even though they know it is important. In fact, BNER says that the majority of businesses spend less than 3 percent of their total budget on business-recovery planning. Yet 47 percent of businesses that experience a fire or major theft go out of business within

FIGURE 13.2 Arup Emergency Web Page.

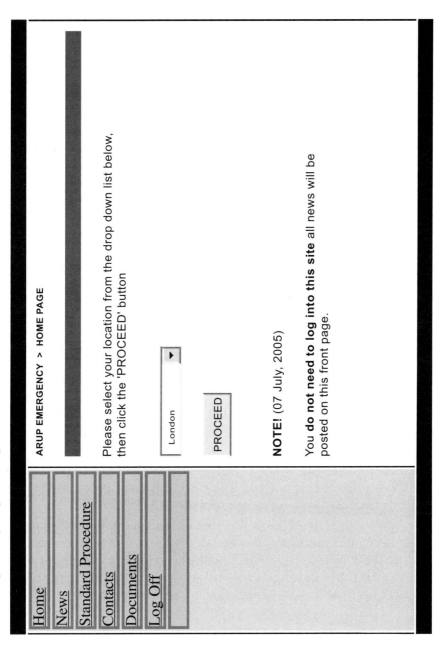

ARUP EMERGENCY > HOME PAGE

Home
News
Standard Procedure
Contacts
Documents
Log Off

Please select your location from the drop down list below, then click the 'PROCEED' button

London ▶

PROCEED

NOTE! (07 July, 2005)

You **do not need to log into this site** all news will be posted on this front page.

(*Source:* Arup.)

two years, 44 percent of companies that lose records in a disaster never resume business, and 93 percent of companies that experience a significant data loss are out of business within five years [2].

___POLICY DEVELOPMENT_____

To efficiently and effectively support IT&T systems and services during both normal operations and extreme events, it is important to understand the nature of the facility or organization and determine what its requirements and needs are. Once these issues are addressed, then availability needs must be determined. *Availability* is a measure of the experience of users of a system or service. When systems have high availability, the user perceives the system or service to be continuously available. Although high availability is always desirable, it is also expensive—the cost increases exponentially as availability increases beyond 99.9 percent (8.8 hours of downtime per year).

Understanding the Business

The first step in developing IT&T policies and procedures and designing the IT&T infrastructure is to understand the nature of the facility or organization. Issues that must be addressed include the following:

- *Facility*. What does the facility or organization do? What is the facility used for? Is it or any of its neighbors a potential terrorist target, such as a foreign mission or an animal laboratory?
- *Organization size*. What is the number of staff, the number of locations, and so forth?
- *IT&T services, systems, and infrastructure role*. Will failure of such services and systems potentially result in loss of life or injury? Will failure cause business to shut down?
- *IT&T failure cost*. What is the cost of failure on a per second, per minute, per hour, per day, and per week basis? Note that following IT&T service and systems failures, it generally takes between 4 to 10 times as long as the duration of the failure for the business or organization to return to normal operations.

Identifying IT&T Requirements

Understanding the nature of the organization is important in determining availability and identifying the communications bandwidth and information-processing and storage requirements of the facility and the organizations it houses.

Communications Bandwidth. Bandwidth requirements are determined by what needs to be communicated and the timeliness required. Organizations using video (CCTV) or Voice over Internet Protocol (VoIP) will find that these services are generally the two most demanding applications and that they often dictate the bandwidth requirements of the facility or organization. VoIP and CCTV dictate bandwidth requirements because they require the highest quality of service (continuous delivery of data) at a relatively high volume. Most other applications can tolerate brief interruptions in delivery of interruption without impacting service.

Information Processing and Storage. Information-processing and storage requirements are determined by the amount of data that must be processed, stored, and archived. Other factors include whether the information must be available in real time or near-real time and how long of a delay in recovering the information is acceptable. *Real time* implies that information is recorded, archived, and distributed as it is entered into the system. *Near-real time* means that a momentary delay, typically less than 1 second, in the recording, distribution, and archiving of information is acceptable. The need for real time versus near-real time information is determined by the size and the types of services supported by the IT&T systems. VoIP, video, and multimedia applications generally have real-time or near–real-time requirements. Internet, extranet, and other data-processing applications can generally tolerate momentary delays.

Some businesses have intense bandwidth, quality-of-service, availability, and information-processing requirements, whereas others have less intense requirements. Businesses that leverage lots of technology typically have higher bandwidth requirements than those that do not. For example, facilities that utilize image processing, such as CCTV cameras at transit facilities or medical diagnostic images at health-care facilities, have much greater bandwidth requirements than organizations whose primary requirement is word processing, such as in law firms or bank offices.

Assessing Availability Needs

Availability is determined by the *mean time between failure (MTBF)* and the *mean time to repair (MTTR)* of the IT&T systems supporting the service in question. When availability requirements for a service are high, the IT&T systems and infrastructure supporting the service must be resilient. Resilience is achieved through redundancy and diversity in both systems and staff.

Availability can be defined generally as the probability that a system will be ready to perform its mission or function under predefined conditions when required to do so at a random time. Availability is a function of the rate of failure of the system (its reliability) and how long it takes to restore the system to an operational condition following a failure (a function of maintenance). There are two basic types of system availability: inherent availability *(Ai)* and operational availability *(Ao)*.

Inherent Availability. Inherent availability *(Ai)* is applicable when ideal support (i.e., unlimited numbers of spare parts, no delays, etc.) is available and only design-, manufacturing- and installation-related failures are considered. *Ai* reflects the level of reliability and maintainability defined in the design and is realized through the manufacturing, assembly, and installation processes. *Ai* is an ideal maximum achievable level of availability for a system; it is suitable as a design parameter. *Ai* is calculated as follows:

$$Ai = \frac{MTBF}{MTBF + MTTR} \tag{1}$$

Where:

MTBF = Mean time between failures (a measure of reliability)
MTTR = Mean time to repair (a measure of maintainability)

Operational Availability. Operational availability *(Ao)* applies within a realistic support environment where all maintenance actions (including those not required as a result of design/manufacturing/installation failures) are considered. *Ao* is a function of reliability, maintainability, and supportability and is calculated as follows:

$$Ao = \frac{MTBM}{MTBM + MDT} \tag{2}$$

Where:

MTBM = Mean time between maintenance (including all corrective and preventive maintenance)

MDT = Mean downtime (including actual time to perform maintenance and accounting for delays in getting needed personnel, parts, etc.)

The information and communications technology industry uses a number of known levels of inherent availability. These levels of availability are listed in Table 13.1.

If a system is carrier class, for example, it is considered to be 99.999 percent available (also known as five nines). This level is the standard for public switched telephone networks (PSTNs). This means that there could be one failure a year that lasts just over 5 minutes, or there can be five failures that each last 1 minute. This applies similarly to all availability levels.

One of the fundamental laws of availability is the *law of diminishing returns*. The higher the level of availability, the greater is the incremental cost of achieving a small improvement. A general rule is that each additional nine after the second nine in an availability value will double the cost to build, operate, and maintain the system. As a system approaches 100-percent availability, the cost of increasing availability increases exponentially. The relationship between cost and availability is illustrated in Figure 13.3. Achieving absolute availability (i.e., A = 100 percent) is cost prohibitive; only so much availability can be built into the infrastructure.

TABLE 13.1 Availability Levels

Availability (%)	Annual Downtime	Description
98	175.2 hours	Too frequent failures
99	87.6 hours	Failures rare
99.5	43.8 hours	Considered high availability
99.9	8.8 hours	Three nines (often used for data storage systems)
99.99	52.6 minutes	Considered fault resilient
99.999	5.3 minutes	Fault tolerant (called carrier class for PSTN infrastructure)
99.99966	1.8 minutes	Six sigma (often used in manufacturing)
99.9999	31.5 seconds	Six nines
100	0	Continuous availability

Source: Arup.

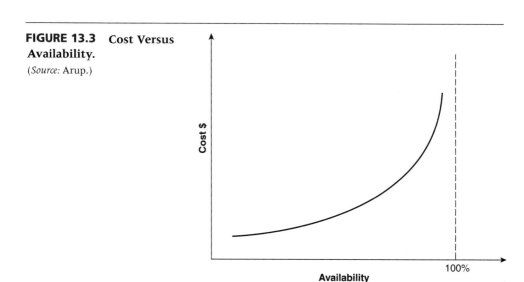

FIGURE 13.3 **Cost Versus Availability.**

(*Source:* Arup.)

Reliability is defined generally as the probability that a system will not fail to perform its functionality when used under stated conditions over a defined time period. Reliability is often expressed as *MTBF,* which applies to a system's normal life (as indicated in Figure 13.4).

With respect to a system or a system component, it is important to specify both the *MTBF* and a separate value for service life to describe both the expected failure rate during the normal/useful life period (as indicated in the bathtub curve shown in Figure 13.4) and the point in time at which the system is expected to move up the wear-out part of the bathtub curve. The relationship between avail-

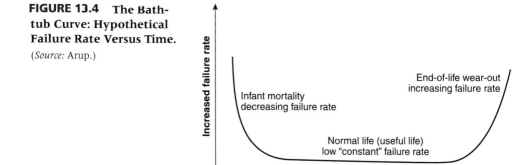

FIGURE 13.4 **The Bathtub Curve: Hypothetical Failure Rate Versus Time.**

(*Source:* Arup.)

ability and *MTBF* is shown in Figure 13.5. It is important to note that the *MTBF* of a system diminishes significantly when the system operates outside its design parameters (environmental, air-cleanliness, temperature, humidity, etc.).

Maintainability and Redundancy. *Maintainability* is often expressed in terms of *MTTR*. Availability is affected by system or network recovery procedures and time to repair. Decreasing the *MTTR* can have a significant effect on improving availability. Thus, any measures that can be used to reduce the *MTTR* for a system can help improve overall availability. Two areas impacting *MTTR* are maintainability and redundancy.

Table 13.2 depicts how the *MTBF* of a component/system must increase with increasing *MTTR* values in order to maintain a specific availability value. Figure 13.6 shows the impact of changes in *MTTR* on availability.

Availability is achieved through engineered diversity and redundancy in staff, services, systems, and infrastructure. Maximizing availability for organizations and businesses is different than maximizing it for a facility. Organizations and businesses often have the ability to locate operations in different parts of the country or the world or to equip staff with the systems needed to telecommute. This remote communications capability provides many organizations and

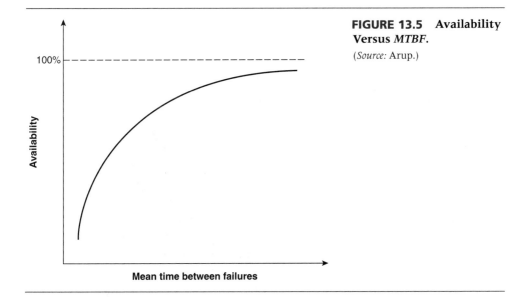

FIGURE 13.5 Availability Versus *MTBF*.

(*Source:* Arup.)

FIGURE 13.6 Impact of Changes in *MTTR* on Availability.

(*Source:* Arup.)

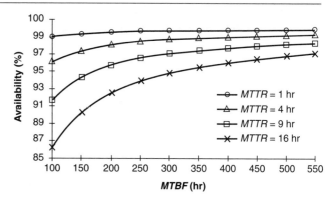

MTBF = Mean time between failures
MTTR = Mean time to repair

TABLE 13.2 *MTTR* and Availability Values

MTTR (hr)	Availability 99% MTBF (hr)	Availability 99.9% MTBF (hr)	Availability 99.95% MTBF (hr)	Availability 99.97% MTBF (hr)	Availability 99.99% MTBF (hr)	Availability 99.999% MTBF (hr)
1	100	1000	2000	3333.33	10,000	100,000
2	200	2000	4000	6666.66	20,000	200,000
4	400	4000	8000	13,333.33	40,000	400,000
8	800	8000	16,000	26,666.66	80,000	800,000

Source: Arup.

businesses with an ability to readily implement a greater degree of geographic diversity than that available to any one facility.

Internal Communications. Although the geographic diversity available to businesses and organizations is not as available to any one facility, the availability of the IT&T systems and services supporting a given facility can be greatly enhanced by incorporating diversity and redundancy into the design. Although this does not protect against external communications failures or failures of the entire facility, it does protect against failure of a portion of the facility. To ensure the availability of intrafacility communications, the IT&T services and systems must be redundant and diverse. Redundancy is achieved via duplication of systems; it protects against failure of a system or component. Diversity is achieved by locating primary and redundant IT&T facilities, such as risers, cable pathways, main equipment rooms, and closets, as far from each other as possible. This mitigates the possibility of a single event impacting both primary and redundant facilities. The appropriate degree of intrafacility redundancy and diversity is determined by the potential impact of a failure of internal communications. Fire and life safety systems are often designed with a great degree of diversity and redundancy—the goal being to protect property and life. This is achieved by equipping facilities with diversely located redundant backbones to support detection of alarm conditions via smoke detectors and other alarm-initiating devices and annunciation of alarm events via redundant audible and visual alarm annunciation devices (speakers and strobe lights).

Today, many facilities, businesses, and organizations have incorporated a similar approach to the design of the systems upon which their businesses depend. For example, many financial institutions incorporate a "salt-and-pepper" or "checkerboard" approach to the cabling of trading facilities, whereby a single failure will not impact the service at more than 50 percent of the trading desks. Additionally, operational procedures are adopted such that traders will share desks, thus helping to minimize the impact. This strategy makes failure of a portion of the IT&T services, systems, or infrastructure transparent to customers and other constituents of the firm. It prevents an extraordinary event from becoming an extreme event.

External Communications. To ensure availability of external communications, it is critical that IT&T systems and the service providers that they are connected to be redundant and diverse. Ideally, this network redundancy means that the facility should incorporate at least two service entries supported by at least two service providers connected via physically diverse routes (no manholes, duct banks, or central offices are shared). This redundancy and diversity mitigates the possibility of operations the facility houses being impacted by an extraordinary or extreme event that affects a service provider.

The nature of the organization determines the importance of IT&T systems and services to the organization and is the foundation for the development of the IT&T systems and services policies. The policies of some organizations will dictate that facilities be designed and built with diversely located redundant IT&T infrastructures and systems and only be located where redundant diversely located services from multiple communications service providers are available.

___INFRASTRUCTURE DESIGN___

Typical Infrastructure

IT&T infrastructures and services support both wired and wireless communications. Typical IT&T infrastructure includes the rooms, cable routes, and risers required to house and interconnect IT&T systems and the building services and systems required to support the IT&T systems. This would include enough space for new system/ technologies to be installed before old system/technologies are removed so that service is not interrupted. Cable routes and pathways should be sized to facilitate installation of new and future cabling as well as removal of abandoned cabling.

Key Point   Because the IT&T infrastructure will likely support several generations of technology, it should be designed to support both current and anticipated needs.

The complexity and cost of the infrastructure is determined by the size and nature of the facility and the organizations it houses. The infrastructure can range from a small system of relatively few rooms with a single connection to the main communications room and communications service providers and one source of power to a large infrastructure characterized by several rooms and diversely routed risers connected to multiple service providers and supported by redundant electrical power and cooling systems.

To determine the most appropriate IT&T infrastructure for a given facility, an understanding of the requirements of the organizations and businesses that will be located in the facility, as well as the needs of the owners and managers of the facility, must be developed. The nature and size of the businesses and organizations using a facility determine the nature, size, and sophistication of the IT&T infrastructure needed to support the facility. Businesses and organizations that will incur large costs due to interruptions in IT&T services can justify the capital and life-cycle expense of sophisticated redundant and diverse IT&T infrastructures and systems. Businesses and organizations that will not experience as severe an impact will not be able to justify the cost.

Figure 13.7 depicts a communications infrastructure for a facility with moderate availability requirements. Note that there are two separate, independent connections to the public network, and each

FIGURE 13.7   Communications Infrastructure for Facility with Moderate Availability Requirements.

TR = Telecommunications room
MER = Main equipment room

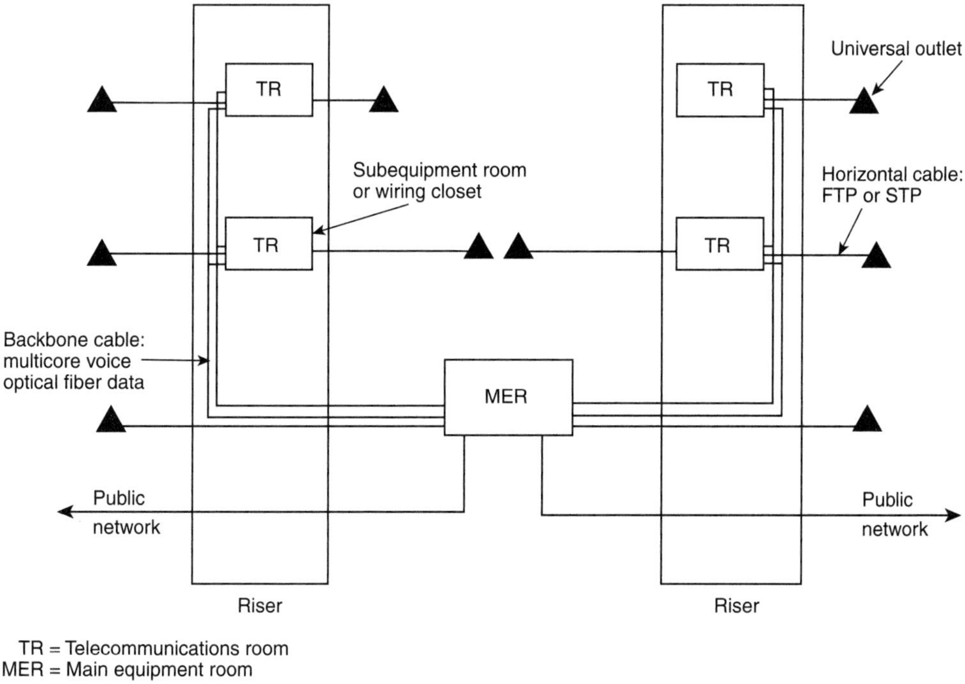

(*Source:* Arup.)

floor is supported by two telecommunications rooms (TRs) connected to the main equipment room by two independent risers. The single point of failure is the main equipment room, which would typically be a *hardened facility*; that is, a facility that is physically hardened by such features as robust construction and redundant systems. Availability of IT&T services is achieved via system redundancy without physical diversity. Because loss would result in interruption of service, it is located in a secure part of the facility, equipped with redundant building services, and provided with better security.

Key Point   In larger facilities and those with more intensive availability requirements, it often makes sense to build an infrastructure with no points of failure.

Figure 13.8 depicts an infrastructure for a large facility with intense availability requirements. Note that there are three main communications equipment rooms, each independently connected to multiple service providers, and each telecommunications closet is connected to two main communications rooms. This topology provides a high degree of availability and assures no single points of failure. This type of infrastructure is appropriate for campuses with high availability requirements, such as airports, data centers, pharmaceutical laboratories, or production facilities.

When facilities house businesses and organizations with limited IT&T requirements, such as bank office facilities or large shopping malls or outlets, the availability requirements of the facility may be greater than those of the organizations it houses. This higher availability requirement is due to the fact that the facility may distribute CCTV images to multiple security consoles. Transmission of images from each camera to a console typically requires approximately 1 to 10 megabytes of bandwidth, depending on image quality and frame rate. At large facilities with 100 to 1000 or more cameras, this rapidly leads to the need for a network backbone with a capacity of several gigabytes. As shown in Figure 13.9, distribution of images and multimedia applications has some of the most demanding bandwidth requirements.

This use of technology presents an opportunity to provide the businesses and organizations housed in the facility with more robust services at a competitive cost by sharing the building's IT&T infrastructure with the occupants. Instead of each occupant providing its own systems/infrastructure and independently negotiating and con-

FIGURE 13.8 Infrastructure for a Large Facility with Intense Availability Requirements.

(*Source:* Arup.)

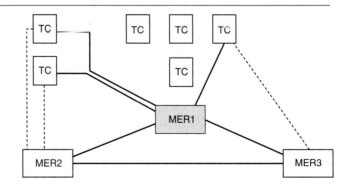

TC = Telecommunications closet
MER = Main equipment room

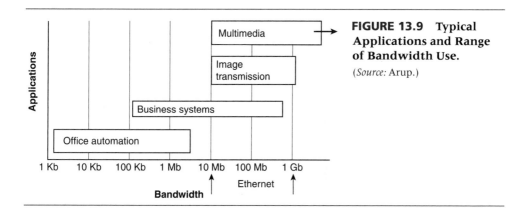

FIGURE 13.9 Typical Applications and Range of Bandwidth Use. (*Source:* Arup.)

tracting with telephone and data communications service providers, such as the telephone company, a facility is equipped with shared infrastructure and systems, and communications services are aggregated, reducing both initial infrastructure/systems costs as well as recurring communications service costs. In facilities occupied by several organizations, the initial and recurring total cost of providing redundant infrastructure, systems, and services that are shared will be less than the initial and recurring cost of each organization providing independent infrastructure, systems, and services with no redundancy. The greater the number of organizations sharing the infrastructure, systems, and services, the greater is the potential for savings.

During extreme events, normal operation of the businesses and organizations housed in a facility generally stops. This slowdown or interruption in operations means that bandwidth requirements will decrease at the same time that the facility needs to respond more effectively to extreme events. This fact often provides opportunities to reduce overall costs of communications and IT&T systems while providing systems with more availability for all users. To take advantage of this opportunity, it is critical that risks and rewards be assessed to determine whether it is best for the facility owner/operator to provide the service or to act as an intermediary between a preferred service provider and the tenants.

Figure 13.10 depicts the relationship of the potential risks and rewards. As the facility owner or operator/manager assumes more control and responsibility for providing the service and becomes the service provider, the facility owner or operator/manager assumes a greater risk but will receive more of the revenues. When facility owners/operators/managers cede delivery of communications ser-

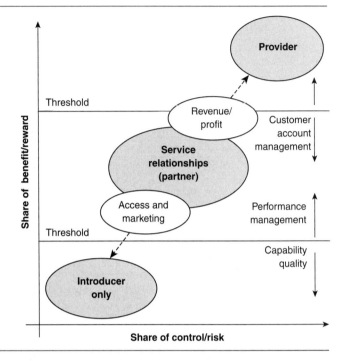

FIGURE 13.10   Relationship of Potential Risks and Rewards.
(*Source:* Arup.)

vices to services providers, as shown in the lower left corner of Figure 13.10, they also give up control and potential revenue streams.

Wireless Infrastructure

Demand continues to increase for support of wireless services ranging from cellular telephones and wireless enabled personal digital assistants (PDAs) to 2-way radios for emergency service personnel and first responders. Although such systems and services are called "wireless," they require a great deal of infrastructure, cabling, and antennas.

Key Point   Much of the infrastructure, cabling, and antennas put in place to support potentially revenue-generating commercial services can also be designed to support 2-way radio service during emergencies.

Money can often be saved by installing a single, shared, ubiquitous wireless infrastructure that supports the needs of all carriers as well as the needs of emergency personnel and first responders. In the past, when cellular service providers wanted to provide coverage in a facility, they worked out an arrangement with the landlord and installed an exclusive-use system. This resulted in facilities that only provided coverage for one carrier. In other cases, duplicate infrastructure, cabling, and systems were installed by each carrier to provide coverage in areas with the most commercial demand. The result is that many facilities are equipped with infrastructure, cabling, and systems that support the wireless communications needs of one (or more) carriers only in areas where they can generate the most revenues.

Some facility owners are now telling providers that if they want to provide service in their facility, it must be ubiquitous. In addition, instead of dedicated infrastructures for each carrier, a single shared infrastructure is installed. The result is better coverage at a lower cost. The challenge is getting the carriers to agree to share the common infrastructure. One great advantage of this approach is that it is possible to interface the emergency service and first responder radio system(s) with the infrastructure so that the wireless infrastructure can be used to support emergency communications during an extreme event.

Figure 13.11 depicts a wireless infrastructure that can be used to support both commercial and emergency communications. As opposed to providing separate antennas, cabling, and so on for each system, tri-band or multi-band antennas are used, thus reducing the number of antennas from 3 or more to 1 and decreasing the amount of infrastructure required to support service.

Service providers' cellular transmissions and radio signals for first responders and others are delivered to the primary communications room, where the signals are combined and transmitted throughout the facility via a shared IT&T infrastructure. If an extreme event happens, the system can be dedicated to first responders to ensure that they have the best communications possible.

—SUMMARY

Properly designed, installed, maintained, and managed IT&T infrastructures are critical to supporting organizations during both normal operations and extreme events. Using a common shared infrastructure to support all of these needs enables organizations to have the most appropriate level of communications and IT&T services at the lowest possible cost. An added advantage of using shared

FIGURE 13.11   Wireless Infrastructure for Commercial and Emergency Communications.

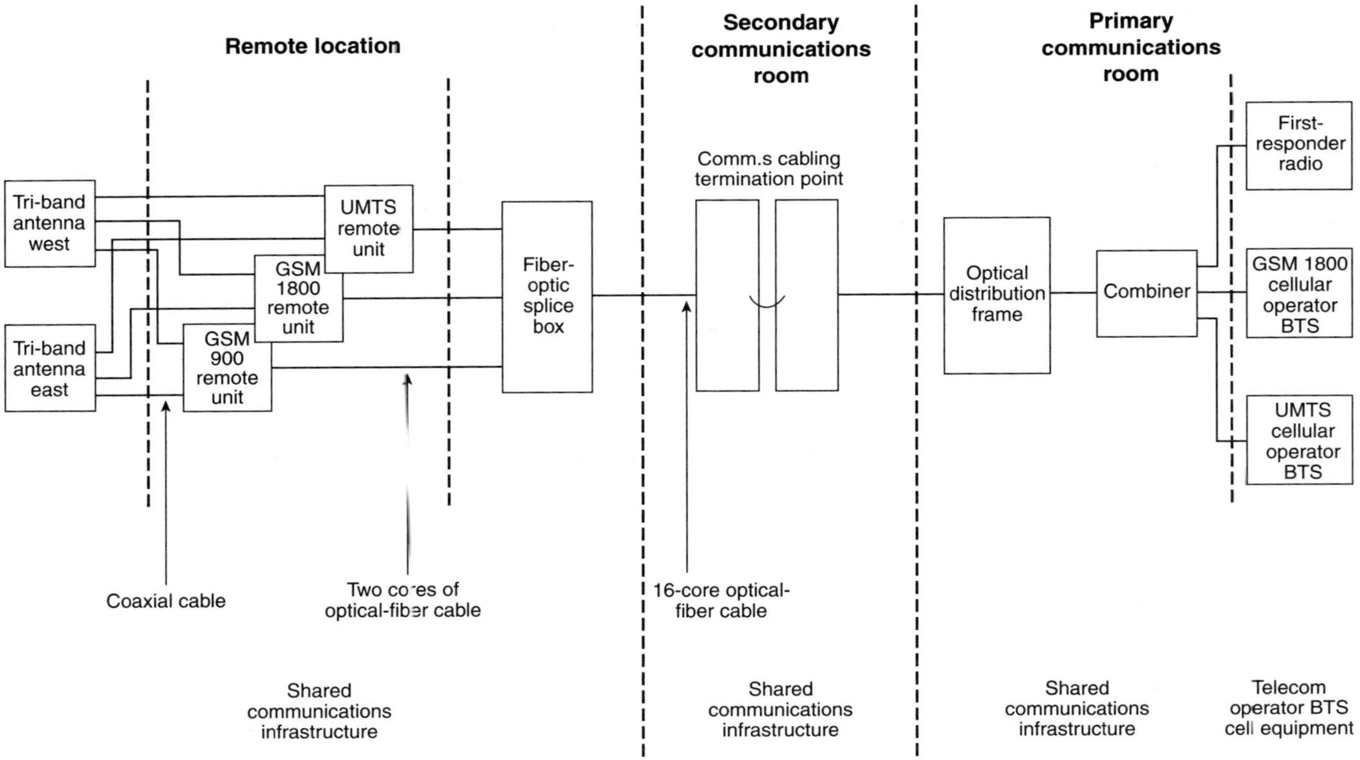

(*Source:* Arup.)

or common infrastructures and systems to support both normal and emergency communications requirements is that they are used continuously. This regular usage ensures that services will be available in emergencies.

BIBLIOGRAPHY

References Cited

1. CEAS. Corporate Emergency Access System, http://ceas.com.
2. BNER. Business Network of Emergency Resources, Inc., http://bnetinc.org/home.html.

Additional Readings

BOMA. Building Owners and Managers Association International (BOMA), http://boma.org.

BOMA. Building Owners and Managers Association International (BOMA), New York Chapter, http://bomany.com.

FSDANY. Fire Safety Directors Association of New York, www.fsdany.org/emp.htm.

14

Emergency Response Planning

Stanley Dawe

The goal of this chapter is to provide assistance to those responsible for developing an extreme event response plan (EERP). An EERP is for a specified area, which is usually defined by the entity developing the plan, such as a city, county, or regional organization. The individuals responsible for developing the plan are usually specified by the governing authority.

This chapter presents suggestions on how to approach and organize the development of an EERP. It also discusses how to determine the resources and personnel that should be included in the plan. The level of resources needed for an appropriate response to an extreme event will likely require the cooperation of many agencies and many levels of government. Therefore, the importance of establishing policies for response and control of resources from outside jurisdictions is also discussed.

This chapter also discusses the importance of establishing a clear chain of command, planning for the control and supervision of resources, and creating systematic, continued training for all response personnel. Other topics presented in this chapter include the use of information technology to support the EERP; the establishment of secure, reliable voice and data communications; and the importance of redundant resources and their management. Deployment of resources to conserve response capability and ensure availability throughout the duration of the response is also considered. The chapter also examines the importance of site access control and the security of resources and personnel. It concludes with discussions on anticipating equipment needs, ensuring availability of resources, encouraging emergency action planning for buildings within the response area of the EERP, providing counseling services for persons impacted by the event, and funding issues.

EMERGENCY RESPONSE PLAN DEVELOPMENT

Two early steps in the development of a response plan for extreme events are assessing the possible event scenarios and determining where possible causes and event locations may converge.

Assessment of Event Scenarios

EERP development begins with a thorough assessment of the possible extreme event scenarios. Possible extreme event scenarios occur when both the possible cause and the likely location of an extreme event are present at the same time and place. What are the causes of an extreme event that could occur within the area of concern? Where might such an extreme event occur? Of course, in the post-9/11 era, everyone is concerned with the possibility of terrorist-related activities. Beyond that concern, however, natural disasters, such as tornadoes and earthquakes, should be considered, as should accidental events. Criminal actions not associated with terrorism may also result in situations that could escalate into extreme events.

Possible Causes. In determining the possible causes of an extreme event, it will be necessary to use good judgment to develop a realistic view of the dangers presented. Although it can be argued that all areas of the United States are potential terrorist targets, in reality, terrorists will likely target high-profile locations where large numbers of people gather. However, note that the cause of an extreme event can be introduced into a location. The cause it need not preexist within the area under consideration. For example, no large liquefied petroleum gas (LPG) storage facilities may be located in a particular area, but LPG rail cars or tank trucks may transit through the community. Criminal activity, natural disasters, or accidental actions involving any number of fixed or mobile properties may cause an extreme event.

Locations and Targets. Locations that represent the U.S. government or military or that are associated with multinational companies are likely terrorist targets. Of course, any location that presents the possibility for a high number of casualties (e.g., sports arenas) or where casualties would produce a high emotional reaction, such as hospitals, schools, or places of worship, should be considered high on the list of possible terrorist targets.

Identifying possible causes and locations will require the knowledge and expertise of government officials, business and community leaders, and emergency response personnel. Additional support for this endeavor should be sought from county, state, federal, and private planning and disaster agencies and organizations. The process should also solicit participation and input from the general public and community groups.

Areas of Convergence

Having identified the possible causes and locations of an extreme event will enable planners to identify situations where these causes and locations may converge. These areas of convergence become the subject of all further work on the EERP. Proceeding from this juncture, the following options should be considered:

- Disrupt convergence
- Prevent event escalation
- Develop a resource matrix
- Determine criteria for selecting resources

Disrupt Convergence. Can actions be taken to disrupt the convergence, thereby reducing the likelihood that an extreme event will occur? Returning to an earlier example, if a convergence of cause and location is created by LPG tank trucks using a roadway that passes near a hospital, can the tank trucks utilize another route to avoid passing the hospital? However, consideration must be given to the possibility of creating a new convergence of cause and location by taking a particular action (i.e., the rerouted tank trucks may now pass near the local high school). In many instances, disrupting the convergence will be difficult, involving cost or inconvenience. However, the benefit to be gained must also be measured. Do not overlook the cost associated with providing the resources needed for the EERP if a potential extreme event threat is permitted to continue.

Prevent Event Escalation. What steps can be taken to reduce the likelihood of an event at the point of convergence from escalating into an extreme event? Are all existing safety practices and rules being followed? Can more stringent rules and regulations be enacted? Will increased security or fire protection reduce the likelihood of the event? Can implementing an emergency action plan (see the section "Other EERP Considerations" in this chapter) reduce the probability of the escalation of an extreme event? Any and all of these options should be considered and implemented when possible.

Develop a Resource Matrix. Most likely, one or more extreme-event scenarios will remain, leading to the third stage of EERP planning: Consideration of the actions that will have to be taken should cause and location come together to result in an extreme event. Planning for a response to an extreme event requires the development of a resource matrix that lists the necessary response resources needed to respond to and mitigate the possible events that have been identified in the assessment process. This matrix enables the identification of available resources and highlights those needs that cannot be addressed with current resources. With this information, the plan developers and managers will be able to prioritize resource needs. This prioritization will facilitate the rational allocation of funding to acquire the most-needed resources and will help in obtaining funding for these resources from local, state, and federal sources. Resources include personnel for plan development, event response, and training, as well as apparatus and equipment and their maintenance, including communications and compatible hardware and software to facilitate control and coordination of the response (see Figure 14.1).

Determine Criteria for Selecting Resources. Criteria should be identified that can be used to determine the resources that should be included in the EERP. Care must be taken to ensure that any resources included will actually be an asset to the response. Various questions can be asked to help determine resource-selection criteria including the following:

- Do the individuals have the proper level of training?
- Can personnel respond in timely manner?
- Are emergency personnel willing to participate? Will they take part in drills and training?
- Is the equipment being considered in good working order and can it be maintained?
- Are spare parts readily available at reasonable cost?

___EQUIPMENT, PERSONNEL, AND TRAINING___

Equipment Supply and Availability

The vast amount of equipment that will be necessary to carry out the functions within the EERP must be included in the framework of the plan. Under an incident command system (ICS), this is the function of the logistics branch. The ICS system is discussed in more detail

FIGURE 14.1 Sample Resource Matrix.

Category		Search and Rescue		Kind	Team
Minimum Capabilities		**Type I**	**Type II**	**Type III**	**Type IV**
Component	**Metric**				
Personnel	Number of people per response	70-person response	28-person response		
Personnel	Training	NFPA 1670 Technician Level in area of specialty, Support personnel at Operations Level.	NFPA 1670 Technician Level in area of specialty. Support personnel at Operations Level.		
Personnel	Areas of specialization	High-angle rope rescue (including highline systems); confined-space rescue (permit required); Advanced life support (ALS) intervention; communications; WMD/HM operations; defensive water rescue	Light frame construction and basic rope rescue operations; ALS intervention; HazMat conditions; communications; trench and excavation rescue		
Personnel	Sustained operations	24-hour S&R operations. Self-sufficient for first 72 hours.	12-hour S&R operations. Self-sufficient for first 72 hours.		
Personnel	Organization	Multidisciplinary organization of Command, Search, Rescue, Medical, HazMat, Logistics, and Planning	Multidisciplinary organization of Command, Search, Rescue, Medical, HazMat, Logistics, and Planning		
Equipment	Sustained operations	Potential mission duration of up to 10 days	Potential mission duration of up to 10 days		
Equipment	Rescue equipment	Pneumatic powered tools, electric powered tools, hydraulic powered tools, hand tools, electrical, heavy rigging, technical rope, safety	Pneumatic powered tools, electric powered tools, hydraulic powered tools, hand tools, electrical, heavy rigging, technical rope, safety		
Equipment	Medical equipment	Antibiotics/antifungals, patient comfort medication, pain medications, sedatives/anesthetics/paralytics, steroids, IV fluids/volume, immunizations/immune globulin, canine treatment, basic airway, intubation, eyecare supplies, IV access/administration, patient assessment care, patient immobilization/extrication, patient/PPE, skeletal care, wound care, patient monitoring	Antibiotics/antifungals, patient comfort medication, pain medications, sedatives/anesthetics/paralytics, steroids, IV fluids/volume, immunizations/immune globulin, canine treatment, basic airway, intubation, eyecare supplies, IV access/administration, patient assessment care, patient immobilization/extrication, patient/PPE, skeletal care, wound care, patient monitoring		
Equipment	Technical equipment	Structures specialist equip, technical information specialist equip, HazMat specialist equip, technical search specialist equip, canine search specialist equip	Structures specialist equip, technical information specialist equip, HazMat specialist equip, technical search specialist equip, canine search specialist equip		
Equipment	Communications equipment	Portable radios, charging units, telecommunications, repeaters, accessories, batteries, power sources, small tools, computer	Portable radios, charging units, telecommunications, repeaters, accessories, batteries, power sources, small tools, computer		
Equipment	Logistics equipment	Water/fluids, food, shelter, sanitation, safety, administrative support, personal bag, task force support, cache transportation/support, base of operations, equip maintenance	Water/fluids, food, shelter, sanitation, safety, administrative support, personal bag, task force support, cache transportation/support, base of operations, equip maintenance		
Comments		Federal asset. There are 28 FEMA US&R Task Forces, totally self-sufficient for the first 72 hours of a deployment, spread throughout the continental United States trained and equipped by FEMA to conduct physical search-and-rescue in collapsed buildings; provide emergency medical care to trapped victims; assess and control gas, electrical services and hazardous materials; and evaluate and stabilize damaged structures.			

(*Source:* DHS, 2004. U.S. Department of Homeland Security, National Incident Management System, Table B-4.)

later in this chapter. The EERP must ensure that this vital function is performed by personnel who have received appropriate training. Hand tools, power tools, generators, lighting, copy machines, and file cabinets are just a few examples of the many and varied items that will be needed. Ensuring that tools and equipment are available when and where they are needed must be addressed. These tools and equipment should be identified and procured before an event, whenever possible.

Agreements must be established with suppliers for items that cannot be procured beforehand due to fiscal limitations, such as pay loaders and cranes. These agreements must contain firm commitments that the supplier will deliver the items on an established timeline. Absence of a firm, continuous supply chain of tools and equipment or failure to meet the established timeline will disrupt the entire plan and may well condemn it to failure.

Wherever possible, tools and equipment should be held in caches disbursed throughout the response area of the plan. The plan must also address the reliability of the tools and equipment in the caches. Security and maintenance must be provided. Vehicles and manpower for transport from the cache to the area of operations must be ready. An inventory system—a computer-based one—if possible, that is compatible with operational objectives should be established and be part of the EERP training and drill cycle. On-scene caches will also require the same functions. The EERP should include the continuation of the security, accountability, supply, and maintenance functions at the extreme event scene.

Personnel and Basic Equipment

The personnel included in the EERP are the key element to a successful response. Properly equipped, trained, and motivated personnel are fundamental to the success of the EERP. Ensuring that only those organizations and individuals that will be an asset to the EERP are included in the response matrix will place the plan on a firm foundation, which will go a long way in ensuring that the EERP will meet the jurisdiction's needs should its activation be necessary.

Individuals or groups must possess several attributes in order to be considered for inclusion in the EERP. Primary among these attributes is knowledge and training in the duties and functions that have been identified as necessary resources for the EERP response matrix. Of course, fire fighters, police officers, and emergency medical providers immediately come to mind. But it is also likely that the

EERP evaluation process will have identified the need for such items as large numbers of handheld power tools, heavy earth-moving equipment, laptop computers, cell phones, hardwired telephones, gasoline, tents, cots, portable space heaters, and on and on. Who will procure, stockpile, maintain, transport, and operate all of these resources during an extreme event?

Emergency response personnel can be trained for many of these duties, but is this the most productive use of their time and abilities? In most jurisdictions, the EERP relies on materials, equipment, and support personnel from outside the emergency response community. Civic and fraternal organizations may prove a fertile source for many of these resources, especially in areas where funding is limited.

Personal Protective Equipment

One of the universal resources that every EERP must make provisions for is that the proper personal protective equipment (PPE) is available for all EERP responders and participants. PPE is necessary to enable responders and participants to operate at the scene of the event, or in proximity to it, without endangering themselves. At a minimum, PPE should provide for basic protection from injury, such as respiratory protection and helmets, gloves, boots, and eye shields. The level of PPE available must be matched to the training and duties of individual responders and participants. Maintenance of equipment and continued training in proper use must be an ongoing component of the EERP. Figure 14.2 shows an example of typical PPE that is often worn by fire fighters.

Most emergency response agencies will provide PPE for their personnel; however, the EERP may have to supplement equipment if duties under the plan differ from the normal responsibilities of emergency responders. For example, fire departments will be able to supply all fire fighters with positive-pressure self-contained breathing apparatus (SCBA), but many police departments will not be able to supply their officers with such equipment. Depending on the duties that the police officers will assume under the EERP, such PPE may be required for some or all of them.

An effort should be made to standardize PPE so that all personnel are familiar with its use, care, and maintenance. If it is not possible to standardize PPE across all personnel, training should include all PPE that could possibly be used during EERP activation. This training will allow for reallocation of PPE as necessary during prolonged operations.

FIGURE 14.2   Example of Typical PPE.

(*Source:* NFPA, 2001. *Introduction to Employee Fire & Life Safety,* National Fire Protection Association, Quincy, MA, Figure 8.9.)

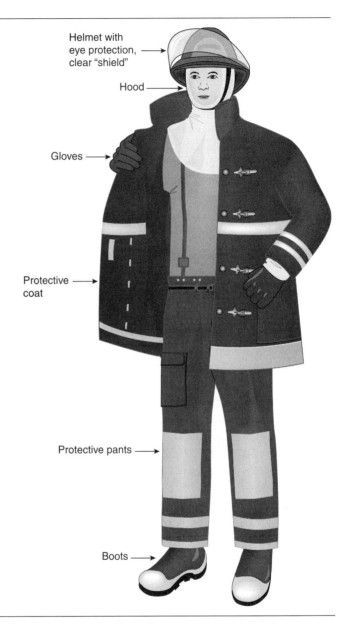

Helmet with eye protection, clear "shield"

Hood

Gloves

Protective coat

Protective pants

Boots

Different types of PPE providing different levels of protection will be required to properly equip the EERP responders and participants. EERP participants assigned to record-keeping duties at initial response points or staging areas remote from event operations will not require the same level of protection as responders operating in the immediate event location. Changes in the operational situation (e.g., unexpected discovery of illegally stored hazardous materials) and extreme weather conditions are two of the many factors that may change PPE needs. Economic factors should also be assessed. In general, the level of PPE required for safe operations will decrease as the mitigation process progresses.

Key Point Having a supply of less costly, lower-level PPE on hand will save wear and tear on more expensive equipment.

Matching the appropriate level of PPE to the conditions under which it is used also impacts the productivity of personnel, not only by preventing injury, but by allowing for longer operational time, because lower-level protection is usually less stressful to work in.

Identification Systems

Standardized documentation of all personnel training and equipment maintenance is vital to the continuous availability of resources and rapid implementation of the EERP. Development of a standardized identification system will be an operational asset, especially for large jurisdictions with response matrices involving many organizations and individuals. The use of identifying colors, lettering, and numbering on helmets and outer garments will enable rapid identification of personnel, especially when multiple groups or agencies with differing capabilities, training, and responsibilities will be operating.

Personal Identification. Personal identification is an important consideration. All potential responders should be issued a unique identification device that can be used to ensure positive identification of all individuals responding to the event. Such identification has many possible uses: site access control; personnel accountability; access to medical history; confirmation of training, certification, and organization affiliation; and more. All EERP responders and participants should be required to prominently display this identification at all times when participating in any activity associated with the EERP.

Equipment Identification. A standardized system for identification of equipment should also be included in the EERP. Such a system should provide for rapid identification of ownership, maintenance history, and operational capabilities and limitations. Personal and equipment identification systems should be developed to facilitate sharing of resources. The identification systems should present information indicating the certification of personnel to work with the various types of tools, apparatus, and equipment that are included in the EERP response matrix.

Communications Equipment

Ensuring that all personnel can communicate with one another is essential to the EERP. All individuals and groups included in the plan must be furnished with compatible equipment that enables them to receive orders, instructions, and assignments and to provide feedback to those individuals responsible for coordination and oversight. In addition to the proper equipment, the individuals must have training to understand the communications network that will be used if the EERP is activated and the rules for use of the network and the importance of communications discipline. It only takes one or two "chatty" individuals to overload the network.

Key Point   The communications network must be designed to accommodate the entire response matrix. It must anticipate the need for a high volume of voice and data exchange over a large area in adverse conditions.

Mutual Aid

Response to an extreme event will be beyond the capabilities of most jurisdictions. Plans for augmenting response resources is an essential part of the EERP. Responders from nearby jurisdictions will most likely be needed to provide the level of response required. It is important that a written "memorandum of understanding" (MOU) be established with each outside resource. An MOU is a legal document that delineates the duties and responsibilities of all entities. Establishment of an MOU will likely mean discussions involving agencies at the federal, state, county, and local levels. These discussions may be protracted, but they are necessary and should be one of the first steps when establishing an EERP. The written MOU will enable the participating agency heads to meet to formulate the EERP and will allow for EERP responders to participate in training and drills. MOUs are also helpful in obtaining funding for the EERP.

The MOU must address issues of activation and availability. The resources that will be supplied under the MOU must be identified and the circumstances under which they will be made available. The number of personnel, the type and number of apparatus and equipment, assurance of equipment maintenance, and the training of personnel must also be part of the MOU. Activation protocols—who is authorized and under what circumstances mutual aid will be activated—are also a necessary component of the MOU. The activation authorization should be as direct as possible, because an extreme event may occur at any time, with little or no advance warning. Time lost trying to contact several individuals to activate mutual aid agreements may result in additional casualties and property loss.

Another reason for the MOU is to ensure control of response resources. Every ambulance within a 50-mile radius may well be needed at an extreme event, but will they all be needed within the first hour? The prevention of unauthorized response or self-dispatch must be addressed in the MOU.

Training

Providing ongoing EERP training for all responders and participants may prove to be one of the greatest obstacles in developing and implementing a viable EERP. Very few jurisdictions have the luxury of being able to provide all required personnel resources. Responders and participants will come from many agencies and organizations, many of which may not be under the direct control of the jurisdictional government. They may work and reside long distances from the jurisdictional area of the EERP. The duties and requirements of their everyday employment may require training that is related to the EERP or the only training they receive may be that provided by the EERP. Work schedules will differ, making scheduling cumbersome. Identical training sessions will often have to be scheduled at various locations at multiple times. Gathering large numbers of responders and participants at one time in one location may be next to impossible.

Dedicated Training Staff. Many of the problems just mentioned can be resolved through the use of dedicated EERP training staff. If funding is available, professional educators should be hired to develop training programs and schedules. Developing a small, dedicated training staff will reduce training costs and ensure a consistent level of training. A dedicated training staff will enable the establishment of long-term training schedules so that responders and participants have an opportunity to adjust their schedules to attend.

Existing Protocols. When several large organizations or agencies provide a sizable portion of the EERP personnel, EERP developers should draw from the standards and procedures of those groups when developing the EERP. This use of other organizations' protocols will reduce the number of personnel requiring training directly under the EERP. These organizations and agencies may also be able to provide or supplement training for other EERP personnel.

Interagency Training. As much as possible, training sessions should involve personnel from different agencies simultaneously. This diversity will promote the development of personal relationships and build confidence in the abilities and knowledge of personnel from other groups.

Drills. Classroom instruction must be supported by drills. When possible, drills should be conducted at locations identified during the assessment process. Large-scale drills in which large numbers of responders and participants take part should be conducted several times a year. These drills will enable evaluation of the command, control, and supervision functions of the EERP. Small-scale drills should be held more frequently and should be designed to reinforce and evaluate individual knowledge and skills.

COMMAND, CONTROL, AND SUPERVISION

Incident Command System

The use of an incident command system (ICS) to control and coordinate operations at an extreme event is imperative. An ICS is the combination of facilities, equipment, personnel, procedures, and communications operating within a common organizational structure with responsibility for the management of assigned resources to effectively accomplish stated objectives pertaining to an incident or training exercise, according to NFPA 1670, *Standard on Operations and Training for Technical Search and Rescue Incidents*. Figure 14.3 shows the major elements of the ICS.

It is not possible to ensure the unity of command and provide the central control necessary for efficiency and responder safety unless all responding individuals and groups are participants in the ICS. Ad-

FIGURE 14.3 **Major Elements of the Incident Command System.**

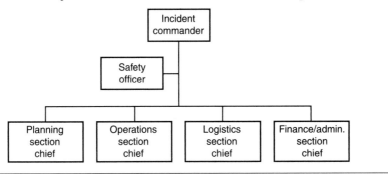

(*Source:* NFPA, 2004. *Fundamentals of Fire Protection,* National Fire Protection Association, Quincy, MA, Figure 10.1.)

ditionally, use of an ICS is mandated by federal and state statutes; failure to adopt and follow the ICS may have several detrimental effects.

Key Point Persons in authority, as well as government entities, involved in event planning, training, or response who do not follow the Incident Command System may be placing themselves in a position of liability in the event of injuries or fatalities to responders or victims of an extreme event.

Complete information on the incident command system is available from the Federal Emergency Management Agency (FEMA) web site at www.fema.gov. NFPA 1561, *Standard on Emergency Services Incident Management System,* also provides specific requirements for the management of various emergency events.

Incident Commander. The basic premise of an incident command system is that *one* individual, the incident commander (IC), is in overall command. All responders, regardless of their organizational affiliation, report to the IC and follow orders and directions issued by that individual. Given the need for the EERP to provide rapid response at any time, day or night, several individuals will have to be designated and trained to fill this position. The fact that the possible extreme event scenarios will likely involve a wide range of events of diverse cause and location will dictate that these individuals come from several different professions, allowing for the individual with the appropriate expertise to assume the position of incident commander.

Incident Command Post. An incident command post (ICP) is the field location at which the primary tactical-level, on-scene incident command functions are performed [1]. An ICP is established by the IC, and all responding agencies and organizations must have a representative at the ICP. This representative serves as liaison between the various agencies and organizations on scene and is the principal contact between the ICP and these agencies and organizations. From the ICP, the IC issues orders to sectors and groups that are established to address particular problems (groups) or geographic areas (sectors) of the extreme event. The members of a group or sector may be drawn from several responding agencies or organizations or they may all be from a single agency, as directed by the IC. Individual agencies, especially when they have many members on scene, should have their own agency command post (ACP) to assist with personnel assignment and accountability and to address such issues as relief of personnel. However, all activity must be approved by the IC and coordinated with other ICS functions (logistics, finance, etc.).

As part of the ICS, there will be one ICP. One representative from each agency, organization, or entity providing personnel or resources should be assigned to the ICP. All groups and agencies with personnel at the extreme event must be represented at the ICP at all times. The individual representative must have immediate direct communications with the group/agency on-scene commander, who in turn must give communications from this individual and the ICP highest priority. Orders, inquiries, and the like from the IC must be acknowledged and complied with immediately.

Provisions for human comfort at the ICP should also be addressed as soon as possible; any extreme event will result in prolonged operations. Basic human needs must be met for operations personnel, as well as command and control staff. Food, shelter, and sanitary facilities must be provided. Records of resource expenditures and operations must be maintained. The ICS provides for a logistics branch to address these issues.

Selection of a location for the ICP rests with the IC. The ICP should not be located too close to the extreme event. The noise and confusion of the operational area of an extreme event could serve as a distraction; command personnel may become involved in operations if the ICP is located in proximity to the area of operations. The ICP must be in an area clear of danger from events in the operation zone (e.g., away from windborne contaminants from hazardous materials). Security must be provided, and access control to the ICP must begin immediately. The ICP will be a priority target if the extreme event is the result of a terrorist act. Exclusion of unauthorized personnel is important to control information flow, provide for a positive work environment, and ensure proper interaction with the media.

Incident Communications. The ICP must have reliable instantaneous communication with all commanders of responding organizations and individuals. It must also be able to communicate directly with all responders on the scene in the event of an emergency. As soon as possible, radio communications should be backed up with hard-wire capabilities. This will increase security and often allow for better understanding and quicker communications between the ICP and the various subordinate posts. Communication to local, state, and federal governments and agencies should be provided as soon as possible and maintained throughout the event.

As per the ICS, a press liaison should be designated. Personnel in this position will facilitate communications between the IC and the public, providing an avenue for dissemination of instructions and information that may be vital to public safety. Selection of personnel for the press liaison function is an important aspect of the EERP.

Chain of Command

Chain of command is a series of command, control, executive, or management positions in hierarchical order of authority. The importance of establishing a clear chain of command for the EERP cannot be overstated. All participants must be fully trained in the organization and function of the command system designated for use within the EERP and be prepared to act within this framework.

Single chain of command indicates that all communication flows from the IC to the resources on one line of communication and that information from resources flows to the IC on the same line. Orders and directions all originate at the ICP with the IC.

Establishing Who Is in Charge. Responders must know who is in charge, and they must be prepared to receive instructions and orders from this person. This chain of command is necessary to avoid confusion and to ensure that all assignments are covered without duplication of effort and that all resources are used appropriately.

Establishment of a credible chain of command may prove to be one of the biggest obstacles to be overcome when establishing the EERP. Organizations and agencies, both those from within a jurisdiction and those from outside (mutual aid), have different missions and operational organizations. All plan participants must accept the concept of a single chain of command under the EERP. Failure to sell this concept will adversely impact the outcome. EERP drills and training sessions will highlight the importance of the single chain of command for the success of operations. Drills and training sessions will bring to light any shortcomings in this area that must be addressed.

Increasing Levels of Supervision. Operations at extreme events will place responders under very high levels of physical and emotional stress. Especially in the early stages of response, operations will tax the physical abilities of responders. As operations proceed and the immediate actions closely associated with search and rescue efforts are replaced by the still physical, but now more emotional, work of recovery and removal, responders will also be subject to an emotional assault. If the event is such that operations stretch over days into weeks or even months, the physical and emotional strain will continue to heighten.

Under such conditions, responders may initially react by calling on past experience for guidance; however, such experience may not lead to the most appropriate actions. Planning, training, and drills in EERP operations must stress the differences between routine operations and actions at extreme events. A higher than normal level of supervision will be necessary to ensure compliance with the EERP. Again, training and drills will be necessary to indoctrinate all levels of supervision to the need of providing close supervision to ensure that the EERP is carried out as planned and to make sure that responders are safe.

The EERP must provide for shortening the lines of communications at all levels of the plan. The supervisory span of control, especially near the point of operations, must be continually monitored and adjusted. Many situations that will be encountered during operations at an extreme event will require a span of control of no more than two or three responders per supervisor.

Addressing Disputes. Increased supervision may necessitate that the EERP include provisions for responders to be supervised by personnel from outside their affiliated agency or organization. This may raise issues of competence along with petty interagency rivalries and jurisdictional disputes carried over from past routine operations. Well-planned training for supervisory personnel will help resolve some of these problems, as will frequent and well-organized training and drill session at which personnel from different organizations and agencies work together to accomplish EERP-related goals. Where they exist, interagency rivalries and jurisdictional disputes must be recognized, and careful planning and training must be utilized to ensure that they do not adversely impact the EERP.

TECHNOLOGY FOR RESPONSE MANAGEMENT

In addition to clearly establishing command, control, and supervision functions, the EERP should address the need for information technology (IT) to assist with management of the extreme event response. The EERP should help with the efforts to acquire and allocate computers with Internet access and secure e-mail as part of the EERP resource matrix. The EERP should also address the issue of access: The IT equipment of all responders should be compatible, and the necessary software and access should be provided. Also, the EERP needs to provide for the appropriate exchange of information. Organizations and agencies committing to participate in the EERP must agree to cooperate with all other responders and to allow access to electronically stored information as appropriate and necessary. Such standardized IT is essential for personnel accountability and equipment management. A standardized personnel and equipment identification system incorporating bar code technology will provide an invaluable management tool for the EERP, both for record keeping and operational command and control.

Personnel Accountability

Information technology can be used as a tool to facilitate personnel accountability within the EERP. Identification cards that utilize barcode or microchip technology can be matched with a database containing vital information on individual responders and provide real time records access for EERP management. This information needs to be centrally available, but it also must be secure.

Technology Compatibility. The EERP must address the issue of IT hardware and software compatibility. Hardware and software used by different response groups may not be readily shareable, either due to incompatibility or lack of knowledge. These issues must be resolved.

Cross-training must take place when necessary. When possible, all response groups should use compatible hardware and software for their day-to-day functions. If this cannot be accomplished, specific EERP hardware and software should be designated. It may be necessary to purchase this equipment and provide the necessary training.

All EERP participants must be indoctrinated into the concept of shared response information. Although it is important that IT used within the EERP be secure, those within the EERP need to have access to information in a timely manner.

Time and effort should be spent on ensuring that IT capability is balanced across responders. For example, if one agency is performing on-scene personnel identification by pencil and paper, it will compromise personnel identification across the entire operation.

Key Point   If the information technology of one or two responding agencies is below the capabilities of other organizations, the flow of information will drop to the level of the slowest agency.

Communications Network

The EERP must contain provisions to provide for reliable, secure radio communications for all responders. The EERP should also address equipment compatibility, the designated frequency that will be used, individual and unit identification, establishment of radio priority for command functions, and radio discipline.

Other parties, of good intention or otherwise, may attempt to gain information about the event and the response to it. Controlling access to the information contained within EERP communications should be a high priority. Establishing of a press liaison is a must. An extreme event will be the subject of intense media coverage. If members of the media cannot get reliable, timely information about the event from persons within the EERP, they will go elsewhere for the information. The information they receive from outside the EERP may not be accurate.

Keeping unwanted listeners off the EERP communications network is also a priority. Untrained individuals or those unfamiliar with the EERP may misunderstand or misinterpret EERP communications, resulting in the dissemination of false reports and contributing to the spread of panic among the public. Establishing secure communications as quickly as possible must be part of the EERP. This security can be accomplished through hardwire communications or the use of voice encryption devices.

The EERP must recognize the use of specialized vocabulary and jargon by various agencies and responders from dissimilar areas or that perform different daily missions. Some responders may use different words for the same piece of equipment; for example, to an EMS provider a mask may mean medical oxygen, whereas to a fire fighter it may mean an SCBA. Training and drills should be used to address this problem and highlight the difficulties dual terminology can cause in order to discourage its use.

Another issue is the use of radio "10" codes. This is a system of shorthand that uses numbers in place of words. Almost universally, "10-4" usually means "understood, will comply," and most police agencies use "10-13" to indicate "officer needs assistance." Different agencies often use the same 10-code numbers to indicate different messages due to different missions, needs, and historical use. Again, this inconsistency should be highlighted during drills. Establishing a unique code for EERP use is usually unproductive; it may lead to even more confusion. A more promising approach is to avoid use of these codes in the EERP.

RESOURCE MANAGEMENT

An important part of EERP is the economic management of resources. To ensure optimum use, the EERP must identify similar resources that can be used for similar tasks and provide for the continued availability of these resources over the anticipated time of operation. Another issue is determining what roles community organizations have during an emergency. Table 14.1 shows an example of how roles and resources can be allocated.

Resource Redundancy

Many organizations and agencies participating in the EERP may have more than one unit of a particular resource within their group (e.g., an ambulance corps may have two or three ambulances). Even more likely is that more than one organization or group will have identical or similar resources (e.g., two fire departments with heavy rescue units). This redundancy is an asset to the EERP, because it will ensure response of needed capability. However, the EERP must recognize the redundancy and take advantage of it, deploying needed resources to immediate tasks, while at the same time creating a ready

TABLE 14.1   Roles of Community Organizations During an Emergency

Organization	Emergency Roles
City manager/mayor	Overall coordination and policy making
Fire department	Fire control, hazardous material control, physical rescue (extrication from vehicles and buildings), flood rescue, emergency medical service
Police department	Crowd control, traffic control, area evacuation, maintenance of order
Public works department	Heavy lift, barricades, diking
Library department	Public information
Health department	Air monitoring
Building department	Building safety surveys
Hospital consortium	Victim care
Social services department	Temporary housing
School district	Busing, food services

Source: NFPA, 2004. *Fundamentals of Fire Protection,* National Fire Protection Association, Quincy, MA, Table 10.2.

reserve of additional resources to be assigned to future needs. The need for resource management highlights the importance of EERP managers knowing the capabilities of all responders.

Designations used within organizations and agencies are not always helpful; for example, one agency's emergency service unit (ESU) may be another's special operations team. Individuals and units may have different capabilities, even when identified similarly. The ESU from one town may be Hazardous Materials Level A trained and equipped, but the ESU from another town may only be Level C capable.

The EERP response matrix must clarify the similarities and differences among resources. Redundant resources must be identified and a clear response protocol established to ensure the optimal utilization of resources and the provision for on-scene and long-term reserves.

Conservation of Resources

Operations at an extreme event will be prolonged. The EERP must recognize the anticipated extended duration and incorporate a phased commitment of resources to mitigate the event. All similar resources cannot be committed at once, and in most cases this would be counterproductive. Nor should an inordinate number of similar resources be committed to the same problem or to operations within a limited area.

Resource Security. One reason to avoid over-committing redundant resources is security. If all or most similar resources are operating in one small geographic area, they would more likely be adversely affected by a single event, be it a criminal (terrorist) act or an accident.

Maintaining Regional Coverage. Another consideration when deploying redundant resources is the need to maintain response capability through a region, not just at the extreme event. The EERP must recognize the importance of the initial response. Not only will a controlled, well-coordinated initial response save lives, but it will also set the tone for ensuing operations.

Schedule Planning. Ongoing, sustainable schedules for personnel should be established as part of the EERP. Multiple schedules must be prearranged. These schedules must address the number of personnel to be on scene, the number necessary to provide a safe reserve, the amount and type of equipment available, and the immediacy of the tasks to be performed, while at the same time giving consideration to needs outside the extreme event and the personal needs of responders and participants. Another major consideration in schedule planning is the capability of the participating organizations and agencies to provide the resources while at some point resuming routine activities.

Rapid Response Groups. The EERP must provide for at least one, and in most instances several, rapid response groups (RRGs) that are charged exclusively with providing rescue or assistance for injured responders or participants. The RRG must be established and maintained throughout the duration of the extreme event. The number of personnel operating, the functions being performed, and the size of the area of operations will dictate the size, number, and location(s) of the RRG(s). The equipment and training needed by the RRG will depend on the nature and location of the event. In many cases, the personnel assigned to the RRG will require training and knowledge above that of most emergency responders. The EERP must recognize this requirement and include proper training and equipment for these teams.

__SITE SECURITY, ACCESS CONTROL,__
AND SITE SAFETY

Site security, access control, and site safety must be addressed in the EERP. These issues are especially important for a terrorist-related event, but they are necessary at all extreme events. It is becoming more and more common for terrorists to target responders. This practice of targeting responders as part of the initial act or in a secondary attack increases overall injuries and fatalities by delaying rescue efforts, adversely impacting the morale of civilians and responders, and destroying equipment, thus impairing response to future attacks. Providing site security, access control, and site safety is also important for natural or accidental events, because responders may become a target of opportunity, enabling terrorists to accomplish the same goals at lower cost. The issue of responder safety should be considered and addressed for any large emergency response, not just an extreme event.

Site Security and Access Control

The EERP would logically make use of responders from the local law enforcement community to direct and provide site security. Controlling site access must also be part of the EERP, and again these responders will likely be the logical providers. Controlling site access involves directing unauthorized persons who are not part of the EERP to safe areas remote from the event site as well as controlling when and where EERP responders and participants enter the site. This function of site access is intimately related to command, control, and supervision. Control of site access should include tracking of EERP responders and participants, not only as they enter the site, but also as they depart. The EERP must provide for accurate, reliable, real time recording of responder arrival and departure. Ideally, this information will make use of IT and will be immediately available at the ICP. Tracking of arrival, departure, assignments, and other dispositions of responders and participants should continue at all locations within the event perimeter. If it is not possible to establish a computer-based personnel and resource-tracking system under the EERP, the issue must still be addressed and a workable paper-based system be included in the plan.

Site Access Procedures. Only authorized responders should be admitted to the site. All dispatch decisions made at the ICP must be relayed to site security and access control personnel so that they are aware of what resources are responding and are able to direct personnel to the proper locations and functions when they arrive.

A unique EERP identification system will ease the burden placed on those individuals responsible for site security and access control. If it is not possible to create a unique EERP identification system, the various identification systems, such as ID cards or badges, used by the participating agencies and organizations should be known to those who will be controlling site access.

At a minimum, the EERP must establish standard site access procedures so that this function starts immediately upon response. All EERP participants must know that they will be challenged when responding and that they will be required to provide positive prearranged identification. This procedure must be reinforced at training and drills.

Preplanned Response Routes. Preplanning of response routes will help with site security and access control. All responders that are part of the EERP should respond using prearranged routes whenever possible. Preplanned response routes will facilitate the arrival of responders and participants by allowing for vehicular and pedestrian traffic control along these roads. In planning for response routes, consideration must be given to the likelihood of the need for egress routes for large numbers of people and vehicles from the event area. The preplanned response routes should begin as close as possible to the starting point of every organization and agency participating in the EERP.

Primary Response Locations.

Key Point When the assessment process identifies multiple possible event locations within a small geographic area, primary response locations should be designated for those areas.

As dispatched resources arrive at these primary response locations, site access and security personnel will direct them to their assignments along response routes established between the initial response point and the event site. Many EERP responders and participants may arrive at the initial response location in personal vehicles or with apparatus or other equipment that is not immediately needed at the point of operations. The initial response location should have provision for secure storage of these personal vehicles and a staging area for apparatus and equipment. Transportation between initial response locations and the area of operations must be provided when these points are not within walking distance. In those situations where event locations may be isolated, it may be possible to preplan response routes directly to staging areas within the event site. Security and access control managers should work with the IC at the early stages of EERP activation to further define response routes, access locations, staging areas, and operation positions.

Vehicle and pedestrian traffic must be controlled on and along response routes and in the vicinity of the extreme event, all staging areas, and rest and recuperation areas. Traffic control will also enhance civilian safety and security. A unique identification marking for vehicles, apparatus, and equipment should be part of the EERP.

Site Safety

Site safety, although related to site security and access control, encompasses other functions. Protecting EERP resources to ensure their continuous availability so that the response plan can be implemented and accomplish its goals should be considered as a separate function under the EERP.

Preventing Injuries. Within the ICS framework, this function of safety is responsible for preventing injury to personnel. Personnel for this function should be designated under the EERP and they must be provided with the appropriate training to fulfill this important duty.

Monitoring Conditions and Unsafe Practices. The EERP must also ensure that an appropriate number of competent supervisors are assigned to monitor conditions throughout the site for unsafe situations and to ensure that all safety precautions and guidelines (e.g., use of proper PPE) are followed. Conditions at the event site will often present situations where responders must go in harm's way to accomplish the goals of the EERP. In such situations, the benefit to be gained must be balanced with the possible costs. The EERP must afford the safety supervisors the authority to discontinue activity that endangers personnel and offer them the opportunity to confer often and freely with the IC and other supervisors to ensure safety. Training for all EERP responders and participants should include knowledge of the importance and authority of the safety supervisors, recognition and avoidance of unsafe situations, full-time compliance with PPE use, and all other safety requirements.

Monitoring Event Site Environment. EERP planners must provide for monitoring of the event site environment and ensure that EERP personnel and participants are not unnecessarily exposed to harm.

Key Point   All areas within the event site must be monitored to prevent exposure to hazardous materials; it may be unknown whether such materials are stored at the site or whether they may be introduced into the location accidentally.

The EERP should consider the possibility that hazardous material may be deliberately placed at the location to cause further harm or to increase mitigation problems and costs. Equipment to handle hazardous materials and properly trained personnel who can use it must be included in the EERP.

Monitoring Responder Activities. Fatigue will cloud judgment, resulting in poor decision making, which can result in injury. Monitoring responders and participants for fatigue and providing a safe location for rest and recuperation is an EERP necessity. Under the ICS, the Safety and Logistics branches will work together to establish well-designed rest and recuperation locations.

OTHER EERP CONSIDERATIONS

Emergency Action Planning

Individuals responsible for buildings and groups of people within the EERP response area must prepare their building population for independent action without support from emergency responders. The need for assistance may or may not be related to the extreme event. For some occupancy groups, such as people with special needs, or for buildings with large numbers of people, such as schools, hospitals, and high-rise buildings, the EERP should require mandatory participation in planning for independent action. Without an emergency action plan (EAP), the need to assist these groups would draw resources from the extreme event response.

It is very likely that people and buildings in the vicinity of an extreme event, but not immediately affected by the event, will have to wait a considerable time before assistance can be assigned and arrive at their location. All of the issues mentioned in relation to response to the extreme event itself will of course apply, as well as such factors as the degree of damage and danger at these other locations, delayed notification of the remote need, and a shortage of resources. It is not beyond reason to postulate a situation in which a location experiencing an extreme event-related emergency or an independent emergency would not receive a response from an appropriate agency for an extended period of time. Building personnel and occupants should be prepared for any such eventuality. See Chapter 12 of this book for more detailed information about EAPs.

Key Point   Implementation of an EAP by building personnel should be part of the overall EERP.

At a minimum, the building EAP should provide for the safety of building occupants in the event of an extreme event in the vicinity of the building. Ideally, the EAP should provide a plan of action for a wide range of emergencies that will enhance the safety of the building occupants. If the EERP planners do not have the authority to require EAP implementation, they should strongly advocate for such legislation with the appropriate governmental groups.

Key Point   The EAP should provide for centralization of supervision of emergency functions within the facility where communication with building occupants is provided along with control of facility systems, such as elevators and heating, ventilation, and air-conditioning systems.

One individual should be in charge of all EAP activity. This person should participate in regular training and drill sessions for all building occupants. Egress paths within the building and to assembly areas should be part of the EAP. It should also include a reliable system to ensure accounting for the safety of all building occupants. In this age, failure on the part of those in charge of buildings to take practical steps to provide for the safety of those who occupy their buildings is criminally negligent.

Counseling Services

In addition to the extreme physical stress to which EERP responders and participants will be exposed, personnel will also bear a great emotional burden. Not only will they experience the often gruesome task of recovery and removal, they will suffer disruption of their everyday lives. Mitigation activities for an extreme event will be protracted. Work schedules at the site may call for extended work hours. Time spent with family and friends and recreational opportunities will be greatly curtailed. Experience has shown that the families of responders and participants may be even more affected than the responders themselves. EERP planning must anticipate that many individuals will need assistance to cope with these emotional demands. The EERP should include provisions for providing counseling services for responders, participants, and their families.

Community Education

The occurrence of an extreme event will impact the civilian population. The degree of impact can be lessened if the community is prepared for the possible outcomes. Just as the EERP developers will be called on to assess the causes and locations of possible extreme events, it would be prudent to devote some effort into gauging the impact of such an event on the community. Providing insight into these consequences to the community and offering suggestions and instruction on actions residents can take to reduce these effects on themselves and their families might well be judged to be a legitimate goal of the EERP.

Educating the public on what steps the jurisdiction is taking to be better prepared for an extreme event will help assure their cooperation if and when such an event occurs. If the public is aware that there are preplanned response routes for responders and preplanned egress routes for those endangered, they will be more likely to comply with direction to use the egress routes and avoid congesting the response routes.

The benefit to be gained by giving information about the EERP to the public must be balanced with the need to prevent illegitimate use of such knowledge. Although it is wise to keep in mind that many aspects of an EERP should be kept confidential, a great deal of useful and important information can be provided to increase public safety and further the objectives of the EERP. A good public education program will enhance public safety and advance the mission of the EERP.

Funding

Developing and implementing an EERP will be expensive. Although a jurisdiction can call on a number of resources to provide funding for the EERP, the development of the EERP will highlight the need for many new and often costly items. Procuring funding for the dedicated personnel, equipment, and training that are an integral part of an EERP will be a challenge, especially for smaller jurisdictions. Community organizations and civic-minded individuals may offer some assistance, but their ability to meet the costs associated with an EERP is limited. Grants from federal, state, county, and private organizations will be the most likely source of funding. EERP developers and planners should acknowledge funding needs early in the process and take steps to develop funding sources. In the end, it may prove that the most valuable member of the EERP team is a good grant writer.

Possible funding sources include FEMA and the U.S. Department of Homeland Security at the federal level, and similar agencies at the state level. Private corporations and civic-minded organizations such as Rotary or Lions Club may also be a possible resource.

___SUMMARY___

Planning a response to an extreme event may be an intimidating prospect, but it is a high priority. Time and resources must be committed to ensure that an organized, appropriate response will be implemented. Do not be intimidated by the grand scale of an EERP. Although every jurisdiction will have unique concerns and situations that will necessitate specific solutions that will differ from place to place, all must recognize the necessity of developing and implementing an EERP. The discussions, observations, and suggestions offered in this chapter will provide a good starting point for development of such a plan.

Assessment of the possible locations and causes of an extreme event, choosing the appropriate resource package from among the many available, establishing a strong command and control function, planning for the timely supply of equipment and material, providing safety and communications, planning response routes, controlling site access, and providing security and accountability for personnel and equipment will establish a solid base for the EERP.

Continued refinement and adjustment, along with well-planned and conducted training will ensure that the people and property within a jurisdiction will suffer the least possible impact should an extreme event occur. Common sense and moral responsibility dictate that the possibility of an extreme event must be considered and that every effort must be made to ensure the most appropriate response possible.

BIBLIOGRAPHY

Reference Cited

1. FEMA. Federal Emergency Management Agency, National Incident Management Capability Assessment Support Tool, www.fema.gov/nimcast/Glossary.do.

NFPA Codes, Standards, and Recommended Practices

NFPA Publications.   The following is a list of NFPA codes, standards and recommended practices cited in this chapter. See the latest version of the *NFPA Catalog* for availability of current editions of these documents.

NFPA 1561, *Standard on Emergency Services Incident Management System*

NFPA 1670, *Standard on Operations and Training for Technical Search and Rescue Incidents*

Appendix A
Threat Assessment Tools

This section provides an inherent vulnerability assessment matrix (Table A.1) and a building vulnerability assessment checklist (Table A.2).

TABLE A.1 Site/Building Inherent Vulnerability Assessment Matrix (Partial Risk Assessment)

Criteria	0	1	2	3	4	5	Score
Asset visibility	—	Existence not well known	—	Existence locally known	—	Existence widely known	
Target utility	None	Very low	Low	Medium	High	Very high	
Asset accessibility	Remote location, secure perimeter, armed guards, tightly controlled access	Fenced, guarded, controlled access	Controlled access, protected entry	Controlled access, unprotected entry	Open access, restricted parking	Open access, unrestricted parking	
Asset mobility	—	Moves or is relocated frequently	—	Moves or is relocated occasionally	—	Permanent/fixed in place	
Presence of hazardous materials	No hazardous materials present	Limited quantities, materials in secure location	Moderate quantities, strict control features	Large quantities, some control features	Large quantities, minimal control features	Large quantities, accessible to nonstaff personnel	
Collateral damage potential	No risk	Low risk, limited to immediate area	Moderate risk, limited to immediate area	Moderate risk within 1-mile radius	High risk within 1-mile radius	High risk beyond 1-mile radius	
Site population/capacity	0	1–250	251–500	501–1000	1001–5000	> 5000	

Source: FEMA, 2002. *Integrating Human-Caused Hazards into Mitigation Planning,* Publication 386-7, Federal Emergency Management Agency, Washington, DC. (as presented in FEMA, 2003. *Reference Manual to Mitigate Potential Terrorist Attacks Against Buildings,* Publication 426, Federal Emergency Management Agency, Washington, DC, p. 1–25).

TABLE A.2 Building Vulnerability Assessment Checklist

Section	Vulnerability Question	Guidances
1	**Site**	
1.1	**What major structures surround the facility (site or building)?** **What critical infrastructure, government, military, or recreation facilities are in the local area that impact transportation, utilities, and collateral damage?** (attack at this facility impacting the other major structures or attack on the major structures impacting this facility) **What are the adjacent land uses immediately outside the perimeter of this facility (site or building)?** **Do future development plans change these land uses outside the facility (site or building) perimeter?** Although this question bridges threat and vulnerability, the threat is the man-made hazard that can occur (likelihood and impact) and the vulnerability is the proximity of the hazard to the building(s) being assessed. Thus, a chemical plant release may be a threat/hazard, but vulnerability changes if the plant is 1 mile upwind for the prevailing winds versus 10 miles away and downwind. Similarly, a terrorist attack upon an adjacent building may impact the building(s) being assessed. The Murrah Federal Building in Oklahoma City was not the only building damaged by the explosion of the Ryder rental truck bomb.	**Critical infrastructure to consider:** **Telecommunications infrastructure:** Facilities for broadcast TV, cable TV; cellular networks; newspaper offices, production, and distribution; radio stations; satellite base stations; telephone trunking and switching stations, including critical cable routes and major rights of way **Electric power systems:** Power plants, especially nuclear facilities; transmission and distribution system components; fuel distribution, delivery, and storage **Gas and oil facilities:** Hazardous material facilities, oil/gas pipelines, and storage facilities **Banking and finance institutions:** Financial institutions (banks, credit unions) and the business district; note schedule business/financial district may follow; armored car services **Transportation networks** Airports: carriers, flight paths, and airport layout; location of air traffic control towers, runways, passenger terminals, and parking areas Bus stations Trains/subways: rails and lines, railheads/rail yards, interchanges, tunnels, and cargo/passenger terminals; note hazardous material transported Traffic: interstate highways/ roads/tunnels/bridges carrying large volumes; points of congestion; note time of day and day of week Trucking: hazardous materials cargo loading/unloading facilities; truck terminals, weigh stations, and rest areas Waterways: dams; levees; berths and ports for cruise ships, ferries, roll-on/

(continues)

TABLE A.2 *Continued*

Section	Vulnerability Question	Guidance
		roll-off cargo vessels, and container ships; international (foreign) flagged vessels (and cargo)
		Water supply systems: Pipelines and process/treatment facilities, dams for water collection; wastewater treatment
		Government services: Federal/state/ local government offices: post offices, law enforcement stations, fire/rescue, town/city hall, local mayor's/ governor's residences, judicial offices and courts, military installations (include type—active, reserves, National Guard)
		Emergency services: Backup facilities, communications centers, emergency operations centers (EOCs), fire/emergency medical service (EMS) facilities, emergency medical center (EMCs), law enforcement facilities
		Not critical infrastructure, but having potential collateral damage to considering
		Agricultural facilities: Chemical distribution, storage, and application sites; crop-spraying services; farms and ranches; food-processing, storage, and distribution facilities
		Commercial/manufacturing/indust rial facilities: Apartment buildings; business/corporate centers; chemical plants (especially those with Section 302 Extremely Hazardous Substances); factories; fuel production, distribution, and storage facilities; hotels and convention centers; industrial plants; raw material production, distribution, and storage facilities; research facilities and laboratories; shipping, warehousing, transfer and logistical centers
		Events and attractions: Festivals and celebrations; open-air markets; parades;

TABLE A.2 *Continued*

Section	Vulnerability Question	Guidance
		rallies, demonstrations, and marches; religious services; scenic tours; theme parks
		Health-care system components: Family planning clinics; health department offices; hospitals; radiological material and medical waste transportation, storage, and disposal; research facilities and laboratories, walk-in clinics
		Political or symbolically significant sites: Embassies, consulates, landmarks, monuments, political party and special interest groups offices, religious sites
		Public/private institutions: Academic institutions, cultural centers, libraries, museums, research facilities and laboratories, schools
		Recreation facilities: Auditoriums, casinos, concert halls and pavilions, parks, restaurants and clubs (frequented by potential target populations), sports arenas, stadiums, theatres, malls, and special interest group facilities; note congestion dates and times for shopping centers
		References: *FEMA 386-7, FEMA SLG 101, DOJ NCJ181200*
1.2	**Does the terrain place the building in a depression or low area?**	Depressions or low areas can trap heavy vapors, inhibit natural decontamination by prevailing winds, and reduce the effectiveness of in-place sheltering. Reference: *USAF Installation Force Protection Guide*
1.3	**In dense, urban areas, does curb-lane parking allow uncontrolled vehicles to park unacceptably close to a building in the public right of way?**	Where distance from the building to the nearest curb provides insufficient setback, restrict parking in the curb lane. For typical city streets, this may require negotiating to close the curb lane. *Setback* is common terminology

(continues)

TABLE A.2 *Continued*

Section	Vulnerability Question	Guidance
		for the distance between a building and its associated roadway or parking. It is analogous to standoff between a vehicle bomb and a building. The benefit per foot of increased standoff between a potential vehicle bomb and a building is very high when close to a building and decreases rapidly as the distance increases. Note that the July 1, 1994, Americans with Disabilities Act Standards for Accessible Design states that required handicapped parking shall be located on the shortest accessible route of travel from adjacent parking to an accessible entrance. Reference: *GSA PBS-P100*
1.4	**Is a perimeter fence or other types of barrier controls in place?**	The intent is to channel pedestrian traffic onto a site with multiple buildings through known access control points. For a single building, the intent is to have a single visitor entrance. Reference: *GSA PBS-P100*
1.5	**What are the site access points to the site or building?**	The goal is to have at least two access points: one for passenger vehicles and one for delivery trucks due to the different procedures needed for each. Having two access points also helps if one of the access points becomes unusable, in which case traffic can be routed through the other access point. Reference: *USAF Installation Force Protection Guide*
1.6	**Is vehicle traffic separated from pedestrian traffic on the site?**	Pedestrian access should not be endangered by car traffic. Pedestrian access, especially from public transportation, should not cross vehicle traffic if possible. References: *GSA PBS-P100 and FEMA 386-7*

TABLE A.2 *Continued*

Section	Vulnerability Question	Guidance
1.7	**Is there vehicle and pedestrian access control at the perimeter of the site?**	Vehicle and pedestrian access control and inspection should occur as far from facilities as possible (preferably at the site perimeter) with the ability to regulate the flow of people and vehicles one at a time.
		Control on-site parking with identification checks, security personnel, and access control systems.
		Reference: *FEMA 386-7*
1.8	**Is there space for inspection at the curb line or outside the protected perimeter?**	Design features for the vehicular inspection point include vehicle arrest devices that prevent vehicles from leaving the vehicular inspection area and that prevent tailgating.
	What is the minimum distance from the inspection location to the building?	If screening space cannot be provided, consider other design features such as hardening and alternative location for vehicle search/inspection.
		Reference: *GSA PBS-P100*
1.9	**Is there any potential access to the site or building through utility paths or water runoff?**	Eliminate potential site access through utility tunnels, corridors, manholes, storm-water runoff culverts, etc. Ensure that covers to these access points are secured.
		Reference: *USAF Installation Force Protection Guide*
1.10	**What are the existing types of vehicle antiramming devices for the site or building?**	Passive barriers include bollards, walls, hardened fences (steel cable interlaced), trenches, ponds/basins, concrete planters, street furniture, plantings, trees, sculptures, and fountains. Active barriers include pop-up bollards, swing arm gates, and rotating plates and drums, etc.
	Are these devices at the property boundary or at the building?	Reference: *GSA PBS-P100*
1.11	**What is the antiramming buffer zone standoff distance from the building to unscreened vehicles or parking?**	If the recommended distance for the postulated threat is not available, consider reducing the standoff required through structural hardening or

(continues)

TABLE A.2 *Continued*

Section	Vulnerability Question	Guidance
		manufacturing additional standoff through barriers and parking restrictions. Also, consider relocation of vulnerable functions within the building or to a more hazard-resistant building. More standoff should be used for unscreened vehicles than for screened vehicles that have been searched.
		Reference: *GSA PBS-P100*
1.12	**Are perimeter barriers capable of stopping vehicles?** **Will the vehicle barriers at the perimeter and building maintain access for emergency responders, including large fire apparatus?**	Antiramming protection may be provided by adequately designed: bollards, street furniture, sculpture, landscaping, walls, and fences. The antiramming protection must be able to stop the threat vehicle size (weight) at the speed attainable by that vehicle at impact. If the antiramming protection cannot absorb the desired kinetic energy, consider adding speed controls (serpentines or speed bumps) to limit the speed at impact. If the resultant speed is still too great, the antiramming protection should be improved.
		References: *Military Handbook 1013/14 and GSA PBS-P100*
1.13	**Does site circulation prevent high-speed approaches by vehicles?**	The intent is to use site circulation to minimize vehicle speeds and eliminate direct approaches to structures.
		Reference: *GSA PBS-P100*
1.14	**Are there offsetting vehicle entrances from the direction of a vehicle's approach to force a reduction of speed?**	Single or double 90-degree turns effectively reduce vehicle approach speed.
		Reference: *GSA PBS-P100*
1.15	**Is there a minimum setback distance between the building and parked vehicles?**	Adjacent parking should be directed to more distant or better-protected areas, segregated from employee parking and away from the building. Some publications use the term *setback* in lieu of the term *standoff*.
		Reference: *GSA PBS-P100*

TABLE A.2 *Continued*

Section	Vulnerability Question	Guidance
1.16	**Does adjacent surface parking on site maintain a minimum standoff distance?**	The specific standoff distance needed is based on the design-basis-threat bomb size and the building construction. For initial screening, consider using 25 meters (82 feet) as a minimum, with more distance needed for unreinforced masonry or wooden walls. Reference: *GSA PBS-P100*
1.17	**Do stand-alone, above-ground parking garages provide adequate visibility across as well as into and out of the parking garage?**	Pedestrian paths should be planned to concentrate activity to the extent possible. Limiting vehicular entry/exits to a minimum number of locations is beneficial. Stair tower and elevator lobby design should be as open as code permits. Stair and/or elevator waiting areas should be as open to the exterior and/or the parking areas as possible and well lighted. Impact-resistant, laminated glass for stair towers and elevators is a way to provide visual openness. Potential hiding places below stairs should be closed off; nooks and crannies should be avoided, and dead-end parking areas should be eliminated. Reference: *GSA PBS-P100*
1.18	**Are garage or service area entrances for employee-permitted vehicles protected by suitable antiramming devices?** **This protection is coordinated with other antiramming devices, such as on the perimeter or property boundary to avoid duplication of arresting capability.**	Control internal building parking, underground parking garages, and access to service areas and loading docks in this manner with proper access control, or eliminate the parking altogether. The antiramming device must be capable of arresting a vehicle of the designated threat size at the speed attainable at the location. Reference: *GSA PBS-P100*
1.19	**Do site landscaping and street furniture provide hiding places?**	Minimize concealment opportunities by keeping landscape plantings (hedges, shrubbery, and large plants with heavy

(continues)

TABLE A.2 *Continued*

Section	Vulnerability Question	Guidance
		ground cover) and street furniture (bus shelters, benches, trash receptacles, mailboxes, newspaper vending machines) away from the building to permit observation of intruders and prevent hiding of packages.
		If mail or express boxes are used, the size of the openings should be restricted to prohibit the insertion of packages.
		Reference: *GSA PBS-P100*
1.20	**Is the site lighting adequate from a security perspective in roadway access and parking areas?**	Security protection can be successfully addressed through adequate lighting. The type and design of lighting, including illumination levels, is critical. Illuminating Engineering Society of North America (IESNA) guidelines can be used. The site lighting should be coordinated with the CCTV system.
		Reference: *GSA PBS-P100*
1.21	**Are line-of-sight perspectives from outside the secured boundary to the building and on the property along pedestrian and vehicle routes integrated with landscaping and green space?**	The goal is to prevent the observation of critical assets by persons outside the secure boundary of the site. For individual buildings in an urban environment, this could mean appropriate window treatments, or no windows for portions of the building.
		Once on the site, the concern is to ensure observation by a general workforce aware of any pedestrians or vehicles outside normal circulation routes or attempting to approach the building unobserved.
		Reference: *USAF Installation Force Protection Guide*
1.22	**Do signs provide control of vehicles and people?**	Signage should be simple and have the necessary level of clarity. However, signs that identify sensitive areas should generally not be provided.
		Reference: *GSA PBS-P100*

TABLE A.2 *Continued*

Section	Vulnerability Question	Guidance
1.23	**Are all existing fire hydrants on the site accessible?**	Just as vehicle access points to the site must be able to transit emergency vehicles, so, too, must the emergency vehicles have access to the buildings and, in the case of fire trucks, the fire hydrants. Thus, security considerations must accommodate emergency response requirements. Reference: *GSA PBS-P100*
2	**Architectural**	
2.1	**Does the site and architectural design incorporate strategies from a Crime Prevention Through Environmental Design (CPTED) perspective?**	**The focus of CPTED is on creating defensible space by employing the following:** **Natural access controls:** • Design streets, sidewalks, and building entrances to clearly indicate public routes and direct people away from private/restricted area. • Discourage access to private areas with structural elements and limit access (no cut-through streets). • Separate loading zones from public parking. **Natural surveillance:** • Utilize a design that maximizes visibility of people, parking areas, and building entrances; design doors and windows that look out on to streets and parking areas. • Keep shrubbery under 2 feet in height for visibility. • Keep lower branches of existing trees kept at least 10 feet off the ground. • Design pedestrian-friendly sidewalks and streets to control pedestrian and vehicle circulation.

(continues)

TABLE A.2 *Continued*

Section	Vulnerability Question	Guidance
		• Provide adequate nighttime lighting, especially at exterior doorways. **Territorial reinforcement:** • Use a design that defines property lines. • Use a design that distinguishes private/restricted spaces from public spaces by separation, landscape plantings, pavement designs (pathway and roadway placement), gateway treatments at lobbies and corridors, door placement, walls, barriers, signage, lighting, and "CPTED" fences. • Install traffic-calming devices for vehicle speed control. **Target hardening:** • Prohibit entry or access with window locks, deadbolts for doors, and interior door hinges. • Utilize access control (building and employee/parking) and intrusion detection systems. **Closed circuit television cameras:** • Use CCTV to prevent crime and influence positive behavior while enhancing the intended uses of space (a design that eliminates or reduces criminal behavior and at the same time encourages people to "keep an eye out" for each other). References: *GSA PBS-P100 and FEMA 386-7*

TABLE A.2 *Continued*

Section	Vulnerability Question	Guidance
2.2	**Is it a mixed-tenant building?**	Separate high-risk tenants from low-risk tenants and from publicly accessible areas. Mixed uses may be accommodated through such means as separating entryways, controlling access, and hardening shared partitions, as well as through special security operational countermeasures. Reference: *GSA PBS-P100*
2.3	**Are pedestrian paths planned to concentrate activity to aid in detection?**	Site planning and landscape design can provide natural surveillance by concentrating pedestrian activity, limiting entrances/exits, and eliminating concealment opportunities. Also, prevent pedestrian access to parking areas other than via established entrances. Reference: *USAF Installation Force Protection Guide*
2.4	**Are there trash receptacles and mailboxes in close proximity to the building that can be used to hide explosive devices?**	The size of the trash receptacles and mailbox openings should be restricted to prohibit insertion of packages. Street furniture, such as newspaper vending machines, should be kept sufficient distance (10 meters, or 33 feet) from the building or brought inside to a secure area. References: *USAF Installation Force Protection Guide and DoD UCF 4-010-01*
2.5	**Do entrances avoid significant queuing?**	If queuing will occur within the building footprint, the area should be enclosed in blast-resistant construction. If queuing is expected outside the building, a rain cover should be provided. For manpower and equipment requirements, colocate or combine staff and visitor entrances. Reference: *GSA PBS-P100*

(continues)

TABLE A.2   *Continued*

Section	Vulnerability Question	Guidance
2.6	**Does security screening cover all public and private area?** **Are public and private activities separated?** **Are public toilets, service spaces, or access to stairs or elevators located in any non-secure areas, including the queuing area before screening at the public entrance?**	Retail activities should be prohibited in nonsecured areas. However, the Public Building Cooperative Use Act of 1976 encourages retail and mixed uses to create open and inviting buildings. Consider separating entryways, controlling areas, hardening shared partitions, and using special security operational countermeasures. References: *GSA PBS-P100 and FEMA 386-7*
2.7	**Is access control provided through main entrance points for employees and visitors?** (lobby receptionist, sign-in, staff escorts, issue of visitor badges, checking forms of personal identification, electronic access control systems)	Reference: *Physical Security Assessment for the Department of Veterans Affairs Facilities*
2.8	**Is access to private and public space or restricted area space clearly defined through the design of the space, signage, use of electronic security devices, etc.?**	Finishes and signage should be designed for visual simplicity. Reference: *Physical Security Assessment for the Department of Veterans Affairs Facilities*
2.9	**Is access to elevators distinguished as to those that are designated only for employees and visitors?**	Reference: *Physical Security Assessment for the Department of Veterans Affairs Facilities*
2.10	**Do public and employee entrances include space for possible future installation of access control and screening equipment?**	These include walk-through metal detectors and x-ray devices, identification check, electronic access card, search stations, and turnstiles. Reference: *GSA PBS-P100*
2.11	**Do foyers have reinforced concrete walls and offset interior and exterior doors from each other?**	Consider reinforcing and door offset for exterior entrances to the building or to access critical areas within the building if explosive blast hazard must be mitigated. Reference: *U.S. Army TM 5-853*

TABLE A.2 *Continued*

Section	Vulnerability Question	Guidance
2.12	**Do doors and walls along the line of security screening meet requirements of UL752, *Standard for Safety: Bullet-Resisting Equipment?***	If the postulated threat in designing entrance access control includes rifles, pistols, or shotguns, then the screening area should have bullet resistance to protect security personnel and uninvolved bystanders. Glass, if present, should also be bullet-resistant. Reference: *GSA PBS-P100*
2.13	**Do circulation routes have unobstructed views of people approaching controlled access points?**	Unobstructed views should be provided for building entrances and to critical areas within the building. References: *USAF Installation Force Protection Guide and DoD UFC 4-010-01*
2.14	**Is roof access limited to authorized personnel by means of locking mechanisms?**	References: *GSA PBS-P100 and CDC/NIOSH, Pub 2002-139*
2.15	**Are critical assets (people, activities, building systems and components) located close to any main entrance, vehicle circulation, parking, maintenance area, loading dock, or interior parking?** **Are the critical building systems and components hardened?**	Critical building components include: Emergency generators, including fuel systems, day tank, fire sprinkler, and water supply; normal fuel storage; main switchgear; telephone distribution and main switchgear; fire pumps; building control centers; uninterruptible power supply (UPS) systems controlling critical functions; main refrigeration and ventilation systems if critical to building operation; elevator machinery and controls; shafts for stairs, elevators, and utilities; and critical distribution feeders for emergency power. Evacuation and rescue require emergency systems to remain operational during a disaster, and they should be located away from potential attack locations. Primary and backup systems should be separated to reduce the risk of both being impacted by a single incident, if colocated. Utility systems should be located at least 50 feet from loading docks, front entrances, and parking areas.

(continues)

TABLE A.2 *Continued*

Section	Vulnerability Question	Guidance
		One way to harden critical building systems and components is to enclose them within hardened walls, floors, and ceilings. Do not place them near high-risk areas where they can receive collateral damage. Reference: *GSA PBS-P100*
2.16	Are high-value or critical assets located as far into the interior of the building as possible and separated from the public areas of the building?	Critical assets, such as people and activities, are more vulnerable to hazards when on an exterior building wall or adjacent to uncontrolled public areas inside the building. Reference: *GSA PBS-P100*
2.17	Is high visitor activity away from critical assets?	High-risk activities should also be separated from low-risk activities. Also, visitor activities should be separated from daily activities. Reference: *USAF Installation Force Protection Guide*
2.18	Are critical assets located in spaces that are occupied 24 hours per day? Are assets located in areas where they are visible to more than one person?	Reference: *USAF Installation Force Protection Guide*
2.19	Are loading docks and receiving and shipping areas separated in any direction from utility rooms, utility mains, and service entrances, including electrical telephone/data, fire detection/alarm systems, fire suppression water mains, cooling and heating units?	Loading docks should be designed to keep vehicles from driving into or parking under the building. If loading docks are in close proximity to critical equipment, consider hardening the equipment and service against explosive blast. Consider a 50-foot separation distance in all directions. Reference: *GSA PBS-P100*

TABLE A.2 *Continued*

Section	Vulnerability Question	Guidance
2.20	Are mailrooms located away from building main entrances, areas containing critical services, utilities, distribution systems, and important assets? Is the mailroom located near the loading dock?	The mailroom should be located at the perimeter of the building with an outside wall or window designed for pressure relief. By separating the mailroom and the loading dock, the collateral damage of an incident at one location has less impact upon the other. However, the loading dock may be the preferred mailroom location. Off-site screening stations or a separate delivery processing building on site may be cost-effective, particularly if several buildings may share one mailroom. A separate delivery processing building reduces risk and simplifies protection measures. Reference: *GSA PBS-P100*
2.21	Does the mailroom have adequate space available for equipment to examine incoming packages and for an explosive disposal?	Screening of all deliveries to the building, including U.S. mail, commercial package delivery services, and delivery of office supplies should be provided. Reference: *GSA PBS-P100*
2.22	Are areas of refuge identified, with special consideration given to egress?	Areas of refuge can be safe havens, shelters, or protected spaces for use during specified hazards. Reference: *FEMA 386-7*
2.23	Are stairwells required for emergency egress located as remotely as possible from high-risk areas where blast events might occur? Are stairways maintained with positive pressure or are there other smoke control systems?	Consider designing stairs so that they discharge into areas other than lobbies, parking or loading docks. Maintain positive pressure from a clean source of air (may require special filtering) aids in egress by keeping smoke, heat, and toxic fumes out of the stairway. Pressurize exit stairways in accordance with the National Model Building Code. References: *GSA PBS-P100 and CDC/NIOSH, Pub 2002-139*

(continues)

TABLE A.2 *Continued*

Section	Vulnerability Question	Guidance
2.24	**Are enclosures for emergency egress hardened to limit the extent of debris that might impede safe passage and reduce the flow of evacuees?**	Egress pathways should be hardened and should discharge into safe areas. Reference: *FEMA 386-7*
2.25	**Do interior barriers differentiate level of security within a building?**	Reference: *USAF Installation Force Protection Guide*
2.26	**Are emergency systems located away from high-risk areas?**	The intent is to keep the emergency systems out of harm's way, such that one incident does not take out all capability—both the regular systems and their backups. Reference: *FEMA 386-7*
2.27	**Is interior glazing near high-risk areas minimized?** **Is interior glazing in other areas shatter-resistant?**	Interior glazing should be minimized where a threat exists and should be avoided in enclosures of critical functions next to high-risk areas. Reference: *GSA PBS-P100*
2.28	**Are ceiling and lighting systems designed to remain in place during hazard events?**	When an explosive blast shatters a window, the blast wave enters the interior space, putting structural and nonstructural building components under loads not considered in standard building codes. Connection criteria for these systems in high-seismic-activity areas results in much less falling debris that could injure building occupants. Mount all overhead utilities and other fixtures weighing 14 kilograms (31 pounds) or more to minimize the likelihood that they will fall and injure building occupants. Design all equipment mountings to resist forces of 0.5 times the equipment weight in any direction and 1.5 times the equipment weight in the downward direction. This standard does not preclude the need to design equipment mountings for forces

TABLE A.2 *Continued*

Section	Vulnerability Question	Guidance
		required by other criteria, such as seismic standards.
		Reference: *DoD UCF 4-101-01*
3	**Structural Systems**	
3.1	**What type of construction is it?** **What type of concrete and reinforcing steel are used in construction?** **What type of steel is used in construction?** **What type of foundation is present?**	The type of construction provides an indication of the robustness to abnormal loading and load reversals. A reinforced concrete moment-resisting frame provides greater ductility and redundancy than a flat-slab or flat-plate construction. The ductility of steel frame with metal deck depends on the connection details and pre-tensioned or post-tensioned construction provides little capacity for abnormal loading patterns and load reversals. The resistance of load-bearing wall structures varies to a great extent, depending on whether the walls are reinforced or un-reinforced. A rapid screening process developed by FEMA for assessing structural hazards identifies the following types of construction with a structural score ranging from 1.0 to 8.5. A higher score indicates a greater capacity to sustain load reversals. Wood buildings of all types: 4.5 to 8.5 Steel moment-resisting frames: 3.5 to 4.5 Braced steel frames: 2.5 to 3.0 Light metal buildings: 5.5 to 6.5 Steel frames with cast-in-place concrete shear walls: 3.5 to 4.5 Steel frames with unreinforced masonry infill walls: 1.5 to 3.0 Concrete moment-resisting frames: 2.0 to 4.0

(continues)

TABLE A.2   *Continued*

Section	Vulnerability Question	Guidance
		Concrete shear wall buildings: 3.0 to 4.0
		Concrete frames with unreinforced masonry infill walls: 1.5 to 3.0
		Tilt-up buildings: 2.0 to 3.5
		Precast concrete frame buildings: 1.5 to 2.5
		Reinforced masonry: 3.0 to 4.0
		Unreinforced masonry: 1.0 to 2.5
		References: *FEMA 154 and Physical Security Assessment for the Department of Veterans Affairs Facilities*
3.2	**Do the reinforced concrete structures contain symmetric steel reinforcement (positive and negative faces) in all floor slabs, roof slabs, walls, beams, and girders that may be subjected to rebound, uplift, and suction pressures?** **Do the lap splices fully develop the capacity of the reinforcement?** **Are lap splices and other discontinuities staggered?** **Do the connections possess ductile details?** **Is special shear reinforcement, including ties and stirrups, available to allow large post-elastic behavior?**	Reference: *GSA PBS-P100*
3.3	**Are the steel frame connections moment connections?** **Is the column spacing minimized so that reasonably sized members will resist the design loads and increase the redundancy of the system?** **What are the floor-to-floor heights?**	A practical upper level for column spacing is generally 30 feet. Unless there is an overriding architectural requirement, a practical limit for floor-to-floor heights is generally less than or equal to 16 feet. Reference: *GSA PBS-P100*

TABLE A.2 *Continued*

Section	Vulnerability Question	Guidance
3.4	**Are critical elements vulnerable to failure?**	The priority for upgrades should be based on the relative importance of structural or nonstructural elements that are essential to mitigating the extent of collapse and minimizing injury and damage.
		Primary structural elements provide the essential parts of the building's resistance to catastrophic blast loads and progressive collapse. These include columns, girders, roof beams, and the main lateral resistance system.
		Secondary structural elements consist of all other load-bearing members, such as floor beams, slabs, etc.
		Primary nonstructural elements consist of elements (including their attachments) that are essential for life safety systems or elements that can cause substantial injury if failure occurs, including ceilings or heavy suspended mechanical units.
		Secondary nonstructural elements consist of all elements not covered in primary nonstructural elements, such as partitions, furniture, and light fixtures.
		Reference: *GSA PBS-P100*
3.5	**Will the structure suffer an unacceptable level of damage resulting from the postulated threat (blast loading or weapon impact)?**	**The extent of damage to the structure and exterior wall systems from the bomb threat may be related to a protection level. The following apply to new buildings:**
		Level of protection below antiterrorism standards: Severe damage. Frame collapse/massive destruction. Little left standing. Doors and windows fail and result in lethal hazards. Majority of personnel suffer fatalities.

(continues)

TABLE A.2   *Continued*

Section	Vulnerability Question	Guidance
		Very low-level protection: Heavy damage. Onset of structural collapse. Major deformation of primary and secondary structural members, but progressive collapse is unlikely. Collapse of nonstructural elements. Glazing will break and is likely to be propelled into the building, resulting in serious glazing fragment injuries, but fragments will be reduced. Doors may be propelled into rooms, presenting serious hazards. Majority of personnel suffer serious injuries. There are likely to be a limited number (10 to 25 percent) of fatalities.
		Low level of protection: Moderate damage, unrepairable. Major deformation of nonstructured elements and secondary structural members and minor deformation of primary structural members, but progressive collapse is unlikely. Glazing will break, but fall within 1 meter of the wall or otherwise not present a significant fragment hazard. Doors may fail, but they will rebound out of their frames, presenting minimal hazards. Majority of personnel suffer significant injuries. There may be a few (<10 percent) fatalities.
		Medium level of protection: Minor damage, repairable. Minor deformations of nonstructural elements and secondary structural members and no permanent deformation in primary structural members. Glazing will break, but will remain in the window frame. Doors will stay in frames, but will not be reusable. Some minor injuries, but fatalities are unlikely.
		High level of protection: Minimal damage, repairable. No permanent deformation

TABLE A.2 *Continued*

Section	Vulnerability Question	Guidance
		of primary and secondary structural members or nonstructural elements. Glazing will not break. Doors will be reusable. Only superficial injuries are likely. Reference: *DoD UFC C-010-01*
3.6	**Is the structure vulnerable to progressive collapse?** **Is the building capable of sustaining the removal of a column for one floor above grade at the building perimeter without progressive collapse?** **In the event of an internal explosion in an uncontrolled public ground floor area, does the design prevent progressive collapse due to the loss of one primary column?** **Do architectural or structural features provide a minimum 6-inch standoff to the internal columns (primary vertical load carrying members)?** **Are the columns in the unscreened internal spaces designed for an unbraced length equal to two floors, or three floors where there are two levels of parking?**	Design to mitigate progressive collapse is an independent analysis to determine a system's ability to resist structural collapse upon the loss of a major structural element or the system's ability to resist the loss of a major structural element. Design to mitigate progressive collapse may be based on the methods outlined in ASCE 7-98 (now 7-02). Designers may apply static and/or dynamic methods of analysis to meet this requirement and ultimate load capacities may be assumed in the analyses. Combine structural upgrades for retrofits to existing buildings, such as seismic and progressive collapse, into a single project due to the economic synergies and other cross benefits. Existing facilities may be retrofitted to withstand the design level threat or to accept the loss of a column for one floor above grade at the building perimeter without progressive collapse. Note that collapse of floors or roof must not be permitted. Reference: *GSA PBS-P100*
3.7	**Are there adequate redundant load paths in the structure?**	Special considerations should be given to materials that have inherent ductility and that are better able to respond to load reversals, such as cost in place reinforced concrete, reinforced masonry, and steel construction. Careful detailing is required for material such as prestressed concrete, precast concrete, and masonry to

(continues)

TABLE A.2 *Continued*

Section	Vulnerability Question	Guidance
		adequately respond to the design loads. Primary vertical-load-carrying members should be protected where parking is inside a facility and the building superstructure is supported by the parking structure. Reference: *GSA PBS-P100*
3.8	**Are there transfer girders supported by columns within unscreened public spaces or at the exterior of the building?**	Transfer girders allow discontinuities in columns between the roof and foundation. This design has inherent difficulty in transferring load to redundant paths upon loss of a column or the girder. Transfer beams and girders that, if lost, may cause progressive collapse are highly discouraged. Reference: *GSA PBS-P100*
3.9	**What is the grouting and reinforcement of masonry [brick and/or concrete masonry unit (CMU)] exterior walls?**	Avoid unreinforced masonry exterior walls. Reinforcement can run the range of light to heavy, depending upon the standoff distance available and postulated design threat. Reference: *GSA PBS-P100* recommends fully grouted and reinforced CMU construction where CMU is selected. Reference: *DoD Minimum Antiterrorism Standards for Buildings* states "Unreinforced masonry walls are prohibited for the exterior walls of new buildings. A minimum of 0.05 percent vertical reinforcement with a maximum spacing of 1200 mm (48 in) will be provided. For existing buildings, implement mitigating measures to provide an equivalent level of protection." (This is light reinforcement and based upon the recommended standoff distance for the situation.)

TABLE A.2   *Continued*

Section	Vulnerability Question	Guidance
3.10	**Will the loading dock design limit damage to adjacent areas and vent explosive force to the exterior of the building?**	Design the floor of the loading dock for blast resistance if the area below is occupied or contains critical utilities. Reference: *GSA PBS-P100*
3.11	**Are mailrooms, where packages are received and opened for inspection, and unscreened retail spaces designed to mitigate the effects of a blast on primary vertical or lateral bracing members?**	Mailrooms and unscreened retail spaces located in occupied areas or adjacent to critical utilities, walls, ceilings, and floors should be blast and fragment resistant. Methods to facilitate the venting of explosive forces and gases from the interior spaces to the outside of the structure may include blow-out panels and window system designs that provide protection from blast pressure applied to the outside, but that readily fail and vent if exposed to blast pressure on the inside. Reference: *GSA PBS-P100*
4	**Building Envelope**	
4.1	**What is the designed or estimated protection level of the exterior walls against the postulated explosive threat?**	The performance of the facade varies to a great extent on the materials. Different construction includes brick or stone with block backup, steel stud walls, precast panels, or curtain wall with glass, stone, or metal panel elements. Shear walls that are essential to the lateral and vertical load bearing system and that also function as exterior walls should be considered primary structures and should resist the actual blast loads predicted from the threats specified. Where exterior walls are not designed for the full design loads, special consideration should be given to construction types that reduce the potential for injury. Reference: *GSA PBS-P100*

(continues)

TABLE A.2 *Continued*

Section	Vulnerability Question	Guidance
4.2	**Is there less than a 40 percent fenestration opening per structural bay?** **Is the window system design on the exterior facade balanced to mitigate the hazardous effects of flying glazing following an explosive event?** (glazing, frames, anchorage to supporting walls, etc.) **Do the glazing systems with a ½-inch (¾-inch is better) bite contain an application of structural silicone?** **Is the glazing laminated or is it protected with an anti-shatter (fragment retention) film?** **If an anti-shatter film is used, is it a minimum of a 7-millimeter thick film, or specially manufactured 4-millimeter thick film?**	The performance of the glass will similarly depend on the materials. Glazing may be single pane or double pane, monolithic or laminated, annealed, heat strengthened or fully tempered. The percent fenestration is a balance between protection level, cost, the architectural look of the building within its surroundings, and building codes. One goal is to keep fenestration to below 40 percent of the building envelope vertical surface area, but the process must balance differing requirements: A blast engineer may prefer no windows; an architect may favor window curtain walls; building codes require so much fenestration per square footage of floor area; fire codes require a prescribed window opening area if the window is a designated escape route; and the building owner has cost concerns. Ideally, an owner would want 100 percent of the glazed area to provide the design protection level against the postulated explosive threat (design basis threat—weapon size at the expected standoff distance). However, economics and geometry may allow 80 to 90 percent due to the statistical differences in the manufacturing process for glass or the angle of incidence of the blast wave upon upper-story windows (fourth floor and higher). Reference: *GSA PBS-P100*

TABLE A.2 *Continued*

Section	Vulnerability Question	Guidance
4.3	Do the walls, anchorage, and window framing fully develop the capacity of the glazing material selected? Are the walls capable of withstanding the dynamic reactions from the windows? Will the anchorage remain attached to the walls of the building during an explosive event without failure? Is the facade connected to a backup block or to the structural frame? Are non-load-bearing masonry walls reinforced?	Government produced and sponsored computer programs coupled with test data and recognized dynamic structural analysis techniques may be used to determine whether the glazing either survives the specified threats or the postdamage performance of the glazing protects the occupants. A breakage probability no higher than 750 breaks per 1,000 may be used when calculated loads to frames and anchorage. The intent is to ensure the building envelope provides relatively equal protection against the postulated explosive threat for the walls and window systems for the safety of the occupants, especially in rooms with exterior walls. Reference: *GSA PBS-P100*
4.4	Does the building contain ballistic glazing? Does the ballistic glazing meet the requirements of UL 752, *Standard for Safety: Bullet-Resistant Glazing*? Does the building contain security-glazing? Does the security-glazing meet the requirements of ASTM F1233 or UL 972, *Standard for Safety: Burglary-Resistant Glazing Material*? Do the window assemblies containing forced-entry-resistant glazing (excluding the glazing) meet the requirements of ASTM F 588?	Glass-clad polycarbonate or laminated polycarbonate are two types of acceptable glazing material. If windows are upgraded to bullet resistant, burglar resistant, or forced entry resistant, ensure that doors, ceilings, and floors, as applicable, can resist the same for the areas of concern. Reference: *GSA PBS-P100*
4.5	Do nonwindow openings, such as mechanical vents and exposed plenums, provide the same level of protection required for the exterior wall?	In-filling of blast overpressures must be considered through nonwindow openings such that structural members and all mechanical system mountings

(continues)

TABLE A.2 *Continued*

Section	Vulnerability Question	Guidance
		and attachments should resist interior fill pressures.
		These nonwindow openings should also be as secure as the rest of the building envelope against forced entry.
		Reference: *GSA PBS-P100*
5	**Utility Systems**	
5.1	**What is the source of domestic water?** (utility, municipal, wells, lake, river, storage tank)	Domestic water is critical for continued building operation. Although bottled water can satisfy requirements for drinking water and minimal sanitation, domestic water meets many other needs, such as flushing toilets, heating and cooling system operations, cooling of emergency generators, humidification, etc.
		Reference: *FEMA 386-7*
5.2	**Are there multiple entry points for the water supply?**	If the building or site has only one source of water entering at one location, the entry point should be secure.
		Reference: *GSA PBS-P100*
5.3	**Is the incoming water supply in a secure location?**	Ensure that only authorized personnel have access to the water supply and its components.
		Reference: *FEMA 386-7*
5.4	**Does the building or site have storage capacity for domestic water?** **How many gallons of storage capacity are available and how long will it allow operations to continue?**	Operational facilities will require reliance on adequate domestic water supply. Storage capacity can meet short-term needs and use water trucks to replenish for extended outages. Reference: *Physical Security Assessment for the Department of Veterans Affairs Facilities*

TABLE A.2 *Continued*

Section	Vulnerability Question	Guidance
5.5	**What is the source of water for the fire suppression system?** (local utility company lines, storage tanks with utility company backup, lake, or river)	The fire suppression system water may be supplied from the domestic water or it may have a separate source, separate storage, or nonpotable alternate sources.
	Are there alternate water supplies for fire suppression?	For a site with multiple buildings, the concern is that the supply should be adequate to fight the worst-case situation according to the fire codes. Recent major construction may change that requirement. Reference: *FEMA 386-7*
5.6	**Is the fire suppression system adequate, code compliant, and protected (in a secure location)?**	Standpipes, water supply control valves, and other system components should be secure or supervised. Reference: *FEMA 386-7*
5.7	**Do the sprinkler/standpipe interior control (risers) have fire- and blast-resistant separation?** **Are the sprinkler and standpipe connections adequate and redundant?** **Are there fire hydrant and water supply connections near the sprinkler/ standpipe connections?**	The incoming fire protection water line should be encased, buried, or located 50 feet from high-risk areas. The interior mains should be looped and sectionalized. Reference: *GSA PBS-P100*
5.8	**Are there redundant fire water pumps (e.g., one electric, one diesel)?** **Are the pumps located apart from each other?**	Colocating fire water pumps puts them at risk for a single incident to disable the fire suppression system. References: *GSA PBS-P100 and FEMA 386-7*
5.9	**Are sewer systems accessible?** **Are they protected or secured?**	Sanitary and storm-water sewers should be protected from unauthorized access. The main concerns are backup or flooding into the building, causing a health risk, shorting out electrical equipment, and loss of building use. Reference: *Physical Security Assessment for the Department of Veterans Affairs Facilities*

(continues)

TABLE A.2 *Continued*

Section	Vulnerability Question	Guidance
5.10	**What fuel supplies does the building rely upon for critical operation?**	Typically, natural gas, propane, or fuel oil is required for continued operation. Reference: *Physical Security Assessment for the Department of Veterans Affairs Facilities*
5.11	**How much fuel is stored on the site or at the building and how long can this quantity support critical operations?** **How is it stored?** **How is it secured?**	Fuel storage protection is essential for continued operation. Main fuel storage should be located away from loading docks, entrances, and parking. Access should be restricted and protected (e.g., locks on caps and seals). References: *GSA PBS-P100 and Physical Security Assessment for the Department of Veterans Affairs Facilities*
5.12	**Where is the fuel supply obtained?** **How is it delivered?**	The supply of fuel is dependent on the reliability of the supplier. Reference: *Physical Security Assessment for the Department of Veterans Affairs Facilities*
5.13	**Are there alternate sources of fuel?** **Can alternate fuels be used?**	Critical functions may be served by alternate methods if normal fuel supply is interrupted. Reference: *Physical Security Assessment for the Department of Veterans Affairs Facilities*
5.14	**What is the normal source of electrical service for the site or building?**	Utilities are the general source unless cogeneration or a private energy provider is available. Reference: *Physical Security Assessment for the Department of Veterans Affairs Facilities*
5.15	**Is there a redundant electrical service source?** **Can the site or buildings be fed from more than one utility substation?**	The utility may have only one source of power from a single substation. There may be only single feeders from the main substation. Reference: *Physical Security Assessment for the Department of Veterans Affairs Facilities*

TABLE A.2 *Continued*

Section	Vulnerability Question	Guidance
5.16	**How many service entry points does the site or building have for electricity?**	Electrical supply at one location creates a vulnerable situation unless an alternate source is available.
		Ensure disconnecting requirements according to NFPA 70, *National Electrical Code®,* are met for multiple service entrances.
		Reference: *Physical Security Assessment for the Department of Veterans Affairs Facilities*
5.17	**Is the incoming electric service to the building secure?**	Typically, the service entrance is a locked room, inaccessible to the public.
		Reference: *Physical Security Assessment for the Department of Veterans Affairs Facilities*
5.18	**What provisions for emergency power exist? What systems receive emergency power and have capacity requirements been tested?**	Besides installed generators to supply emergency power, portable generators or rental generators available under emergency contract can be connected quickly to a building with an exterior quick disconnect already installed.
	Is the emergency power collocated with the commercial electric service?	Testing under actual loading and operational conditions ensures that the critical systems requiring emergency power receive it with a high assurance of reliability.
	Is there an exterior connection for emergency power?	Reference: *GSA PBS-P100*
5.19	**By what means do the main telephone and data communications interface the site or building?**	Typically, communication ducts or other conduits are available. Overhead service is more identifiable and vulnerable.
		Reference: *Physical Security Assessment for the Department of Veterans Affairs Facilities*
5.20	**Are there multiple or redundant locations for the telephone and communications service?**	Secure locations of communications wiring entry to the site or building are required.
		Reference: *Physical Security Assessment for the Department of Veterans Affairs Facilities*

(continues)

TABLE A.2 *Continued*

Section	Vulnerability Question	Guidance
5.21	**Does the fire alarm system require communication with external sources?** **By what method is the alarm signal sent to the responding agency? (telephone, radio, etc.)** **Is there an intermediary alarm monitoring center?**	Typically, the local fire department responds to an alarm that sounds at the station or is transmitted over phone lines by an auto dialer. An intermediary control center for fire, security, and/or building system alarms may receive the initial notification at an on-site or off-site location. This center may then determine the necessary response and inform the responding agency. Reference: *Physical Security Assessment for the Department of Veterans Affairs Facilities*
5.22	**Are utility lifelines above ground, underground, or direct buried?**	Utility lifelines (water, power, communications, etc.) can be protected by concealing, burying, or encasing. References: *GSA PBS-P100 and FEMA 386-7*
6	**Mechanical Systems (HVAC and CBR)**	
6.1	**Where are the air intakes and exhaust louvers for the building?** (low, high, or midpoint of the building structure) **Are the intakes and exhausts accessible to the public?**	Air intakes should be located as high on the roof as possible. Otherwise, secure intakes within CPTED-compliant fencing or enclosure. The fencing or enclosure should have a sloped roof to prevent thrown items from getting near the intakes. *GSA PBS-P100* states that air intakes should be on the fourth floor or higher and, on buildings with three floors or fewer, they should be on the roof or as high as is practical. Locating intakes high on a wall is preferred over a roof location. *DoD UFC 4-010-01* states that, for all new inhabited buildings covered by this document, all air intakes should be located at least 3 meters (10 feet) above the ground. *DCD/NIOSH, Pub 2002-139* states: "An extension height of 12 feet (3.7 meters)

TABLE A.2 *Continued*

Section	Vulnerability Question	Guidance
		will place the intake out of reach of individuals without some assistance. Also, the entrance to the intake should be covered with a sloped metal mesh to reduce the threat of objects being tossed into the intake. A minimum slope of 45 degrees is generally adequate. Extension height should be increased where existing platforms or building features (i.e., loading docks, retaining walls) might provide access to the outdoor air intakes." *LBNL Pub 51959* states that exhausts are also a concern during an outdoor release, especially if exhaust fans are not in continuous operation, due to wind effects and chimney effects (air movement due to differential temperature).
6.2	**Is roof access limited to authorized personnel by means of locking mechanisms?** **Is access to mechanical areas similarly controlled?**	Roofs are like entrances to the building and are like mechanical rooms when HVAC is installed. Adjacent structures or landscaping should not allow access to the roof. References: *GSA PBS-P100, CDC/NIOSH Pub 2002-139, and LBNL Pub 51959*
6.3	**Are there multiple air-intake locations?**	Single air intakes may feed several air-handling units. Indicate if the air intakes are localized or separated. Installing low-leakage dampers is one way to provide system separation when necessary. Reference: *Physical Security Assessment for the Department of Veterans Affairs Facilities*
6.4	**What are the types of air filtration? Include the efficiency and number of filter modules for each of the main air-handling systems?**	**Types of air filtration include the following:** MERV—minimum efficiency reporting value HEPA—high efficiency particulate air

(continues)

TABLE A.2 *Continued*

Section	Vulnerability Question	Guidance
	Is there any collective protection for chemical, biological, and radiological contamination designed into the building?	Activated charcoal for gases Ultraviolet C for biologicals Consider a mix of approaches for optimum protection and cost-effectiveness. Reference: *CDC/NIOSH Pub 2002-139*
6.5	**Is there space for larger filter assemblies on critical air-handling systems?**	Air-handling units serving critical functions during continued operation may be retrofitted to provide enhanced protection during emergencies. However, upgraded filtration may have negative effects on overall air-handling-system operation, such as increased pressure drop. Reference: *CDC/NIOSH Pub 2002-139*
6.6	**Are there provisions for air monitors or sensors for chemical or biological agents?**	Duct-mounted sensors are usually found in limited cases in laboratory areas. Sensors generally have a limited spectrum of high reliability and are costly. Many different technologies are being researched to provide this capability. Reference: *CDC/NIOSH Pub 2002-139*
6.7	**By what methods are air intakes and exhausts closed when not operational?**	Motorized (low-leakage, fast-acting) dampers are the preferred method for closure with fail-safe to the closed position so as to support in-place sheltering. References: *CDC/NIOSH Pub 2002-139 and LBNL Pub 51959*
6.8	**How are air-handling systems zoned?** **What areas and functions do each of the primary air-handling systems serve?**	Understanding the critical areas of the building that must continue functioning focuses security and hazard mitigation measures. Applying HVAC zones that isolate lobbies, mailrooms, loading docks, and other entry and storage areas from the rest of the building's HVAC zones

TABLE A.2 *Continued*

Section	Vulnerability Question	Guidance
		and maintaining negative pressure within those areas will contain CBR releases. Identify common return systems that service more than one zone, effectively making a large single zone.
		Conversely, emergency egress routes should receive positive pressurization to ensure that contamination does not hinder egress. Consider filtering of the pressurization air.
		References: *CDC/NIOSH Pub 2002-139 and LBNL Pub 51959*
6.9	**Are there large central air-handling units or are there multiple units serving separate zones?**	Independent units can continue to operate if damage occurs to limited areas of the building.
		Reference: *Physical Security Assessment for the Department of Veterans Affairs Facilities*
6.10	**Are there any redundancies in the air-handling system?** **Can critical areas be served from other units if a major system is disabled?**	Redundancy reduces the security measures required compared to a nonredundant situation.
		Reference: *Physical Security Assessment for the Department of Veterans Affairs Facilities*
6.11	**Is the air supply to critical areas compartmentalized?** **Similarly, are the critical areas or the building as a whole considered tight, with little or no leakage?**	During chemical, biological, and radiological situations, the intent is to either keep the contamination localized in the critical area or to prevent its entry into other critical, noncritical, or public areas. Systems can be cross-connected through building openings (doorways, ceilings, partial wall), ductwork leakage, or pressure differences in the air-handling system. In standard practice, some air is almost always carried between ventilation zones by pressure imbalances due to elevator piston action, chimney effect, and wind effects.

(continues)

TABLE A.2 *Continued*

Section	Vulnerability Question	Guidance
		Smoke testing of the air supply to critical areas may be necessary.
		References: *CDC/NIOSH Pub 2002-139 and LBNL Pub 51959*
6.12	**Are supply, return, and exhaust air systems for critical areas secure?** **Are all supply and return ducts completely connected to their grilles and registers and secure?** **Is the return air ducted?**	The air systems to critical areas should be inaccessible to the public, especially if the ductwork runs through the public areas of the building. It is also more secure to have a ducted air-handling system versus sharing hallways and plenums above drop ceilings for return air. Nonducted systems provide greater opportunity for the introduction of contaminants. References: *CDC/NIOSH Pub 2002-139 and LBNL Pub 51959*
6.13	**What is the method of temperature and humidity control?** **Is it localized or centralized?**	Central systems can range from monitoring only to full control. Local control may be available to override central operation. Of greatest concern are systems needed before, during, and after an incident that may be unavailable due to temperature and humidity exceeding operational limits (e.g., main telephone switch room). Reference: *DOC CIAO Vulnerability Assessment Frame 1.1*
6.14	**Where are the building automation control centers and cabinets located?** **Are they in secure areas?** **How is the control wiring routed?**	Access to any component of the building automation and control system could compromise the functioning of the system, increasing vulnerability to a hazard or precluding their proper operation during a hazard incident. The HVAC and exhaust system controls should be in a secure area that allows rapid shutdown or other activation based on location and type of attack. References: *FEMA 386-7, DOC CIAO Vulnerability Assessment Framework 1.1 and LBNL Pub 51959*

TABLE A.2 *Continued*

Section	Vulnerability Question	Guidance
6.15	**Does the control of air-handling systems support plans for sheltering in place or other protective approaches?**	The micrometeorological effects of building and terrain can alter travel and duration of chemical agents and hazardous material releases. Shielding in the form of sheltering in place can protect people and property from harmful effects. To support in-place sheltering, the air handling systems require the ability for authorized personnel to rapidly turn off all systems. However, if the system is properly filtered, then keeping the system operating will provide protection as long as the air handling system does not distribute an internal release to other portions of the building. Reference: *CDC/NIOSH Pub 2002-139*
6.16	**Are there any smoke evacuation systems installed?** **Does it have purge capability?**	For an internal blast, a smoke removal system may be essential, particularly in large, open spaces. The equipment should be located away from high-risk areas, the system controls and wiring should be protected, and it should be connected to emergency power. This exhaust capability can be built into areas with significant risk on internal events, such as lobbies, loading docks, and mailrooms. Consider filtering of the exhaust to capture CBR contaminants. References: *GSA PBS-P100, CDC/NIOSH Pub 2002-139, and LBNL Pub 51959*
6.17	**Where is roof-mounted equipment located on the roof?** (near perimeter, at center of roof)	Roof-mounted equipment should be kept away from the building perimeter. Reference: *U.S. Army TM 5-853*
6.18	**Are fire dampers installed at all fire barriers?** **Are all dampers functional?** **Do they seal well when closed?**	All dampers (fire, smoke, outdoor air, return air, bypass) must be functional for proper protection within the building during an incident. Reference: *CDC/NIOSH Pub 2002-139*

(continues)

TABLE A.2 *Continued*

Section	Vulnerability Question	Guidance
6.19	**Do fire walls and fire doors maintain their integrity?**	The tightness of the building (both exterior, by weatherization to seal cracks around doors and windows, and internal, by zone ducting, fire walls, fire stops, and fire doors) provides energy conservation benefits and functional benefits during a CBR incident. Reference: *LBNL Pub 51959*
6.20	**Do elevators have recall capability and elevator emergency message capability?**	Although a life safety code and fire response requirement, the control of elevators also has benefit during a CBR incident. The elevators generate a piston effect, causing pressure differentials in the elevator shaft and associated floors that can force contamination to flow up or down. Reference: *LBNL Pub 51959*
6.21	**Is access to building information restricted?**	Information on building operations, schematics, procedures, plans, and specifications should be strictly controlled and available only to authorized personnel. References: *CDC/NIOSH Pub 2002-139 and LBNL Pub 51959*
6.22	**Does the HVAC maintenance staff have the proper training, procedures, and preventive maintenance schedule to ensure that CBR equipment is functional?**	Functional equipment must interface with operational procedures in an emergency plan to ensure the equipment is properly operated to provide the protection desired. The HVAC system can be operated in different ways, depending on an external or internal release and where in the building an internal release occurs. Thus, maintenance and security staff must have the training to properly operate the HVAC system under different circumstances, even if the procedure is to turn off all air-movement equipment. References: *CDC/NIOSH Pub 2002-139 and LBNL Pub 51959*

TABLE A.2 *Continued*

Section	Vulnerability Question	Guidance
7	**Plumbing and Gas Systems**	
7.1	**What is the method of water distribution?**	Central shaft locations for piping are more vulnerable than multiple-riser locations. Reference: *Physical Security Assessment for the Department of Veterans Affairs Facilities*
7.2	**What is the method of gas distribution?** (heating, cooking, medical, process)	Single storage or main supplies are more vulnerable than distributed storage and local piping systems. Reference: *Physical Security Assessment for the Department of Veterans Affairs Facilities*
7.3	**Is there redundancy to the main piping distribution?**	Looping of piping and use of section valves provide redundancies in the event section of the system are damaged. Reference: *Physical Security Assessment for the Department of Veterans Affairs Facilities*
7.4	**What is the method of heating domestic water?** **What fuel(s) is used?**	A single source of hot water with one fuel source is more vulnerable than multiple sources and multiple fuel types. Domestic hot water availability is an operational concern for many building occupancies. Reference: *Physical Security Assessment for the Department of Veterans Affairs Facilities*
7.5	**Where are gas storage tanks located?** **How are they piped to the distribution system?** (above or below ground)	The concern is that the tanks and piping could be vulnerable to a moving vehicle or a bomb blast either directly or by collateral damage due to proximity to a high-risk area. Reference: *Physical Security Assessment for the Department of Veterans Affairs Facilities*
7.6	**Are there reserve supplies of critical gases?**	Localized gas cylinders should be available in the event of damage to the central tank system Reference: *Physical Security Assessment for the Department of Veterans Affairs Facilities*

(continues)

TABLE A.2 *Continued*

Section	Vulnerability Question	Guidance
8	**Electrical Systems**	
8.1	**Are there any transformers or switchgears located outside the building or accessible from the building exterior?** **Are they vulnerable to public access?** **Are they secured?**	The concern is that external transformers may be unprotected. Some protection is needed. Reference: *Physical Security Assessment for the Department of Veterans Affairs Facilities*
8.2	**What is the extent of the external building lighting in utility and service areas and at normal entryways used by the building occupants?**	Lighting should be sufficient to see all areas. There should not be dark places to hide. Reference: *Physical Security Assessment for the Department of Veterans Affairs Facilities*
8.3	**How are the electrical rooms secured and where are they located relative to other higher-risk areas, starting with the main electrical distribution room at the service entrance?**	Critical electrical rooms and distribution points should be protected. Reference: *Physical Security Assessment for the Department of Veterans Affairs Facilities*
8.4	**Are critical electrical systems colocated with other building systems?** **Are critical electrical systems located in areas outside of secured electrical areas?** **Is security system wiring located separately from electrical and other service systems?**	Colocation concerns include rooms, ceilings, raceways, conduits, panels, and risers. Reference: *Physical Security Assessment for the Department of Veterans Affairs Facilities*
8.5	**How are electrical distribution panels serving branch-circuit security?** **Are they in secure locations?**	Should avoid electrical distribution panels in unsecure locations. Reference: *Physical Security Assessment for the Department of Veterans Affairs Facilities*
8.6	**Does emergency backup power exist for all areas within the building or for critical areas only?** **How is the emergency power distributed?**	There should be no single critical node that allows both the normal electrical service and the emergency backup power to be affected by a single incident. Automatic transfer switches

TABLE A.2 *Continued*

Section	Vulnerability Question	Guidance
	Is the emergency power system independent from the normal electrical service, particularly in critical areas?	and interconnecting switchgear are the initial concerns. Emergency and normal electrical equipment should be installed separately, at different locations, and as far apart as possible. Reference: *GSA PBS-P100*
8.7	**How is the primary electrical system wiring distributed?** **Is it colocated with other major utilities?** **Is there redundancy of distribution to critical areas?**	Central utility shafts may be subject to damage, especially if there is only one for the building. Reference: *Physical Security Assessment for the Department of Veterans Affairs Facilities*
9	**Fire Alarm Systems**	
9.1	**Is the building fire alarm system centralized or localized?** **How are alarms made known both locally and centrally?** **Are critical documents and control systems located in a secure, yet accessible, location?**	Fire alarm systems must first warn building occupants to evacuate for life safety. Then they must inform the responding agency to dispatch fire equipment and personnel. Reference: *Physical Security Assessment for the Department of Veterans Affairs Facilities*
9.2	**Where are the fire alarm panels located?** **Can unauthorized personnel access them?**	Should avoid locating fire alarm control panels in unsecure locations. Reference: *Physical Security Assessment for the Department of Veterans Affairs Facilities*
9.3	**Is the fire alarm system stand-alone or integrated with other functions, such as security and environmental or building management systems?** **What is the interface?**	Concern for single points of failure. If combined systems are used, more protection and higher reliability may be warranted. Reference: *Physical Security Assessment for the Department of Veterans Affairs Facilities*
9.4	**Do key fire alarm system components have fire- and blast-resistant separation?**	This is especially necessary for the fire command center or fire alarm control center. The concern is to similarly protect critical components as described in Sections 2.19, 5.7, and 10.3 of this table.

(continues)

TABLE A.2 *Continued*

Section	Vulnerability Question	Guidance
9.5	Is there redundant off-premises fire alarm reporting?	Fire alarms can ring at a fire station, at an intermediary alarm monitoring center, or autodial someone else. See Sections 5.21 and 10.5 of this table.
10	**Communications and IT Systems**	
10.1	Where is the main telephone distribution room and where is it in relation to higher-risk areas? Is the main telephone distribution room secure?	One can expect to find voice, data, signal, and alarm systems to be routed through the main telephone distribution room. Reference: *FEMA 386-7*
10.2	Does the telephone system have an uninterruptible power supply (UPS)? What is its type, power rating, and operational duration under load, and location? (battery, on-line, filtered)	Many telephone systems are now computerized and need a UPS to ensure reliability during power fluctuations. The UPS is also needed to await any emergency power coming on line or allow orderly shutdown. Reference: *DOC CIAO Vulnerability Assessment Frame 1.1*
10.3	Where are communications system wiring closets located? (voice, data, signal, alarm) Are they colocated with other utilities? Are they in secure areas?	Wiring closets should be distanced from other utilities and higher-risk areas to avoid collateral damage. Security approaches on the closets include door alarms, CCTV, swipe cards, or other logging notifications to ensure that only authorized personnel have access to these closets. Reference: *FEMA 386-7*
10.4	How is the communications system wiring distributed? (secure chases and risers, accessible public areas)	The intent is to prevent tampering with the systems. Reference: *Physical Security Assessment for the Department of Veterans Affairs Facilities*
10.5	Are redundant communications systems available?	Critical areas should be supplied with multiple or redundant means of communication. Power-outage phones can provide redundancy because they connect directly with the local commercial telephone switch-off site

TABLE A.2 *Continued*

Section	Vulnerability Question	Guidance
		and not through the building telephone switch in the main telephone distribution room.
		A base radio communication system with antenna can be installed in stairwells, and portable sets distributed to floors.
		References: *GSA PBS-P100 and FEMA 386-7*
10.6	**Where are the main distribution facilities, data centers, routers, firewalls, and servers located? Are they secure?** **Where are the secondary and/or intermediate distribution facilities? Are they secure?**	Concern is collateral damage from manmade hazards and redundancy of critical functions. Reference: *DOC CIAO Vulnerability Assessment Framework 1.1*
10.7	**What type and where are the wide area network (WAN) connections?**	Critical facilities should have two minimum-points-of-presence (MPOPs) where the telephone company's outside cable terminates inside the building. It is functionally a service-entrance connection that demarcates where the telephone company's property stops and the building owner's property begins. MPOPs should not be collocated, and they should connect to different telephone company central offices so that the loss of one cable or central office does not reduce capability. Reference: *Physical Security Assessment for the Department of Veterans Affairs Facilities*
10.8	**What are the type, power rating, and location of the uninterruptible power supply?** (battery, online, filtered) **Are the UPSs also connected to emergency power?**	UPSs should be located at all computerized points from the main distribution facility to individual data closets and at critical personal computers/terminals. Critical LAN sections should also be on backup power. Reference: *DOC CIAO Vulnerability Assessment Framework 1.1*

(continues)

TABLE A.2 *Continued*

Section	Vulnerability Question	Guidance
10.9	**What type of local area network (LAN) cabling and physical topology is being used?** (Category 5, Gigabit Ethernet, Ethernet, Token Ring)	The physical topology of a network is the way in which the cables and computers are connected to each other. The main types of physical topologies are bus, star, and ring.
		Bus: Single radial where any damage on the bus affects the whole system, especially all portions downstream.
		Star: Several computers are connected to a hub, and many hubs can be in the network. The hubs may be critical nodes but the other hubs continue to function if one fails.
		Ring: A bus with a continuous connection. This is the least often used. It can tolerate some damage because if the ring fails at a single point it can be rerouted, much like a looped electrical or water system.
		The configuration and the availability of surplus cable or spare capacity on individual cables can reduce vulnerability to hazard incidents.
		Reference: *Physical Security Assessment for the Department of Veterans Affairs Facilities*
10.10	**For installed radio/wireless systems, what are their types and where are they located?** [radio frequency (RF), high frequency (HF), very high frequency (VHF), medium wave (MW)]	Depending on the function of the wireless system, it could be susceptible to accidental or intended jamming or collateral damage.
		Reference: *Physical Security Assessment for the Department of Veterans Affairs Facilities*
10.11	**Do IT systems meet requirements of confidentiality, integrity, and availability?**	Ensure access to terminals and equipment for authorized personnel only and ensure system up-time to meet operational needs.
		Reference: *DOC CIAO Vulnerability Assessment Framework 1.1*

TABLE A.2 *Continued*

Section	Vulnerability Question	Guidance
10.12	**Where is the disaster recovery or mirroring site?**	A site with suitable equipment that allows continuation of operations or that mirrors (operates in parallel to) the existing operation is beneficial if equipment is lost during a natural or manmade disaster. The need is based on the criticality of the operation and how quickly replacement equipment can be put in place and made operational. Reference: *DOC CIAO Vulnerability Assessment Framework 1.1*
10.13	**Where is the backup tape/file storage site?** **What is the type of safe environment?** (safe, vault, underground) **Is there redundant refrigeration in the site?**	If equipment is lost, data are most likely lost, too. Backups are needed to continue operations at the disaster recovery site or when equipment can be delivered and installed. Reference: *DOC CIAO Vulnerability Assessment Framework 1.1*
10.14	**Are there any satellite communications (SATCOM) links?** (location, power, UPS, emergency power, spare capacity/capability)	SATCOM links can serve as redundant communications for voice and data if configured to support required capability after a hazard incident. Reference: *DOC CIAO Vulnerability Assessment Framework 1.1*
10.15	**Is there a mass-notification system that reaches all building occupants?** (public address, pager, cell phone, computer override, etc.) **Will one or more of these systems be operational under hazard conditions?** (UPS, emergency power)	Depending on the building's size, a mass-notification system will provide warning and alert information, along with actions to take before and after an incident if there is redundancy and power. Reference: *DoD UFC 4-010-01*
10.16	**Do control centers and their designated alternate locations have equivalent or reduced capability for voice, data, mass notification, etc.?** (emergency operations, security, fire alarms, building automation) **Do the alternate locations also have access to backup systems, including emergency power?**	Alternate control center locations should be able to operate in emergencies with critical functions provided. Reference: *GSA PBS-P100*

(continues)

TABLE A.2 *Continued*

Section	Vulnerability Question	Guidance
11	**Equipment Operations and Maintenance**	
11.1	**Are there composite drawings indicating location and capacities of major systems? Are they current?** (electrical, mechanical, and fire protection systems and date of last update) **Do updated operations and maintenance (O&M) manuals exist?**	The current configuration and capacity of all critical systems must be understood to ensure they meet emergency needs. Manuals must also be current to ensure operations and maintenance keeps these systems functioning properly. The system must function during an emergency unless directly affected by the hazard incident. Reference: *Physical Security Assessment for the Department of Veterans Affairs Facilities*
11.2	**Have critical air systems been rebalanced?** **If so, when and how often?**	Although the system may function, it must be tested periodically to ensure it is performing as designed. Balancing is also critical after initial construction to set equipment to proper performance per the design. Rebalancing may only occur during renovation. Reference: *CDC/NIOSH Pub 2002-139*
11.3	**Is air pressurization monitored regularly?**	Some areas require positive or negative pressure to function properly. Pressurization is critical in a hazardous environment or emergency situation. Measuring pressure drop across filters is an indication that filters should be changed; it may also indicate that low pressures are developing downstream, which could result in loss of expected protection. Reference: *CDC/NIOSH Pub 2002-139*
11.4	**Does the building have a policy or procedure for periodic recommissioning of major mechanical/electrical/plumbing (M/E/P) systems?**	Recommissioning involves testing and balancing of systems to ascertain their capability to perform as described. Reference: *Physical Security Assessment for the Department of Veterans Affairs Facilities*

TABLE A.2 *Continued*

Section	Vulnerability Question	Guidance
11.5	**Is there an adequate O&M program, including training of facilities management staff?**	If O&M of critical systems is done with in-house personnel, management must know what needs to be done and the workforce must have the necessary training to ensure systems reliability. Reference: *CDC/NIOSH Pub 2002-139*
11.6	**What maintenance and service agreements exist for M/E/P systems?**	When an in-house facility maintenance workforce does not exist or does not have the capability to perform the work, maintenance and service contracts are the alternative to ensure critical systems will work under all conditions. The facility management staff requires the same knowledge to oversee these contracts as if the work was being done by in-house personnel. Reference: *Physical Security Assessment for the Department of Veterans Affairs Facilities*
11.7	**Are backup power systems periodically tested under load?**	Loading should be at or above the maximum connected load to ensure available capacity, and automatic sensors should be tested at least once per year. Periodically (once a year at a minimum) check the duration of capacity of backup systems by running them for the expected emergency duration or estimating operational duration through fuel consumption, water consumption, or voltage loss. Reference: *FEMA 386-7*
11.8	**Is stairway and exit sign lighting operational?**	The maintenance program for stairway and exit sign lighting (all egress lighting) should ensure that all lights function under normal and emergency power conditions. Expect building codes to be updated as emergency egress lighting is moved from upper walls and over doorways to floor level as heat and smoke drive

(continues)

TABLE A.2 *Continued*

Section	Vulnerability Question	Guidance
		occupants to crawl along the floor to get out of the building. Signs and lights mounted high have limited or no benefit when obscured.
		Reference: *FEMA 386-7*
12	**Security Systems**	
	Perimeter Systems	
12.1	**Are black/white or color CCTV cameras used?** **Are they monitored and recorded 24 hours per day, 7 days per week? By whom?** **Are they analog or digital by design?** **What are the number of fixed, wireless, and pan-tilt-zoom cameras used?** **Who are the manufacturers of the CCTV cameras?** **What is the age of the CCTV cameras in use?**	Security technology is frequently considered to complement or supplement security personnel forces and to provide a wider area of coverage. Typically, these physical security elements provide the first line of defense in deterring, detecting, and responding to threats and reducing vulnerabilities. They must be viewed as an integral component of the overall security program. Their design, engineering, installation, operation, and management must be able to meet daily security challenges from a cost-effective and efficiency perspective. During and after an incident, the system, or its backups, should be functional per the planned design. Consider color CCTV cameras to view and record activity at the perimeter of the building, particularly at primary entrances and exits. A mix of monochrome cameras should be considered for areas that lack adequate illumination for color cameras. Reference: *GSA PBS-P100*
12.2	**Are the cameras programmed to respond automatically to perimeter building alarm events?** **Do they have built-in video motion capabilities?**	The efficiency of monitoring multiple screens decreases as the number of screens increases. Tying the alarm system or motion sensors to a CCTV camera and a monitoring screen improves the man–machine interface by drawing attention to a specific

TABLE A.2 *Continued*

Section	Vulnerability Question	Guidance
		screen and its associated camera. Adjustment may be required after installation due to initial false alarms, usually caused by wind or small animals.
		Reference: *Physical Security Assessment for the Department of Veterans Affairs Facilities*
12.3	**What type of camera housings are used and are they designed to protect against exposure to heat and cold weather elements?**	Cameras should be appropriate to the environment.
		Reference: *Physical Security Assessment for the Department of Veterans Affairs Facilities*
12.4	**Are panic/duress alarm buttons or sensors used?** **Where are they located?** **Are they hardwired or portable?**	Call buttons should be provided at key public contact areas and as needed in offices of managers and directors, in garages and parking lots, and other high-risk locations by assessment.
		Reference: *GSA PBS-P100*
12.5	**Are intercom call boxes used in parking areas or along the building perimeter?**	See Section 12.4 of this table.
12.6	**What is the transmission media used to transmit camera video signals** (fiber, wire line, telephone wire, coaxial, wireless)	The mode of communication may have an impact on reliability.
		Reference: *Physical Security Assessment for the Department of Veterans Affairs Facilities*
12.7	**Who monitors the CCTV system?**	Reference: *DOC CIAO Vulnerability Assessment Framework 1.1*
12.8	**What is the quality of video images both during the day and during hours of darkness?** **Are infrared camera illuminators used?**	Sufficient lighting should be provided in monitored areas to enable viewing of the image.
		Reference: *Physical Security Assessment for the Department of Veterans Affairs Facilities*
12.9	**Are the perimeter cameras supported by UPS, battery, or building emergency power?**	Camera systems with emergency power provide greater protection.
		Reference: *Physical Security Assessment for the Department of Veterans Affairs Facilities*

(continues)

TABLE A.2   *Continued*

Section	Vulnerability Question	Guidance
12.10	**What type of exterior Intrusion Detection System (IDS) sensors are used?** [electromagnetic; fiber-optic; active infrared; bistatic microwave; seismic; photoelectric; ground; fence; glass break (vibration/shock); single, double, and roll-up door magnetic contacts or switches]	Consider balanced magnetic contact switch sets for all exterior doors, including overhead/roll-up doors, and review roof-intrusion detection. Consider glass-break sensors for windows up to scalable heights. Reference: *GSA PBS-P100*
12.11	**Is a global positioning system (GPS) used to monitor vehicles and asset movements?**	Reference: *Physical Security Assessment for the Department of Veterans Affairs Facilities*
	Interior Security	
12.12	**Are black/white or color CCTV cameras used?** **Are they monitored and recorded 24 hours per day, 7 days per week? By whom?** **Are they analog or digital by design?** **What are the number of fixed, wireless, and pan-tilt-zoom cameras used?** **Who are the manufacturers of the CCTV cameras?** **What is the age of the CCTV cameras in use?**	See Section 12.1 of this table. Reference: *Physical Security Assessment for the Department of Veterans Affairs Facilities*
12.13	**Are the cameras programmed to respond automatically to interior building alarm events?** **Do they have built-in video motion capabilities?**	The efficiency of monitoring multiple screens decreases as the number of screens increases. Tying the alarm system or motion sensors to a CCTV camera and a monitoring screen improves the man–machine interface by drawing attention to a specific screen and its associated camera. Reference: *Physical Security Assessment for the Department of Veterans Affairs Facilities*

TABLE A.2 *Continued*

Section	Vulnerability Question	Guidance
12.14	**What type of camera housings are used and are they designed to protect against exposure or tampering?**	Reference: *Physical Security Assessment for the Department of Veterans Affairs Facilities*
12.15	**Do the camera lenses used have the proper specifications, especially distance viewing and clarity?**	Reference: *Physical Security Assessment for the Department of Veterans Affairs Facilities*
12.16	**What is the transmission media used to transmit camera video signals?** (fiber, wire line, telephone wire, coaxial, wireless)	Reference: *Physical Security Assessment for the Department of Veterans Affairs Facilities*
12.17	**Are the interior camera video images of good visual and recording quality?**	Reference: *Physical Security Assessment for the Department of Veterans Affairs Facilities*
12.18	**Are the interior cameras supported by UPS, battery, or building emergency power?**	Reference: *Physical Security Assessment for the Department of Veterans Affairs Facilities*
12.19	**What are the first costs and maintenance costs associated with the interior cameras?**	Reference: *Physical Security Assessment for the Department of Veterans Affairs Facilities*
12.20	**What type of access control system is used?** **Are the devices used for physical security also used (integrated) with security computer networks (e.g., in place of or in combination with user ID and system passwords)?**	Reference: *Physical Security Assessment for the Department of Veterans Affairs Facilities*
12.21	**What type of access control transmission media is used to transmit access control system signals (same as defined for CCTV cameras)?**	Reference: *Physical Security Assessment for the Department of Veterans Affairs Facilities*
12.22	**What is the backup power supply source for the access control systems?** (battery, UPS)	Reference: *Physical Security Assessment for the Department of Veterans Affairs Facilities*

(continues)

TABLE A.2 *Continued*

Section	Vulnerability Question	Guidance
12.23	What access control system equipment is used? How old are the systems and what are the related first and maintenance service costs?	Reference: *Physical Security Assessment for the Department of Veterans Affairs Facilities*
12.24	Are panic/duress alarm sensors used? Where are they located? Are they hardwired or portable?	Call buttons should be provided at key public contact areas and as needed in offices of managers and directors, in garages and parking lots, and other high-risk locations by assessment. Reference: *GSA PBS-P100*
12.25	Are intercom call boxes or a building intercom system used throughout the building?	See Section 12.24 of this table.
12.26	Are magnetometers (metal detectors) and x-ray equipment used? At what locations within the building?	Reference: *DOC CIAO Vulnerability Assessment Framework 1.1*
12.27	What type of interior IDS sensors are used? [electromagnetic; fiber optic; active infrared-motion detector; photoelectric; glass break (vibration/shock); single, double, and roll-up door magnetic contacts or switches]	Consider magnetic reed switches for interior doors and openings. Reference: *GSA PBS-P100*
12.28	Are mechanical, electrical, gas, power supply, radiological material storage, voice/data telecommunication system nodes, security system panels, elevator and critical system panels, and other sensitive rooms locked continuously, under electronic security, CCTV camera, and intrusion alarm systems surveillance?	Reference: *DOC CIOA Vulnerability Assessment Framework 1.1*

TABLE A.2 *Continued*

Section	Vulnerability Question	Guidance
12.29	**What types of locking hardware are used throughout the building? Are manual and electromagnetic cipher, keypad, pushbutton, panic bar, door strikes, and related hardware and software used?**	At a minimum, electric utility closets, mechanical rooms, and telephone closets should be secured. The mailroom should also be secured, allowing only authorized personnel into the area where mail is screened and sorted. Separate the public access area from the screening area for the postulated mailroom threats. All security locking arrangements on doors used for egress must comply with *NFPA 101, Life Safety Code.* Reference: *GSA PBS-P100*
12.30	**Are any potentially hazardous chemicals, combustible, or toxic materials stored on site in nonsecure and nonmonitored areas?**	The storage, use, and handling locations should also be kept away from other activities. The concern is that an intruder need not bring the material into the building if it is already there and accessible. Reference: *Physical Security Assessment for the Department of Veterans Affairs Facilities*
12.31	**What security controls are in place to handle the processing of mail and protect against potential biological, explosive, or other threatening exposures?**	Reference: *Physical Security Assessment for the Department of Veterans Affairs Facilities*
12.32	**Is there a designated security control room and console in place to monitor security, fire alarm, and other building systems? Has a backup control center been designated and equipped? Is there off-site 24-hour monitoring of intrusion detection systems?**	Monitoring can be done at an off-site facility, at an on-site monitoring center during normal duty hours, or at a 24-hour on-site monitoring center. Reference: *GSA PBS-P100*

(continues)

TABLE A.2   *Continued*

Section	Vulnerability Question	Guidance
12.33	**Is the security console and control room adequate in size and does it provide room for expansion?** **Does it have adequate environment controls?** (a/c, lighting, heating, air circulation, backup power) **Is it ergonomically designed?**	Reference: *Physical Security Assessment for the Department of Veterans Affairs Facilities*
12.34	**Is the location of the security room in a secure area with limited, controlled, and restricted access controls in place?**	Reference: *Physical Security Assessment for the Department of Veterans Affairs Facilities*
12.35	**What are the means by which facility and security personnel can communicate with one another?** (portable radio, pager, cell phone, personal data assistants) **What problems have been experienced with these and other electronic security systems?**	Reference: *Physical Security Assessment for the Department of Veterans Affairs Facilities*
12.36	**Is there a computerized security incident reporting system used to prepare reports and track security incident trends and patterns?**	Reference: *Physical Security Assessment for the Department of Veterans Affairs Facilities*
12.37	**Does the current security force have access to a computerized guard tour system?**	This system allows for the systematic performance of guard patrols with validation indicators built in. The system notes stations/locations checked or missed, dates and times of such patrols, and who conducted them on what shifts. Management reports can be produced for recordkeeping and manpower analysis purposes. Reference: *Physical Security Assessment for the Department of Veterans Affairs Facilities*
12.38	**Are vaults or safes in the building?** **Where are they located?**	Basic structural design requires an understanding of where heavy concentrations of floor loading may occur so as to strengthen the floor and

TABLE A.2 *Continued*

Section	Vulnerability Question	Guidance
		structural framing to handle this downward load. Security design also needs this information to analyze how this concentrated load affects upward and downward loadings under blast conditions and its impact upon progressive collapse. Location is important because safes can be moved by blast. They should be located away from people and away from exterior windows.
		Vaults, on the other hand, require construction above the building requirements with thick masonry walls and steel reinforcement. A vault can provide protection in many instances due to its robust construction.
		Safes and vaults may also require security sensors and equipment, depending upon the level of protection and defensive layers needed.
		Reference: *U.S. Army TM 5-85*
	Security System Documents	
12.39	**Have security system as-built drawings been generated and are they ready for review?**	Drawings are critical to the consideration and operation of security technologies, including the overall design and engineering processes. These historical reference documents outline system specifications and layout security devices used, as well as their application, location, and connectivity. They are a critical resource tool for troubleshooting system problems, and replacing and adding other security system hardware and software products.
		Reference: *Physical Security Assessment for the Department of Veterans Affairs Facilities*
12.40	**Have security system design and drawing standards been developed?**	Reference: *Physical Security Assessment for the Department of Veterans Affairs Facilities*

(continues)

TABLE A.2 *Continued*

Section	Vulnerability Question	Guidance
12.41	Are security equipment selection criteria defined?	Reference: *Physical Security Assessment for the Department of Veterans Affairs Facilities*
12.42	What contingency plans have been developed or are in place to deal with security control center redundancy and backup operations?	Reference: *Physical Security Assessment for the Department of Veterans Affairs Facilities*
12.43	Have security system construction specification documents been prepared and standardized?	Reference: *Physical Security Assessment for the Department of Veterans Affairs Facilities*
12.44	Do all security system documents include current as-built drawings?	Reference: *Physical Security Assessment for the Department of Veterans Affairs Facilities*
12.45	Have qualifications been determined for security consultants, system designers/engineers, installation vendors, and contractors?	Reference: *Physical Security Assessment for the Department of Veterans Affairs Facilities*
12.46	Are security systems decentralized, centralized, or integrated? Do they operate over an existing IT network or are they a stand-alone method of operation?	Reference: *Physical Security Assessment for the Department of Veterans Affairs Facilities*
12.47	What security systems manuals are available?	Reference: *Physical Security Assessment for the Department of Veterans Affairs Facilities*
12.48	What maintenance or service agreements exist for security systems?	Reference: *Physical Security Assessment for the Department of Veterans Affairs Facilities*
13	**Security Master Plan**	
13.1	Does a written security plan exist for this site or building? When was the initial security plan written and last revised? Who is responsible for preparing and reviewing the security plan?	The development and implementation of a security master plan provides a roadmap that outlines the strategic direction and vision, goals, and objectives and operational, managerial, and technological mission of the organization's security program. Reference: *DOC CIAO Vulnerability Assessment Framework 1.1*

TABLE A.2 *Continued*

Section	Vulnerability Question	Guidance
13.2	Has the security plan been communicated and disseminated to key management personnel and departments?	The security plan should be part of the building design so that the construction or renovation of the structure integrates with the security procedures to be used during daily operations. Reference: *Physical Security Assessment for the Department of Veterans Affairs Facilities*
13.3	Has the security plan been benchmarked or compared against related organizations and operational entities?	Reference: *Physical Security Assessment for the Department of Veterans Affairs Facilities*
13.4	Has the security plan ever been tested and evaluated from a benefit/cost and operational efficiency and effectiveness perspective?	Reference: *Physical Security Assessment for the Department of Veterans Affairs Facilities*
13.5	Does the security plan define mission, vision, and short- and long-term security program goals and objectives?	Reference: *Physical Security Assessment for the Department of Veterans Affairs Facilities*
13.6	Are threats/hazards, vulnerabilities, and risks adequately defined and security countermeasures addressed and prioritized relevant to their criticality and probability of occurrence?	Reference: *DOC CIAO Vulnerability Assessment Framework 1.1*
13.7	Has a security implementation schedule been established to address recommended security solutions?	Reference: *Physical Security Assessment for the Department of Veterans Affairs Facilities*
13.8	Have security operating and capital budgets been addressed, approved, and established to support the plan?	Reference: *Physical Security Assessment for the Department of Veterans Affairs Facilities*
13.9	What regulatory or industry guidelines/standards were followed in the preparation of the security plan?	Reference: *Physical Security Assessment for the Department of Veterans Affairs Facilities*

(continues)

TABLE A.2 *Continued*

Section	Vulnerability Question	Guidance
13.10	Does the security plan address existing security conditions from an administrative, operational, managerial, and technical security systems perspective?	Reference: *Physical Security Assessment for the Department of Veterans Affairs Facilities*
13.11	Does the security plan address the protection of people, property, assets, and information?	Reference: *Physical Security Assessment for the Department of Veterans Affairs Facilities*
13.12	Does the security plan address the following major components: access control, surveillance, response, building hardening, and protection against CBR and cyber-network attacks?	Reference: *Physical Security Assessment for the Department of Veterans Affairs Facilities*
13.13	Has the level of risk been identified and communicated in the security plan through the performance of a physical security assessment?	Reference: *Physical Security Assessment for the Department of Veterans Affairs Facilities*
13.14	When was the last security assessment performed? Who performed the security risk assessment?	Reference: *DOC CIAO Vulnerability Assessment Framework 1.1*
13.15	Are the following areas of security analysis addressed in the security master plan? Asset analysis: Does the security plan identify and prioritize the assets to be protected in accordance to their location, control, current value, and replacement value? Threat analysis: Does the security plan address potential threats; causes of potential harm in the form of death, injury, destruction, disclosure, interruption of operations, or denial of services? [possible criminal acts (documented	This process is the input to the building design and what mitigation measures will be included in the facility project to reduce risk and increase safety of the building and people. Reference. *USA TM 5-853, Security Engineering*

TABLE A.2 *Continued*

Section	Vulnerability Question	Guidance
	and review of police/security incident reports) associated with forced entry, bombs, ballistic assault, biochemical and related terrorist tactics, attacks against utility systems infrastructure and buildings]	
	Vulnerability analysis: Does the security plan address other areas associated with the site or building and its operations that can be taken advantage of to carry out a threat?	
	Risk analysis: Does the security plan address the findings from the asset, threat/hazard, and vulnerability analyses in order to develop, recommend, and consider implementation of appropriate security countermeasures?	

Reference: FEMA, 2003. *Reference Manual to Mitigate Potential Terrorist Attacks Against Buildings,* Publication 426, Federal Emergency Mangement Agency, Washington DC, pp. 1-46–1-93.

Sources: CDC/NIOSH, 2002. *Guidance for Protecting Building Environments from Airborne Chemical, Biological, or Radiological Attack,* Publication 2002-139, Centers for Disease Control and Prevention/National Institute for Occupational Safety and Health (CDC/NIOSH), Atlanta, GA; DoD, 2002. *DoD Minimum Antiterrorism Standards for Buildings,* Unified Facilities Criteria (UFC), UFC 4-010-01, U.S. Department of Defense, Washington, DC; DOJ, 2000. *Fiscal Year 1999 State Domestic Preparedness Equipment Program, Assessment and Strategy Development Tool Kit,* National Criminal Justice (NCJ) NCK181200, U.S. Department of Justice, Washington, DC; FEMA, 1988. *Rapid Visual Screening of Buildings for Seismic Hazards: A Handbook,* FEMA 154, (also, Applied Technology Council (ATC-21) by same name), Federal Emergency Management Agency, Washington, DC; FEMA, 2002. *Integrating Human-Caused Hazards Into Mitigation Planning,* FEMA 386-7, Federal Emergency Management Agency, Washington, DC; FEMA, 2001, SLG 101, *Guide for All-Hazard Emergency Operations Planning,* Chapter 6, Attachment G, Terrorism, Federal Emergency Management Agency, Washington, DC; GSA, 2002. *Facilities Standards for Public Buildings Service,* PBS-P100, General Services Administration, Washington, DC; LBNL, 2003. *Protecting Buildings from a Biological or Chemical Attack: Actions to Take Before or During a Release,* LBNL PUB-51959, Lawrence Berkeley National Laboratory, Berkeley, CA; USAF, 1997 *Installation Force Protection Guide,* U.S. Air Force; U.S. Army, 1994. *Security Engineering,* Technical Manual (TM) 5-853-1/-2/-3/-4; DOC CIAO, 1998. *Vulnerability Assessment Frame 1.1,* U.S. Department of Commerce, Critical Infrastructure Assurance Office, Washington, DC; VA, 2002. Physical Security Assessment for the Department of Veterans Affairs Facilities, *Recommendations of the National Institute of Building Sciences Task Group to the Department of Veterans Affairs,* U.S. Department of Veterans Affairs, Washington, DC.

Definitions

Active fire protection system   A system that takes direct action to limit the growth rate of a fire or control the movement of smoke and fire. Examples include automatic sprinklers or the use of fans to exhaust or control the movement of smoke.

Air-based HVAC system   A mechanical system that uses air to provide heating, cooling, and ventilation throughout a building. Air is often recirculated for energy saving reasons.

Arson   The crime of deliberately or recklessly initiating a fire or explosion.

Availability   The probability that a system will be ready to perform its mission or function under pre-defined conditions, when required to do so at a random time.

Biological weapon   The use of living organisms or the inanimate by-products of living organisms (toxins) as weapons.

Catenary   A form of resistance where all loads are carried in tension rather than by bending or shear.

Chain of command   A series of command, control, executive, or management positions in hierarchical order of authority.

Chemical warfare agent   A chemical substance, whether gaseous, liquid or solid, that might be employed because of its direct toxic effects on man, animals and plants. [13]

Combination fire and smoke damper   A device that meets both the fire damper and smoke damper requirements. [NFPA 90A]

Compartmentation   A form of passive fire protection that involves dividing buildings or spaces by using fire-rated separations to isolate compartments from the compartment of fire origin, and thus to limit the fire spread both horizontally and vertically.

Consequence analysis   Analysis that focuses on the extent of damage that may be expected for unmitigated design basis threat scenarios, with respect to protection targets, tolerable performance levels, tolerable loss levels, or other metrics agreed on for the TARA/TVA analysis.

Criticality   A key component of risk analysis that is based on the valuation of the stakeholder and the capacity of the building to perform adequately during the extreme event.

Delay time   The time it takes for an occupant to receive and understand evacuation cues and initiate the exiting process.

Design fire scenario   A set of conditions that defines or describes the critical factors for determining outcomes of trial designs. [11]

Design objective   An objective stated in engineering or design terms, which can be readily translated into quantifiable terms. Design objectives are often used to bridge the gap between stakeholder goals and design or performance criteria.

Design scenario   A limited set of likely, risk-significant event scenarios that can be used for the evaluation of a proposed design.

Deterministic fire model   A model based on specific physical situations that employs calculations based on physical laws or correlations developed from fire test data to predict fire outcomes. [1]

Detonation   Occurs when materials of the type often referred to as high explosives undergo an extremely rapid and violent chemical reaction. The rise to peak pressure in the surrounding air happens almost instantaneously with a subsequent rapid decay while the wave front advances away from the seat of the explosion at supersonic velocity.

Disproportionate damage   Damage that is more extensive than would generally be expected in consideration of the event that triggered it.

Ductility   The ability of an element or structure to deform without a significant loss in load carrying capacity.

Earthquake   An earthquake occurs when the strength of the rock forming the crust is exceeded by the accumulated strain energy, causing the rock to break. When the rock ruptures, it causes sudden ground motion and seismic waves are propagated in all directions.

Event scenario   A set of conditions that defines an initiating event and its subsequent impact throughout a building or part of a building.

Exit   That portion of a means of egress that is separated from all other areas of a building or structure by construction or equipment as required to provide a protected way of travel to the exit discharge. [NFPA *101*]

Exit access   Exit access is the portion of the means of egress that lead to an exit. This includes open stairwells, corridors, ramps and pathways from all areas within a building. [NFPA *101*]

Exit discharge   Exit discharges are the portion of a means of egress between the termination of an exit and a public way. [NFPA *101*]

Explosion   A chemical reaction or change of state effected in an exceedingly short period of time with the generation of a high temperature and generally a large quantity of gas. An explosion produces a shock wave in the surrounding medium. [10]

Extraordinary event   An unplanned event that could become an extreme event and have an extreme impact but does not because the systems, policies, and procedures work as designed and the event does not have an extreme impact on the organization or facility.

Failure analysis   A logical, systematic examination of an item, component, assembly, or structure and its place and function within a system conducted in order to identify and analyze the probability, causes, and consequences of potential and real failures. [NFPA 921]

Failure modes and effects analysis   A systematic method involving analysis of the possible failure modes of individual components and the resulting impact(s) of each failure, either on the system in general or on other components of the system. [11]

Fire cause   The circumstances, conditions, or agencies that bring together a fuel, ignition source, and oxidizer (such as air or oxygen) resulting in a fire or a combustion explosion. [NFPA 921]

Fire damper   A device, installed in an air distribution system, designed to close automatically upon detection of heat, to interrupt migratory airflow, and to restrict the passage of flame. [NFPA 90A]

Fire origin   The point or area where an ignition source and the first fuel ignited come together and a fire begins.

Flashover   The point at which the radiant energy in the hot gases in the upper portions of the compartment raises the temperature of unignited fuels, resulting in rapid transition from only one or two items burning to full room involvement. [6]

Fractional effective dose   The Fractional Effective Dose provides a method for accounting for the fact that in some cases exposures to lower doses over a long period of time may be as severe as a higher dose over a shorter exposure.

Fully-tempered glass (toughened glass)   Glass that has been thermally processed to increase its breaking strength. When it shatters under blast load it tends to form dice-shaped particles rather than the elongated razor-sharp shards that are produced when annealed glass breaks.

Game theory   The interaction between two or more persons with opposed or mixed views where the outcomes depend on the strategy of each person.

Heat release rate   The heat energy output of a burning material expressed as a function of time.

HEPA filter   A high efficiency particulate air (HEPA) filter that removes radioactive dust particles from the air. These filters are 99.97 percent efficient in capturing 0.3 micron diameter particles. They are composed of pleated glass microfiber paper supported by aluminum fins and housed in a cartridge.

Hot combustion products   Superheated combustion gases, such as carbon monoxide, carbon dioxide, and hydrogen cyanide, and particulate matter (smoke) that are evolved during a fire.

Improvised explosive device (IED)   Although generally composed of small amounts of military-grade explosive to act as a booster that initiates detonation in a larger mass of a more easily obtainable material, such as certain agricultural fertilizers, physical evidence from actual IEDs shows that when skillfully manufactured they can display all the devastating characteristics of high explosive.

Incendiary fire   A deliberately caused fire that comes about as the result of human action when the person or persons know the fire should not be ignited.

Incident command post   The field location at which the primary tactical-level, on-scene incident command functions are performed. [3]

Incident command system   The combination of facilities, equipment, personnel, procedures, and communications operating within a common organizational structure that has responsibility for the management of assigned resources to effectively accomplish stated objectives pertaining to an incident or training exercise. [NFPA 1670]

Incident commander   The individual in overall command of an emergency incident. [NFPA 1561]

Initiating devices   Devices, such as smoke and heat detectors, that activate suppression systems, close doors in passive systems such as fire walls, activate smoke management systems and activate notification appliances.

Intelligibility   How well a voice alarm signal is understood by occupants during an evacuation notification.

IT&T infrastructure   The rooms, routes, and risers required to house and interconnect information technology and telecommunications (IT&T) systems and the building services/systems required to support the IT&T systems.

Judgment Analysis   Type of analysis used to design a safety indicator for a given building or public space that is based on a consensus judgment of a group of technical experts.

Liquefaction   A physical phenomenon that occurs when water-saturated cohesionless soil deposits (sand and silts) experience shaking strong enough to densify the soil fabric. Soil liquefaction can lead to foundation failure, lateral ground movement, settlement and sand boils when specific materials behave like a viscous fluid.

Means of egress   A continuous and unobstructed way of travel from any point in a building or structure to a public way consisting of three separate and distinct parts: (1) the exit access, (2) the exit, and (3) the exit discharge. [NFPA *101*]

Mixed HVAC system   A mechanical system that uses pipes to distribute water to provide heating and/or cooling and uses air, usually much less than in all air systems, for fresh air ventilation only. In most mixed systems (e.g., fan coils) all the air is exhausted after use and there is no recirculation. Energy savings are achieved through the recirculation of water.

Natural disaster   A destructive event that includes gale force winds, sudden floods, releases of deadly chemicals, fire, ice, and even upheavals of the earth itself. [2]

Natural ventilation   This system involves vents that are either automatically or manually opened upon detection of a fire to allow the smoke to be vented from the building or compartment due to its natural buoyancy.

Objective   A statement used to provide more direction as to how a goal might be met, and normally stated in quantifiable terms.

Passive fire protection system   A fixed system, including fire-rated walls used to limit spread of fire and smoke once ignition has occurred.

Performance criteria   Quantified metrics stated in engineering terms against which the results of a performance analysis can be measured to show achievement (or lack thereof) of objectives or performance requirements.

Performance group   Buildings of various uses that have requirements for similar levels of importance can be grouped together into a performance group. [5, 8, 9]

Performance-based analysis and design   A process of engineering a solution to meet specific levels of performance, where performance may be stated in terms of qualitative or quantitative objectives, criteria, or limiting states of damage or injury. [7]

Performance-based fire safety design   An engineering approach to fire protection design based on (1) agreed upon fire safety goals, loss objectives, and design objectives; (2) deterministic and probabilistic evaluation of fire initiation, growth, and development; (3) the physical and chemical properties of fire and fire effluents; and (4) quantitative assessment of the effectiveness of design alternatives against loss objectives and performance objectives.

Physical access control measures   Security measures that prevent building access, ranging from "temporary" concrete barriers, to planters and street furniture, to permanent bollards, walls, and plinths.

Plug holing   The process of smoke exhaust fans drawing clear air from below the smoke layer. This reduces the effectiveness of the smoke removal system, and it can be avoided by limiting the exhaust air velocity.

Plume   The column of hot combustion products and particulates (smoke) produced by combustion that rises from a fire.

Possible extreme event scenario   An assessment of a projected event, which occurs when both the possible cause and the likely location of an extreme event are present at the same time and place.

Possible fire scenario   A set of conditions that defines the development of a fire and the spread of combustion products throughout a building or part of a building. [11]

Probabilistic fire model   A model that deals with the statistical likelihood of the occurrence of fire and fire outcomes, based on the random nature of fire and the likelihood of occurrence. [1]

Progressive collapse   The spreading of the collapse of one part of the structure to other parts that were initially not affected by the damage event.

Rapid response group   Personnel assigned to a group charged exclusively with response to incidents within the extreme event area involving rescue or assistance for injured responders or participants.

Response resources   The necessary support required to mitigate a possible event. This support comprises personnel for plan development, event response, and training; as well the equipment needed to facilitate control and coordination of the response.

Risk   Viewed quantitatively as the combination of three components: an unwanted event, the likelihood that the event will occur, and the potential consequences should the event occur.

Risk characterization   A process that brings together analytical data and stakeholder concerns in a way that allows agreement to be reached on levels of tolerable risk through deliberation. [8, 12]

Robustness   A fundamental concept in engineering design that implies a certain degree of reserve strength to deal with variations in loading that a building may see in its lifetime and which are not entirely predictable.

Shock wave   An intense compression wave produced by the detonation of an explosive. [10]

Smoke   The airborne solid and liquid particulates and gases evolved when a material undergoes pyrolysis or combustion, together with the quantity of air that is entrained or otherwise mixed into the mass. [NFPA 921]

Smoke damper   A device within an air distribution system to control the movement of smoke. [NFPA 90A]

Strain-rate effects   The changes in the functional characteristics of material under a load depending on the rate at which loads are applied (e.g. significant increases in strength and stiffness are commonly observed, as is a reduction in ductility).

Terrorism   The unlawful use of force and violence against persons or property to intimidate or coerce a government, the civilian population, or any segment thereof, in furtherance of political or social objectives. [4]

Tornado   A rapidly rotating funnel of air extending groundward from a cumulonimbus cloud that is typically spawned by a severe thunderstorm.

Toxin A poisonous substance produced and derived from a living plant, animal, or microorganism; some toxins may also be produced or altered by chemical means.

Tropical cyclone A low pressure area that originates over warm tropical waters and has winds circulating around a characteristic eye. Hurricanes, tropical storms, and typhoons are collectively known as tropical cyclones and affect many coastal areas worldwide, often with devastating effect.

Vulnerability assessment An assessment that focuses on two components: the ability of an aggressor to gain access to a facility in order to carry out an action and the response of the asset to the action. Some TARA/TVA approaches use vulnerability to mean only one of these factors, so care should be taken to understand what vulnerability means in the context of the approach used.

"What if?" analysis A simplified technique that involves hypothesizing, based on the available knowledge of the stakeholders and often through brainstorming amongst multiple stakeholders, about what will happen if a certain failure or event occurs. [11]

References Cited

1. Custer, R. L. P. and Meacham, B. J., 1997. *Introduction to Performance-Based Fire Safety*, Society of Fire Protection Engineers, Bethesda, MD.

2. FEMA. Disaster Fact Sheets and Backgrounders, www.fema.gov/library/factshts.shtm.

3. FEMA. National Incident Management Capability Assessment Support Tool, www.fema.gov/nimcast/Glossary.do.

4. GPO, 2003. Title 28, U.S. Code of Federal Regulations, Part 0.85, U.S. Government Printing Office, Washington, DC.

5. ICC, 2001. *ICC Performance Code for Buildings and Facilities*, International Code Council, Falls Church, VA.

6. Karlsson, B. and Quintiere, J. G., 2000. *Enclosure Fire Dynamics*, CRC Press, Boca Raton, FL.

7. Meacham, B. J., 1998. *Assessment of the Technological Requirements for the Realization of Performance-Based Fire Safety Design in the United States*, NIST-GCR-98-763, National Institute of Standards and Technology, Gaithersburg, MD.

8. Meacham, B. J., 2000. *A Process for Identifying, Characterizing and Incorporating Risk Concepts into Performance-Based Building and Fire*

Regulation Development, Ph.D. Dissertation, Clark University, Worcester, MA.

9. Meacham, B. J., 2004. "Risk Characterization and Performance Concepts," Chapter 4, *Performance-Based Building Design Concepts*, International Code Council, Falls Church, VA, pp. 4-1–4-34.

10. Meyer, R. et al., 1987. *Explosives*, 3rd edition, VCH, New York.

11. SFPE, 2000. *SFPE Engineering Guide to Performance-Based Fire Protection Analysis and Design of Buildings*, National Fire Protection Association, Quincy, MA.

12. Stern, P. C. and Fineburg, H. V. (Eds.), 1996. *Understanding Risk: Informing Decisions in a Democratic Society*, National Research Council, National Academy Press, Washington, DC.

13. U.N., 1969. *Chemical and Bacteriological Weapons, and the Effect of Their Possible Use*, United Nations, New York.

NFPA Codes, Standards, and Recommended Practices

NFPA Publications. The following is a list of NFPA codes, standards, and recommended practices cited in this chapter. See the latest version of the *NFPA Catalog* for availability of current editions of these documents.

NFPA *101®, Life Safety Code®*

NFPA 90A, *Standard for the Installation of Air-Conditioning and Ventilating Systems*

NFPA 921, *Guide for Fire and Explosion Investigations*

NFPA 1561, *Standard on Emergency Services Incident Management System*

NFPA 1670, *Standard on Operations and Training for Technical Search and Rescue Incidents*

Index

About the Authors

Fiona Cousins Fiona Cousins joined Arup in 1985 as a pre-university trainee. Following graduation from university, she spent one year in Arup Research and Development developing building analysis software. She has worked as a building mechanical consulting engineer in London, Berlin, Tanzania, San Francisco, and New York. Fiona has a broad range of design, analysis, and construction experience in corporate, high-rise, industrial, residential, commercial, and institutional buildings located both in the United States and abroad. Her major projects include corporate offices for Sun Microsystems and General Motors, gallery spaces for the High Museum in Atlanta and the Jack S. Blanton Museum at the University of Texas, and the renovation of the British Airways terminal at JFK International Airport. In addition, she has been active in the field of sustainable construction. Projects with a sustainable focus include the solar-heated California College of Arts and Crafts in San Francisco and master-planning work for Denver Union Station and the American University in Cairo. Fiona is currently a director of the United States Green Building Council New York Chapter. She has presented papers at a number of conferences, including EnvironDesign 2, 1998; Sustainable Steel 1998; Earth Day New York, 1998; Green Building Challenge 1998; EnvironDesign 6, 2002; Greenbuild 2002 and Greenbuild 2005. She has also contributed to a book on the design of spaces for worship. Fiona holds an M.A. in Engineering Science and an M.St. in Interdisciplinary Design for the Built Environment from Cambridge University, England.

Richard Custer Richard Custer is an Associate Principal with Arup in its Westborough, Massachusetts, office and is Technical Director for Arup Fire in the Americas. Richard has over 35 years of experience in fire research, small- and large-scale fire testing, development of international codes and standards, and undergraduate and graduate fire safety engineering education. A Fellow of the Society of Fire Protection Engineers (SFPE), Richard has served on the Steering Committee and the Task Group for SFPE's Design Guidelines for Performance-Based Fire Protection Engineering. He is the coauthor of the text *Introduction to Performance-Based Fire Safety,* published by SFPE and NFPA. He is also editor of *The SFPE Handbook of Fire Protection Engineering* section on design methods and coauthor of the chapter "Design of Detection Systems" in that handbook. He currently serves on the NFPA Committee for Fire Protection of Telecommunications Facilities, the *NFPA 5000® Building Construction and Safety Code* Technical Committee on Building Materials and the NFPA Committee on Hazard and Risk of Contents and Furnishings. Richard has also served as the Associate Director of the Center for Firesafety Studies at Worcester Polytechnic Institute in Massachusetts, Associate Director of the Center for Fire Research at the U.S. National Bureau of Standards (now NIST), and on the faculty of the Fire Protection Engineering Department at the University of Maryland.

Stanley Dawe   Stanley Dawe recently ended a 30-year career with the Fire Department of New York (FDNY), retiring with the rank of Assistant Chief. During his career with FDNY, Chief Dawe held operational assignments in all areas of the city. The majority of these assignments were in midtown Manhattan. His administrative assignments included service as Technical Editor of *WNYF,* the FDNY training magazine and as Chief in Charge of the Bureau of Health Services. He was instrumental in establishing the Certified First Responders Training Program during the merger of emergency medical services into FDNY and was Chief in Charge of CFR-D training during the inaugural class of over 800 fire fighters and company officers to be trained and certified as medical first responders. Chief Dawe's final assignment was as chief of the Bureau of Fire Prevention, during which time he also performed duty as Citywide Command Chief, having responsibility for all FDNY activity throughout the city. Chief Dawe has a B.A. from C.W. Post College of Long Island University and an M.A. from the State University of New York at Stony Brook.

J. David Hadden   David Hadden is an Associate Director with Arup in its London office and leads the blast-engineering team within Arup Security Consulting. He has extensive experience in appraising bomb-damaged buildings and advising building owners, occupiers and designers on blast-safety matters. Additionally, he has wide knowledge and experience of both the design and construction of building and civil engineering projects. While with Arup, he has worked on the design of some notable public and commercial sector buildings and has led the planning and implementation of improvements and modifications to a range of existing facilities. David has served on several committees, including the British Council for Offices Security Committee, the British Council for Offices Risk Management Working Party, and the Advisory Committee for Concrete Structures M.Sc. Course—Imperial College, London. David holds an M.A. in Engineering from Cambridge University, and an M.Sc. with Distinction in Concrete Structures from Imperial College, London. He has lectured on blast mitigation and security strategy in the United Kingdom, the United States, Europe, Asia, and Australasia to a wide range of clients, designers, and government representatives. He is a chartered member of the Institution of Civil Engineers and a Fellow of The Security Institute.

John Haddon   John Haddon is a Director of Arup in its London office and is the leader of Arup Security Consulting. He has practiced security engineering since his appointment as a graduate engineer at Arup in 1978. In 1995, he was responsible for setting up the specialist security team within Arup, pulling together a multidisciplinary team of specialists from throughout the organization. He has been responsible for the development of the business and technical services provided by that group, and in June 2001 it was renamed as Arup Security Consulting. He was appointed as a visiting professor at the Royal Military College of Science, Shrivenham, University of Cranfield in October 2003 and is a Fellow of the Security Institute. His main interests are in threat and risk assessment and security planning. He has been responsible for the development of a number of in-house and external design guides on the design of security and counterterrorist measures for new and refurbished buildings. He currently works with a number of U.K. Government agencies and other organizations on the preparation of a design guide on resilience against terrorist attack. He has been responsible for the technical delivery as well as the direction and management of a wide range of security projects in the United Kingdom and overseas. These projects have included transport infrastructure projects, including rail and air terminals and river crossings; retail developments; commercial and government offices; headquarters buildings; financial services buildings; data centers; theaters; galleries; industrial developments; hospitals; research facilities, including pharmaceutical research facilities; leisure facilities; and business and mixed-development estates.

David Jacoby   David Jacoby is an Associate with Arup in its New York City office. David has developed numerous performance-based fire-engineering analyses, including fire-modeling studies, fire scenario evaluations, timed egress analyses, smoke-filling studies, and hazard assessment. He has developed fire protection programs/fire strategies, fire protection/life safety surveys, fire alarm system designs, and conceptual smoke-control designs. His experience includes large mixed-use high-rise facilities, airports, arenas, convention centers, assembly facilities, casinos, residential facilities, hospitals, federal courthouses, and office buildings. David has been involved in these projects from initial feasibility studies or concept development to negotiating acceptance, developing designs, overseeing construction, and conducting final acceptance testing and commissioning of systems. He also has experience with laboratory testing and composite materials related to his master's thesis. He was a lab coordinator at Worcester Polytechnic Institute. He has been involved with various committees in the fire industry, including New York City Department of Buildings—New NYC Building Code Committees—Fire Protection Committee; New York City Fire Code Revision Project—Advisory Committee member; and is a principal member of the fundamentals Committee of NFPA *101®/NFPA 5000®*. David is actively involved in SFPE and has been president of the NYC Metro Chapter of SFPE. David holds a B.S. in Mechanical Engineering and an M.S. in Fire Protection Engineering from Worcester Polytechnic Institute.

Matthew Johann   Matt Johann is a Fire Specialist with Arup in its Westborough, Massachusetts, office. He has experience in a wide range of fire protection engineering analyses, including computational fluid dynamics, fire modeling, design of smoke-control systems, and life safety design. Matt's research and education have focused on the performance and analysis of structures under fire conditions. He has developed finite element analyses of fire-impacted structures and has carried out laboratory tests of fire effects on structural components. His laboratory experience also includes testing of fire-growth and flame-spread behavior. Matt is a certified fire and explosion investigator, with experience investigating and analyzing fires and blasts in a wide range of occupancies. Matt holds a B.S. in Civil Engineering and an M.S. in Fire Protection Engineering from Worcester Polytechnic Institute.

Tony Jones Tony Jones, Ph.D., is an Associate Director within Arup Research and Development. He specializes in structural concrete and provides design advice on projects throughout Arup. Tony sits on the U.K. committee responsible for the update of structural concrete codes of practice and was part of the European committee responsible for drafting *EC2*, the Eurocode for structural concrete. He has been involved with the investigation of a number of building failures, providing expert opinion on causes. He maintains strong links with researchers in his field and is currently involved with several research projects investigating the real behavior of buildings in service. Tony has published in a number of areas related to structural concrete. He was responsible for drafting the section on structural behavior in the recent Office of the Deputy Prime Minister Scoping Study to investigate the potential changes to the Building Regulations (England and Wales) following the events of September 11, 2001.

Ann Marie Kammerer Ann Kammerer is a Risk Consultant with Arup in its San Francisco office. She has a general background in geotechnical earthquake engineering and natural hazard risk assessment, with special expertise in probabilistic seismic hazard assessment, liquefaction triggering and deformation analyses, probable maximum loss studies, soil–structure interaction, laboratory testing of soils, modeling of soil behavior, and seismic slope stability assessments. Her recent hazard- and risk-based work has included probabilistic natural hazard assessments and liquefaction assessments for projects worldwide (Egypt, Indonesia, Japan, Philippine Islands, Turkey, the United Kingdom, and the United States). Past experiences include several major Northern California projects, including the seismic retrofit of the Oakland–San Francisco Bay Bridge, the seismic upgrade of the East Bay MUD aqueduct, and the expansion of San Francisco International Airport.

Gayle Katzman Gayle Katzman is a Senior Risk Consultant with Arup in its New York City office. Her focus is risk assessments for high-rise buildings and transportation infrastructure. Using analysis techniques such as Monte Carlo simulation, she performed research as a graduate student on the risks associated with the New York Citicorp Center under extreme wind forces. Gayle has worked on all aspects of analysis and design for buildings ranging from 5 to 65 stories, as well as large-scale cultural structures such as museums. Her experience extends to wind engineering for high rises and blast-protection design for federal structures. Gayle has performed a number of risk analyses and served as Risk Manager for the preliminary design phase of the Fulton Street Transit Center, a transportation hub in lower Manhattan. She was also a risk analyst for a comprehensive assessment of options for maintaining, rehabilitating, modifying, and/or replacing the Tappan Zee Bridge in New York. Gayle holds a B.S. in Civil Engineering from McGill University and an M.S. in Civil Engineering from Princeton University, and she is pursuing an M.B.A. at New York University. She is a Spencer Educational Fellow of the Risk and Insurance Management Society.

Stuart Knoop   Stuart L. Knoop is cofounder and president of Oudens and Knoop Architects, PC, of Chevy Chase, Maryland. He has been involved in design for security for 25 years, particularly for the U.S. State Department, Office of Overseas Buildings Operations. He has extensive experience designing security upgrades for more than 60 embassies and consulates worldwide and has provided physical security consultation to the National Institutes of Health, the Walter Reed Army Medical Center, the General Services Administration, the U.S. Marshals Service, and the Department of Veterans Affairs. Stuart has served on National Research Council (NRC) committees for the security of future U.S. embassy buildings, on protecting buildings from bomb damage, and for oversight and assessment of blast effects and related research. Stuart participated in drafting the Interagency Security Criteria (ISC) and their subsequent revisions. He chaired the NRC committee to review the ISC Criteria, and compiled the first edition of the State Department's A/E Design Guidelines. He is the author of various articles on security and the introduction to *Security Planning and Design—A Guide for Architects and Building Design Professionals*, published by the American Institute of Architects and John Wiley & Sons. Stuart is a registered architect, a Fellow of the American Institute of Architects, and a member of the American Society for Industrial Security and the Construction Specifications Institute. He holds a B.Arch. from Carnegie Mellon University and was a Fulbright Scholar.

Richard G. Little   Richard Little is Director of the Keston Infrastructure Institute at the University of Southern California. Prior to this appointment, Richard served as Director of the Board on Infrastructure and the Constructed Environment of the National Research Council (NRC), where he developed and directed a program of studies in building and infrastructure research. He has directed NRC study activities, participated in workshops and panels, and written several papers dealing with choicemaking for physical security and critical-infrastructure protection. He served as the Study Director for the 1995 NRC report, "Protecting Buildings from Bomb Damage," and the 2001 report, "Protecting People and Buildings from Terrorism: Technology Transfer for Blast-effects Mitigation." Richard has over 30 years of experience in planning, management, and policy development relating to public facilities. He is a member of the American Institute of Certified Planners, the American Planning Association, and the Society for Risk Analysis. Richard holds a B.S. in Geology and an M.S. in Urban-Environmental Studies, from Rensselaer Polytechnic Institute.

Al Lyons Al Lyons is a Principal in the New York City office of Arup, where he leads the Information Communications Technology Consulting Team and is responsible for maintaining high-quality standards on all projects. Specific responsibilities include project management; design; engineering and integration of electronic systems, including voice and data communications; audio evacuation; environmental control; energy management; facilities (building and plant) management; and audiovisual systems. Al is recognized as a leader in incorporating technology into the built environment. He has lectured on and written articles about creating built environments with the infrastructure needed to support current, emerging, and future technologies and the flexibility needed to support emerging alternative operational and management strategies. Al has a successful track record for helping clients develop and upgrade facilities and create procurement strategies that enable them to standardize on particular systems/vendors without exposing them to predatory pricing practices. He has helped several clients develop the policies and procedures needed to capitalize on the benefits of new and emerging technologies and develop business plans to generate revenue from these systems. Al is chairman of the BOMA NY Telecommunications Subcommittee, co-chair of the BOMA NY Security Subcommittee, and is a member of the 7X24 Exchange and several other industry organizations. He speaks regularly about how organizations can benefit from new and emerging technologies and how these technologies can be integrated into the built environment. Al holds a B.S. from Cornell University and an M.B.A. from New York University.

Christopher Marrion Chris Marrion is an Associate Principal with Arup in its New York City office, where he leads the local Arup

Fire group. Chris has worked for various fire engineering consulting firms in the United States, United Kingdom, Hong Kong, and Europe for the last 15 years. During this time, he has been involved with numerous projects, including airports, rail/transit facilities, assembly facilities, commercial buildings, museums, and historic buildings. Chris has written and presented numerous papers on performance-based design for fire engineering, protection of heritage structures, and addressing extreme events. He has been involved with several committees in the fire industry, including New York City Department of Buildings—New York City Building Code Committees for Egress and Fire Protection Systems; New York City Fire Prevention Code Committees; SFPE Performance-Based Design Committee—Steering Committee; SFPE Design Basis Fires Committee—chair; ICC/SFPE Code Authority's Guide to Performance Based Design Review; *NFPA 72®*, Annex B—*Engineering Guide for Automatic Fire Detection*—Technical Committee chair, and the SFPE/NIST—National R&D Roadmap for Fire Safety Design and Retrofit of Structures Workshop—Steering Committee. Chris was also a member of the FEMA/ASCE Building Performance Assessment Team for the World Trade Center assessment and coauthored the WTC1, WTC2, and WTC7 chapters. Chris holds an M.S. in Fire Protection Engineering, is a Fellow of SFPE, and is a registered Professional Engineer in Fire Protection Engineering.

Chad McArthur   Chad McArthur is a Senior Research Engineer at Weidlinger Associates in its New Mexico office. He is responsible for providing threat and vulnerability assessments for new and existing facilities and draws on his extensive experience with non-linear structural dynamic behavior to perform consequence analyses. Chad is a leading developer of the application of advanced computational methods for solving engineering design, assessment, and retrofit problems related to extreme events including blast, fire, impact, and seismic design. With over 10 years of experience performing advanced structural analysis using finite element software, Chad is an expert user of programs such as LS-DYNA along with other industry standard programs for solving cutting edge blast design problems related to structural engineering. He has been heavily involved in the design and construction of a number of international landmark buildings and has led the blast assessment, design, and retrofit of major building and infrastructure projects such as airports, subways, and financial institutions. Chad holds a B.S. in Aerospace Engineering and an M.S. in Civil Engineering from the University of Colorado.

Brian Meacham Brian is a Principal with Arup, where he leads the risk consulting business for Arup worldwide, and consults on risk, fire and regulatory issues. Brian has more than 20 years of experience in these areas, and his project experience includes fire risk assessment, terrorism threat and risk assessment, fire engineering analysis and design, strategic planning, risk and uncertainty research, and regulatory assessment and development. Brian has written more than 100 publications and given more than 100 presentations on the topics of fire, risk, and building performance. He has served on numerous committees, including the NFPA Technical Committee on Fire Risk Assessment Methods, the SFPE Engineering Task Group on Fire Risk Analysis, the New York Department of Buildings, Risk & Security Advisory Committee, which he chairs, and the National Research Council Committee on *Developing a Performance-Based Approach for Security-Related Design of Federal Facilities*. He is currently Associate Team Leader—Risk Management Products, for the ATC-58 project to develop Performance-Based Seismic Design Guidelines. Brian holds an M.S. in Fire Protection Engineering from Worcester Polytechnic Institute (WPI), and a Ph.D. in Risk and Public Policy from Clark University. He is a licensed Professional Engineer in Connecticut, a chartered engineer member of the Institute of Fire Engineers in the United Kingdom, and a Fellow of the SFPE. Brian holds the appointments of adjunct associate professor in Fire Protection Engineering at WPI, and research associate professor and Director of the Center for Risk and Security at Clark University.

Andrew C. T. Thompson Andy Thompson is a Senior Engineer and Risk Consultant with Arup in its San Francisco office. Andy specializes in assessing the behavior of critical physical assets (buildings, facilities, and infrastructure) and associated business continuity, when subjected to natural hazards and terrorist attacks. He has extensive experience in site-specific loss estimation, structural analysis, business impact analysis, risk mitigation options analysis, and retrofit design gained on a variety of international projects and post-disaster reconnaissance missions. He holds a M.S. in Earthquake Engineering from the University of California at Berkeley, and is a licensed Civil Engineer in the State of California.

Jeffrey Tubbs Jeff Tubbs is an Associate Principal with Arup in its Westborough, Massachusetts, office, where he is Staff Group Leader and leader of the Fire Design group. Jeff has a broad range of experience with unique projects. He has focused upon providing innovative, pragmatic solutions in the context of both prescriptive and performance codes throughout the United States and internationally. He has developed many prescriptive egress approaches and performance or dynamic egress analyses for new, existing, and historic facilities. Jeff is a member of the NFPA *101®Life Safety Code®*, and *NFPA 5000®, Building Construction and Safety Code®* Assembly Occupancies Committees, chair of the ad-hoc Sub-Committee to Review Sprinkler Thresholds in Nightclubs, a member of ASHRAE TC5.6: Control of Fire and Smoke, a corresponding member of ASHRAE TC5.9: Enclosed Vehicular Facilities, and a member of the Society of Fire Protection Engineer's Computer Fire Model Evaluation Task Group. He has provided postgraduate lectures and dozens of seminars and papers on developing engineered life safety solutions. Jeff is the author of the "Occupant Movement and Safety" chapter of *Performance-Based Building Design Concepts* (ICC, 2004), and he led the Arup component of the National Construction Safety Team investigation of the February 20, 2002 fire at the Station Nightclub in Warwick, Rhode Island. He is a registered Fire Protection Engineer in California, Massachusetts, and Oregon, and holds a B.S. in Mechanical Engineering and an M.S. in Fire Protection Engineering from Worcester Polytechnic Institute.

Faith Wainwright   Faith Wainwright is a Director of Arup based in the Advanced Technology Group in London. In 22 years with Arup, Faith has led the structural design for several prominent projects, including high-rise buildings, such as HSBC Canary Wharf in London. Faith is also the Skills Director for Arup, promoting learning, technical development, and the exchange of best practice across the firm. Faith served on the Extreme Events Mitigation Task Force within Arup that addressed the concerns raised by the events of September 11, 2001, and the Institution of Structural Engineers Working Party, which produced the report "Safety in Tall Buildings" in July 2002. She subsequently led a scoping study undertaken by Arup for the Office of the Deputy Prime Minister related to potential changes to the Building Regulations (England and Wales) following the events of September 11, 2001. Faith continues to be active in issues related to structural safety as a committee member of the Standing Committee on Structural Safety that is jointly sponsored by the Institution of Structural Engineers, Institution of Civil Engineers and the U.K. Government's Health and Safety Executive. She also serves on the Joint Board of Moderators, responsible for accrediting engineering degree courses in the United Kingdom. Faith is a Fellow of the Royal Academy of Engineering, a Fellow of the Institution of Structural Engineers and a Fellow of the Institution of Civil Engineers.

Andrew Whittaker   Andrew Whittaker is a Professor in the Department of Civil, Structural, and Environmental Engineering at the University at Buffalo. He is an active member of the structural-engineering research community, focusing on the development and implementation of seismic protective systems for buildings, bridges, and infrastructure; performance-based earthquake and blast engineering of buildings, bridges, nuclear structures and other mission-critical infrastructure; and progressive collapse of building structures due to blast loading. Andrew serves as the University at Buffalo's representative on the CUREE Board of Directors and is currently the CUREE President. He has led NSF-funded earthquake reconnaissance teams to Kobe, Japan, in 1995, and Izmit, Turkey, in 1999, and participated in a three-person, NSF-funded structural engineering reconnaissance team at the site of the former World Trade Center.